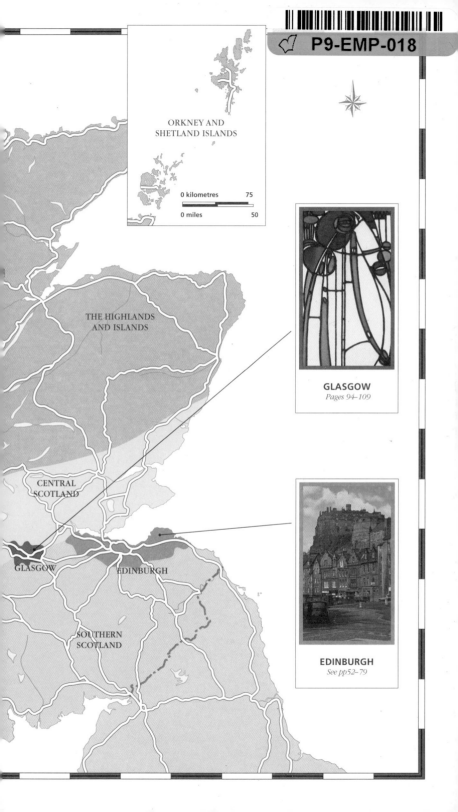

ORKNEY AND
SHETLAND ISLANDS

0 kilometres 75

0 miles 50

THE HIGHLANDS
AND ISLANDS

GLASGOW
Pages 94–109

CENTRAL
SCOTLAND

GLASGOW

EDINBURGH

SOUTHERN
SCOTLAND

EDINBURGH
See pp52–79

EYEWITNESS TRAVEL

SCOTLAND

LONDON, NEW YORK, MELBOURNE, MUNICH AND DELHI
www.dk.com

PROJECT EDITOR Rosalyn Thiro
ART EDITOR Marisa Renzullo
EDITORS Felicity Crowe, Emily Green
DESIGNER Paul Jackson
MANAGING EDITORS Fay Franklin, Louise Bostock Lang
MANAGING ART EDITOR Annette Jacobs
SENIOR EDITOR Helen Townsend
EDITORIAL DIRECTOR Vivien Crump
ART DIRECTOR Gillian Allan
PUBLISHER Douglas Amrine
PICTURE RESEARCH Brigitte Arora
DTP DESIGNERS Maite Lantaron, Lee Redmond

CONTRIBUTORS
Juliet Clough, Keith Davidson, Alan Freeman, Sandie Randall,
Alastair Scott, Roger Smith

MAPS
Ben Bowles, Rob Clynes (Colourmap Scanning, London)

PHOTOGRAPHERS
Joe Cornish, Paul Harris, Stephen Whitehorn

ILLUSTRATORS
Richard Bonson, Gary Cross, Jared Gilby, Paul Guest, Kevin Jones
Associates, Claire Littlejohn, Chris Orr & Associates, Ann Winterbotham

Reproduced by Colourscan, Singapore.
Printed and bound in Malaysia by Vivar Printing Sdn Bhd.

First American Edition, 1999
12 13 14 15 10 9 8 7 6 5 4 3 2

Published in the United States by DK Publishing, 375 Hudson Street,
New York, New York 10014

Reprinted with revisions 2000, 2001, 2002, 2004, 2004, 2006, 2008, 2010, 2012

Copyright 1999, 2012 © Dorling Kindersley Limited, London
A Penguin Company

Published in Great Britain by Dorling Kindersley Limited.

A CATALOG RECORD FOR THIS BOOK IS AVAILABLE FROM THE LIBRARY OF CONGRESS.

ISSN 1542-1554
ISBN 978-0756-684-204

THROUGHOUT THIS BOOK, FLOORS ARE REFERRED TO IN ACCORDANCE WITH
EUROPEAN USAGE IE THE "FIRST FLOOR" IS ONE FLOOR ABOVE GROUND LEVEL

*Front cover main image: Inverlochy Castle,
with snow-capped Ben Nevis is the background*

MIX
Paper from
responsible sources
FSC
www.fsc.org   FSC™ C018179

**The information in this
DK Eyewitness Travel Guide is checked regularly.**
Every effort has been made to ensure that this book is as up-to-date as
possible at the time of going to press. Some details, however, such as
telephone numbers, opening hours, prices, gallery hanging
arrangements and travel information, are liable to change. The
publishers cannot accept responsibility for any consequences arising
from the use of this book, nor for any material on third party websites,
and cannot guarantee that any website address in this book will be a
suitable source of travel information. We value the views and
suggestions of our readers. Please write to:
Publisher, DK Eyewitness Travel Guides,
Dorling Kindersley, 80 Strand, London, Great Britain WC2R 0RL,
or email: travelguides@dk.com.

The dramatic, sunlit ruins of Tantallon Castle

CONTENTS

INTRODUCING SCOTLAND

Detail of the decorated vaulting in
Rosslyn Chapel, in the Pentland Hills

◁ The tranquil river, lush greenery and snowy peaks of Glencoe, in the Highlands

EYEWITNESS TRAVEL

SCOTLAND

MAIN CONTRIBUTORS: JULIET CLOUGH, KEITH DAVIDSON,
SANDIE RANDALL & ALASTAIR SCOTT

DK

on the southeast coast

SCOTLAND REGION BY REGION

Mary, Queen of Scots (1542–87)
of the House of Stuart

Kestrel in the Highlands

SURVIVAL GUIDE

Royal Scots Greys Memorial to the
Scottish soldiers of the Boer War

Walkers enjoying a glorious
summer's day in Glen Etive

Edinburgh Castle on its volcanic
rock above the city centre

INTRODUCING SCOTLAND

DISCOVERING SCOTLAND

Scotland is home to some of the UK's most impressive areas of true wilderness. Mountains and lochs present scenes of breathtaking beauty, as does the varied, island-strewn coastline. If you are not a fan of the great outdoors, Scotland's hospitable towns and cities

Wild thistle, the national flower

proclaim the legacies of an intensely enterprising people. In architecture and engineering, arts and crafts, and thriving cultural traditions, the spirit of Scotland is as distinctive as the other national spirit, the malt whisky distilled from the clear, peaty streams of Speyside.

The Military Tattoo, in the shadow of Edinburgh Castle

EDINBURGH

- **The historical Royal Mile**
- **The Georgian New Town**
- **Museums and galleries**
- **The International Festival**

Enhanced status as capital of a devolved Scotland has boosted Edinburgh's civic pride. The **Scottish Parliament building** *(see p67)* is the latest addition to 1,000 years of history visible along the Royal Mile, a stately thoroughfare linking **Edinburgh Castle** *(see pp60–61)* and the **Palace of Holyroodhouse** *(see pp66–7)*. Around Castle Rock lie the huddled, hilly alleys of the Old Town, lined with tall tenements and crow-stepped gables, while north of Princes Street are the gracious urban grids of the **Georgian New Town** *(see pp64–5)*. Two buildings house the **National Museum of Scotland** *(see pp62–3)*, while the **National Gallery of Scotland** *(see p63)* contains the pick of the country's paintings. Fine views can be enjoyed from the natural belvederes of Edinburgh's volcanic hills,

pleasantly endowed with parks and gardens. Each August, crowds converge on the capital for its **International Festival** *(see pp78–9)*, a banquet of performing arts encompassing outlandish fringe events and the ever-popular Military Tattoo.

SOUTHERN SCOTLAND

- **Abbeys and castles**
- **Tranquil coastline**
- **Historic and literary links**
- **Idyllic rural scenery**

Ruined abbeys *(see p85)* and mighty castles such as **Culzean** *(see p92)* and **Caerlaverock**

(see p90) bear witness to the turbulent relations between Scotland and neighbouring England through the ages.

Southern Scotland's soft green hills and placid shores are ideal for a host of varied tours. Follow in the footsteps of literary giants such as Sir Walter Scott and Robert Burns, or visit the 15th-century **Rosslyn Chapel** *(see p87)* in the Pentland Hills, famed for its role in *The Da Vinci Code*. Alternatively, take a stroll through the **Galloway Forest Park** *(see pp90–91)* or the nature reserve of **St Abb's Head** *(see p84)*, haunt of countless nesting seabirds in early summer.

GLASGOW

- **Cultural diversity**
- **World-class art and architecture**
- **Maritime heritage**
- **Designer shopping**

Triumphantly reincarnated from the ashes of its industrial past, Glasgow is a worthy challenger to its age-old rival Edinburgh for cultural and economic

Melrose Abbey, in the Scottish Borders

◁ **15th-century manuscript showing King David of Scotland at the Battle of Neville's Cross in 1346**

Kelvingrove Art Gallery, Glasgow

supremacy. Whatever your taste in art or music, food or fashion, you can probably find it here. Not for nothing was Glasgow chosen as a European City of Culture in 1990, and named the UK City of Architecture and Design in 1999. Its clutch of dazzling art museums includes the **Burrell Collection** *(see pp104–5)*, the **Hunterian Art Gallery** *(see pp102–3)* and **Kelvingrove** *(see p102)*. The multimillion-pound **Science Centre** *(see p102)* adds a new dimension to the revitalized Clydeside Docklands, while the **Glasgow School of Art** *(see p100)* and the **House for an Art Lover** *(see p103)* delight Mackintosh fans. Meanwhile, a range of classy shops and a busy, vibrant nightlife keep this city buzzing nonstop.

CENTRAL SCOTLAND

- **Loch Lomond and Trossachs National Park**
- **Stirling Castle**
- **Historic towns**
- **The Home of Golf**

Scotland's waistline, dividing the Anglicised Lowlands from the Gaelic Highlands, is a watery zone, tapered on either side by the Firths of Forth and Clyde. Its delights include woodland walks and views across Loch Lomond in the **Trossachs National Park** *(see pp116–17)*, historic towns such as **Dundee** *(see p123)*, **Dunfermline** *(see pp124–5)* and **Culross** *(see p125)*, and the quieter retreats of **Arran** *(see p114)* and **Bute** *(see*

p115). There are ancient castles to explore too, notably at **Stirling** *(see pp120–21)*, **Falkland** *(see p124)*, **Doune** *(see p122)* and **Glamis** *(see pp122–3)*. This area is also renowned for golf. The wide variety of courses scattered around Glasgow, Fife and Perthshire includes the hallowed ground of **St Andrews** *(see p123)*, where this game originated, and the championship golfing mecca of Gleneagles.

The approach to Glamis Castle, a medieval castle in Tayside

THE HIGHLANDS AND ISLANDS

- **Stunning wilderness**
- **The Loch Ness Monster**
- **Malt whisky**
- **Offshore excursions**

This sparsely populated area at the remotest limits of the United Kingdom embodies the true essence of Scottishness. Here the

scenery is wilder and grander, and the traditions of the Highlanders, with their crofts and ceilidhs, seem most archetypal.

Highlights include the west coast, where peninsulas trail towards the Atlantic in settings of peerless beauty, and the **Road to the Isles** *(see pp136–7)*, winding from the foot of **Ben Nevis** *(see p135)* to the harbour town of **Mallaig** *(see p137)*, springboard for the **Isle of Skye** *(see pp152–3)*. Scenic Glencoe *(see pp134)* is popular with hikers.

Inland are the **Cairngorms** *(see pp140–41)*, challenging walkers, climbers and skiers to a year-round schedule of rugged outdoor pursuits. Virtually severing the region along a massive glacial rift is the **Great Glen** *(see pp148–9)*, a chain of four slender lochs linked by the Caledonian Canal. Loch Ness, famed for its legendary monster, is the best known. East coast highlights include the malt-whisky distilleries of **Speyside** *(see pp144–5)* and the gritty charm of **Aberdeen** *(see pp142–3)*.

Offshore, reached by a maze of land-bridges, ferry routes and short-hop flights, lie some 800 other worlds, including the **Orkney** *(see pp158–9)* and **Shetland** *(see pp160–61)* islands, with their abundance of seabirds, and the **Western Isles** *(see pp162–3)*, where Gaelic is still widely spoken.

The snowy peaks of the Cairngorms, in the Scottish Highlands

Putting Scotland on the Map

Separated from Continental Europe by the North Sea, Scotland forms the northern part of Great Britain. It is a mountainous, sparsely populated land. The highest peak is Ben Nevis, at 1,344 m (4,406 ft). The coastline is also ringed by hundreds of islands; at the farthest extreme Shetland lies just six degrees south of the Arctic Circle. Edinburgh is the historic capital, and Glasgow is the largest city with a population of 578,000. The country has good road, rail and ferry connections.

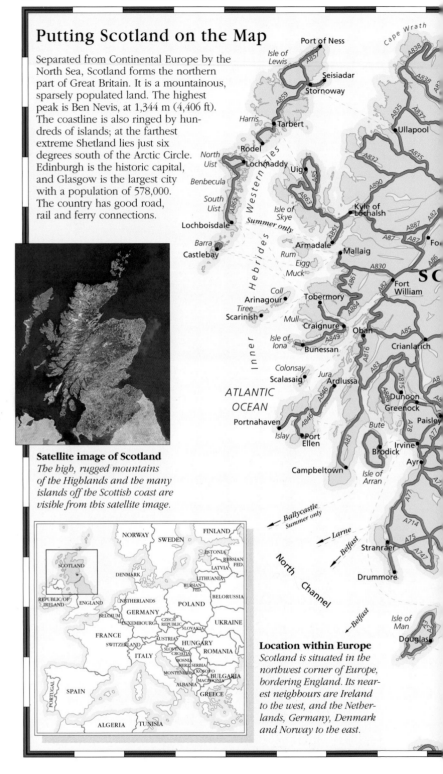

Satellite image of Scotland
The high, rugged mountains of the Highlands and the many islands off the Scottish coast are visible from this satellite image.

Location within Europe
Scotland is situated in the northwest corner of Europe, bordering England. Its nearest neighbours are Ireland to the west, and the Netherlands, Germany, Denmark and Norway to the east.

Cape Wrath

Port of Ness
Isle of Lewis
A857
Seisiadar
A859
Stornoway
A838
A838
A835
A837
Harris
Tarbert
Ullapool
A832
A835
Rodel
North Uist
Lochmaddy
Uig
A865
Benbecula
A890
A863
South Uist
Isle of Skye
Kyle of Lochalsh
A887
A87
A87
Lochboisdale
Summer only
A831
Barra
Castlebay
Armadale
Mallaig
Fo
A830
Rum
Eigg
Muck
Fort William
SC
A861
A884
Coll
Arinagour
Tobermory
Tiree
Scarinish
Mull
Craignure
Oban
A85
A849
Isle of Iona
Bunessan
Crianlarich
A816
A82
Colonsay
Scalasaig
Jura
Ardlussa
A815
A8
ATLANTIC OCEAN
A846
Dunoon
Greenock
Portnahaven
Bute
Paisley
Islay
Port Ellen
A83
Irvine
A77
Brodick
Ayr
Campbeltown
Isle of Arran

North Channel
Ballycastle
Summer only
Larne
Belfast
Stranraer
A75
A714
A741
Drummore

Belfast
Isle of Man
Douglas

NORWAY
SWEDEN
FINLAND
SCOTLAND
ESTONIA
RUSSIAN FED.
DENMARK
LATVIA
LITHUANIA
REPUBLIC OF IRELAND
ENGLAND
NETHERLANDS
RUSSIAN FED.
BELORUSSIA
BELGIUM
GERMANY
POLAND
LUXEMBOURG
CZECH REPUBLIC
UKRAINE
FRANCE
SLOVAKIA
AUSTRIA
HUNGARY
SWITZERLAND
SLOVENIA
CROATIA
ROMANIA
ITALY
BOSNIA HERZ.
SERBIA
MONTENEGRO
KOSOVO
BULGARIA
MACEDONIA
ALBANIA
PORTUGAL
SPAIN
GREECE
ALGERIA
TUNISIA

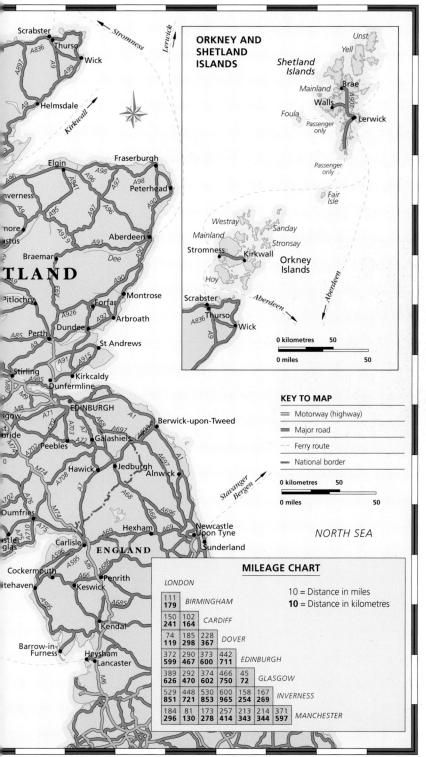

ORKNEY AND SHETLAND ISLANDS

Unst
Yell

Shetland Islands

Mainland
Brae
Walls
Foula
Lerwick

Passenger only

Passenger only

Fair Isle

Westray
Sanday
Mainland
Stronsay
Stromness
Kirkwall

Orkney Islands

Hoy

Scrabster
Thurso
Wick

Aberdeen
Aberdeen

0 kilometres 50
0 miles 50

Scrabster
Thurso
Wick
Helmsdale

Stromness
Lerwick
Kirkwall

Elgin
Fraserburgh
Peterhead
Inverness
Aberdeen
Braemar
Dee
Pitlochry
Forfar
Montrose
Dundee
Arbroath
Perth
St Andrews

SCOTLAND

Stirling
Kirkcaldy
Dunfermline
EDINBURGH
Berwick-upon-Tweed
Glasgow
Peebles
Galashiels
Hawick
Jedburgh
Alnwick
Dumfries

Stavanger
Bergen

Newcastle Upon Tyne
Hexham
Sunderland
Carlisle
ENGLAND

NORTH SEA

Cockermouth
Penrith
Whitehaven
Keswick
Kendal
Barrow-in-Furness
Heysham
Lancaster

KEY TO MAP

═══	Motorway (highway)
▬▬	Major road
- - -	Ferry route
━━	National border

0 kilometres 50
0 miles 50

MILEAGE CHART

LONDON							
111 / **179**	BIRMINGHAM						
150 / **241**	102 / **164**	CARDIFF					
74 / **119**	185 / **298**	228 / **367**	DOVER				
372 / **599**	290 / **467**	373 / **600**	442 / **711**	EDINBURGH			
389 / **626**	292 / **470**	374 / **602**	466 / **750**	45 / **72**	GLASGOW		
529 / **851**	448 / **721**	530 / **853**	600 / **965**	158 / **254**	167 / **269**	INVERNESS	
184 / **296**	81 / **130**	173 / **278**	257 / **414**	213 / **343**	214 / **344**	371 / **597**	MANCHESTER

10 = Distance in miles
10 = Distance in kilometres

A PORTRAIT OF SCOTLAND

With such a distinctive national dress, drink, bagpipe music, landscape and folklore, Scotland has shaped an identity recognizable the world over. It is a land of contrasts and often possesses a magical quality, whether seen shrouded in mist or rising majestically above the mirror of a loch.

Red deer in the Highlands

In a straight line from the far south to the far north, the Scottish mainland reaches about 440 km (275 miles), yet its coastline stretches nearly 10,000 km (6,200 miles). There are 787 major islands, almost all lying off the northern or western coasts. The topography is generally extremely mountainous with wild heather moorlands in the north and west, pine forests mixed with quality pasture in the middle, fertile farmland in the east and, in the south, the rounded, grass-covered hills of the Lowlands. Picturesque lochs and rivers are scattered throughout. Most of Scotland's five million people live in the country's Central Belt. The Scots cherish the differences that set them apart from the English, and cling tenaciously to the distinctions that differentiate them region by region – their customs, dialects and the Gaelic language. It is perhaps more by their differences than similarities that the Scots can be defined but, for all that, they are immensely proud of their nation and its separate institutions, such as education and law. The Scots can be dour but equally they can flash with inspiration. They delight in self-deprecating humour and continue to honour a long tradition of hospitality.

A view from Edinburgh Castle over the rooftops of the capital to Calton Hill

◁ **Isolated dwellings set among the lofty mountains on Skye, the largest island of the Inner Hebrides**

POLITICS AND THE ECONOMY

Ever since the Treaty of Union in 1707, which combined the parliaments of Scotland and England into one governing body convening in Westminster (London), Scotland has often felt estranged from the mechanisms of government, and short-changed by the small allocation of time given to Scottish affairs. The 2011 election gave the SNP a majority, which means there is currently enough support to hold a referendum on Scottish independence. In 1997 the Scots voted for the re-establishment of a Scottish parliament, which began in 1999. This parliament has a wide-ranging administrative role, though major financial controls and decisions of national interest are retained by Westminster.

A hammer-thrower at the Braemar Games

Scotland's economy has fluctuated in the last 100 years. It has had to fight back from the demise of its heavy industries: shipbuilding, coal mining and steel production. Today, the major contributors to the economy are North Sea oil, tourism and services, aided by a range of light industries. Chief among these is the manufacture of electronic components and microchips, giving rise to the notion of a "Silicon Glen", but this industry, has become shaky in response to the global market.

The Viking fire festival, *Up Helly Aa* in Shetland

Whisky production is a leading source of revenue, although it employs few people. Agriculture retains its importance but has been beleaguered by disastrous markets. Fishing remains an important industry, though there is increasing competition for dwindling stocks. Scotland's level of unemployment is on a par with the UK, though in some areas, such as the Western Isles, it reaches 15 per cent.

SOCIETY

The Scots are a gregarious people and enjoy company, whether this be in a small group at a Highland *ceilidh* (literally, a "visit"), a bar, or as part of the Saturday armies of football (soccer) fans. Sometimes they have to travel far to find company; the Highland region has a population density of eight people per square kilometre (20 per sq mile), and the lack of public transport means a car is vital.

Edinburgh bagpiper

Church attendance is in decline in all but the Gaelic-speaking areas, where Sundays are observed as days of rest. In most towns, and all cities, a full range of leisure activities and entertainment runs into the wee hours, but in rural areas opening hours are shorter, and restaurants may stop serving early.

Scotland is renowned as the home of golf, but football is the national passion. Other popular sports include hill-walking, skiing, rugby, shinty and curling. There are also annual Highland Games – great gatherings of whisky, music, craft stalls and tests of stamina and strength *(see p31)*. Despite their love of sports, the Scots are statistically speaking an unhealthy race. Their appetite for red meat and

Small-scale farming in the Western Isles

greasy food contributes to a high incidence of heart problems, and they have the highest consumption of alcohol in the UK. Tobacco sales, however, are in decline after smoking was banned in public places in 2006.

CULTURE AND THE ARTS

Scotland offers an excellent programme of performing arts, subsidized by the Scottish Arts Council. The Edinburgh Festival and Fringe *(see pp78–9)* is the largest celebration of its kind in the world, and there are many smaller festivals that take place throughout the year. The Scottish film industry is small but creative and lively. The music scene is also enjoying a time of vibrancy, ranging from opera, Gaelic song and *pibroch* (the classical music of the bagpipes) to such varied international acts as Franz Ferdinand and Snow Patrol, not to mention a strong electronic music scene. Traditional music has experienced a renaissance using rhythms and instruments from around the world. Bands like Salsa Celtica combine Scottish folk and jazz with Latin American sounds. With an estimated four Scots living abroad for every one in the homeland, outside influences are not surprising. In dance, there are the varied delights of Scottish country, Highland and *ceilidh* dancing and step dancing, as well as the Scottish ballet. Although only about 50,000 people speak Gaelic, the language has been boosted by increased funding for Gaelic radio and TV shows. Literature also has a strong following, with no shortage of Scottish authors and poets *(see pp26–7)*.

Edinburgh's Festival
Fringe Office detail

The blue waters of Loch Achray in the heart of the Trossachs, north of Glasgow

The Geology of Scotland

Scotland is a geologist's playground, with rocks displaying three billion years of geological time. Starting with the hard granitic gneiss in the Western Isles, which was formed before life developed on earth, the rocks tell a story of lava flows, eras of mountain-building, numerous ice ages and even a time when the land was separated from England by the ancient Iapetus Ocean. Four major fault and thrust lines, running across Scotland from north-east to southwest, define the main geological zones.

FAULT AND THRUST LINES

– – Moine Thrust
– – Great Glen Fault (see pp148–9)
– – Highland Boundary Fault
– – Southern Uplands Fault

The gabbro *(dark rock) of the Cuillin Hills on Skye was created by subterranean magma in the Tertiary period, a time when the dinosaurs had died out and mammals were flourishing.*

CHANGING EARTH

Scotland Equator
Iapetus Ocean
England

▢ Ancient landmass

About 500 million years ago
Scotland was part of a landmass that included North America, while England was part of Gondwana. After 75 million years of continental breakup and drift, the two countries "collided", not far from the modern political boundary.

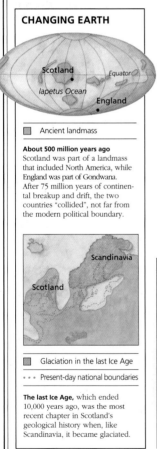

Scandinavia
Scotland

▢ Glaciation in the last Ice Age
• • • Present-day national boundaries

The last Ice Age, which ended 10,000 years ago, was the most recent chapter in Scotland's geological history when, like Scandinavia, it became glaciated.

Rock layers in a stepped effect

The action of sea tides and waves continually erodes the existing coastline.

Plateau-topped hills on the island are the exposed remains of a basalt lava flow.

Lewisian gneiss *is one of earth's oldest substances, created in the lower crust three billion years ago and later thrust up and exposed. Hard, infertile and grey, it forms low plateaus filled with thousands of small lochs in the Western Isles.*

U-shaped valleys *in the Highlands are a legacy of the last Ice Age. The weight and movements of glaciers broke off spurs, deepening and rounding out the existing river valleys.*

Quartzite peaks soar above a base of sandstone in parts of the Torridon range. The quartzite can be mistaken for snow from a distance.

Freshwater loch

Deep sea loch

The basalt columns *of the Isle of Staffa (see p133) were formed 60 million years ago. A flow of lava cooled slowly, contracting and fracturing in a distinctive hexagonal pattern similar to the Giant's Causeway in Ireland.*

The Highland Boundary Fault runs from Stonehaven, on the east coast, to Arran on the west as an obvious line of hills.

Serpentine

Old lava flow

TYPICAL FEATURES

This cross-section is an idealized representation (not to scale) of some of the distinctive geology of the Highlands and islands of northwest Scotland. The tortuously indented coastline of this part of the country is a result of high precipitation in the area during the last Ice Age which heavily eroded the layers of ancient rocks, leaving a beautiful and contrasting landscape of boulder-strewn glens and deep lochs.

Devonian sandstone *is prevalent in the Orkney Islands (see pp158–9). In places, the sea has eroded the horizontally layered rock into spectacular cliffs and stacks, as with the 137-m (450-ft) Old Man of Hoy.*

The Landscape and Wildlife of Scotland

Scotland is a land of contrasts, from the austere majesty of the mountains to the subtle undulations of the Lowland valleys, and from dramatic coastal cliffs to dense forests. It is in the wilds of the Highlands and islands that you are most likely to encounter Scotland's wealth of wildlife. Many once-prolific species are under threat; preserving them and their habitats is now paramount.

A tiny goldcrest

NATIVE ANIMALS

There are no large or dangerous wild animals in Scotland, but there are a few which are rarely found living wild elsewhere in the British Isles. Shetland ponies and Highland cattle, by their names alone, are instantly associated with Scotland, and you are unlikely to see a golden eagle outside of the Scottish Highlands.

COASTAL

The immense, windswept coastline of Scotland provides some of the best chances to view the country's wildlife. Islands such as Skye (*see pp152–3*), pictured above, sustain myriad nesting seabirds, including puffins, guillemots and kittiwakes, while the Bass Rock, off the east coast near North Berwick, has a breeding colony of gannets. The Scottish coast is also home to seals, whales and dolphins.

Puffin

Grey seals *have long inhabited the rocky Scottish coasts, such as in Shetland or in North Rona, and are easily spotted.*

Kittiwakes, *with their white and grey plumage, are widespread along the Scottish cliffs, from St Abb's Head on the east coast to Handa Island off the north-west coast (see p157).*

LOCHS AND RIVERS

Scotland has an abundance of sea lochs, fresh water lochs and rivers, enabling a wide range of animal and insect life to flourish. Sea lochs, such as those shown above on the western isle of North Uist, may contain wild salmon and otters, although the latter are more likely to be spotted at a man-made sanctuary, such as the one at Kylerhea on Skye. Many Scottish rivers, the Tay being just one example, provide a wonderful opportunity for fishermen to catch salmon and trout.

Dragonfly

Wild otters *breed along many parts of Scotland's coast and in its sea lochs. Unlike their Asian cousins, they have webbed feet with which they catch and eat their prey.*

Salmon *swim into Scotland's lochs and rivers every year to breed. They travel miles upstream and up steep waterfalls in order to spawn.*

Shetland ponies are indigenous to the windswept, northerly isles of the same name, but can also be found on the mainland. The ponies are small, with thick, wiry coats.

Highland cattle, *bred in Scotland since the 1500s, are recogniz- able by their long horns and shaggy coats.*

The golden eagle *is one of Scotland's most enduring emblems. Found at high alti- tudes, this majestic bird takes its prey in one silent swoop.*

MOUNTAIN AND MOORLAND

The hills and mountains of Scotland are a refuge for rare arctic and alpine plants, while heather and grasses flourish on the moorlands and Lowlands. This contrast of landscapes can be seen right across the Scottish Highlands and islands, as shown here on Mull. Birds of prey, such as eagles and kestrels, favour this terrain; red deer graze on the bleak moorland.

Kestrel

Sheep *roam freely on the moorland and hills of Scot- land, but they are usually marked so they can be identi- fied by the farmer.*

Red deer *are the most com- mon deer in Europe and can often be sighted in the High- lands of Scotland. Their sig- nature coats are at their most vibrant in summer. The stags shed their antlers in spring.*

WOODLAND AND FOREST

Some of Scotland's forests form part of a protected Forest Park. Woodland refuges, such as the one in the Borders shown above, are home to red squirrels and goldcrests, while pine martens and wildcats favour the rockier terrain of the Highland forests. Birch and oak woods are dotted around the country.

Pine marten

Wildcats *can still be found in forest areas, but their num- bers are dwindling. A stocky body, thick fur and short, blunt tail distinguish them from a domestic cat.*

Red squirrels *are far rarer than their grey counterparts, but they share the same bushy tail for agility and commu- nication, and sharp, hooked claws for a sure grip on trees.*

Evolution of the Scottish Castle

Few sights can match the romance of a Scottish castle set upon a small island in the middle of a quiet loch. These formidable retreats, often in remote settings, were built all over the Highlands, where incursions and strife between the clans were common. From the earliest Pictish *brochs* (Iron Age stone towers) and Norman-influenced motte and bailey castles, the distinctively Scottish stone tower-house evolved, first appearing in the 14th century. By the mid-17th century fashion had become more important than defence, and there followed a period in which numerous huge Scottish palaces were built.

Detail of the Baroque façade, Drumlanrig

MOTTE AND BAILEY

These castles first appeared in the 12th century. They stood atop two adjacent mounds enclosed by a wall, or palisade, and defensive ditches. The higher mound, or motte, was the most strongly defended as it held the keep and chief's house. The lower bailey was where the ordinary people lived.

The keep contained the chief's house, lookout and main defence.

Duffus Castle, Morayshire

Duffus Castle
(c.1150) was atypically made of stone rather than wood. Its fine defensive position dominates the surrounding flatlands north of Elgin.

The Motte of earth or rock was sometimes partially man-made.

The Bailey enclosed dwellings and storehouses.

EARLY TOWER-HOUSE

Designed to deter local attacks rather than a major assault, the first tower-houses appeared in the 13th century, and their design lived on for 400 years. They were built initially on a rectangular plan, with a single tower divided into three or four floors. The walls were unadorned, with few windows. Defensive structures were on top, and extra space was made by building adjoining towers. Extensions were vertical, to minimize the area open to attack.

Crenellated parapet for sentries

Claypotts Castle (c.1570), with uniquely projecting garrets above its towers

Braemar Castle (c.1630), a conglomeration of extended towers

Neidpath Castle, *standing upon a steep rocky crag above the River Tweed, is an L-shaped tower-house dating from the late 14th century. Once a stronghold for Charles II, its walls still bear damage from a siege conducted by Oliver Cromwell.*

Featureless, straight walls contain arrow slits for windows.

LATER TOWER-HOUSE

Though the requirements of defence were being replaced by those of comfort, the style of the early tower-house remained popular. By the 17th century wings for accommodation were being added around the original tower (often creating a courtyard). The battlements and turrets were kept more for decorative than defensive reasons.

Drum Castle, near Aberdeen, a 13th-century keep with a mansion house extension from 1619

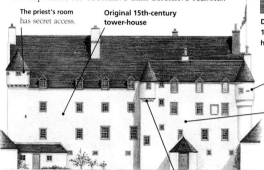

The priest's room has secret access.

Original 15th-century tower-house

This round angle tower contains a stairway.

Sixteenth-century horizontal extension

Traquair House (see p87), *by the Tweed, is the oldest continuously inhabited house in Scotland. The largely unadorned, roughcast exterior dates from the 16th century, when a series of extensions were built around the original 15th-century tower-house.*

Decorative, corbelled turret

Blair Castle (see p139), incorporating a medieval tower

CLASSICAL PALACE

By the 18th century the defensive imperative had passed and castles were built in the manner of country houses; the vertical tower-house was rejected in favour of a horizontal plan (though the building of imitation fortified buildings continued into the 19th century with the mock-Baronial trend). Outside influences came from all over Europe, including Renaissance and Gothic revivals, with echoes of French châteaux.

Dunrobin Castle (c.1840), Sutherland

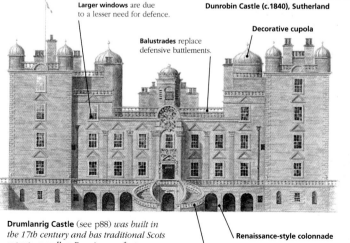

Larger windows are due to a lesser need for defence.

Balustrades replace defensive battlements.

Decorative cupola

Drumlanrig Castle (see p88) *was built in the 17th century and has traditional Scots aspects as well as Renaissance features, such as the decorated stairway and façade.*

Renaissance-style colonnade

Baroque horseshoe stairway

Scottish Gardens

Scotland has a great number of diverse and beautiful gardens. Some are renowned for their layout, such as Pitmedden, or for particular plants. Rhododendrons flourish in Scotland's acidic, peaty soil, and the Royal Botanic Garden in Edinburgh is famous for its spectacular, colourful display. Some gardens have a striking backdrop of lakes or mountains, while others form the grounds of a stately home. Gulf Stream gardens like Inverewe offer visitors a rare chance to view exotic, subtropical flora at a northern latitude. The gardens shown here are some of Scotland's finest.

Inverewe Garden *(see p156) is renowned for its lush, exotic, subtropical flora. Ferns, lilies, giant forget-me-nots and rare palms are just some of the 2,500 species that thrive in the mild climate.*

Crarae Gardens (see p130) *are sited on a slope overlooking Loch Fyne, surrounded by mature woodland. There are many walks, all designed to cross a picturesque burn at the centre. The gardens are riotous with spectacular rhododendrons in spring and ablaze with golden and russet leaves during the autumn.*

The Botanic Gardens, *Glasgow* (see p103), *have a wonderful collection of orchids, begonias and cacti. Kibble Palace, a domed, iron conservatory designed by engineer John Kibble, houses tropical tree ferns from around the world.*

Logan Botanic Garden *is an outpost of the Royal Botanic Garden in Edinburgh. The garden is divided into two main areas – a walled garden with cabbage palms, and a woodland area. The Gulf Stream enables subtropical plants to grow here.*

Inverewe
Garden

Angus
Garden

Crarae
Gardens

Arduaine
Garden

Younger
Botanic
Garden

Botani
Garden
Glasgo

Logan
Botanic
Garden

THE RHODODENDRON

These examples illustrate three of the 900 rhododendron varieties. The first is tropical, grown under glass in Scotland; the second is evergreen; the third is an azalea, which used to be considered a separate species. Rhododendrons also fall into scaly-leaved and non-scaly groups.

Macgregoriae

Augustini

Medway

Drummond Castle Gardens *are laid out as a large boxwood parterre in the shape of a St Andrew's Cross. Yellow and red roses and antirrhinums provide the colour, and a sundial forms the centrepiece.*

THE GULF STREAM

The west coast of Scotland is the surprising location for a number of gardens where tropical and subtropical plants bloom. Although on the same latitude as Siberia, this area of Scotland lies in the path of a warm water current from the Atlantic. Inverewe is the most famous of the Gulf Stream gardens, with plants from South America, South Africa and the South Pacific. Other gardens include Achamore on the Isle of Gigha and Logan Botanic Garden near Stranraer.

Tree ferns warmed by the Gulf Stream, Logan Botanic Garden

Pitmedden Garden *was created in 1675 and later restored to its full glory as a formal garden by the National Trust for Scotland. Split into two levels, it has four parterres, two gazebos, box hedges and a splendid fountain at its centre.*

Pitmedden Garden •

Crathes Gardens •

Drummond Castle Gardens •

• Royal Botanic Garden, Edinburgh

Kailzie Gardens •

Dawyck Botanic Garden

Priorwood Gardens

0 kilometres 50

0 miles 50

Crathes Gardens' *topiary and scented borders are centred around the beautiful tower house, Crathes Castle (see p145). There are eight different themed gardens, such as the Golden Garden designed in the style of Gertrude Jekyll.*

Dawyck Botanic Garden *is another branch of Edinburgh's Royal Botanic Garden, and specializes in rare trees, such as the Dawyck Beech, flowering shrubs and blankets of narcissi.*

The Royal Botanic Garden, Edinburgh *(see p68), is internationally renowned as a base for scientific research. With almost 17,000 species, the garden has a marvellous range of plants. Exotic plants are found in the many glasshouses, and the grounds are enhanced by beautifully maintained lawns.*

Great Scottish Inventions

Marmalade

Despite its relatively small size and population, Scotland has produced a remarkable number of inventors over the centuries. The late 1700s and 1800s were years of such intense creativity that the period became known as the Scottish Enlightenment. Many technological, medicinal and mechanical breakthroughs were made at this time, including the invention of the steam engine, antiseptic and the telephone. Out of the country's factories, universities and laboratories came a breed of men who were intrepid and forward-thinking. Their revolutionary ideas and experiments produced inventions that have shaped our modern, progressive society.

Logarithm tables *(1594) were devised by John Napier as a practical way of multiplying and dividing large numbers. Though easy to use, the tables took 20 years to create.*

Continous electric light *(1834) was invented by James Bowman Lindsay using galvanic cells in a revolutionary design.*

Parallel motion operated all the valves in time.

The pneumatic tyre/tire *(John Dunlop, 1887), was originally patented by RW Thomson and then developed by Dunlop for use on bicycles and, later, cars.*

Piston rod

A flywheel stored energy so that the engine ran smoothly.

Golf clubs *were originally wooden and hand-crafted by carpenters such as Old Tom Morris. By 1890, aluminium-headed clubs had been introduced.*

The rotative steam engine *(James Watt, 1782) was a refinement of the existing steam engine. This new model soon became the driving force behind the Industrial Revolution in Britain, powering all manner of machinery. Watt's success led to his name being given to the modern unit of power.*

The bicycle *(Kirkpatrick Macmillan, 1839) was originally known as a veloci-pede. Macmillan's version was an important stage in the development of cycling.*

Colour photography *(1861) was developed by the Scottish physicist, James C Maxwell. The first to experiment with three-colour photography, he photographed this tartan ribbon using coloured water as a filter.*

Spray nozzle

Steam generator

Antiseptic *(Joseph Lister, 1865) in the form of carbolic acid was a most important breakthrough in surgery. Lister discovered that, applied to wounds and sprayed around the theatre, the acid helped to prevent germs and infection.*

Carbolic acid reservoir

The thermos flask *(Sir James Dewar, 1892) was first designed as a vacuum for storing low-temperature gases. The flask was later mass produced as the thermos, for maintaining the temperature of hot and cold drinks.*

The telephone *(Alexander Graham Bell, 1876) was the scientific breakthrough that revolutionized the way the world communicated, introducing the transmission of sound by electricity.*

Penicillin *(Alexander Fleming, 1928) is a discovery that has changed the face of medicine. Fleming's brainchild was the first antibiotic drug to treat diseases, and by 1940 it was being used to save the lives of wounded soldiers.*

The radar receiver *(Robert Watson-Watt, 1935) was in use long before World War II, since Watson-Watt's team had built the first working radar defence system by 1935. Radar is an acronym for "radio detection and ranging".*

The first television *(John Logie Baird, 1926), or "televisor", was black and white, and unable to produce sound and pictures together, but it was nevertheless hailed as a monumental invention. In 1928, Baird demonstrated the possibilities of creating colour images.*

Dolly the cloned sheep *was created in 1996 by a team of scientists at Edinburgh's Roslin Institute. Dolly, the first successful clone of an adult animal in the world, gave birth in 1998.*

Writers and Intellectuals

From medieval poets through Robert Burns to Irvine Welsh, writers in the three literary languages of Scotland – Scots, English and Gaelic – have created a body of literature expressing both their place in the European mainstream and the diversity within Scotland. In 1999, a new parliament was established in Scotland, three centuries after the dissolution of the last one. Political devolution followed three decades of ferment in which literature reached new heights of success.

Robert Burns encircled by images of his literary creations

THE GOLDEN AGE BEFORE ENLIGHTENMENT

Often regarded as the golden age of Scottish literature, the century leading up to the Reformation of 1560 was characterized by strong links with the Continent and a rich tradition of poetry, culminating in the achievements of William Dunbar and Robert Henryson. John Barbour established the mythic heroism of the national hero in *The Bruce* (c.1375). Other early works were James I's *Kingis Quair* (c.1424) and Blind Harry's *Wallace* (c.1478).

Dunbar rose to pre-eminence for his polished art, from *Lament for the Makars* (1508), an elegy to poets, to his insult poetry known as "flyting". Henryson's work is rich in insight, as in *The Testament of Cresseid* (c.1480), which tells the legend from the woman's point of view. Gavin Douglas translated Virgil's *Aeneid* into Scots in 1513. The golden age ended with Sir David Lindsay's much-revived play, *A Satire of the Three Estates*, in 1540.

ENLIGHTENMENT AND ROMANTICISM

The intellectual triumphs of the Enlightenment in Scotland were fuelled by the expanding educational system.

Among the great thinkers of the time were Adam Smith (1723–90), who theorized on political economy, and Adam Ferguson (1723–1816), who founded modern sociology. Other prominent figures were William Robertson (1721–93) and David Hume (1711–76), both of whom helped to define modern history. Hume's greatest legacy was in philosophy – his rigorous empiricism offended Christian orthodoxy and foretold crises of faith versus scientific knowledge. James Macpherson published the *Ossian Chronicles* in 1760, supposedly the documentation of his discovery of an old Celtic tradition in the Hebrides. This fictional work tapped a nostalgia for ancient civilizations and, allied to fears about progress, Romanticism was born. Allan Ramsay wrote poems in Scots, as did the tragic Robert Fergusson, who died in poverty aged 25.

Philosopher David Hume

The country's most fêted literary figure, Robert Burns (1759–96), was a man of his time. His popular "heaven-taught ploughman" image belied a sound education. His works ranged from love lyrics to savage satire (*Holy Willie's Prayer*), nationalism to radical ideals (*A Man's a Man for a' That*).

THE 19TH CENTURY

Despite the importance of Edinburgh in British culture, it was the pattern of leaving Scotland to achieve fame in London, initiated in the mid-18th century by James Boswell and Tobias Smollett, that would predominate in the Victorian period.

The poetry of Walter Scott (1771–1832) enjoyed phenomenal success. His novels, especially *Waverley* (1814), rose to greater glory. Francis Jeffrey's Whig-orientated *Edinburgh Review* led opinion, challenged by *Blackwood's* Tory alternative. James Hogg was published by the latter before writing his startling,

Map of Robert Louis Stevenson's Treasure Island, based on an island in the Firth of Forth

gothic *Private Memoirs and Confessions of a Justified Sinner* (1824). Following Susan Ferrier and John Galt, standards were modest, despite the prodigious career of Margaret Oliphant. Thomas Carlyle noted the provinciality of Edinburgh in the 1830s.

A later response to anxieties of the age came from Robert Louis Stevenson (1850–94) in *Dr Jekyll and Mr Hyde*. This contrasted with the sentimentality of home-spun or so-called kailyard (literally "cabbage patch") fiction, led by JM Barrie and SR Crockett. Barrie's dramas often catered for bourgeois tastes, as did the *Sherlock Holmes* stories of Arthur Conan Doyle (1859–1930), which endure today.

Arthur Conan Doyle's sleuth, Sherlock Holmes, in *The Graphic* (1901)

Poster for the film *Rob Roy* (1995), based on Walter Scott's 1817 novel

EARLY 20TH-CENTURY RENAISSANCE

George Douglas Brown's fierce anti-kailyard novel, *The House with the Green Shutters* (1901), opened the century and serious art was reborn. Hugh MacDiarmid's poetry in the 1920s carried literature into the stream of modernism. *A Drunk Man Looks at the Thistle* (1926) combines disparate Scottish dialects with political and social commentary in one of the century's great symbolist works. Edwin Muir also won international acclaim. Successors included Sidney Goodsir

Smith and William Soutar. Fiction reached epic and innovative proportions with Neil Gunn (*Butcher's Broom*, 1933) and Lewis Grassic Gibbon (*A Scots Quair*, 1932–4). Others included Willa Muir, Nan Shepherd and Fionn MacColla. John Buchan attempted serious work and popular thrillers. Nationalist impetus was dissipated by the rise of fascism, and new directions were sought after World War II.

POST-1945

Sorley Maclean wrote in his native Gaelic of the ancient Highland culture's plight. Norman MacCaig began a career characterized by metaphysical whimsy, and George Bruce and Robert Garioch evoked the strictures of nature and social class.

Edwin Morgan has celebrated art and modernity (*Sonnets from Scotland*, 1984), Liz Lochhead continues to produce fresh drama and poetry, and Jackie Kay explores the experience of being a black Scottish citizen. While James Bridie, Bill Bryden and John Byrne made an impact in the theatre, Muriel Spark rose to international acclaim

for her blackly comic novels (*The Prime of Miss Jean Brodie*, 1961). Urban realism developed quietly before William MacIlvanney's breakthrough with *The Big Man* (1985).

Following Alasdair Gray's bizarre *Lanark* (1981), a powerful wave propelled fiction into the highly productive present, in which Iain Banks remains a bestseller (*The Crow Road*, 1992). Tom Leonard's poems initiated a tradition using urban demotic speech. James Kelman elevated this to new levels, winning the Booker Prize for *How Late It Was, How Late* (1994).

Irvine Welsh's portrayal of drug culture is now world famous, though the energy of *Trainspotting* (1993) is absent from its successors. The private dramas articulated in AL Kennedy's stories are poignant and mysterious (*So I Am Glad*, 1995), while Ian Rankin's thrillers receive international acclaim, as do JK Rowling's hugely successful *Harry Potter* books.

Poster for the film version of Irvine Welsh's novel

Clans and Tartans

The clan system, by which Highland society was divided into tribal groups led by autocratic chiefs, can be traced to the 12th century, when clans were already known to wear the chequered wool cloth later called tartan. All members of the clan bore the name of their chief, but not all were related by blood. Though they had noble codes of hospitality, the clansmen had to be warriors to protect their herds, as can be seen from their mottoes. After the Battle of Culloden *(see p146)*, all the clan lands were forfeited to the Crown, and the wearing of tartan was banned for nearly 100 years.

The Mackays, *also known as the Clan Morgan, won lasting renown during the Thirty Years War.*

The MacLeods *are of Norse heritage. The clan chief still lives in Dunvegan Castle, Skye.*

The MacDonalds *were the most power-ful of all the clans, holding the title of Lords of the Isles.*

The Mackenzies *received much of the lands of Kintail* (see p151) *from David II in 1362.*

CLAN CHIEF

The chief was the clan's patriarch, judge and leader in war, commanding absolute loyalty from his clansmen who gave mili-tary service in return for his protection. The chief sum-moned his clan to do battle by sending a run-ner across his land bearing a burning cross.

Bonnet with eagle feathers, clan crest and plant badge.

Dirk

Sporran, or pouch, made of badger's skin.

Feileadh-mor, or "great plaid" (the early kilt), wrap-ped around waist and shoulder.

Basket-hilted sword

The Campbells *were a widely feared clan who fought the Jacobites in 1746* (see p147).

The Black Watch, *raised in 1729 to keep peace in the Highlands, was one of the Highland regiments in which the wearing of tartan sur-vived. After 1746, civilians were punished by exile for up to seven years for wearing tartan.*

The Sinclairs *came from France in the 11th century and became Earls of Caithness in 1455.*

The Frasers *came over to Britain from France with William the Conqueror and his followers in 1066.*

George IV, *dressed as a Highlander, visited Edinburgh in 1822, the year of the tartan revival. Many tartan "setts" (patterns) date from this time, as the original ones were lost.*

The Gordons *were famously good soldiers; the clan motto was "by courage, not by craft".*

The Stuarts *were Scotland's royal dynasty. Their motto was "no one harms me with impunity".*

The Douglas *clan was prominent in Scottish history, though its origin is unknown.*

CLAN TERRITORIES

The territories of 10 major clans are marked here with their clan crests and tartan. The patterns shown are modern versions of original tartan designs.

PLANT BADGES

Each clan had a plant associated with its territory. It was worn on the bonnet, especially on the day of battle.

Scots pine was worn by the MacGregors of Argyll.

Rowan berries were worn by the Clan Malcolm.

Ivy was worn by the Clan Gordon of Aberdeenshire.

Spear thistle, now a national symbol, was a Stuart badge.

Cotton grass was worn by the Clan Henderson.

HIGHLAND CLANS TODAY

Once the daily dress of the clansmen, the kilt continues to be a symbol of national pride. The one-piece *feileadh-mor* has been replaced by the *feileadh-beag*, or "small plaid", made from approximately 7 m (23 ft) of material with a double apron fastened at the front with a silver pin. Though they exist now only in name, the clans are still a strong source of pride for Scots, and many still live in areas traditionally belonging to their clans. Many visitors to Britain can trace their Scots ancestry back to the Highlands.

Modern Highland formal dress

Highland Music and Games

The Highlands and Islands of Scotland have been the focus of Gaelic culture for hundreds of years. Although the language itself is little spoken today, the legacy of the Gaelic lifestyle lives on in the music and activities of the people. The bagpipes, a traditional Highland instrument, are an important part of Scotland's identity around the world, and the Highland Games are an amalgamation of the Gaelic customs of music, dancing and contests of strength.

The blow-pipe is used to inflate the bag by blowing air, as continuously as possible, into the pipe's mouthpiece.

A piper's hat is made traditionally from ostrich feathers.

Pibroch *is the classical music of the piping world. Played by solo pipers, these slow, melancholy tunes produce a haunting sound that is easier on the ear than the almost discordant sound a group of bagpipers makes.*

The chanter pipe has eight finger-holes, used to play the melody.

The drones or "borduns", are the three pipes that give the pitch. They are pitched on a fixed note, one bass and the other two higher, each at intervals of a fifth.

The bag, made from animal hide, is inflated by air from the blow-pipe; the air is then expelled under pressure applied by the piper's elbow.

THE BAGPIPES

Bagpipes have been the traditional sound of the Highlands for many centuries and are thought to have been introduced to Britain by the Romans. After the Battle of Culloden in 1746 they were banned for 11 years, along with Highland dress, for inspiring the Highlanders to rebel against English rule. The pipes have now become one of the most recognized emblems of Scotland.

TRADITIONAL GAELIC MUSIC

Music has always featured strongly in the Highlands' Gaelic communities. Solo instruments include the harp and accordion, and *ceilidh* bands are still common.

Accordions *have accompanied ceilidhs ever since the dances began in the crofting communities of the Scottish Highlands and islands.*

The harp *is Irish in origin but was introduced to Scotland in the 1800s. The "clarsach", as it is known, has enjoyed a revival in recent years.*

Ceilidh bands *are an alternative to the solo accordion as accompaniment for the modern ceilidh (a Gaelic word for "visit"). The band's instruments usually include fiddles, accordions and penny whistles.*

Re-enacting Highland battles *is popular with modern-day clansmen to commemorate their forefathers' fight for freedom. The above occasion was the 250th anniversary of the Battle of Culloden, where over 2,000 Highland warriors died.*

HIGHLAND GAMES AND ACTIVITIES

As well as music, the Highlands of Scotland are famous for their Games. The first Games took place many hundreds of years ago, and may have served a military purpose by allowing clan chiefs to choose the strongest men from those competing in contests of strength. Highland Games are held annually at Braemar *(see p38)*, as well as at Oban and Dunoon, among others. Another activity in the Highlands is the re-enactment of past battles and rebellions.

The Highland Games (or Gatherings) *as they are played today date from the 1820s. The most common contests and events are tossing the caber, weight shifting, piping, singing, dancing and throwing the hammer. The result is a cacophony of sound and activity, which can be overwhelming to a first-time spectator.*

Tossing the caber *is one of the most famous Highland sports, and requires strength and skill. The athlete must run with the tree trunk and toss it so that it flips over 180° and lands vertically, straight ahead.*

Throwing the hammer *involves revolving on the spot to gather speed, while swinging the hammer (a weight on the end of a long pole) around the head, before launching it across the field. The winner is the contestant whose hammer reaches the furthest distance.*

Highland dancing *is an important part of the Games, and the dances often have symbolic meanings – for instance the circle in a reel represents the circle of life. In the sword dance, the feet skip nimbly over the swords without touching them.*

Weight shifting *is a severe test of strength and stamina. Here, the man stands with his back to a bar, over which he must throw the huge weight. The bar is raised after each successful attempt, until only one person is left in the competition.*

Scotch Whisky

Whisky is to the Scots what Champagne is to the French, and a visit to Scotland would not be complete without sampling this fiery, heart-warming spirit. All malt whiskies are produced using much the same process, but the environment, maturity and storage of the whisky have such a strong bearing on its character that every one is a different experience. There is no "best" malt whisky – some are suited to drinking at bedtime, others as an aperitif. All the distilleries named below produce highly rated Single Malt Scotch Whiskies, a title that is revered by true whisky connoisseurs.

A 1920s steam wagon transporting The Glenlivet to the nearby railways

Talisker *is a highly distinctive malt with an extremely hot, peppery, powerful flavour that is guaranteed to warm the toes.*

Glenmorangie *is the biggest selling single malt in Scotland, with a light, flowery taste and strong perfume.*

Lochnagar *is reputed to have been a favourite with Queen Victoria, who visited this distillery located near Balmoral. This is a sweet whisky with overtones of sherry.*

Lagavulin *is a classic Islay whisky with a dry, smoky palate. Islay is thought to be the best of the whisky-producing islands.*

Edradour *is the smallest distillery in Scotland but it succeeds in producing a deliciously minty, creamy whisky.*

SPEYSIDE WHISKIES

The region of Speyside *(see p144)*, where barley is widely grown, is the setting for over half of Scotland's malt whisky distilleries.

MALT REGIONS

Single malts vary according to regional differences in the peat and stream water used. This map illustrates the divisions of the traditional whisky distilling regions in Scotland. Each whisky has subtle but recognizable regional flavour characteristics.

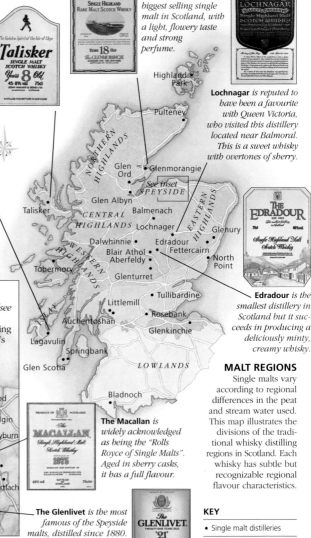

The Macallan *is widely acknowledged as being the "Rolls Royce of Single Malts". Aged in sherry casks, it has a full flavour.*

The Glenlivet *is the most famous of the Speyside malts, distilled since 1880.*

KEY

● Single malt distilleries

HOW WHISKY IS MADE

Traditionally made from just barley, yeast and stream water, Scottish whisky (from the Gaelic *usquebaugh*, or the "water of life") takes a little over three weeks to produce, though it must be given at least three years to mature. Maturation usually takes place in oak casks, often in barrels previously used for sherry. The art of blending was pioneered in Edinburgh in the 1860s.

Barley grass

1 *Malting is the first stage. Barley grain is soaked in water and spread on the malting floor. With regular turning the grain germinates, producing a "green malt". Germination stimulates the production of enzymes which turn the starches into fermentable sugars.*

2 *Drying of the barley halts germination after 12 days of malting. This is done over a peat fire in a pagoda-shaped malt-kiln. The peat-smoke gives flavour to the malt and eventually to the mature whisky. The malt is gleaned of germinated roots and then milled.*

3 *Mashing of the ground malt, or "grist", occurs in a large vat or "mash tun", which holds a vast quantity of hot water. The malt is soaked and begins to dissolve, producing a sugary solution called "wort", which is then extracted for fermentation.*

4 *Fermentation occurs when yeast is added to the cooled wort in wooden vats, or "washbacks". The mixture is stirred for hours as the yeast turns the sugar into alcohol, producing a clear liquid called "wash".*

5 *Distillation involves boiling the wash twice so that the alcohol vaporizes and condenses. In copper "pot stills", the wash is distilled – first in the "wash still", then in the "spirit still". Now purified, with an alcohol content of 57 per cent, the result is young whisky.*

6 *Maturation is the final process. The whisky mellows in oak casks for a legal minimum of three years. Premium brands give the whisky a 10- to 15-year maturation, though some are given up to 50 years.*

Traditional drinking vessels, or *quaichs*, made of silver

Blended whiskies *are made from a mixture of up to 50 different single malts.*

Single malts *are made in one distillery, from pure barley malt that is never blended.*

Touring Scotland by Car

The ten routes marked on this map are excellent examples of the options open to motorists touring Scotland. Some routes are circular, using a major city as a base; some can be combined into longer itineraries. Main roads are few and far between in the Highlands, but driving conditions are generally good, and traffic is light outside the peak July and August holiday period. The driving times given in the key assume normal conditions without lengthy stops. Further information about road travel is on pages 230–31.

The far northwest *can be visited in a circular tour starting at Braemore Junction, near Ullapool, heading west on a series of single-track roads past tiny crofting settlements and some of the oldest rocks in Britain. The route rejoins the two-lane road near Unapool.*

From Kyle of Lochalsh, *this route along the west coast encompasses the magnificent mountains and coastline of Wester Ross, taking in Loch Carron, Torridon, Loch Maree, Gairloch and Inverewe Gardens.*

KEY TO TOURING ROUTES

▬	The Border Abbeys & Scott's View *195 km (120 miles), 3–4 hours*
▬	Walter Scott's Country *185 km (115 miles), 3–4 hours*
▬	Fife Fishing Villages & St Andrews *195 km (120 miles), 3–4 hours*
▬	Eastern Grampians & Royal Deeside *180 km (110 miles), 4 hours*
▬	High Mountains of Breadalbane *180 km (110 miles), 4 hours*
▬	Loch Lomond & the Trossachs *225 km (140 miles), 5 hours*
▬	Inveraray & the Mountains of Lorne *225 km (140 miles), 4 hours*
▬	Glencoe & the Road to the Isles *160 km (100 miles), 3 hours*
▬	Sea Lochs of the West Coast *195 km (120 miles), 4 hours*
▬	The Far Northwest *160 km (100 miles), 3–4 hours*

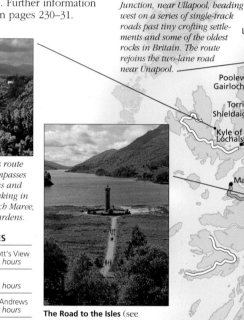

The Road to the Isles (see pp136–7) *begins in Crianlarich, then crosses desolate Rannoch Moor to Glencoe (see p134) and past Fort William. The rugged scenery shown here is near the end of the tour route.*

0 kilometres   50

0 miles   50

Loch Lomond *is the first point of interest on a tour of Inveraray and the Mountains of Lorne. After Tarbet is a pass known as "The Rest and Be Thankful", then a drive to the 18th-century town of Inveraray (see p130), and on past Kilchurn Castle.*

Unapool
Lochinver
Ullap
Poolewe
Gairloch
Braemo
Torridon
Shieldaig   Achnasheer
Kyle of
Lochalsh
A87
Mallaig
A830
Fort
Willia
Crainlaric
A85
A819   A83
A816
Inveraray
Tarbet
A78
A77
A75
A835
A832
A8

Passing through Royal Deeside *in the eastern Grampians, this route links Perth with Aberdeen, crossing a 700-m (2,000-ft) pass before descending to Balmoral Castle. The stretch from Braemar is on pages 144–5.*

St Andrews (see p123) *and the historic fishing villages of East Fife can be reached from Edinburgh over the Forth Bridge, and back via the hunting palace of the Stuart kings at Falkland (see p124).*

A tour of Walter Scott's Country takes in the River Tweed Valley, with its attractive hills, market towns and an arboretum at Dawyck.

Melrose Abbey *is one of the highlights of a tour taking in attractive Border towns, the famous Border Abbeys and Scott's View – one of the finest viewpoints in southern Scotland. More details of part of this tour are on page 85.*

From Glasgow, this route includes Loch Lomond, Lochearnhead and Balquhidder. Just north of Callander, it turns west into the Trossachs. Heading back via Drymen, there is access to Loch Lomond.

Stirling, *with its castle, is the base from which to explore the high mountains of Breadalbane. The route passes through Callander, past Rob Roy's grave and Loch Earn. It then climbs over a mountain pass down to Glen Lyon, one of the most beautiful glens, and on through Crieff.*

SCOTLAND THROUGH THE YEAR

Most visitors come to Scotland between May and August, when they enjoy the best weather, long hours of daylight and the chance to sample world-class events such as the Edinburgh International Festival or the Glasgow International Jazz Festival. The countryside lures tourists and Scots alike, and at the height of summer, it gets very busy in areas such as Loch Ness (monster spotting) or Royal Deeside (site of Balmoral Castle, the British Royal Family's Scottish residence). Out of season, a good winter snowfall in the Highlands provides an opportunity for snowboarding or skiing. Edinburgh's organized celebration at New Year – known locally as Hogmanay – has seen a rise in visitor numbers. During most weeks of the year, but especially in the summer, a festival is held somewhere across the country.

Poster for the Edinburgh Fringe

Full colours of gorse in springtime

SPRING

The snow clears off the mountains after April, the salmon swim upstream and the country prepares for visitors. There are some excellent festivals and a series of important sporting events. British Summer Time, when the clocks go forward one hour, starts at the end of March.

MARCH

Cairngorm Snow Festival (*third weekend*), Aviemore. Daytime events at the Cairngorm ski area and evening street parades in Aviemore.

Glasgow International Comedy Festival (*mid- to late Mar*). Comedy acts from around the world.

APRIL

Puppet and Animation Festival (*first two weeks*). Workshops and displays at 70 venues nationwide.
International Science Festival (*two weeks, early Apr*), Edinburgh. The world's largest science festival.
Scottish Grand National (*mid-Apr*), Ayr Racecourse. Scotland's top steeplechase event.
The Melrose Sevens (*mid-Apr or early May*), Melrose, Borders. International seven-a-side rugby union event.

Glasgow Art Fair (*late Apr*). Commercial art show in various galleries.
Beltane (*30 Apr*), Calton Hill, Edinburgh. Pagan celebration to welcome start of summer.
Scottish Rugby Union Cup Final (*30 Apr*), Murrayfield Stadium, Edinburgh. Scotland's showpiece club rugby event.

MAY

Shetland Folk Festival (*first week*). Traditional Scottish music in an island setting.
Scottish Cup Final (*mid-May*), Hampden Park, Glasgow. Scottish football's showpiece club event.
International Children's Festival (*fourth week*), Edinburgh. Performing arts event.
Wigtown Book Fair (*21–22*), Wigtown, Dumfries and Galloway. Scotland's National Book Town welcomes book lovers and collectors.

An inter-Scotland rugby match at Murrayfield Stadium, Edinburgh

AVERAGE DAILY HOURS OF SUNSHINE

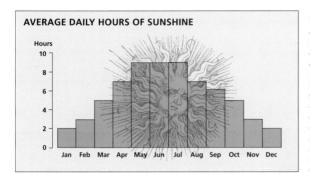

Hours: 10, 8, 6, 4, 2, 0

Jan Feb Mar Apr May Jun Jul Aug Sep Oct Nov Dec

Sunshine Chart
Although Scotland is not in any way synonymous with sunshine, its summers are marked by very long hours of daylight, due to the country's northerly latitude. Thus there is a relatively high proportion of hours of sunshine between the months of May and July.

SUMMER

This is the busiest time of year. Many towns and villages stage their own version of the Highland Games, at varying scales. Days are long – in Shetland there is no proper night at midsummer, while even the south sees sunrise around 4:30am, sunset around 10pm.

The traditional event of tossing the caber at the Highland Games

JUNE

Gardening Scotland *(late May/ early Jun)*, Edinburgh. Large gardening show.
Rockness Music Festival *(second weekend)*, Inverness. Rock festival at Loch Ness.
Edinburgh International Film Festival *(mid-Jun)*, Edinburgh. The world's oldest film festival.
Glasgow International Jazz Festival *(late Jun)*. Various venues across the city.
St Magnus Festival *(third week)*, Orkney. Arts event.
Royal Highland Show *(late Jun)*, Ingliston, Edinburgh.

Agricultural and food fair.
Traditional Boats Festival *(last weekend)*, Portsoy harbour, Banffshire. Displaying Scotland's fisheries heritage.

JULY

Game Conservancy Scottish Fair *(first weekend)*, Scone Palace, Perth. Major shooting and fishing event.
T in the Park *(second weekend)*, Balado, Fife. Scotland's biggest rock festival.
The Barclays Scottish Open *(mid-Jul)*, Alexandria. Fixture on European golf tour.

AUGUST

Traquair Fair *(first weekend)*, Innerleithen, Borders. Folk music, theatre and food stalls.
Eyemouth Maritime Festival *(12–15)*, Berwickshire. Music, crafts and seafood.
Edinburgh Festival *(various dates in Aug)*. "The Festival" comprises an international arts festival, an extensive fringe festival and other events

Grouse shooting on the "Glorious Twelfth" of August

dedicated to television, comedy, books, jazz and blues music *(see pp78–9)*.
Edinburgh Military Tattoo *(throughout Aug)*. Martial music and displays on Edinburgh Castle Esplanade.
Glorious Twelfth *(12 Aug)*. Grouse shooting season opens.
World Pipe Band Championships *(mid-Aug)*, Glasgow Green. Bagpipe music competition with some Highland Games events.
Great Scottish Run *(third Sun)*, Glasgow. A half-marathon for all to enter.
Connect Festival *(date varies)*, Inveraray. A grown-up alternative to T in the Park.

Drums and marching at the Edinburgh Military Tattoo in August

AVERAGE MONTHLY RAINFALL (EDINBURGH)

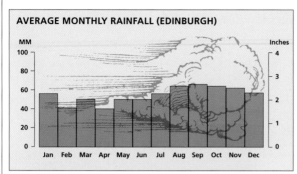

MM: 100, 80, 60, 40, 20, 0

Jan Feb Mar Apr May Jun Jul Aug Sep Oct Nov Dec

Inches: 4, 3, 2, 1, 0

Rainfall Chart

The east coast has a consistently lower rainfall in comparison with the rest of the country. The Northern Isles, Inner and Outer Hebrides (Western Isles) and Western Highlands are likely to have three times as much precipitation as Edinburgh, Fife or Tayside.

The soft colours of autumn in Tayside

AUTUMN

Catch a fine day in the countryside and the autumn colours can be spectacular. Scotland may be beginnning to wind down after the summer, but there are still some attractions to be found for the attentive visitor. Schools have a week's holiday in October, which was traditionally a break to allow the children to work on the potato harvest.

Shot-putting at Braemar

SEPTEMBER

Ben Nevis Hill Race *(first Sat)*, Fort William. Annual race up and down the highest mountain in Britain.
Braemar Gathering *(first weekend)*, Braemar, Aberdeenshire. One of the country's leading Highland Games *(see p31)* with members of the Royal Family usually in attendance.
Leuchars Air Show *(mid-Sep)*, RAF Leuchars, Fife. Airshow with flying displays and other attractions.
Ayr Gold Cup *(mid-Sep)*, Ayr Racecourse. Prestigious flat-race for horses.
Open Doors Day *(last Sat)*, different cities across Scotland. A number of the city's finest private buildings are opened to the public (0131 557 8686 or www.doorsopendays.org.uk).
Hairth O' Knokrach Festival *(mid-Sep)*, a weekend of live Celtic, world and roots music, song and dance at Craigshiels meadow in the Forest of Ae, Galloway Forest Park. Fire spectaculars, workshops and stalls.

OCTOBER

Highland Feast *(first week)*, the Highland's largest food festival with events throughout the region.
Royal National Mod *(second week)*, venue changes yearly. Performing arts competition promoting Gaelic language and Gaelic culture in general.

NOVEMBER

St Andrew's Week *(last week)*. Various venues in St Andrews host ceilidh evenings and festivals of Scottish food and drink.
St Andrew's Night *(30 Nov)*. National day of Scotland's patron saint. Many private and society dinners.

PUBLIC HOLIDAYS

These public holidays are observed throughout Scotland. Some local authorities declare extra holidays that apply only to their own areas.

New Year *(1–2 Jan)*. Two days in Scotland, compared with just the one day in England.
Good Friday *(late Mar or early Apr)*. Easter Monday is not an official holiday in Scotland.
May Day *(first Monday in May)*.
Spring Bank Holiday *(last Monday in May)*.
Summer Bank Holiday *(first Monday in Aug)*.
Christmas Day *(25 Dec)*.
Boxing Day *(26 Dec)*.

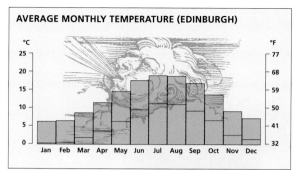

AVERAGE MONTHLY TEMPERATURE (EDINBURGH)

°C | Jan Feb Mar Apr May Jun Jul Aug Sep Oct Nov Dec | °F

Temperature Chart
This bar chart illustrates the average minimum and maximum monthly temperatures recorded in Edinburgh. The west of Scotland tends to be warmer than the east, while the Highlands can be arctic-like, with heavy snowfalls during the winter.

WINTER

This is a season of short days and cold weather, but Christmas and New Year celebrations provide a welcome antidote. Haggis sales peak in late January with Burns Night parties. This quiet period is probably the best time of year to visit Scotland's museums and galleries.

DECEMBER

Edinburgh's Hogmanay *(late Dec into early Jan).* World's biggest New Year celebration. Several days of events, including processions and street theatre, in the capital. The centrepiece is a vast street party on 31 December.

Edinburgh's Royal Mile over-flowing with Hogmanay revellers

JANUARY

The Ba' Game *(1 Jan),* Kirkwall, Orkney Isles. A centuries-old tradition to welcome the New Year

involving the young men of Kirkwall playing a ball game on the town's streets.
Celtic Connections *(second half of month),* Glasgow. Two weeks of music and *ceilidhs* on a Celtic theme, held in various venues.
Burns Night *(25 Jan).* Scotland celebrates the birth of its national poet with readings and "Burns Suppers". Haggis, potatoes, turnips and whisky are on the menu.
Up Helly Aa *(last Tue),* Lerwick, Shetland Isles. Midwinter fire festival.

FEBRUARY

Glasgow Film Festival *(mid-Feb),* Glasgow. Showcases a range of blockbusters and independent films.

Walker surveying the winter landscape in the Mamores in the Scottish Highlands

THE HISTORY OF SCOTLAND

*S*cotland has been torn apart by religion and internal politics, coveted by a richer and more powerful neighbour and wooed and punished for 400 years as the vital partner in the power struggles between England, France and Spain. She has risen and fallen through the ages, acquiring romance from tragedy, producing genius out of poverty and demonstrating an irrepressible spirit.

"They spend all their time in wars, and when there is no war, they fight one another" is a description of the Scots written in about 1500. For the visitor, the chief delight in this turbulent history is that so much is still tangible and visible.

An elaborately carved Pictish stone at Aberlemno, Angus

The earliest settlers in the country are believed to have been Celtic-Iberians, who worked their way north along the coast from the Mediterranean, and arrived in Scotland about 8,000 years ago. Around 2000 BC their descendants erected majestic standing stones, which are found all over the country. The layout of those at Callanish in the Western Isles shows an advanced knowledge of astronomy. These people also built underground round-houses and an abundance of forts, indicating that they were no strangers to invasion and warfare.

In AD 82 the Romans penetrated deep into " Caledonia", as they called the country, and Tacitus recorded victories against the Picts (the "painted people") and other tribes. Yet the Romans never conquered Caledonia because their resources were stretched too thin. Instead, they built Hadrian's Wall from Wallsend on the east coast to Bowness-on-Solway in the west, and later the Antonine Wall, a shorter wall further north, thereby endeavouring to shut out the Caledonians. Despite the country's relative isolation from the rest of Britain, however, it is believed that the original form of the Scottish kilt derived from the Roman tunic, or toga.

By AD 400 the Romans had abandoned their northern outposts, and Scotland was divided between four races, each with its own king. These were the predominant Picts, the Britons and Angles in the south, and the smallest group – the Scots – who originally came from Ireland and occupied southwest of the country.

In the late 4th century AD a Scot, St Ninian, travelled to Rome and, upon his return, built a church at Whithorn, thereby introducing Christianity to "Dalriada", the Kingdom of the Scots.

TIMELINE

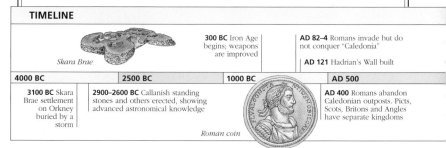

Skara Brae

300 BC Iron Age begins; weapons are improved

AD 82–4 Romans invade but do not conquer "Caledonia"

AD 121 Hadrian's Wall built

4000 BC	2500 BC	1000 BC	AD 500

3100 BC Skara Brae settlement on Orkney buried by a storm

2900–2600 BC Callanish standing stones and others erected, showing advanced astronomical knowledge

Roman coin

AD 400 Romans abandon Caledonian outposts. Picts, Scots, Britons and Angles have separate kingdoms

◁ *Return of Mary, Queen of Scots to Edinburgh* in 1561, by James Drummond (1816–77)

CHRISTIANITY AND UNIFICATION

Christianity remained in an isolated pocket centred around Whithorn on the Solway Coast, until the great warrior-missionary, St Columba, arrived from Ireland and established his monastery on the small Hebridean island of Iona in 563. Fired by his zeal, the new religion spread rapidly. By 800, Iona had achieved widespread influence, and Columban missionaries worked all over Europe. The Celtic Church developed along monastic lines and remained predominantly reclusive by nature, dedicating itself to worship and scholarship. Among its surviving works of art is the famous *Book of Kells*. This lavish, illuminated 8th- to 9th-century manuscript is thought to have been started on Iona, and later moved to Ireland for safe-keeping.

An illustrated page from the ornate *Book of Kells*, now kept in Trinity College, Dublin

The consolidation of a common religion helped to ease the merging of tribes. In 843 the Picts and Scots united under Kenneth MacAlpin. Curiously, the once-mighty Picts were the ones to lose their identity. They remain a mystery, except for their exquisite stone carvings depicting interwoven patterns, warriors and a wondrous mythology.

A long era of terrible Viking raids began in 890, resulting in the Norse occupation of the Western Isles for 370 years, and Shetland and Orkney for almost 600 years. The Norse threat possibly encouraged the Britons to join "Scotia", and in 1018 the Angles were defeated. Scotland became one united kingdom for the first time.

Viking axe

FEUDALISM AND THE CLANS

Under the powerful influence of Margaret, the English wife of Malcolm III (1057–93), a radical shift occurred during the king's reign away from the Gaelic-speaking culture of most of Scotland to the English-speaking culture of the south. This divide was widened under "good king" David I (1124–53). Under his reign Royal Burghs were created – towns built on the king's land and given special trading privileges in exchange for annual payments to him. He also introduced a national system of justice and weights and measures and, in the Lowlands, a feudal system based on Anglo-Norman lines.

Power devolved through an introduced aristocracy, largely French-speaking, and a structure bonded through land tenure. David I tried to impose this system in the north, but the region remained out of his control and, indeed, had its own "kings" –

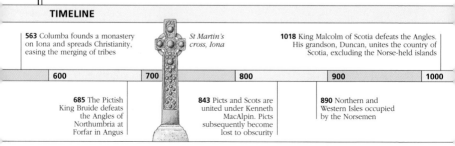

TIMELINE

563 Columba founds a monastery on Iona and spreads Christianity, easing the merging of tribes

St Martin's cross, Iona

1018 King Malcolm of Scotia defeats the Angles. His grandson, Duncan, unites the country of Scotia, excluding the Norse-held islands

600	700	800	900	1000

685 The Pictish King Bruide defeats the Angles of Northumbria at Forfar in Angus

843 Picts and Scots are united under Kenneth MacAlpin. Picts subsequently become lost to obscurity

890 Northern and Western Isles occupied by the Norsemen

the Lords of the Isles. In the Highlands a different social structure based on kinship – that of families, or clans – had evolved. The chief was a patriarch who held land, not privately, but on behalf of his people. It was an inheritable position, but the chief remained accountable to the clan and could be removed by common consent, unlike the feudal landlords whose power was vested through legal title to the land. This subtle difference was mirrored on a national level – in England, the monarch was the King of England; in Scotland, he was known as the King of Scots.

The lion of Scotland, dating from 1222

THE WARS OF INDEPENDENCE AND THE BATTLE OF BANNOCKBURN

In 1222 the lion of Scotland's coat of arms first appeared on the great seal of Alexander II. This was during a relatively peaceful interlude among frequent periods of turmoil when it seemed that Scotland was in danger of breaking apart.

When Alexander III's infant daughter died in 1290, there was no heir to the throne. Edward I of England installed a puppet king and, in 1296, led a devastating invasion that carried off the Stone of Destiny – the Scots' coronation throne – and earned him the title "Hammer of the Scots". Scotland was crushed and, but for one man, lost. William Wallace rose and led a revolt that rekindled

hope until his capture and execution six years later. His cause was taken up by Robert the Bruce who, against all odds, won support and raised an army that changed the course of history by winning a decisive victory over the English at the Battle of Bannockburn, near Stirling, on 23 June 1314.

Confronted by the largest English army to cross the border, the Scots were outnumbered three to one, and their arms were inferior. Yet Bruce had chosen his ground and his strategy carefully and, despite the enemy's skilful bowmen and heavy cavalry, the Scots gained the victory they so badly needed. Scotland had won back its independence, but it was not until 1329 that its sovereign status was recognized and secured by a Papal bull (six days after Bruce had died). Even so, the wars with England would continue for another 300 years.

Robert the Bruce in combat at the Battle of Bannockburn (1314)

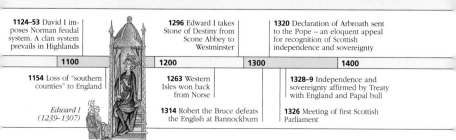

1124–53 David I imposes Norman feudal system. A clan system prevails in Highlands		1296 Edward I takes Stone of Destiny from Scone Abbey to Westminster		1320 Declaration of Arbroath sent to the Pope – an eloquent appeal for recognition of Scottish independence and sovereignty
1100		**1200**	**1300**	**1400**
1154 Loss of "southern counties" to England		1263 Western Isles won back from Norse		1328–9 Independence and sovereignty affirmed by Treaty with England and Papal bull
Edward I (1239–1307)		1314 Robert the Bruce defeats the English at Bannockburn		1326 Meeting of first Scottish Parliament

THE STUARTS

In 1371 began the long dynasty of the House of Stuart, a family distinguished by intelligence and flair but prone to tragedy. James I introduced wide legal reforms and approved the first university. James III won Orkney and Shetland from King Christian of Denmark and Norway through marriage to his daughter. James IV ended his illustrious reign with uncharacteristic misjudgement at the Battle of Flodden, in which 10,000 Scots died. But the most famous of the Stuarts was Mary, Queen of Scots (1542–87) who acceded to the throne as an infant.

Woodcut of Protestant martyr George Wishart being burned at the stake in 1546

Raised in France, Mary was beautiful, clever, gentle and spirited, but her reign was destined to be difficult. She was a Catholic in a country changing to Protestantism, and a threat to her cousin, Elizabeth I, whose claim to the English throne was precarious. Had Mary married wisely she might have ruled successfully, but her husbands alienated her potential supporters.

Mary returned to Scotland aged 18, already a widow and Dowager Queen of France, and spent just six turbulent years as Scotland's queen. She married again and following the public scandal of her secretary's murder by her second husband and his subsequent murder, she married for a third time. However, her choice was unacceptable to both the public and the church. She was deposed and held captive, making a daring escape from an island castle to England, only to be imprisoned there for 18 years and then finally executed on the orders of her cousin, Elizabeth.

Mary, Queen of Scots, of the House of Stuart

THE REFORMATION

Until Mary's reign, Scotland's national religion, like the rest of Europe, was the Church of Rome. It had become extremely rich and powerful and, in many ways, self-serving and divorced from the people. When Martin Luther sparked the Reformation in Germany in 1517, the ripples of Protestantism spread. In Scotland the most vociferous leader was the firebrand preacher John Knox *(see p58)*, who fearlessly denounced Mary.

There followed a long period of religious tension and strife. At first the main contentions were between Roman Catholics and Protestants. As Catholicism was purged, albeit with revivals and impregnable strongholds in the Highlands and islands, the conflicts shifted to Presbyterians versus Episcopalians. The differences lay in the structures of the churches and in their forms of worship. The feuds blazed and spluttered for 150 years.

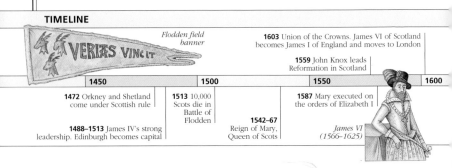

TIMELINE

Flodden field banner

VERITAS VINCIT

1603 Union of the Crowns. James VI of Scotland becomes James I of England and moves to London

1559 John Knox leads Reformation in Scotland

| 1450 | 1500 | 1550 | 1600 |

1472 Orkney and Shetland come under Scottish rule

1513 10,000 Scots die in Battle of Flodden

1587 Mary executed on the orders of Elizabeth I

1488–1513 James IV's strong leadership. Edinburgh becomes capital

1542–67 Reign of Mary, Queen of Scots

James VI (1566–1625)

UNION WITH ENGLAND

Mary's son, James VI, had reigned for 36 years when he became heir to the English throne. In 1603 he moved his court to London (taking his golf clubs), thus removing the monarchy from a permanent presence in Scotland for good. Scotland still retained its own parliament but found it increasingly difficult to trade in the face of restrictive English laws. In 1698 it tried to break the English monopoly on foreign trade by starting its own colony in Panama, a scheme that failed and brought financial ruin.

Articles of Union between England and Scotland, signed 22 July 1706 and accepted in 1707

The first proposal to unite the two parliaments received a hostile reception from the public. Yet influential Scots saw union as a means of securing equal trading rights. The English saw it as a means of securing the Protestant line of succession to the throne, for by now the deposed Stuarts were threatening to reinstate the Catholic line. James VII was deposed in 1689 and fled to France. In 1707 the Act of Union was passed and the Scottish Parliament was dissolved.

Protestant preacher John Knox

BONNIE PRINCE CHARLIE AND THE JACOBITES

In 1745 James VII's grandson, Prince Charles Edward Stuart, secretly entered Scotland, landing on the west Highland coast with seven men and a promise of French military support, which never materialized. His call to arms to overthrow the Hanoverian usurper, George II, drew a poor response and only a few Highland chiefs offered support. From this dismal start his campaign achieved remarkable success, but indecisive leadership weakened the side.

The rebel army came within 200 km (125 miles) of London, throwing the city into panic, before losing heart and retreating. At Culloden, near Inverness, the Hanoverian army (which included many Scots, for this was not an issue of nationalism) defeated the Jacobites on a snowy 16 April 1746. The cause was lost. Bonnie Prince Charlie became a fugitive hotly pursued for six months, but despite a £30,000 reward on his head he was never betrayed.

Feather-capped Scottish Jacobites being attacked by Royalists at Glen Shiel in the Highlands, 1719

1642 Civil war in England

1692 Massacre of Glencoe – a Campbell-led force murders its hosts, the MacDonalds, as an official punitive example

MacDonald shield

1745–6 Jacobite rising. Bonnie Prince Charlie tries to recover throne, but loses the Battle of Culloden and flees

| 1650 | 1700 | 1750 |

1746 Abolition of Feudal Jurisdictions

1689 James VII loses throne as he tries to restore Catholicism

1726 Roadbuilding under General Wade

1698 First Darien (Panama) Expedition to found a trading colony. Bank of Scotland established

1706–7 Union of Parliaments. Scottish Parliament dissolved

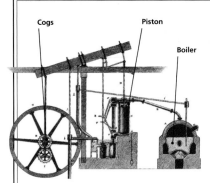

Cogs   Piston

Boiler

James Watt's steam engine, which shifted the
source of industrial power from water to steam

THE AFTERMATH OF CULLODEN
AND THE CLEARANCES

Culloden was the turning point in
Highland history, such was the severity
of the oppressive measures following
the battle. An Act was passed banning
the wearing of tartan, the playing of
pipes and the carrying of arms. The
ties of kinship between chief and
people were severed, and a way of life
was extinguished. From then on chiefs
assumed the roles of feudal landlords,
and the land, once held for the people,
became their private prop-
erty. When sheep were
found to thrive profitably
on the land, the people
became a hindrance and,
as a result, were removed.

The evictions, or so-
called Clearances, began
in the 1760s. Some were
achieved quite peacefully
through financial incen-
tives, but increasingly they
were enforced through
violence and burning, the
most notorious taking
place on the Duke of
Sutherland's estate in 1814.

In the 1860s, by which time Queen
Victoria had made the Highlands
popular and sporting estates all the
rage for hunting deer, the inland glens
were as empty as they are today.

INDUSTRIALIZATION AND THE
SCOTTISH ENLIGHTENMENT

While the Highlands were emptying,
parts of southern Scotland were
booming. For a large part of the 18th
century Glasgow's tobacco lords
operated a lucrative stranglehold on
the European market, and linen,
cotton and coal in their turn became
important national industries.

The Industrial Revolution, made
possible by Scotsman James Watt's
revolutionary contribution to the
steam engine, brought wealth to the
nation (yet at the expense of health
and social conditions) and turned
Glasgow into the "Workshop of the
Empire"– a reputation it retained until
the demise of its famous shipbuilding
industry in the 20th century.

A flowering of original thinkers also
emerged in Scotland in the 18th
century *(see pp26–7)*, most notably

Shipbuilding factory in Clydeside, now closed

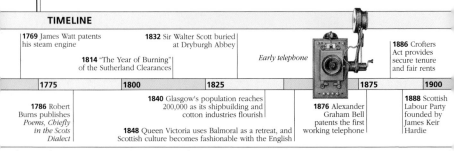

TIMELINE

1769 James Watt patents
his steam engine

1786 Robert
Burns publishes
*Poems, Chiefly
in the Scots
Dialect*

1814 "The Year of Burning"
of the Sutherland Clearances

1832 Sir Walter Scott buried
at Dryburgh Abbey

1840 Glasgow's population reaches
200,000 as its shipbuilding and
cotton industries flourish

1848 Queen Victoria uses Balmoral as a retreat, and
Scottish culture becomes fashionable with the English

Early telephone

1876 Alexander
Graham Bell
patents the first
working telephone

1886 Crofters
Act provides
secure tenure
and fair rents

1888 Scottish
Labour Party
founded by
James Keir
Hardie

1775   1800   1825   1875   1900

the philosopher David Hume, economist Adam Smith and the "Bard of Humanity", Robert Burns.

In the 19th century, Scotland's architecture led the way in Europe, as epitomized by the development of Edinburgh's New Town *(see pp64–5)*. This bold plan to create a residential centre away from the congested Old Town was begun in 1770, and the design was greatly expanded in 1822 to produce a model of elegance that is outstanding to this day. Among the more famous of those who have occupied these classic Georgian houses was Sir Walter Scott, one of the world's earliest best-selling novelists.

In this same period, known as the Scottish Enlightenment, Thomas Telford excelled in engineering and, ever increasingly, Scots were finding fame and fortune abroad by exploring and developing foreign lands.

A North Sea oil rig, providing prosperity in the late 20th century

The Scottish National Party (SNP), founded in 1934, is seen by many as too extremist, and its popularity has fluctuated. The exploration of North Sea oil since the late 1960s boosted Scotland's economy and its ability to self govern. In 1997 the Labour government held a referendum in which, by a large majority, the Scots voted for the re-establishment of a Scottish Parliament in 1999.

Although its tax-raising powers are restrained, the Scottish Parliament has devolved authority over many policies including health, education and local government.

In 2011, the Scottish National Party won an overall majority vote and began a second term in government. The party is expected to hold a referendum on Scottish independence later in the term.

THE PROCESS OF DEVOLUTION

For a long time, following the Act of Union, it was clear that England and Scotland were never intended to be equal. The political centre moved to Westminster and accordingly forced any Scot with a talent or aptitude for politics to leave Scotland. This, and an imbalance in the system weighted in favour of English affairs, caused a general feeling of apathy and impotence to take root in the Scottish psyche. Various reforms adjusted the imbalance, but the sense of political estrangement continued to fester.

SNP demonstrations in 1997, encouraging voters to say "Yes" to Scottish devolution

1925	1950	1975	2000	2025

1914–18 74,000 Scots die in World War I

1945 Alexander Fleming wins Nobel Prize

1967 North Sea oil exploration begins

1996 Stone of Destiny *(see p60)* returns to Scotland

1999 Scottish Parliament re-established

2011 SNP win landslide majority vote and begin a second term in government

1920s Hugh MacDiarmid reinstates Scots as literary language

1934 Scottish National Party founded

1931 Economic slump – 65 per cent unemployment in Clyde shipyards

2004 Opening of new Scottish Parliament building

Stone of Destiny

SCOTLAND REGION BY REGION

Scotland at a Glance

Stretching from the rich farmlands of the
Borders to a chain of isles only a few degrees
south of the Arctic Circle, the Scottish landscape
has a diversity without parallel in Britain. The
vibrant cities of Glasgow and Edinburgh offer
numerous attractions. The northeast is an area
rich in wildlife, and as you travel northwest,
the land becomes more mountainous and its
archaeological treasures more numerous.
In the far northwest, in the Western Isles,
Scotland's earliest relics stand upon some
of the oldest rock on earth.

Western Isles

The Isle of Skye
(see pp152–3),
*renowned for its
dramatic scenery,
has one of Scotland's
most striking coast-
lines. On the east
coast, a stream
plunges over Kilt
Rock, a cliff of
hexagonal basalt
columns named
after its likeness
to the Scottish
national dress.*

**THE HIGHLANDS
AND ISLANDS**
(see pp126–63)

The Trossachs (see pp116–17) *are a beautiful range
of hills straddling the border between the Highlands
and the Lowlands. At their heart, the forested slopes of
Ben Venue rise above the still
waters of Loch Achray.*

Strathclyde

GLASGOW
(see pp94–109)

Culzean Castle (see pp92–3)
*stands on a cliff's edge on the
Firth of Clyde, amid an extensive
country park. One of the jewels of
southern Scotland, Culzean is a
magnificent showcase for the work
of the Scottish-born architect,
Robert Adam (1728–92).*

◁ **Loch Lomond in the Highlands**

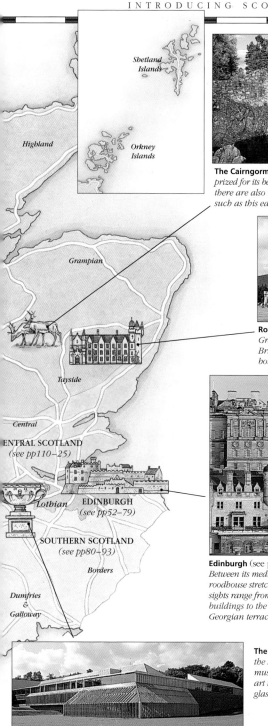

The Cairngorms (see pp140–41) *cover an area prized for its beauty and diversity of wildlife, though there are also many historical relics to be found, such as this early 18th-century arch at Carrbridge.*

Royal Deeside (see pp144–5) *in the Grampians has been associated with British royalty since Queen Victoria bought Balmoral Castle in 1852.*

Edinburgh (see pp52–79) *is the capital of Scotland. Between its medieval castle and The Palace of Holyroodhouse stretches the Royal Mile. Here, the historic sights range from the old Scottish Parliament buildings to the house of John Knox. By contrast, Georgian terraces predominate in the New Town.*

The Burrell Collection (see pp104–5), *on the southern outskirts of Glasgow, is a museum of some of the city's greatest art treasures. It is housed in a spacious, glass building opened in 1983.*

Shetland
Islands

Orkney
Islands

Highland

Grampian

Tayside

Central

CENTRAL SCOTLAND
(see pp110–25)

Lothian   **EDINBURGH**
(see pp52–79)

SOUTHERN SCOTLAND
(see pp80–93)

Borders

Dumfries
&
Galloway

0 kilometres   50

0 miles   50

EDINBURGH

The historic status of Edinburgh, the capital of Scotland, is beyond question, with ancient buildings scattered across the city, and the seat of Scotland's parliament lying close to the royal residence of The Palace of Holyroodhouse. The range of historical and artistic attractions draws visitors from all over the world.

Castle Rock in Edinburgh has been occupied since around 1,000 BC in the Bronze Age, which is no surprise given its strategic views over the Firth of Forth. The Castle itself houses the city's oldest building, St Margaret's Chapel, dating from the 11th century. A few years after it was built, Margaret's son, King David I, founded Holyrood Abbey a mile to the east. The town that grew along the route between these buildings, the "Royal Mile", became a popular residence of kings, although not until the reign of James IV (1488–1513) did Edinburgh gain the status of Scotland's capital. James built The Palace of Holyroodhouse as a royal residence in 1498 and made the city an administrative centre.

Overcrowding made the Old Town a dirty and difficult place to live, and threw rich and poor together. The construction of a Georgian New Town to the north in the late 1700s gave the wealthy an escape route, but even today Edinburgh has a reputation for social extremes. It has major law courts, is second only to London as a financial centre in the British Isles and houses the Scottish parliament. Bankers and lawyers form the city's establishment, and the most ambitious architectural developments have been for financial sector companies. Yet outlying housing estates, built after World War II, still have echoes of the Old Town poverty.

Edinburgh is best known today as a major tourist centre. There are wonderful museums and galleries to visit, and the city enjoys a widely renowned nightlife. At the height of the International Festival, in August, it is estimated that the population doubles from 400,000 to 800,000.

A juggler performing at the annual arts extravaganza, the Edinburgh Festival

◁ The Grassmarket area of the city, dominated by the imposing edifice of Edinburgh Castle

Exploring Edinburgh

The centre of Edinburgh is divided neatly in half by Princes Street, the principal shopping area. To the south lies the Old Town, site of the ancient city, which grew along the route of the Royal Mile, from the Castle Rock in the west to The Palace of Holyroodhouse in the east. At the end of the 18th century, building for the New Town started to the north of Princes Street. The area is still viewed today as a world-class example of Georgian urban architecture, with its elegant façades and broad streets. Princes Street has lots to offer, including shopoing, art galleries, the towering Scott Monument and the landmark Balmoral Hotel clock tower, as well as the city's main train station, Waverley.

Edinburgh Castle's Royal Scots soldiers

North Bridge, opened in 1772 – the main route connecting the Old and New Towns

GETTING AROUND

Central Edinburgh is compact, so walking is an excellent way to explore the centre. Other options include a comprehensive bus service and a multitude of black taxis. Avoid exploring the centre by car, because the streets tend to be congested with traffic, and parking may be difficult; car use is discouraged by the local authority. On main routes special lanes are provided for buses, taxis and bicycles, and in the suburbs there is also a good network of bicycle paths. A tram network should be operational by 2014.

SIGHTS AT A GLANCE

Historic Areas, Streets and Buildings

Edinburgh Castle pp60–61 **2**
The Exchange **3**
Greyfriars Kirk **4**
New Town pp64–5 **9**
Palace of Holyroodhouse **11**
The Royal Mile pp56–9 **1**
Scottish Parliament **13**

Monuments

Scott Monument **7**

Landmarks

Calton Hill **10**
Holyrood Park and Arthur's Seat **14**

Museums, Galleries and Exhibitions

National Gallery of Scotland **6**
Our Dynamic Earth **12**
National Museum of Scotland **5**
Scottish National Portrait Gallery **8**

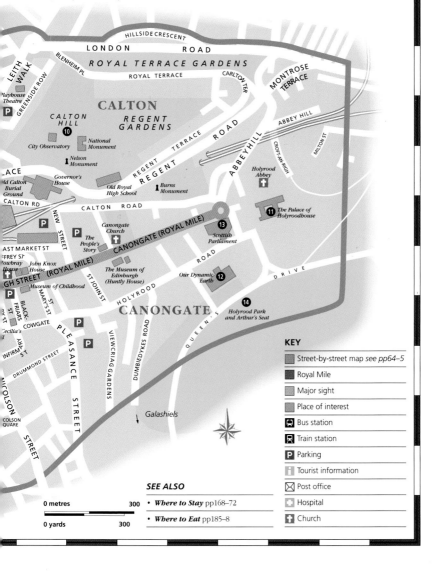

KEY

▨	Street-by-street map *see pp64–5*
▨	Royal Mile
▨	Major sight
▨	Place of interest
🚌	Bus station
🚉	Train station
🅿	Parking
ℹ	Tourist information
⊠	Post office
✚	Hospital
✚	Church

SEE ALSO

• *Where to Stay* pp168–72
• *Where to Eat* pp185–8

0 metres   300
0 yards   300

The Royal Mile ❶

The Royal Mile is a stretch of four ancient streets (from Castlehill to Canongate) which formed the main thoroughfare of medieval Edinburgh, linking the castle to the Palace of Holyroodhouse. Confined by the city wall, the "Old Town" grew upwards, with some tenements climbing to 20 floors. It is still possible, among the 66 alleys and closes off the main street, to imagine Edinburgh's medieval past.

Eagle sign outside Gladstone's Land

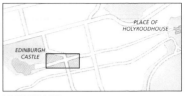

LOCATOR MAP

Gladstone's Land is a preserved 17th-century merchant's house.

Scotch Whisky Heritage Centre introduces visitors to Scotland's national drink.

The Camera Obscura contains an observatory from which to view the city.

Edinburgh Castle

CASTLEHILL

LAWNMARKET

Writer's Museum
This 17th-century house is now a museum of the lives and works of writers Burns, Scott and Stevenson.

The Hub is the headquarters of the Edinburgh Festival.

🛈 Camera Obscura
Tel (0131) 226 3709. ◯ daily. Apr–Oct: 9:30am–6pm (to 7:30pm Jul & Aug); Nov–Mar: 10am–5pm. 🔲 🔲
The lower floors of this building date from the early 17th century and were once the home of the Laird of Cockpen. In 1852, Maria Short added the upper floor, the viewing terrace and the Camera Obscura – a large pinhole camera that pictures life in the city centre as it happens. A marvel at the time, it remains one of Edinburgh's most popular attractions.

🛈 Gladstone's Land
(NTS) 477B Lawnmarket. **Tel** (0844) 493 2120. ◯ Apr–Oct: 10am–5pm daily (to 6pm Jul & Aug). 🔲 🔲
This restored 17th-century merchant's house provides a window on life in a typical Old Town house before overcrowding drove the rich inhabitants northwest to the Georgian New Town. "Lands", as they were then known, were tall, narrow buildings erected on small plots of land. The six-floor Gladstone's Land was named after Thomas Gledstanes, the merchant who built it in 1617. The house still has the original arcade booths on the street façade as well as a painted ceiling.

Although the house is extravagantly furnished, it also contains items, such as wooden overshoes that had to be worn in the dirty streets, which serve as a reminder of the less salubrious features that were part of the old city.

A chest in the beautiful Painted Chamber is said to have been given by a Dutch sea captain to a Scottish merchant who saved him from a shipwreck. A similar house, named Morocco's Land (*see p59*), can be found further to the east, on Canongate.

The bedroom of Gladstone's Land

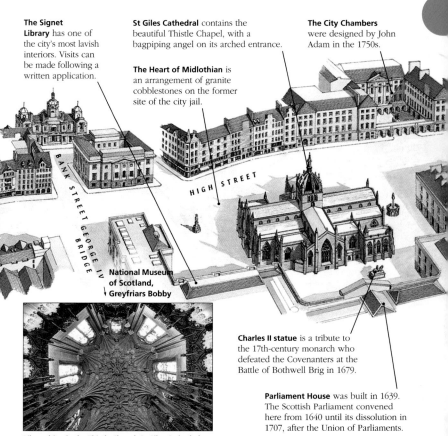

The Signet Library has one of the city's most lavish interiors. Visits can be made following a written application.

St Giles Cathedral contains the beautiful Thistle Chapel, with a bagpiping angel on its arched entrance.

The City Chambers were designed by John Adam in the 1750s.

The Heart of Midlothian is an arrangement of granite cobblestones on the former site of the city jail.

HIGH STREET

BANK STREET

GEORGE IV BRIDGE

National Museum of Scotland, Greyfriars Bobby

Charles II statue is a tribute to the 17th-century monarch who defeated the Covenanters at the Battle of Bothwell Brig in 1679.

Parliament House was built in 1639. The Scottish Parliament convened here from 1640 until its dissolution in 1707, after the Union of Parliaments.

Rib-vaulting in the Thistle Chapel, St Giles Cathedral

🏛 Writers' Museum
Lady Stair's Close. *Tel (0131) 529 4901.* ◯ *10am–5pm Mon–Sat (Aug: noon–5pm Sun).*
This fine Old Town mansion was built in 1622. In the 1720s it was acquired by Elizabeth, Dowager Countess of Stair, and has since been called Lady Stair's House. Its official title reflects its role as a museum of memorabilia from Robert Burns, Sir Walter Scott and Robert Louis Stevenson.

🏛 Parliament House
Parliament Sq, High St. *Tel (0131) 225 2595.* ◯ *9am–4:30pm Mon–Fri.* 🚹 *limited.*
This majestic, Italianate building was constructed in the 1630s for the Scottish Parliament. It has been home to the Court of Session and the High Court since the Union of Parliaments *(see p45)* in 1707. It is well worth seeing, as much for the

spectacle of its many gowned and wigged advocates as for the beautiful stained-glass window in the Great Hall, commemorating the inauguration of the Court of Session by King James V in 1532.

🔒 St Giles Cathedral
Royal Mile. *Tel (0131) 225 9442.* ◯ *May–Sep: 9am–7pm Mon–Fri, 9am–5pm Sat, 1–5pm Sun. Oct–Apr: 9am–5pm Mon–Sat, 1–5pm Sun.*
Properly known as the High Kirk (church) of Edinburgh, St Giles is popularly known as a cathedral. Though it was twice the seat of a bishop in the 17th century, it was from here that John Knox directed the Scottish Reformation, with its

Bagpiping angel from the entrance of the cathedral

emphasis on individual worship freed from the authority of bishops. A tablet marks the place where Jenny Geddes, a local market stallholder, scored a victory for the Covenanters in 1637 by hurling her stool at a preacher as he read from an English prayer book.
St Giles's Gothic exterior has a 15th-century tower, the only part to escape heavy renovation in the 1800s.
Inside, the Thistle Chapel, with its rib-vaulted ceiling and carved heraldic canopies, honours the knights of the Most Ancient and Most Noble Order of the Thistle. The carved royal pew in the Preston Aisle is used by Queen Elizabeth II when staying in Edinburgh.

Exploring Further Down the Royal Mile

The section of the Royal Mile from High Street to Canongate passes two monuments to the Reformation: John Knox's house and the Tron Kirk. The Canongate was once an independent district, owned by the canons of the Abbey of Holyrood, and sections of its south side have been restored. Beyond Morocco's Land, the road stretches for the final half-mile (800 m) to the Palace of Holyroodhouse.

LOCATOR MAP

HIGH STREET

SOUTH BRIDGE STREET

The Mercat Cross marks the city centre. It was here that Bonnie Prince Charlie *(see p153)* proclaimed his father king in 1745.

The Tron Kirk
was built in 1630 for the Presbyterians who left St Giles Cathedral when it came under the control of the Bishop of Edinburgh.

🏠 John Knox House

45 High St. **Tel** *(0131) 556 9579.*
⬜ *10am–6pm Mon–Sat, noon–6pm Sun (mid-Jun–Aug only).* ♿ *limited.* 📷 📹 *by appointment.*

As a leader of the Protestant Reformation and minister at St Giles, John Knox (1513–72) was one of the most important figures in 16th-century Scotland. Ordained as a priest in 1536, Knox later became convinced of the need for religious change. He took part in the Protestant occupation

of St Andrews Castle in 1547 and served two years as a galley slave in the French navy as punishment. On release, Knox went to London and Geneva to espouse the Protestant cause, returning to Edinburgh in 1559. This townhouse on the Royal Mile dates from 1450, and it was here that he spent the last few months of his life. Displays tell the story of Knox's life in the context of the political and religious upheavals of his time. The building also incorporates the Scottish Storytelling Centre.

🏛 Museum of Childhood

42 High St. **Tel** *(0131) 529 4142.*
⬜ *10am–5pm Mon–Sat, noon–5pm Sun.* ♿ *limited.*

This museum is not merely a toy collection but an insight into childhood, with all its joys and trials. Founded in 1955 by a city councillor, Patrick Murray (who claimed

to eat children for breakfast), it was the world's first museum of childhood. The collection includes medicines, school books and old-fashioned toys. With its nickelodeon and antique slot machines, this has been called the world's noisiest museum.

🏛 Canongate Tolbooth: The People's Story Museum

163 Canongate. **Tel** *(0131) 529 4057.*
⬜ *10am–5pm Mon–Sat (to 6pm Jun–Sep) (Sun during Edinburgh Festival).*

Edinburgh's social history museum is housed in the Canongate Tolbooth, dating

An 1880 automaton of the Man on the Moon, Museum of Childhood

John Knox House
Dating from 1450, the oldest house in the city was the home of the preacher John Knox during the 1560s. He is said to have died in an upstairs room. It contains relics of his life.

Morocco's Land is a reproduction of a 17th-century tenement house. It takes its name from the statue of a Moor which adorns the entrance.

**Museum of Edinburgh
Canongate Tolbooth**

CANONGATE

Museum of Childhood
Though created as a museum for adults by a city councillor who was known to dislike children, this lively musem now attracts flocks of young visitors.

Moubray House was to be the signing place of the Act of Union in 1707, until a mob forced the authorities to retreat to another venue.

from 1591. With its distinctive clock tower, this was the focal point for life in the Burgh of Canongate. Until the mid-19th century it contained law courts, a jail and the meeting place for the burgh council. It has been a museum since 1954.

Focusing on the lives of ordinary citizens from the late 18th century to the present, it covers subjects such as public health, recreation, trade unions and work. The riots, disease and poverty of the 19th century are also covered, and with subjects as diverse as wartime, football and punk rock, this collection gives a valuable insight into life in Edinburgh.

LIFE BELOW THE OLD TOWN
Until the 18th century most residents of Edinburgh lived along and beneath the Royal Mile and Cowgate. The old abandoned cellars and basements, which lacked any proper water supply, daylight or ventilation, were once centres of domestic life and industry. Under these conditions, cholera, typhus and smallpox were common. Mary King's Close, under the City Chambers, is one of the most famous of these areas – its inhabitants were all killed by the plague around 1645.

In 2003 many of these closes were opened up for the first time and guided visits are now possible through The Real Mary King's Close (0870) 243 0160.

A prison cell in the Canongate Tolbooth: The People's Story Museum

🏛 The Museum of Edinburgh
142–146 Canongate. **Tel** *(0131) 529 4143.* ☐ *10am–5pm Mon–Sat (noon–5pm Sun during Aug).*

Huntly House was built in the early 16th century and damaged in the English raid on Edinburgh in 1544. First used as a family townhouse, it was later divided into apartments but by the 19th century it was little more than a slum. In 1924 the local authority bought the property and opened the museum in 1932. The collection includes exhibits such as Neolithic axe heads, Roman coins, military artifacts and glassware. A section is also dedicated to Field Marshal Earl Haig, Commander-in-Chief of the British Army during World War I.

Edinburgh Castle ❷

Beam support in
the Great Hall

Standing upon the basalt core of an extinct volcano, Edinburgh Castle is an assemblage of buildings dating from the 12th to the 20th century, reflecting its changing role as fortress, royal palace, military garrison and state prison. Though there is evidence of Bronze Age occupation of the site, the original fortress was built by the 6th-century Northumbrian king, Edwin, from whom the city takes its name. The castle was a favourite royal residence until the Union of the Crowns *(see p45)* in 1603, after which the king resided in England. After the Union of Parliaments in 1707, the Scottish regalia were walled up in the Palace for over a hundred years. The Palace is now the zealous possessor of the so-called Stone of Destiny, a relic of ancient Scottish kings which was seized by the English and not returned to Scotland until 1996.

The Honours of Scotland
The Crown was restyled by James V of Scotland in 1540.

Military
Prison

Governor's House
Complete with Flemish-style crow-stepped gables, this building was constructed for the governor in 1742 and now serves as the Officers' Mess for the castle garrison.

MONS MEG

Positioned outside St Margaret's Chapel, this siege gun (or *bombard*) was made in Belgium in 1449 for the Duke of Burgundy, who gave it to his nephew, James II of Scotland. It was used by James against the Douglas family in their stronghold of Threave Castle *(see p89)* on the Dee in 1455, and later by James IV against Norham Castle in England. After exploding during a salute to the Duke of York in 1682, it was kept in the Tower of London until it was returned to Edinburgh in 1829, at Sir Walter Scott's request.

Vaults
This French graffiti, dating from 1780, recalls the many prisoners who were held in the vaults during the wars with France in the 18th and 19th centuries.

STAR SIGHTS

★ Great Hall

★ Palace

VISITORS' CHECKLIST

Castle Hill. **Tel** *(0131) 225 9846.*
☐ *Apr–Sep: 9:30am–6pm daily;*
Oct–Mar: 9:30am–5pm daily (last
admission: 45 mins before
closing). 🏷 ♿ 🎧 🏛 🍴 🖥
www.edinburghcastle.gov.uk

Argyle Battery

*These battlements offer a panoramic
view north over Princes Street to the
city's New Town, the Firth of Forth
and Fife.*

★ Palace

*Mary, Queen of
Scots, gave birth to
James VI in this
15th-century palace,
where the Stone of
Destiny and Crown
Jewels are displayed.*

Entrance

**Royal
Mile**

The Esplanade is the
location of the Military
Tattoo *(see p79).*

**The Half Moon
Battery** was built in
the 1570s as a plat-
form for the artillery
defending the eastern
wing of the castle.

St Margaret's Chapel

*This stained glass
window depicts Malcolm
III's saintly queen, to
whom the chapel is
dedicated. Probably built
by her son, David I, in
the early 12th century,
the chapel is the castle's
oldest existing building.*

★ Great Hall

*With its restored open-timber
roof, the hall dates from the
15th century and was the
meeting place of the Scottish
Parliament until 1639.*

The Standard Life Building, at the heart of the city's financial centre

The Exchange ❸

Lothian Rd, West Approach Rd and Morrison St.

The Exchange, once an unsightly area, was rejuvenated when Festival Square and the Sheraton Grand Hotel were built in 1985. Three years later the local authority published a plan to promote the area as a financial centre. In 1991 investment management firm Baillie Gifford opened Rutland Court on West Approach Road. The ambitious **Edinburgh International Conference Centre**, on Morrison Street, was designed by Terry Farrell and opened in 1995. Standard Life opened a headquarters on Lothian Road in 1997, and in 1998, Scottish Widows opened a bold building. The Exchange has grown into a trendy area, with restaurants, shops and the famous Filmhouse Cinema on Lothian Road (Tel: 0131 228 2688).

Edinburgh International Conference Centre *Tel (0131) 300 3000.* www.eicc.co.uk

Greyfriars Kirk ❹

Greyfriars Place. *Tel (0131) 226 5429.* Apr–Oct: 10:30am–4:30pm Mon–Fri, 10:30am–2:30pm Sat; Nov–Mar: 1:30–3:30pm Thu.

Greyfriars Kirk occupies a key role in the history of Scotland, as this is where the National Covenant was signed in 1638, marking the Protestant stand against the imposition of an episcopal church by King Charles I. Greyfriars was then a relatively new structure, having been completed in 1620 on the site of a Franciscan friary.

Throughout the 17th century, during years of bloodshed and religious persecution, the kirkyard was used as a mass grave for executed Covenanters. The kirk also served as a prison for Covenanter forces captured after the 1679 Battle of Bothwell Brig. The Martyrs' Monument is a sobering reminder of those times. The original kirk building was severely damaged by fire in 1845 and substantially rebuilt. Greyfriars is best known for its association with a dog, Bobby, who kept a vigil by his master's grave from 1858 to 1872. Bobby's statue stands outside Greyfriars Kirk.

A tribute to Greyfriars Bobby

National Museum of Scotland ❺

Chambers St. *Tel (0131) 225 7534.* 10am–5pm Mon–Sun. www.nms.ac.uk

The National Museum of Scotland comprises two radically different buildings, which stand side by side on Chambers Street. The older of the two is a great Victorian palace of self improvement. Designed by Captain Francis Fowke of the Royal Engineers, the building was completed in 1888, and was substantially restored and expanded in 2011. It includes an eclectic assortment of exhibits, which range from stuffed animals to ethnographic and technological items, displayed in rooms leading off the large and impressive central hall. There are also absorbing exhibits on world cultures, science and technology, art and design and the natural world.

As far back as the 1950s, recommendations were made that a new facility be built to house Scotland's own historical treasures. Work on a site next door to the Victorian building on Chambers Street started in 1993, and took five years to complete. The result is a contemporary flourish of confident design by architects Gordon Benson and Alan Forsyth, which opened to the public in December 1998. Described as one of the most important buildings erected in Scotland in the second half of the 20th century, the National Museum of Scotland tells the story of the country, starting with its geology and natural history. It then moves through to the early peoples of Scotland, the centuries when Scotland was a kingdom in its own right, and then on to later industrial developments. Some stunning items are on show, including St Fillan's Crozier, which was said to have been carried at the head of the Scottish army at Bannockburn in 1314, and the famous Lewis Chessman, carved from walrus ivory in the twelfth century. The Monymusk Reliquary is also

The 9th-century Monymusk Reliquary on display at Edinburgh's National Museum of Scotland

on display. Dated to around AD 800, it was a receptacle for the remains of the Christian missionary, St Columba *(see p42)*.

A museum highlight of a different kind is The Tower (www.tower-restaurant.com), a glamorous rooftop restaurant at the highest point of the new building, which appropriately enough uses seasonal Scottish ingredients.

National Gallery of Scotland ❻

The Mound. **Tel** *(0131) 624 6200.* ☐ *10am–5pm daily (to 7pm Thu).* 🔥 🍴 ♿ 📷 📷 **www**.national galleries.org

One of Scotland's finest art galleries, the National Gallery of Scotland is worth visiting for its 15th- to 19th-century British and European paintings alone, though plenty more can be found to delight art-lovers.

Some of the highlights among the Scottish works exhibited are the society portraits by Allan Ramsay and Sir Henry Raeburn, including the latter's *Reverend Robert Walker Skating on Duddingston Loch*, thought to date from the beginning of the 19th century.

The collection of early German pieces contains Gerard David's almost comic-strip treatment of the *Three Legends of St Nicholas*, from around the beginning of the 16th century. Works by Raphael, Titian and Tintoretto accompany other southern European paintings, including Velazquez's *An Old Woman Cooking Eggs*, from 1620.

There is an entire room devoted to *The Seven Sacraments* by Nicholas Poussin, dating from around 1640. Flemish painters represented include Rembrandt, Van Dyck and Rubens, while among the British offerings are important works by Ramsay, Reynolds and Gainsborough.

Rev Robert Walker Skating on Duddingston Loch

Scott Monument ❼

Princes Street Gardens East. ☐ *Apr–Sep: 10am–7pm Mon–Sat, 10am–6pm Sun; Oct–Mar: 9am–4pm Mon–Sat, 10am–6pm Sun).* 📷

Sir Walter Scott (1771–1832) is one of the most important figures in Scottish literature *(see p86)*. Born in Edinburgh, Scott initially pursued a legal career but he soon turned to writing full time as his ballads and historical novels began to bring him success. His works looked back to a time of adventure, honour and chivalry, and did much to promote this image of Scotland abroad.

In addition to being a celebrated novelist, Sir Walter was also a major public figure – he organized the visit of King George IV to Edinburgh in 1822. After Scott's death in 1832, the Monument was constructed on the south side of Princes Street as a tribute to his life and work. This Gothic tower was designed by George Meikle Kemp and reaches a height of 61 m (200 ft). It was completed in 1840, and includes a statue of Sir Walter at its base, sculpted by Sir John Steell. Inside the huge structure, 287 steps give access to the topmost platform. The rewards for those who climb up are great views around the city centre and across the Forth to Fife.

The imposing Gothic heights of the Scott Monument on Princes Street

Scottish National Portrait Gallery ❽

1 Queen St. **Tel** *(0131) 556 8921.* ☐ *10am–5pm daily.* 🔥 📷 **www**.nationalgalleries.org

An exhibition on the 12 generations of the Royal House of Stuart, from the time of Robert the Bruce to Queen Anne, is a highlight here. Memorabilia include Mary, Queen of Scots' jewellery and a silver travelling canteen left by Bonnie Prince Charlie *(see p153)* at the Battle of Culloden. The upper gallery has a number of portraits of famous Scots, including a picture of Robert Burns.

The museum was completely refurbished in 2011, in order to display more of the collecion.

Van Dyck's *Princess Elizabeth and Princess Anne*, **National Portrait Gallery**

Street-by-Street: New Town 🄈

Albert Monument, Charlotte Square

The first phase of Edinburgh's "New Town" was built in the 18th century, to relieve the congested and unsanitary conditions of the medieval old town. Charlotte Square at the western end formed the climax of this initial phase, and its new architectural concepts were to influence all subsequent phases. Of these, the most magnificent is the Moray Estate, where a linked series of very large houses forms a crescent, an oval and a twelve-sided circus. The walk shown here explores this area of monumental Georgian town planning.

Moray Place
The crowning glory of the Moray Estate, this circus consists of a series of immense houses and apartments, many still inhabited.

The Water of Leith is a small river running through a delightful gorge below Dean Bridge. There is a riverside walkway to Stockbridge.

Dean Bridge
This was built in 1829 to the design of Thomas Telford. It gives views down to the Water of Leith and upstream to the weirs and old mill buildings of Dean Village.

Ainslie Place, an oval pattern of town houses, forms the core of the Moray Estate, linking Randolph Crescent and Moray Place.

STAR SIGHTS

★ Charlotte Square

★ The Georgian House

NEW TOWN ARCHITECTS

The driving force behind the creation of the New Town was George Drummond (1687–1766), the city's Provost, or Mayor. James Craig (1744–95) won the overall design competition in 1766. Robert Adam (1728–92) introduced Classical ornamentation to Charlotte Square. Robert Reid (1774–1856) designed Heriot Row and Great King Street, and William Playfair (1790–1857) designed Royal Circus. The monumental development of the Moray Estate was the work of James Gillespie Graham (1776–1855).

Robert Adam

No. 14 was the residence of judge and diarist Lord Cockburn from 1813 to 1843.

| 0 metres | 100 |
| 0 yards | 100 |

KEY

- - - Suggested route

For hotels and restaurants in this region see pp168–72 and pp185–8

★ The Georgian House

No. 7 is owned by the National Trust for Scotland and is open to the public. It has been repainted in its original colours and furnished with appropriate antiques, and is a testament to the lifestyle of the upper sector of 18th-century Edinburgh society.

LOCATOR MAP
See Edinburgh Map pp54–5

Bute House is the official residence of the First Minister of the Scottish Parliament.

★ Charlotte Square

The square was built between 1792 and 1811 to provide a series of lavish town houses for the most successful city merchants. Most of the buildings are now used as offices.

No. 39 Castle Street was the home of the writer Sir Walter Scott *(see p86).*

Princes Street Gardens
Princes Street was part of the initial building phase of the New Town. The north side is lined with shops; the gardens to the south lie below the castle.

No. 9 was the home of surgeon Joseph Lister *(see p25)* from 1870 to 1877. He developed methods of preventing infection both during and after surgery.

West Register House was originally St George's Church, designed by Robert Adam.

York Place

A view from Edinburgh Castle across the towers and spires of the city to Calton Hill in the distance

Calton Hill ⑩

City centre east, via Waterloo Pl.

Calton Hill, at the east end of Princes Street, has one of Edinburgh's most memorable and baffling landmarks – a half-finished Parthenon. Conceived as the National Monument to the dead of the Napoleonic Wars, building began in 1822 but funds ran out and it was never finished. Public shame over its condition has given way to affection, as attitudes have softened over the last 170 years or so.

Fortunately, the nearby tower commemorating the British victory at Trafalgar was completed, in 1816. Named the **Nelson Monument**, the tower is designed to resemble a telescope standing on its end. It provides a fine vantage point from which to admire the views of Edinburgh and the surrounding area.

The Classical theme continues on top of Calton Hill with the old **City Observatory**, designed by William Playfair in 1818 and based on Athens' Tower of the Winds. At present it is closed to the public, but it's still worth a trip to see the impressive exterior.

Another Classical building, the **Royal High School**, was created during the 1820s on the Regent Road side of Calton Hill. It was designed by Thomas Hamilton, with the Temple of Theseus at Athens in mind. Often cited as a possible home for a Scottish parliament, the building was the focus for the Vigil for Scottish Democracy, which campaigned from 1992 to 1997 for self government. A discreet cairn marking this effort stands a little way east of the National Monument on Calton Hill. The cairn contains several "gift" stones, including one from Auschwitz in memory of a Scottish missionary who died there.

The final resting place of Thomas Hamilton is the **Old Calton Cemetery**, south of Waterloo Place, which he shares with philosopher David Hume and other celebrated Edinburgh residents.

🏛 Nelson Monument
Tel (0131) 556 2716. ⏰ Apr–Sep: 1–6pm Mon, 10am–6pm Tue–Sat; Oct–Mar: 10am–3pm Mon–Sat 🅿

🏛 City Observatory
Calton Hill. *Tel* (0131) 556 4365.
⬤ to the public.

The grand façade of the Palace of Holyroodhouse, renovated in the 17th century following a fire

Palace of Holyroodhouse ⑪

East end of the Royal Mile. **Palace & Queen's Gallery** *Tel* (0131) 556 1096. ⏰ Nov–Mar: 9:30am–4:30pm daily; Apr–Oct: 9:30am–6pm daily. 🅿 🅿 🅿

Known today as Queen Elizabeth II's official Scottish residence, the Palace of Holyroodhouse was built by James IV in the grounds of an abbey in 1498. It was later the home of James V and his wife, Mary of Guise, and was remodelled in the 1670s for Charles II. The Royal Apartments (including the Throne Room and Royal Dining Room)

City Observatory, Calton Hill, based on Classical Greek architecture

are used for investitures and for banquets whenever the Queen visits the palace. A chamber in the so-called James V tower is famously associated with the unhappy reign of Mary, Queen of Scots (see p44). It was probably in this room, in 1566, that Mary saw the murder of her trusted Italian secretary, David Rizzio, authorized by her jealous husband, Lord Darnley. She was six months pregnant when she witnessed the murder, during which Rizzio's body was pierced "with fifty-six wounds".

In the early stages of the Jacobite uprising of 1745 (see p45), the last of the pretenders to the British throne, Charles Edward Stuart (Bonnie Prince Charlie) held court at Holyroodhouse, dazzling Edinburgh society with his magnificent parties.

James V's arms, Holyroodhouse

The new **Queen's Gallery** displays works from the Royal Collection.

Our Dynamic Earth ⑫

Holyrood Road. **Tel** (0131) 550 7800.
⬜ Apr–Oct: 10am–5pm daily; Nov–Mar: Wed–Sun. 🈹 🗗 ♿ 🖵
www.dynamicearth.co.uk

Our Dynamic Earth is a permanent exhibition about the planet. Visitors are taken on a journey from the earth's volcanic beginnings to the first appearance of life. Further displays concentrate on the world's climatic zones and dramatic natural phenomena such as tidal waves and earthquakes. State-of-the-art lighting and interactive techniques produce the special effects for 90 minutes of learning and entertainment.

The exhibition building is fronted by a 1,000-seat stone amphitheatre designed by Sir Michael Hopkins, and it incorporates a translucent tented roof. Situated beneath Salisbury Crags, the modern lines of Our Dynamic Earth contrast sharply with the natural landscape.

Scottish Parliament ⑬

Holyrood. **Tel** 0131 348 5200.
⬜ 10am–5:30pm Mon & Fri (to 4pm Oct–Mar), 9am–6:30pm Tue–Thu, 11am–5:30pm Sat. 🗗 ♿ 🖵
www.scottish.parliament.uk

Following decades of Scottish calls for more political self-determination, a 1997 referendum on the issue of whether or not to have a Scottish parliament, with some powers devolved from the UK parliament in London, resulted in a majority "yes" vote (see p47). Designed by the late Enric Miralles, known for his work on buildings at the 1992 Barcelona Olympics, the parliament building was opened in October 2004 by Queen Elizabeth II. It's well worth taking one of the regular tours of this architecturally exciting public building.

Holyrood Park and Arthur's Seat ⑭

Main access via Holyrood Park Rd, Holyrood Rd and Meadowbank Terrace.

Holyrood Park, adjacent to the Palace of Holyroodhouse, covers over 260 hectares (640 acres) of varying terrain, topped by a rugged 250-m (820-ft) hill. Known as

Arthur's Seat, the hill is actually a volcano that has been extinct for 350 million years. The area has been a royal hunting ground since at least the time of King David I, who died in 1153, and a royal park since the 16th century.

The name Holyrood, which means "holy cross", comes from an episode in the life of David I when, in 1128, he was knocked from his horse by a stag while out hunting. Legend has it that a cross appeared miraculously in his hands to ward off the animal and, in thanksgiving, the king founded the Abbey of the Holy Cross, Holyrood Abbey. The name Arthur's Seat is probably a corruption of Archer's Seat, a more prosaic explanation for the name than any link with the legendary King Arthur.

The park has three small lochs. St Margaret's near the Palace is the most romantic, with its resident swans and position under the ruins of St Anthony's Chapel. Dunsapie Loch is the highest, sitting 112 m (367 ft) above sea level under Arthur's Seat. Duddingston Loch, on the south side of the park, is home to a large number of wildfowl.

The **Salisbury Crags** are among the park's most striking features. Their dramatic profile, along with that of Arthur's Seat, can be seen from many kilometres away. The Crags form a parabola of red cliffs that sweep round and up from Holyrood Palace, above a steep supporting hillside. A rough track, called the Radical Road, follows their base.

Arthur's Seat and the Salisbury Crags, looming above the city

Further Afield

Although inextricably linked to the rest of Edinburgh, the inhabitants of Leith insist that they do not live in the city itself. More than just a docks area, Leith has plenty of attractions for the visitor. Close by is the magnificent Royal Botanic Garden. Dean Village offers riverside walks, galleries and antique shops. To the west of the city are the historic Hopetoun House and Linlithgow Palace, to the east is Haddington and a dramatic coastline.

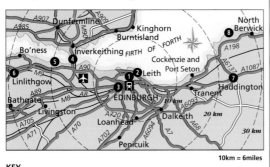

10km = 6miles

KEY

▦	Urban area
✈	Airport
🚉	Train station
—	Intercity train line
▬	Motorway (highway)
▬	Major road
═	Minor road

SIGHTS AT A GLANCE

Dean Village ❸
East Lothian Coast ❽
Forth Bridges ❹
Haddington ❼
Hopetoun House ❺
Leith ❷
Linlithgow Palace ❻
Royal Botanic Garden ❶

A specimen from the Palm House in the city's Royal Botanic Garden

Royal Botanic Garden ❶

Inverleith Row. **Tel** *(0131) 552 7171.*
▦ ◯ *Feb–Oct: 10am–6pm daily;*
Nov–Feb 10am–4pm daily. ⬛ 🍴 ▦
📷 www.rbge.org.uk

This magnificent garden lies a short way to the north of the New Town, across the Water of Leith (a river that runs from the Pentland Hills down through Edinburgh and into the Firth of Forth at Leith). The garden is a descendant of a Physic Garden near Holyroodhouse that was created by two doctors in 1670. It was moved to its present location in 1820, and since then has been progressively enlarged and developed. Public access is from the east (well served by buses) and from the west (offering better car parking). The garden benefits from a hill site, giving southerly views across the city.

There is a rock garden in the southeast corner and an indoor exhibition and interpretation display in the northeast corner. There are also extensive greenhouses in traditional and modern architectural styles, offering fascinating hideaways on rainy days. Be sure not to miss the alpine display to the northwest of the greenhouses, or the beautiful and fragrant rhododendron walk.

Leith ❷

Northeast of the city centre, linked by Leith Walk.

Leith is a historic port that has traded for centuries with Scandinavia, the Baltic and Holland, and has always been the port for Edinburgh. It was incorporated into the city in 1920, and now forms a northeastern suburb.

The medieval core of narrow streets and quays includes a number of historic warehouses and merchants' houses dating from the 13th and 14th centuries. There was a great expansion of the docks in the 19th century, and many port buildings date from this period.

Shipbuilding and port activities have diminished, but there has been a renaissance in recent years in the form of conversions of warehouse buildings to offices, residences and, most notably, restaurants and bars. The Shore and Dock Place now has Edinburgh's most dense concentration of seafood bistros and varied restaurants *(see pp187–8).*

The tourist attractions have been further boosted by the presence of the former British **Royal Yacht Britannia**, which is on display in Leith's Ocean Terminal.

🚢 **Royal Yacht Britannia**
Ocean Terminal, Leith Docks. **Tel**
(0131) 555 5566. ◯ *daily.* 📷 ⬛
🍴 www.royalyachtbritannia.co.uk

The British Royal Yacht Britannia, berthed at Leith's Ocean Terminal

For hotels and restaurants in this region see pp168–72 and pp185–8

Forth Bridges ❹

Lothian. ⚡🚇 Dalmeny, Inverkeithing.

The small town of South Queensferry is dominated by the two great bridges that span 1.5 km (1 mile) across the River Forth to the town of Inverkeithing. The spectacular rail bridge, the first major steel-built bridge in the world, was opened in 1890 and remains one of the greatest engineering achievements of the late Victorian era. Its massive cantilevered sections are held together by more than eight million rivets, and the painted area adds up to some 55 ha (135 acres). The saying "it's like painting the Forth Bridge" has become a byword for non-stop, repetitive endeavour.

The neighbouring road bridge was the largest suspension bridge outside the US when it was opened in 1964 by Her Majesty Queen Elizabeth II. The two bridges make an impressive contrast, best seen from the promenade at South Queensferry. The town got its name from Queen Margaret (see p61), who reigned with her husband, King Malcolm III, in the 11th century. She used the ferry here on her frequent journeys between Edinburgh and the royal palace at Dunfermline in Fife (see p124). From Queensferry you can take a boat trip down the River Forth to visit the island of Inchcolm with its exceptionally well-preserved 12th-century abbey. A new Forth bridge is due for completion in 2016.

Leger's *The Team at Rest* (1950), Scottish National Gallery of Modern Art

Dean Village ❸

Northwest of the city centre.

This interesting, tranquil area lies in the valley of the Water of Leith, just a few minutes' walk northwest from Charlotte Square (see map p54). A series of water mills along the river have been replaced by attractive buildings of all periods..

Access to Dean Village can be gained by walking down Bell's Brae from Randolph Crescent. A riverside walk threads its way between the historic buildings, crossing the river on a series of footbridges. Upstream from Dean Village the riverside walk leads in a few minutes to a footbridge and a flight of steps giving access to the **Scottish Gallery of Modern Art and Dean Gallery**. The main access for vehicles, and less energetic pedestrians, is on Belford Road.

Downstream from Dean Village, the riverside walkway passes under the magnificent high level bridge designed by Thomas Telford. It then passes St Bernard's Well before

arriving in the urban village of Stockbridge. Antiques, curios, vintage clothes and jewellery can be found in the shops on the south side of the river in St Stephen Street. The riverside walk continues north-east, close to the Royal Botanic Garden. The city centre is a short walk away, via Royal Circus and Howe Street.

17th-century stone houses on the historic Bell's Brae

🏛 **Scottish Gallery of Modern Art & Dean Gallery**
75 Belford Rd. **Tel** (0131) 624 6200.
⭕ daily. 🖼 special exhibitions only.
♿ 🖥 www.nationalgalleries.org

The huge, cantilevered Forth Rail Bridge, seen from South Queensferry

Hopetoun House ❺

West Lothian. **Tel** (0131) 331 2451.
�+ Dalmeny then taxi. ⏱ mid-Apr–
Sep: 10am–5:30pm daily. 🎦 ♿ 🅿
🖥 www.hopetoun.co.uk

An extensive parkland by
the Firth of Forth, designed
in the style of Versailles, is the
setting for one of Scotland's
finest stately homes. The
original house was completed
in 1707 and later absorbed
into William Adam's grand
extension. The dignified,
horseshoe-shaped plan and
lavish interior represent
Neo-Classical 18th-century
architecture at its best. The
red and yellow state drawing
rooms, with their Rococo
plasterwork and ornate
mantelpieces, are particularly
impressive. A highlight of a
visit here is the afternoon
tea available in the stables
tearoom, with the option
of a champagne tea.

A wooden panel above the main
stairs depicting Hopetoun House

Linlithgow Palace ❻

Kirk Gate, Linlithgow, West Lothian.
Tel (01506) 842896. 🚄 🅿
⏱ Apr–Sep: 9:30am–5:30pm daily;
Oct–Mar: 9:30am–4:30pm daily. 🎦
♿ limited.

Standing on the edge of
Linlithgow Loch, the former
royal palace of Linlithgow is
one of the country's most-
visited ruins. It dates back
largely to the building

Ornate fountain in the ruins of Linlithgow Palace

commissioned by James I
in 1425, though some sections
date from the 14th century.
The vast scale of the building
is best seen in the 28-m-
(94-ft-) long Great Hall, with
its huge fireplace and
windows. The restored
fountain in the courtyard was
a wedding present in 1538
from James V to his wife, Mary
of Guise. His daughter, Mary,
Queen of Scots *(see p44)*, was
born at Linlithgow in 1542.

The adjacent Church of St
Michael is Scotland's largest pre-
Reformation church and a fine
example of the Scottish Decorated style. Consecrated in the
13th century, the church was
damaged by the fire of 1424.

Haddington ❼

East Lothian. 🛈 Edinburgh &
Lothians (0845) 225 5121.

This attractive county town is
situated about 24 km (15 miles)
east of Edinburgh. It was
destroyed on various
occasions during the Wars
of Independence in the

13th–14th
centuries, and
again in the
16th century.
The agricultural
revolution
brought great
prosperity, giving
Haddington
many historic
houses, churches,
and other public
buildings. A
programme of
restoration has
helped the town
to retain its char-
acter. The River
Tyne encloses the town, and
there are attractive riverside
walks and parkland. ("A walk
around Haddington" guide is
available from newsagents.)
The parish church of St Mary's,
southeast of the centre, dates
from 1462 and is one of the
largest in the area. Parts of
the church have been rebuilt
in later years, having been
destroyed in the siege of 1548.
A short way south of the
town lies **Lennoxlove House**,
with its ancient tower house.

🏛 **Lennoxlove House**
Tel (01620) 823720. ⏱ Easter–Oct:
pm only Wed–Thu, Sat & Sun. 🎦 🅿

East Lothian Coast ❽

🛈 Edinburgh Lothians (0845) 225
5121. **www**.visitscotland.com

Stretching east from Musselburgh for some 65 km (40
miles), the coast of East Lothian
offers many opportunities for
beach activities, windsurfing,
golf, viewing seabirds and
coastal walks. The coastline is
a pleasant mixture of beaches,

The historic and tranquil town of Haddington on the River Tyne

For hotels and restaurants in this region see pp168–72 and pp185–8

low cliffs, woodland, golf courses and some farmland. Although the A198 and A1 are adjacent to the coast for only short distances, they give easy access to a series of public car parks (a small charge is made in summer) close to the shore. Among these visitor points is Gullane, perhaps the best beach for seaside activities. Yellowcraig, near Dirleton, is another lovely bay, lying

Tantallon Castle, looking out to the North Sea

about 400 m (440 yds) from the car park. Limetree Walk, near Tyninghame, has the long, east-facing beach of Ravensheugh Sands (a ten-minute walk along a woodland track). Belhaven Bay, just west of Dunbar, is a large beach providing walks along the estuary of the River Tyne. Barns Ness, east of Dunbar, offers a geological nature trail and an impressive lighthouse. Skateraw Harbour is an attractive small bay, despite the presence of Torness nuclear power station to the east. Finally, there is another delightful beach to be found at Seacliff, reached by a private toll road that leaves the A198 about 3 km (2 miles)

east of North Berwick. This sheltered bay has spectacular views of the Bass Rock, home to one of the largest gannet (a type of marine bird) colonies in Britain. The rock itself can be seen at close quarters by taking the boat trip from North Berwick harbour (summer only). At the town's **Scottish Seabird Centre** it is possible to control cameras on the rock and on the Island of Fidra, for live coverage of the birdlife without disturbing it. Also of interest along this coastline are **Dirleton Castle** and **Tantallon Castle**, perched on a cliff top near Seacliff beach. There is a small industrial museum at Prestonpans. North Berwick and Dunbar are towns worthy of a visit.

Scottish Seabird Centre
Tel (01620) 890202. ☐ daily. 🌐
♿ 🔲 www.seabird.org
Dirleton Castle
Tel (01620) 850330. ☐ daily. 🌐
Tantallon Castle
Tel (01620) 892727. ☐ 9:30am–4:30pm Sat–Wed. ● Nov–Mar. 🌐

EAST LOTHIAN COASTAL WALK

For a very attractive longer coast walk, there is easy public access along the footpath from Gullane Bay to North Berwick. The path follows the coastline, crossing grassy heathland between the alternating sandy bays and low rocky headlands, with views of the coast of Fife to the north. There are small islands along the way. The last part of the walk into North Berwick has wonderful views east to the white slopes of the Bass Rock.

TIPS FOR WALKERS

Starting point: *Gullane Bay.*
Finishing point: *North Berwick.*
Length: *10 km (6 miles); 3 hours.*
Getting there: *by car; a bus service between Edinburgh and North Berwick gives access to both ends.*
Level: *easy (one steep section).*

Dirleton

North Berwick

Muirfield

Gullane

KEY

▬	Major road
═	Minor road
┼┼┼	Train line
☀	Viewpoint
P	Parking

| ☐ | Urban area |
| - - | Route |

0 kilometres 2
0 miles 1

SHOPPING IN EDINBURGH

Despite the growth of new out-of-town malls, Princes Street remains one of the top 12 retail centres in the British Isles. With the ancient Castle rising above the gardens along the street's south side, it is a unique and picturesque place to shop. Although many familiar chain stores can be found here, the capital also boasts its very own

Colourful Wemyssware china

department store, Jenners, a marvellous institution that has been in business for over 150 years. But there are shopping attractions away from Princes Street, too, including Scotland's best delicatessen (Valvona & Crolla), several excellent wine merchants, a selection of Highland clothing outfitters and an appealing collection of specialist stores.

DEPARTMENT STORES

Princes Street has several good department stores, with **House of Fraser** at the west end being one of the best. Located opposite the Scott Monument, is **Jenners**. Founded on a different site in the late 1830s, it has gained a reputation as Edinburgh's top store. During the Christmas season it is famed for its central atrium housing a Christmas tree. **John Lewis**, belonging to a nationwide chain of stores, is in a contemporary building on Leith Street. The famous **Harvey Nichols** is on St Andrew Square.

CLOTHING

Designer labels for men and women can be found in both Jenners and House of Fraser *(see Department Stores)*. **Corniche** on Jeffrey Street offers more interesting and

Traditional Highland dress and accessories, for sale on the Royal Mile

exciting women's fashion by designers such as Jean-Paul Gaultier and Vivienne Westwood, while **Jane Davidson** is home to a more traditional, chic look. George Street contains a number of women's stores, including **Phase Eight** and **Whistles**. **Cruise** has separate shops for men and women. Men can also go to **Thomas Pink**, and **Austin Reed** for smart suits and shirts. The **Schuh** chain has fashionable footwear for men and women. Several shops on the Royal Mile, including **Ragamuffin**, sell interesting knitwear. The Royal Mile also boasts Highland outfitters offering made-to-measure kilts; **Hector Russell** is one of the best. **Kinloch Anderson** in Leith is also a leading example, and the shop has a small display on the history of tartan. Outdoor equipment and waterproof clothing can be found at leading supplier **Graham Tiso**.

FOOD AND DRINK

Edinburgh has a reputation as Scotland's top city for eating out, and it matches this status on the shopping front, with some very good food stores. **Valvona & Crolla**, a family-run delicatessen trading since the 1930s, is acknowledged as one of the best of its kind in the UK, let alone Scotland, and stocks good breads and an award-winning Italian wine selection. The **Peckham's** chain is present here, while **Glass & Thompson** is a good deli serving the New Town. Celebrated cheesemonger **Iain Mellis** started his business in Edinburgh, **MacSweens** are master haggis makers, and **Real Foods** is one of Scotland's longest-established wholefood stores.

Specialist wine merchants include **Peter Green** and **Villeneuve Wines**, as well as chains such as **Oddbins**, while **Cadenheads** supplies rare whiskies. **Justerini & Brooks** is the most distinguished wine and

Princes Street from the top of Calton Hill

spirit merchant in the city centre, and **Henderson Wines** has an extensive selection of wines, beers and malts.

BOOKS AND NEWSPAPERS

The high-street **Waterstone's** chain has two stores in Princes Street (the west end branch has a fine coffee shop) and a third branch on George Street nearby. There are also several small, friendly independent bookshops, such as the design-focused **Analogue Books** and **Beyond Words**, which specializes in photographic books. **The International Newsagents** offers a good selection of foreign newspapers and magazines.

ART, DESIGN AND ANTIQUES

Original artworks are on sale at a variety of galleries in the city. **The Scottish Gallery** in the New Town has everything from jewellery for under £100, to pieces by well-known Scottish artists sold at £10,000 or more. The prices at the **Printmakers Workshop** are more affordable, with an innovative range of limited-edition prints for sale, and the **Collective Gallery** offers experimental works. **Inhouse** has some remarkable designer furniture. Browsers looking for antiques should try Victoria Street, St Stephen's Street, the Grassmarket and Causeway-side. For large-scale fixtures

and fittings, the **Edinburgh Architectural Salvage Yard** sells everything from Victorian baths to staircases and doors.

Intricately patterned Edinburgh Crystal, a popular souvenir

DIRECTORY

DEPARTMENT STORES

Harvey Nichols
30–34 St Andrew's Sq,
EH2 2AD.
Tel (0131) 524 8388.

House of Fraser
145 Princes St, EH2 4YZ.
Tel (0844) 800 3724.

Jenners
48 Princes St, EH2 2YJ.
Tel (0844) 800 3725.

John Lewis
69 St James Centre,
EH1 3SP.
Tel (0871) 432 1335.

CLOTHING

Austin Reed
39 George St, EH2 2HN.
Tel (0131) 225 6703.

Corniche
2 Jeffrey St, EH1 1DT.
Tel (0131) 556 3707.

Cruise *(men)*
94 George St, EH2 3DF.
Tel (0131) 226 3524.

Cruise *(women)*
31 Castle St, EH2 3DN.
Tel (0131) 220 4441.

Graham Tiso
41 Commercial St,
EH6 6JD.
Tel (0131) 554 0804.

Hector Russell
137–141 High St,
EH1 1SG.
Tel (0131) 558 1254.

Jane Davidson
52 Thistle St, EH2 1EN.
Tel (0131) 225 3280.

Kinloch Anderson
Commercial St, EH6 6EY.
Tel (0131) 555 1390.

Phase Eight
47b George St,
EH2 2HT.
Tel (0131) 226 4009.

Ragamuffin
278 Canongate,
EH8 8AA.
Tel (0131) 557 6007.

Schuh
32 North Bridge,
EH1 1QG.
Tel (0131) 225 6552.

Thomas Pink
32a Castle St,
EH2 3HT.
Tel (0131) 225 4264.

Whistles
97 George St, EH2 3ES.
Tel (0131) 226 4398.

FOOD AND DRINK

Cadenheads
172 Canongate,
EH8 8BN.
Tel (0131) 556 5864.

Glass & Thompson
2 Dundas St, EH3 6HZ.
Tel (0131) 557 0909.

Henderson Wines
109 Comiston Rd,
EH10 6AQ.
Tel (0131) 447 8580.

Iain Mellis
30a Victoria St, EH1 2JW.
Tel (0131) 226 6215.

Justerini & Brooks
14 Alva Street, EH2 4QG.
Tel (0131) 226 4202.

MacSweens
Dryden Rd, Bilston Glen,
Loanhead, EH20 9LZ.
Tel (0131) 440 2555.

Oddbins
Elm Row, 94–96
Brunswick St, EH7 5HN.
Tel (0131) 556 4075.

Peckham's
155 Bruntsfield Place,
EH10 4DG.
Tel (0131) 229 7054.

Peter Green
37 Warrender Park Rd,
EH9 1HJ.
Tel (0131) 229 5925.

Real Foods
37 Broughton St, EH1 3JU.
Tel (0131) 557 1911.

Valvona & Crolla
19 Elm Row, EH7 4AA.
Tel (0131) 556 6066.

Villeneuve Wines
9a Broughton Street,
EH1 3RJ.
Tel (0131) 558 8441.

BOOKS AND NEWSPAPERS

Analogue Books
39 Candlemaker Row,
EH1 2BQ.
Tel (0131) 220 0601.

Beyond Words
42–44 Cockburn St,
EH1 1PR.
Tel (0131) 226 6636.

The International Newsagents
351 High St, EH1 1PW.
Tel (0131) 225 4827.

Waterstone's
128 Princes St, EH2 4AD.
Tel (0131) 226 2666.

ART, DESIGN AND ANTIQUES

Collective Gallery
28 Cockburn St, EH1 1NY.
Tel (0131) 220 1260.

Edinburgh Architectural Salvage Yard
31 West Bowling
Green St, EH6 5NX.
Tel (0131) 554 7077.

Inhouse
28 Howe St, EH3 6TG.
Tel (0131) 225 2888.

Printmakers Workshop
23 Union St, EH1 3LR.
Tel (0131) 557 2479.

The Scottish Gallery
16 Dundas St, EH3 6HZ.
Tel (0131) 558 1200.

What to Buy

Scottish blend tobacco

Scotland offers a wide range of goods and souvenirs to tempt its visitors. Most food and drink items can be found in Edinburgh's food stores and off-licences (liquor stores that also stock tobacco). A number of specialist shops in the city sell more unusual Scottish crafts and products, from handcrafted jewellery to clothing, such as tartan kilts and knitwear. Certain areas of Scotland specialize in particular crafts – Orkney is famed for its jewellery, Caithness and Edinburgh for their beautifully engraved glassware.

Caithness glass paperweight

Edinburgh glass goblet

Scottish glass *is beautifully decorated. The Caithness glass factories in Oban, Perth and Wick offer tours to show how delicate patterns are engraved.*

Celtic earrings

Amethyst brooch

Celtic brooch

Scottish jewellery *reflects either the area in which it was made, a culture (such as Celtic) or an artistic movement such as Art Nouveau. The unbroken, intricate patterns and knotwork in the jewellery pictured above symbolize the wish for eternal life.*

Stag horn *is carved into all manner of objects, both functional, as with this ashtray, and decorative.*

Dagger ("sgian dubh")

Sporran

Classic Scottish kilt

Tartan tie and scarf

Scottish tartan *originally existed in the form of a feileadh-mor (meaning "great plaid" or "great kilt"), an untailored garment draped over the shoulder and around the waist. It was worn by Highlanders in the 15th and 16th centuries. Today, "tartan" refers to the distinctive patterns woven into cloth. Some are based on the designs of centuries past.*

Scottish textiles *vary greatly, but the most distinctive include chunky woollens from the islands; smart tweeds, such as Harris tweed with its fine-toothed check; softest cashmere, used to make sweaters, cardigans and scarves; and fluffy sheepskin rugs.*

Cable-knit sweater

Tweed jacket

PACKAGED FOODS

Food is a popular and accessible form of souvenir or gift to purchase during a visit to Scotland. Teatime is a favourite meal with the Scottish, offering such treats as Dundee cake, butter shortbread, Abernethy biscuits, Scotch pancakes and parlies (ginger cookies). Oatcakes are the traditional accompaniment to cheese in Scotland, although they also complement pâté and sweet toppings such as jam or honey. They are also delicious toasted and served with plenty of butter.

Vegetarian haggis   **Original haggis**

Haggis, the most famous of Scottish foods, traditionally consists of sheep's offal and oatmeal. It is now also available in vegetarian, venison and whisky-laced varieties.

Traditional pure butter shortbread   **Oatcakes**

Scotch Abernethy biscuits

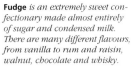

Fudge is an extremely sweet confectionary made almost entirely of sugar and condensed milk. There are many different flavours, from vanilla to rum and raisin, walnut, chocolate and whisky.

Dairy vanilla fudge   **LochRanza whisky fudge**

BOTTLED DRINKS

Home to a large number of distilleries and breweries, Scotland is perhaps associated most with its alcoholic beverages. There is certainly a good range on sale, including locally brewed beers and ales, many varieties of Scotch whisky *(see pp32–3)* and an assortment of spirits and liqueurs, such as Drambuie and Glayva. But Scotland is also famed for its mountain spring water, which is sold still, fizzy (carbonated) or flavoured with fruits such as peach or melon.

Historic Scottish ales

Beers and ales figure prominently in the drink produced in Scotland. Traditionally served by the pint in pubs, they can also be purchased in bottles. Alternative choices include fruit ales and heather ales, brewed using ancient Highland recipes.

Highland spring water

Whisky is undoubtedly the most famous of all Scottish spirits. There are a huge number of whiskies from which to choose, each with a unique taste (see pp32–3). Drambuie is a variation on a theme, being a whisky-based, herb flavoured liqueur.

Drambuie   **Glenfiddich**   **LochRanza**   **Glen Ord**   **Bell's**

ENTERTAINMENT IN EDINBURGH

Although most people associate entertainment in Edinburgh with the festivals that take place in August, the city also benefits from its status as the Scottish capital by acting as a centre for drama, dance and music. The Filmhouse is an important venue on the arthouse cinema circuit and some argue that Edinburgh's nightclubs are as

A postcard advertising the Edinburgh Festival

good as those in Glasgow these days. Many bars offer an excellent range of Scotch whiskies and cask ales, while the expansion of the café-bar scene in the last few years means it is now possible to find a decent cup of coffee later on in the evening. Edinburgh is home to Scotland's national rugby union stadium, Murrayfield, host to international matches.

ENTERTAINMENT GUIDES

The twice-monthly arts and entertainments magazine, *The List* (www.list.co.uk), covers events in both Edinburgh and Glasgow. A similar publication, *The Skinny* (www.theskinny. co.uk), is available free from restaurants and clubs.

THEATRE AND DANCE

Edinburgh's **The King's Theatre** hosts pantomimes and performances by touring companies. Run by the same organization that manages Edinburgh Festival Theatre *(see Classical Music and Opera)*, it focuses on contemporary dance and ballet, but there are children's shows and music hall-style performances too. **Edinburgh Playhouse** often hosts internationally successful musicals, such as "Mamma Mia!" and "Chicago", while **The Traverse** is home to more experimental work and has helped launch

Edinburgh Festival Theatre, venue for dance, classical music and opera

the careers of young Scottish playwrights. **The Royal Lyceum** opts for a repertory of well-known plays and adaptations, but showcases some new work too. Edinburgh University's theatre company stages shows at **Bedlam**, while both **Theatre Workshop** and **St Bride's** present innovative productions.

CLASSICAL MUSIC AND OPERA

Visits from the Glasgow-based Scottish Opera and the Royal Scottish National Orchestra are hosted at the glass-fronted **Edinburgh Festival Theatre**, which opened in 1994. Edinburgh is home to the internationally acclaimed Scottish Chamber Orchestra, which performs at the **Queen's Hall**. Smaller venues host recitals, including Edinburgh University's **Reid Concert Hall** and **St Cecilia's Hall**. **St Giles Cathedral** hosts classical concerts by small groups.

ROCK, JAZZ AND WORLD MUSIC

For major rock concerts, Murrayfield Stadium *(see Sports)* is sometimes called into use. Edinburgh Playhouse *(see Theatre and Dance)* has also played host to major pop stars, as have **Cabaret Voltaire** and **The Liquid Room**. The city has an eclectic nightclub scene, and intimate sessions – including jazz and world music – often take place at clubs *(see Café-bars, Bars and Clubs)*. The Queen's Hall *(see Classical Music and Opera)* also hosts smaller shows. Folk and jazz musicians appear at the **The Tron** and **Henry's Cellar Bar**, respectively.

Some pubs have resident folk musicians and jazz bands; check *The List* magazine for details. **The Assembly Rooms** hosts *ceilidhs* (traditional Highland dance evenings).

CINEMA

Edinburgh, like other cities, has seen a move to multiplex cinemas. However, **Cineworld** and **Odeon Multiplex** are quite far from the centre; the **Odeon Edinburgh** is the most central. A few minutes from Princes Street is the **OMNI** leisure centre, with a 12-screen cinema village. **The Dominion** is an old-fashioned affair, while **The Cameo** shows offbeat modern classics. **The Filmhouse** is the arthouse movie theatre, and centre for the International Film Festival.

EDINBURGH INTERNATIONAL FILM FESTIVAL

Logo for the annual Film Festival

The ornate, colourful interior of The King's Theatre, opened in 1906

For hotels and restaurants in this region see pp168–72 and pp185–8

Opening ceremony of a Five Nations rugby union match at Murrayfield

SPORTS

The impressive **Murrayfield Stadium** is the national centre for Scottish rugby and international matches are played from late January to March. There are two association football (soccer) sides, **Heart of Midlothian** in the west and **Hibernian** in Leith. **Meadowbank Stadium and Sports Centre** hosts league basketball and a range of athletics events throughout the summer.

CAFÉ-BARS, BARS AND CLUBS

Broughton Street is an obvious centre for café-bars. Some are predominantly night-time spots, including **Assembly, Indigo Yard, Po-Na-Na** and **Voodoo Rooms**. Examples of more traditional Edinburgh bars are **The Café Royal, Bennet's, The Cumberland** or **The Bow Bar**. All serve good cask ales and an extensive selection of single-malt Scotch whiskies. Some of the city's acclaimed club venues, which also host live bands from time to time, are **The Bongo Club**, and **The Liquid Room** (*see Rock, Jazz and World Music*). **Opal Lounge**, is a more stylish club that also serves food.

DIRECTORY

THEATRE AND DANCE

Bedlam
11b Bristow Place, EH1 1E2.
Tel (0131) 225 9893.

Edinburgh Playhouse
18–22 Greenside Place, EH1 3AA.
Tel (0870) 6063424.

The King's Theatre
2 Leven St, EH3 9LQ.
Tel (0131) 529 6000.

The Royal Lyceum
30b Grindlay St, EH3 9AX.
Tel (0131) 248 4800.

St Bride's
10 Orwell Terrace, EH11 2DZ.
Tel (0131) 346 1405.

Theatre Workshop
34 Hamilton Pl, EH3 5AX.
Tel (0131) 226 5425.

The Traverse
10 Cambridge St, EH1 2ED.
Tel (0131) 228 1404.

CLASSICAL MUSIC AND OPERA

Edinburgh Festival Theatre
13-29 Nicolson St, EH8 9FT.
Tel (0131) 529 6000.

The Queen's Hall
85–89 Clerk St, EH8 9JG.
Tel (0131) 668 2019.

Reid Concert Hall
Bristo Sq, EH8 9AG.
Tel (0131) 650 4367.

St Cecilia's Hall
Niddry St, EH1 1LG.
Tel (0131) 668 2019.

St Giles Cathedral
High St, EH1 1RE.
Tel (0131) 225 9442.

ROCK, JAZZ AND WORLD MUSIC

Assembly Rooms
54 George St, EH2 2LR.
Tel (0131) 220 4348.

Cabaret Voltaire
36 Blair St, EH1 1QR.
Tel (0131) 220 6176.

Henry's Cellar Bar
8–16a Morrison St, EH3 8BJ.
Tel (0131) 221 1288.

The Liquid Room
9c Victoria St, EH1 2HE.
Tel (0131) 225 2564.

The Tron
9 Hunter Sq, EH1 1QW.
Tel (0131) 225 3784.

CINEMA

The Cameo
38 Home St, EH3 9LZ.
Tel (0131) 228 2800.

Cineworld
130 Dundee Street, EH1 1AF. *Tel (0871) 200 2000.*

The Dominion
18 Newbattle Terrace, EH10 4RT.
Tel (0131) 447 4771.

Edinburgh Odeon
118 Lothian Road, EH3 3BG. *Tel (0871) 224 4007.*

The Filmhouse
88 Lothian Rd, EH3 9BZ.
Tel (0131) 228 2688.

Odeon Multiplex
120 Wester Hailes Rd, EH14 1SW.
Tel (0871) 224 4007.

OMNI Edinburgh
Greenside Place, EH1 3BN.
Tel (0871) 224 0240.

SPORTS

Heart of Midlothian
Tynecastle Stadium, Gorgie Rd, EH11 2NL.
Tel (0131) 200 7200.

Hibernian Football Club Ltd
12 Albion Place, EH7 5QG.
Tel (0131) 661 2159.

Meadowbank Stadium and Sports Centre
139 London Rd, EH7 6AE.
Tel (0131) 661 5351.

Murrayfield Stadium
Murrayfield, EH12 5PJ.
Tel (0131) 346 5000.

CAFÉ-BARS, BARS AND CLUBS

Assembly
41 Lothian St, EH1 1HB.
Tel (0131) 220 4288.

Bennet's
8 Leven St, EH3 9LG.
Tel (0131) 229 5143.

The Bongo Club
37 Holyrood Rd, EH8 8BA.
Tel (0131) 558 7604.

The Bow Bar
80 West Bow, EH1 2HH.
Tel (0131) 226 7667.

The Café Royal
19 W Register St, EH2 2AA.
Tel (0131) 556 1884.

The Cumberland
1–3 Cumberland St, EH3 6RT.
Tel (0131) 558 3134.

Indigo Yard
7 Charlotte Lane, EH2 4QZ. *Tel (0131) 220 5603.*

Opal Lounge
51a George Street, EH2 2HT. *Tel (0131) 226 2275.*

Po-Na-Na
43b Frederick St, EH2 1EP.
Tel (0131) 226 2224.

Voodoo Rooms
19a West Register St, EH2 2AA.
Tel (0131) 556 7060.

The Edinburgh Festival

A masked Fringe street performer

August in Edinburgh means "the Festival", one of the world's premier arts jamborees, covering drama, dance, opera, music and ballet. The more eclectic "Fringe" developed in parallel with the official event, but has now exceeded it in terms of size. Both have been going strong for over 60 years, as has the Edinburgh International Film Festival, which is held in June and has become a renowned festival in its own right. The British Army contributes with the Military Tattoo, and the Edinburgh Book Festival and Jazz & Blues Festival are also staged in August. A total of half a million people visit these events.

Entrance to the Fringe information office, located on the Royal Mile

EDINBURGH INTERNATIONAL FESTIVAL

As a cultural antidote to the austerity of post-war Europe, where many cities were devastated and food rationing was common even in the victorious countries, Edinburgh held its first arts festival in 1947. Over the years it grew in scope and prestige, and it is now one of the top events in the world calendar of performing arts. It boasts a strong programme of classical music, traditional ballet, contemporary dance, opera and drama, and is held in major venues across the city *(see Directory p77)*.

The grand finale of the International Festival is a breathtaking spectacle, with some 250,000 crowding into the city centre to see a magnificent fireworks display based at the Castle. The lucky few with tickets for the Ross Bandstand in Princes Street Gardens also experience the fireworks concert by the Scottish Chamber Orchestra.

THE FRINGE

The Fringe started with a few performances providing an alternative to the official events of the International Festival, in the first year it was staged. A decade later, coming to Edinburgh to appear "on the Fringe" was an established pastime for amateurs, student drama companies or anyone else. All that was needed was a space to perform in the city in August. This haphazard approach has long since given way to a more formal one, with an administrative body running the Fringe and, in recent years, a core of professionally-run venues attracting the bulk of the Fringe audiences. The Assembly Rooms in George Street *(see Directory p77)* and the Pleasance Theatre in The Pleasance host shows by television celebrities whose stand-up comedy or cabaret fails to fit the International Festival format.

The original vibrancy of the Fringe still exists, and in church halls and other odd venues across Edinburgh, including the city's streets, Fringe-goers can find everything from musicals performed by school children to experimental adaptations of Kafka's works.

Enjoying the August sun and street entertainment on the Royal Mile

EDINBURGH INTERNATIONAL FILM FESTIVAL

Dating from 1947, the Edinburgh International Film Festival was one of the world's first international film festivals, and is held in June. Although it started with a focus on documentary cinema, it soon began to widen and include arthouse and popular movies.

The Festival invented "the retrospective" as a means of studying a film-maker's work. It has seen premieres by such noted directors as Woody Allen and Steven Spielberg. Since its 1995 relaunch, the

Crowds throng around the colourful Fringe street performers

The Military Tattoo at Edinburgh Castle, with an audience of thousands

Festival has been broken down into four main sections. There is a showcase for young British talent, a world premieres section, a film study category, and a major retrospective.

Although the showings are screened primarily at The Filmhouse on Lothian Road, every city centre cinema now takes part in the festival to some extent (see Directory p77 for details of all the cinemas).

EDINBURGH MILITARY TATTOO

The enduring popularity of the Military Tattoo never fails to surprise some people, or to charm others. It has been running since 1950, when the British Army decided to contribute to Edinburgh's August events with displays of martial prowess and music on the picturesque Castle Esplanade.

Temporary stands are built on the Esplanade each summer in preparation for the 200,000 visitors who watch the Tattoo over its three-week run. This enormous spectacle heralds the approach of the other, assorted August arts festivals. Marching bands and musicians from the

A painted street performer showing his skill at staying as still as a statue

armed forces of other countries are invited every year to enhance the show. For many, the highlight of the Tattoo is a solo piper playing a haunting pibroch lament (see p30) from the Castle battlements.

A temporary marquee selling books at the Edinburgh Book Festival

EDINBURGH BOOK FESTIVAL

Every August, a mini-village of marquees is erected in the beautiful Georgian surroundings of Charlotte Square Gardens in the city centre. This temporary village plays host to two weeks of book-related events and talks by a variety of writers, from novelists and poets to those who specialize in cook books or children's fiction. Scottish authors are always well represented.

Originally held every other year, the Book Festival became so popular that since 1998 it has been an annual event coinciding with the other festivals.

EDINBURGH JAZZ & BLUES FESTIVAL

For around ten days in early August a selection of international jazz performers comes to Edinburgh to give concerts, accompanied by Scotland's principal jazz musicians.

The HVB and ARE on Clerk Street (see p76) are the main centres, although other venues in the city are used. There is also a free, open-air Mardi Gras day in the Grassmarket, in the Old Town, on the opening Saturday. The Blues element of the Festival is held in its own separate venue and is also very successful, attracting many UK and American performers.

DIRECTORY

Edinburgh International Festival
The Hub, Edinburgh's Festival Centre, Castlehill, Royal Mile, EH1 2NE.
Tel (0131) 473 2099 (info).
Tel (0131) 473 2000 (booking).
www.eif.co.uk

Edinburgh International Film Festival
88 Lothian Rd, EH3 9BZ.
Tel (0131) 228 4051.
www.edfilmfest.org.uk

Edinburgh International Book Festival
5a Charlotte Sq, EH2 4DR.
Tel (0845) 373 5888.
www.edbookfest.co.uk

Edinburgh Jazz and Blues Festival
Assembly Direct,
89 Giles St, EH6 6BZ.
Tel (0131) 553 4000.
Tel Box office: (0131) 467 5200.
www.edinburghjazzfestival.com

The Fringe
The Fringe Office,
180 High St, EH1 1QS.
Tel (0131) 226 0026.
www.edfringe.com

Military Tattoo
Edinburgh Tattoo,
32 Market St, EH1 1QB.
Tel (0131) 225 1188.
www.edintattoo.co.uk

SOUTHERN SCOTLAND

*S*outhern Scotland is a blend of attractive landscapes and historic houses, castles and abbeys. Sadly, many of these ancient buildings exist only in fortified or ruined form due to the frontier wars that dated from the late 13th century. The rounded hills of the Scottish Borders and the more rugged peaks of Dumfries & Galloway bore the brunt of this fierce conflict between Scotland and England.

In 1296 Scotland committed itself to the Wars of Independence against the English, and it was Southern Scotland that suffered the most. The strife caused by the many battles lasted for three centuries, as first Scottish self-determination, and then alliances with France, led to strained relations between Scotland and its southern neighbour, England. Dryburgh, one of the area's magnificent 12th-century abbeys, was burned twice, first by the English in 1322 and then again in 1544.

The virtual independence of the Borders district brought further conflict. Powerful families had operated under local laws set in place since the mid-12th century, and when Scottish kings were not fighting the English, they led raids into the Border country to try and bring it back under central control.

Over the years, some of the great dramas of Scottish history have been played out in the South. Robert the Bruce's guerrilla army defeated an English force at Glen Trool in 1307, but Flodden, near Coldstream, was the scene of the country's worst military reverse in 1513, when King James IV of Scotland and thousands of his men fell in battle.

Today, the quiet countryside around the Borders market towns, and the beautiful mountain scenery in Dumfries & Galloway, seem to belie such violent history. The area is now known for its manufacturing of textiles and for promoting its literary associations, as Sir Walter Scott lived at Abbotsford, near St Boswells. But it is the ruins of the great Border abbeys, castles and battlegrounds that serve as a reminder of Southern Scotland's turbulent past.

Fishing in the tranquil waters of the River Tweed, which weaves its way through the Border country

◁ The majestic ruins and colourful gardens of Melrose Abbey, one of the four great Border abbeys

Exploring Southern Scotland

Southern Scotland has a variety of
landscapes and small towns of great
character, but the region is often
overlooked by visitors keen to reach
Edinburgh, Glasgow or the Highlands.
The hills around Glen Trool in Dumfries & Galloway are beautiful and
dramatic while, further east, the Border
hills are less rugged but offer some
classic panoramas such as Scott's View,
near Melrose. The Ayrshire coast has a
string of holiday resorts; the Solway
Firth coast is fine touring country,
quiet and picturesque; and St Abb's
Head in the east is one of Scotland's
most important wildlife reserves.

The Gothic abbey church at Melrose, once one of the
richest abbeys in Scotland

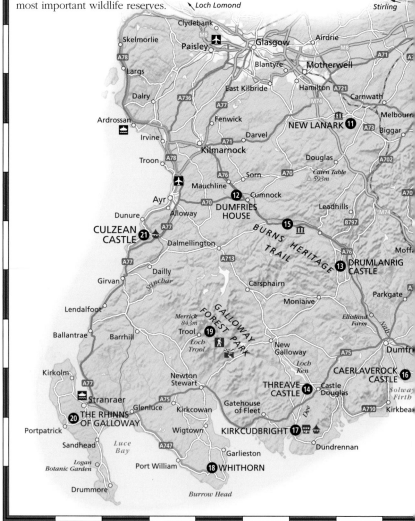

GETTING AROUND

Travelling east to west and vice versa can be problematic as all the main routes run north–south from Edinburgh and Glasgow to England. There are rural bus services but these tend to be infrequent and slow. Rail links down the east coast from Edinburgh, and from Glasgow to Ayrshire, are good, and there is also a train service from Glasgow to Stranraer, the ferry port for Northern Ireland. Exploring scenic areas away from the coasts is best done by car.

KEY

═══	Motorway (highway)
═══	Major road
──	Minor road
══	Other road
──	Scenic route
──	Main line railway
──	Minor railway
△	Summit

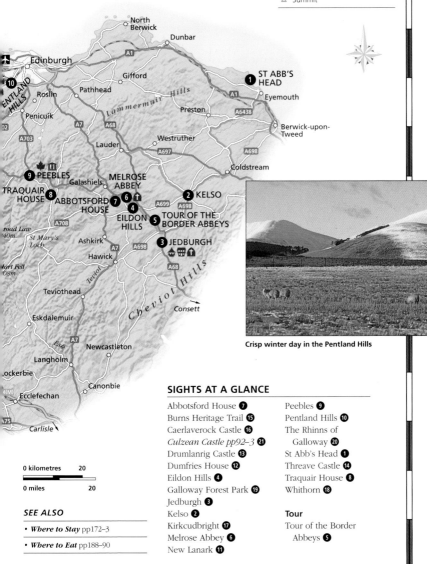

Crisp winter day in the Pentland Hills

SIGHTS AT A GLANCE

Abbotsford House **7**
Burns Heritage Trail **15**
Caerlaverock Castle **16**
Culzean Castle pp92–3 **21**
Drumlanrig Castle **13**
Dumfries House **12**
Eildon Hills **4**
Galloway Forest Park **19**
Jedburgh **3**
Kelso **2**
Kirkcudbright **17**
Melrose Abbey **6**
New Lanark **11**

Peebles **9**
Pentland Hills **10**
The Rhinns of
  Galloway **20**
St Abb's Head **1**
Threave Castle **14**
Traquair House **8**
Whithorn **18**

Tour
Tour of the Border
  Abbeys **5**

SEE ALSO

• *Where to Stay* pp172–3

• *Where to Eat* pp188–90

The shattered crags and cliffs of St Abb's Head

St Abb's Head ①

The Scottish Borders. ⛴ *Berwick-upon-Tweed.* 🚌 *from Edinburgh.* **Tel** *(01890) 771443.* ⏰ *Easter–Oct: 10am–5pm daily.*

The jagged cliffs of St Abb's Head, rising 91 m (300 ft) from the North Sea, offer a spectacular view of thousands of seabirds wheeling and diving below. During the May to June breeding season, this nature reserve becomes an important site for more than 50,000 cliff-nesting sea birds, including fulmars, guillemots, kittiwakes and puffins.

St Abb's village has one of the few unspoiled working harbours on Scotland's east coast. A clifftop trail begins at the visitors' centre, where displays include identification boards and a touch table where young visitors can get to grips with wings and feathers.

Kelso ②

The Scottish Borders. 🏠 *6,035.* 🚉 ℹ️ *The Square (01573) 228 055.* **www**.visitscottishborders.com

Kelso has a charming centre, with a cobbled square surrounded by Georgian and Victorian buildings. Nearby **Kelso Race Course** holds regular horse races. The focus of the town, however, is the ruin of the 12th-century **abbey**. This was the oldest and wealthiest of the four Border Abbeys founded by David I, but it suffered from wars with England and was severely

damaged in 1545. **Floors Castle** on the northern edge of Kelso was designed by William Adam in the 1720s, and reworked by William Playfair after 1837.

ℹ️ **Kelso Race Course**
Tel *(01668) 280800.* 📷 ♿

⚜ **Floors Castle**
Tel *(01573) 223333.* ⏰ *Mar–Oct: daily.* 📷 ♿ 🎬

Jedburgh ③

The Scottish Borders. 🏠 *4,250.* 🚉 ℹ️ *Murray's Green (01835) 863435.* **www**.visitscottishborders.com

The town is home to the mock-medieval **Jedburgh Castle, Jail and Museum**. Built in the 1820s and once the local jail, it now serves as a museum with some good displays on the area's history and life in a 19th-century prison.

Built around 1500, **Mary, Queen of Scots' House** is so-called due to a visit by the queen in 1566. The house was converted into a general

Jedburgh's medieval Abbey church at the centre of the attractive town

museum in the 1930s, and in 1987 (on the 400th anniversary of Mary's execution) it became a centre dedicated to telling her life story. Exhibits include a copy of her death mask.

Jedburgh Abbey is one of the great quartet of 12th-century Border Abbeys, along with Dryburgh, Kelso and Melrose. The Abbey church has some interesting features including a rose window.

⚜ **Jedburgh Castle, Jail and Museum**
Tel *(01835) 863254.* ⏰ *Easter–Oct: daily (Sun: pm).* 📷

⚜ **Mary, Queen of Scots' House**
Tel *(01835) 863331.* ⏰ *Mar–Nov: daily.* 📷

🏰 **Jedburgh Abbey**
Tel *(01835) 863925.* ⏰ *daily.* 📷

A picturesque view of the Eildon Hills in late summer sunshine

Eildon Hills ④

The Scottish Borders. 🚉 ℹ️ *Melrose (01896) 822 283.*

The three peaks of the Eildon Hills dominate the central Borders landscape. Mid Hill is the tallest at 422 m (1,385 ft), while North Hill once had a Bronze Age hill fort dating from before 500 BC, and later a Roman fort. In this part of the country the most celebrated name is Sir Walter Scott *(see p86)*, who had a particular affection for these hills. A panorama of the Eildons called **Scott's View** lies just east of Melrose, near Dryburgh Abbey, and this is the best location to see the hills' position as they rise above the Tweed Valley.

Tour of the Border Abbeys ⑤

The Scottish Borders are scattered with the ruins of
ancient buildings destroyed in conflicts between
England and Scotland. Most poignant of all are the
Border Abbeys, whose magnificent architecture bears
witness to their former spiritual and political power.
Founded during the 12th-century reign of David I,
the abbeys were destroyed by Henry VIII in 1545.
This tour takes in the abbeys
and some other sights.

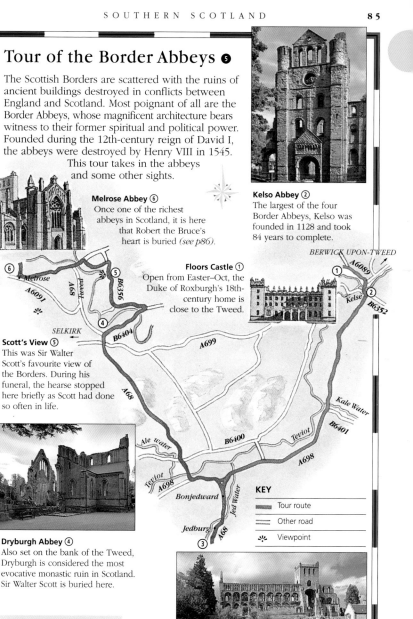

Melrose Abbey ⑥
Once one of the richest
abbeys in Scotland, it is here
that Robert the Bruce's
heart is buried *(see p86)*.

Kelso Abbey ②
The largest of the four
Border Abbeys, Kelso was
founded in 1128 and took
84 years to complete.

Floors Castle ①
Open from Easter–Oct, the
Duke of Roxburgh's 18th-
century home is
close to the Tweed.

BERWICK UPON-TWEED

Scott's View ⑤
This was Sir Walter
Scott's favourite view of
the Borders. During his
funeral, the hearse stopped
here briefly as Scott had done
so often in life.

Dryburgh Abbey ④
Also set on the bank of the Tweed,
Dryburgh is considered the most
evocative monastic ruin in Scotland.
Sir Walter Scott is buried here.

KEY

▬▬	Tour route
—	Other road
☀	Viewpoint

TIPS FOR DRIVERS

Length: 50 km (32 miles).
Stopping-off points: *Leave the
car at Dryburgh Abbey and take
a walk northwards to the footbridge over the River Tweed.*

0 kilometres   5

0 miles   3

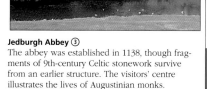

Jedburgh Abbey ③
The abbey was established in 1138, though frag-
ments of 9th-century Celtic stonework survive
from an earlier structure. The visitors' centre
illustrates the lives of Augustinian monks.

The ruins of Melrose Abbey, viewed from the southwest

Melrose Abbey ❻

Melrose, The Scottish Borders.
Tel (01896) 822562. ⬜ Apr–Sep:
9:30am–5:30pm daily; Oct–Mar:
9:30am–4:30pm daily. 🎧 ♿ limited.
www.historic-scotland.gov.uk

The rose-pink ruins of this
beautiful Border abbey bear
testimony to the devastation of
successive English invasions.
Built by David I in 1136 for
Cistercian monks, and also to
replace a 7th-century monastery, Melrose was repeatedly
ransacked by English armies,
most notably in 1322 and
1385. The final blow, from
which none of the abbeys
recovered, came in 1545,
when Henry VIII of England
implemented his destructive

Scottish policy known as the
"Rough Wooing". This resulted
from the failure of the Scots
to ratify a marriage treaty between Henry VIII's son and the
infant Mary, Queen of Scots.
What remains of the abbey are
the outlines of cloisters, the
kitchen, monastic buildings
and the shell of the abbey
church, with its soaring east
window and profusion of
medieval carvings. The decora-
tions of the south exterior wall
include a gargoyle shaped like
a pig playing the bagpipes and
several animated figures, including a cook with his ladle.
    An embalmed heart, found
here in 1920, is probably that
of Robert the Bruce, the
abbey's chief benefactor, who
had decreed that his heart be

taken on a crusade to the
Holy Land. It was returned
to Melrose Abbey after its
bearer, Sir James Douglas,
was killed in Spain.

Abbotsford House ❼

Galashiels, The Scottish Borders.
Tel (01896) 752043. 🚂 from
Galashiels. ⬜ Jun–Sep: 9:30am–5pm
daily; mid-Mar–May & Oct: 2–5pm
daily (Sun: 11am–4pm). 🎧 🎫 📷
♿ limited.

Few houses bear the stamp
of their creator so intimately
as Abbotsford House, the home
of Sir Walter Scott for the final
20 years of his life. He bought
a farm here in 1811, known
as Clarteyhole ("dirty hole"
in Borders Scots), though he
soon renamed it Abbotsford,
in memory of the monks of
Melrose Abbey who used to
cross the River Tweed nearby.
He later demolished the house
to make way for the turreted
building we see today, its
construction funded by the
sales of his popular novels.
    Scott's library contains over
9,000 rare books and his
collections of historic relics
reflect his passion for the
heroic past. The walls display
an extensive collection of arms
and armour, including Rob
Roy's broadsword (see p117).
Stuart mementos include one
of many crucifixes belonging
to Mary, Queen of Scots and a
lock of Bonnie Prince Charlie's
hair. The study in which Scott
wrote his *Waverley* novels, is
open to the public, as is the
room where he died in 1832.

SIR WALTER SCOTT

Sir Walter Scott (1771–1832)
was born in Edinburgh and
trained as a lawyer. He is
best remembered as a major
literary figure and champion
of Scotland, whose poems
and novels (most famously
his *Waverley* series) created
enduring images of a heroic
wilderness filled with the
romance of the clans. His
orchestration, in 1822, of the
state visit of George IV to
Edinburgh was an extrava-
ganza of Highland culture that helped establish tartan as the
national dress of Scotland. He served as Clerk of the Court
in Edinburgh's Parliament House and for 30 years was
Sheriff of Selkirk. He loved Central and Southern Scotland,
putting the Trossachs *(see pp116–17)* firmly on the map
with the publication of the *Lady of the Lake* (1810). His
final years were spent writing to pay off a £114,000 debt
following the failure of his publisher in 1827. He died with
his debts paid, and was buried at Dryburgh Abbey in 1832.

**The Great Hall at Abbotsford,
adorned with arms and armour**

Traquair House ❽

Peebles, The Scottish Borders.
Tel (01896) 830323. █ from Peebles.
☐ Apr, May, Sep: noon–5pm; Jun, Jul,
Aug: 10:30am–5pm; Oct: 11am–4pm;
Nov: 11am–3pm. 🅿️ ☐ ♿ limited.
www.traquair.co.uk

Scotland's oldest continuously
inhabited house has deep
roots in Scottish religious and
political history stretching back over 900
years. Evolving
from a fortified
tower to a 17th-
century mansion
(see p21), the house
was a Catholic Stuart
stronghold for 500
years. Mary, Queen of
Scots was among the
many monarchs to
have stayed here. Her
crucifix is kept in the
house and her bed
is covered by a
counterpane that
she made. Family
letters and engraved
Jacobite drinking
glasses are among the
relics recalling the period
of the Highland rebellions.
Following a vow made by
the fifth Earl, Traquair's Bear
Gates (the "Steekit Yetts"),
which closed after Bonnie
Prince Charlie's visit in 1745,
will not reopen until a Stuart
reascends the throne. A secret

**Mary's crucifix,
Traquair House**

stairway leads to the Priest's
Room, which, with its clerical
vestments that could be disguised as bedspreads, attests
to the problems faced by
Catholic families until Catholicism was legalized in 1829.

Peebles ❾

The Scottish Borders. 🏠 8,000.
🚊 from Galashiels. 🚹 23 High St
(0870) 608 0404.

This charming Borders
town has some fascin-
ating sights, including
the **Tweeddale Museum
and Gallery** which houses
full-scale plaster casts
of part of the Parthenon
Frieze, and casts of a frieze
depicting the entry of
Alexander the Great into
Babylon. Nearby, the
**Scottish Museum of Orna-
mental Plasterwork** is
housed in a quaint work-
shop. The walled **Kailzie
Gardens** attract day-
trippers from Edinburgh.

🏛 **Tweeddale Museum and
Gallery**
Tel (01721) 724820. ☐ Mon–Sat.

🏛 **Scottish Museum of
Ornamental Plasterwork**
Tel (01721) 720212. ☐ Mon–Fri.
🌑 first 2 weeks in Aug. 🅿️ ♿

🌺 **Kailzie Gardens**
Tel (01721) 720007. ☐ daily. 🅿️ 🌑

Pentland Hills ❿

The Lothians. 🚆 Edinburgh, then
bus. 🚹 Regional Park Headquarters,
Edinburgh (0131) 445 3383.

The wilds of the Pentland Hills
stretch for 26 km (16 miles)
southwest of Edinburgh, and
offer some of the best hill-
walking country in Southern
Scotland. Walkers can saunter
along the many signposted
footpaths, while the more
adventurous can take the
chairlift at the Hillend dry ski
slope to reach the higher
ground leading to the 493 m
(1,617 ft) hill of Allermuir. Even
more ambitious is the classic
scenic route along the ridge
from Caerketton to West Kip.

To the east of the A703,
in the lee of the Pentlands,
stands the exquisite and ornate
15th-century **Rosslyn Chapel**,
which features in *The Da Vinci
Code*. It was originally intended
as a church, but after the death
of its founder, William Sinclair,
it was used as a burial ground
for his descendants. The
delicately wreathed Apprentice
Pillar recalls the legend of the
apprentice carver who was
killed by the master stone-
mason in a fit of jealousy at
his pupil's superior skill.

🔒 **Rosslyn Chapel**
Tel (0131) 440 2159. ☐ daily.
🅿️ ♿ **www**.rosslynchapel.com

Details of the highly ornate, decorative carved-stone vaulting in Rosslyn Chapel

The Classical 18th-century tenements of New Lanark on the banks of the Clyde

New Lanark ⓫

Clyde Valley. 185. Lanark. Horsemarket, Ladyacre Rd, Lanark (01555) 661661. www.seeglasgow.com

Situated by the beautiful falls of the River Clyde, with three separate waterfalls, the village of New Lanark was founded in 1785 by the industrial

DAVID LIVINGSTONE

Scotland's great missionary doctor and explorer was born in Blantyre where he began working life as a mill boy at the age of ten. Livingstone (1813–73) made three epic journeys across Africa, from 1840, promoting "commerce and Christianity". He became the first European to see Victoria Falls, and died in 1873 while searching for the source of the Nile. His body is buried in Westminster Abbey in London.

entrepreneur David Dale. Ideally located alongside the river for the working of its water-driven mills, the village had become the largest producer of cotton in Britain by 1800. Dale and his successor, and son-in-law, Robert Owen, were philanthropists whose reforms demonstrated that commercial success need not undermine the wellbeing of the workforce. The manufacturing of cotton continued here until the late 1960s.

The **New Millennium Experience** illustrates New Lanark's significance as a window on to working life in the early 19th century.

Environs

24 km (15 miles) north, the town of Blantyre has a memorial to the Clyde Valley's most famous son, the explorer David Livingstone.

🏛 **New Millennium Experience**
New Lanark Visitor Centre. **Tel** (01555) 661345. 11am–5pm daily. by appointment.

Dumfries House ⓬

Cumnock, Ayrshire. **Tel** (01290) 425 959. Easter–Oct: 11am–4pm daily. www.dumfrieshouse.biz

This wonderful Palladian villa is off the beaten track, but well worth a detour. Sitting in

sweeping parkland, the grand symmetrical villa was built for the fifth Earl of Dumfries, William Crichton Dalrymple. Designed to lure a prospective wife, it was decorated in highly fashionable Rococo style between 1756 and 1760. Amongst the treasures is a priceless collection of Chippendale furniture, some of it purpose built and incorporating Scottish saltires. Up for sale in 2007, the house and contents were saved at the last minute by a trust established by Prince Charles.

Drumlanrig Castle ⓭

Thornhill, Dumfries & Galloway. (01848) 331555. Dumfries, then bus. Easter–Aug: 11am–4pm daily.

Rising squarely from a grassy platform, the massive fortress-palace of **Drumlanrig Castle** was built from pink sandstone between 1679 and 1691 on the site of a 15th-century Douglas stronghold. The castle's multi-turreted,

The Baroque front steps and doorway of Drumlanrig Castle

formidable exterior conceals a priceless collection of art treasures as well as such Jacobite relics as Bonnie Prince Charlie's camp kettle, sash and money box. Hanging within oak-panelled rooms are paintings by Leonardo da Vinci (including *The Madonna of Yarnwinder*, stolen in 2003 but returned in 2007), Holbein and Rembrandt. The emblem of a crowned and winged heart recalls the famous Douglas ancestor "The Good Sir James". Legend has it he bore Robert the Bruce's heart on crusade against the Moors in Spain.

The sturdy island fortress of Threave Castle on the Dee

Threave Castle 14

(NTS) Castle Douglas, Dumfries & Galloway. *Tel* (01556) 502611. Dumfries. Apr–Sep: daily. Times vary. www.historic-scotland.gov.uk

A menacing giant of a tower, this 14th-century Black Douglas stronghold on an island in the Dee commands the most complete medieval riverside harbour in Scotland. Douglas's struggles against the early Stuart kings resulted in his surrender here after a two-month siege in 1455 – but only after James II had brought the cannon Mons Meg to batter the castle. Threave was dismantled after Protestant Covenanters defeated its Catholic defenders in 1640. Only the shell of the kitchen, great hall and domestic levels remain.

The exterior of Burns Cottage, birthplace of Robert Burns

Burns Heritage Trail 15

South Ayrshire, Dumfries & Galloway. Dumfries (01387) 253862, Ayr (0845) 225 5121. www.visitdumfriesandgalloway.co.uk

Robert Burns (1759–96) left behind a remarkable body of work ranging from satirical poetry to tender love songs. His status as national bard is unchallenged and an official Burns Heritage Trail leads visitors around sights in south-west Scotland where he lived.

In Dumfries, the **Robert Burns Centre** focuses on his years in the town, while **Burns House**, where he lived from 1793 to 1796, contains memorabilia. His Greek-style mausoleum can be found in St Michael's Churchyard.

At **Ellisland Farm** there are further displays, with some of Burns' family possessions. Mauchline, some 18 km (11 miles) east of Ayr, has the **Burns House and Museum** in another former residence.

Alloway, just south of Ayr, is the real centre of the Burns Trail. The **Robert Burns Birthplace Museum** is set in beautiful countryside. It incorporates Burns Cottage, the poet's birthplace, which houses memorabilia and a collection of manuscripts. The ruins of Alloway Kirk and the 13th-century Brig o' Doon have the best period atmosphere.

Robert Burns Centre
Mill Rd, Dumfries. *Tel* (01387) 264808. Apr–Sep: 10am–5pm Mon–Sat, 2–5pm Sun; Oct–Mar: 10am–1pm, 2–5pm Tue–Sat.

Burns House
Burns St, Dumfries. *Tel* (01387) 255297. Apr–Sep: 10am–5pm Mon–Sat, 2–5pm Sun; Oct–Mar: 10am–1pm, 2–5pm Tue–Sat.

Ellisland Farm
Holywood Rd, Auldgirth. *Tel* (01387) 740426. Apr–Sep: 10am–1pm, 2–5pm Mon–Sat, 2–5pm Sun; Oct–Mar: 2–5pm Tue–Sat.

Burns House and Museum
Castle St, Mauchline. *Tel* (01290) 550045. 10am–4pm Tue–Sat. limited.

Robert Burns Birthplace Museum
Alloway. *Tel* (01292) 443700. Apr–Sep: 10am–5:30pm daily; Oct–Mar: 10am–5pm daily. www.burnsmuseum.co.uk

SCOTTISH TEXTILES

Weaving in the Scottish Borders goes back to the Middle Ages, when monks from Flanders established a thriving woollen trade with the Continent. Cotton became an important source of wealth in the Clyde Valley during the 19th century, when handloom weaving was overtaken by power-driven mills. The popular Paisley patterns were based on original Indian designs.

A colourful pattern from Paisley

Moated fairy-tale Caerlaverock Castle with its red stone walls

Caerlaverock Castle ⑯

Near Dumfries, Dumfries & Galloway.
🖥 *(01387) 770244.* ⏰ *Apr–Sep: 9:30am–5:30pm daily; Oct–Mar: 9:30am–4:30pm daily.* 🎧 ♿ 📷
🌐 www.historic-scotland.gov.uk

This impressive, three-sided, red stone structure, with its distinctive moat, is the finest example of a medieval castle in southwest Scotland. It stands 14 km (9 miles) south of Dumfries, and was built in around 1270.

Caerlaverock came to prominence in 1300, during the Wars of Independence, when it was beseiged by Edward I, king of England, setting a precedent

for more than three centuries of strife. Surviving chronicles of Edward's adventures describe the castle in much the same form as it stands today, despite being partially demolished and rebuilt many times, due to the clashes between the English and Scottish forces during the 14th and 16th centuries. Throughout these troubles it remained the stronghold of the Maxwell family, and the Maxwell crest and motto remain over the door. It was the struggle between Robert Maxwell, who was the first Earl of Nithsdale and a supporter of Charles I, and a Covenanter army that caused the castle's ruin in 1640.

Kirkcudbright ⑰

Dumfries & Galloway. 👥 *3,600.*
🚉 🖥 *Harbour Sq (01557) 330494.* ⏰ *Feb–Oct: daily.*
www.kirkcudbright.co.uk

By the mouth of the River Dee, at the head of Kirkcudbright Bay, this town has an artistic heritage. The Tolbooth, dating from the late 1500s, is now the **Tolbooth Art Centre**, which exhibits work by Kirkcudbright artists from 1880 to the present day. The most celebrated was Edward Hornel (1864–1933), one of the Glasgow Boys, who painted striking images of

Japanese women. Some of his work is displayed in his former home, Broughton House, on the High Street.

MacLellan's Castle in the town centre was built in 1582 by the then Provost of Kirkcudbright, while outside, the ruins of Dundrennan Abbey date from the 12th century. Mary, Queen of Scots spent her last night there before fleeing to England in May 1568.

🏛 **Tolbooth Art Centre**
High St. **Tel** *(01557) 331556.*
⏰ *11am–4pm Mon–Sat (to 5pm May–Sep), 2–5pm Sun.* ♿
⚓ **MacLellan's Castle**
Tel *(01557) 331856.* ⏰ *Apr–Sep: 9:30am–5:30pm daily.* 📷

Whithorn ⑱

Dumfries & Galloway. 👥 *1,000.*
🚉 *Stranraer.* 🖥 🖥 *Dashwood Sq, Newton Stewart (01671) 402431.*
www.dumfriesandgalloway.co.uk

The earliest site of continuous Christian worship in Scotland, Whithorn (meaning white house) takes its name from the white chapel built by St Ninian in 397. Though nothing remains of the chapel, a guided tour of the archaeological dig reveals evidence of Northumbrian, Viking and Scottish settlements ranging from the 5th to the 19th centuries. **The Whithorn Story** provides audio-visual information on the excavations, and contains a fine collection of ancient carved stones.

🏛 **The Whithorn Story**
45–47 George St. **Tel** *(01988) 500508.*
⏰ *Easter–Oct: 10:30am–5pm.* 📷
📷 ♿ www.whithorn.com

Galloway Forest Park ⑲

Dumfries & Galloway. 🚉 *Stranraer.*
🖥 *Clatteringshaws Visitor Centre (01644) 420285, Glen Trool Visitor Centre (01671) 402420, Kirroughtree Visitor Centre (01671) 402165.*
www.forestry.gov.uk

This is the wildest stretch of country in Southern Scotland, with points of historical interest as well as great beauty.

Traditional stone buildings on the shore at Kirkcudbright

For hotels and restaurants in this region see pp172–3 and pp188–90

Loch Trool, Galloway Forest Park, site of one of Robert the Bruce's victories

The park extends to 670 sq km (260 sq miles) just north of Newton Stewart. The principal focal point is Loch Trool. By Caldons Wood, to the west end of the loch, the Martyrs' Monument marks the spot where six Covenanters were killed at prayer in 1685. Bruce's Stone, above the north shore, commemorates an occasion in 1307 when Robert the Bruce routed English forces. The hills to the north of Loch Trool are a considerable size, and worthy of note. Bennan stands at 562 m (1,844 ft), Benyellary at 719 m (2,359 ft), while Merrick, at 843 m (2,766 ft), is the tallest mountain in Southern Scotland. A round trip from Loch Trool to Merrick's summit and back, via the silver sands of Loch Enoch to the east, is a total of 15 km (9 miles) over rough but very rewarding ground.

The Rhinns of Galloway ⑳

Dumfries & Galloway. 🚢 Stranraer. 🚌 Stranraer, Portpatrick. ⛴ Stranraer. 🛈 28 Harbour St, Stranraer (01776) 702595.

In the extreme southwest of Scotland, this peninsula is almost separated from the rest of the country by Loch Ryan and Luce Bay. It has a number of attractions, including the **Logan Botanic Garden**, near Port Logan. Established in 1900, subtropical species in the garden benefit from the area's mild climate. Stranraer on Loch Ryan is the main centre and ferry port for Northern Ireland. The nearby **Portpatrick** is a prettier town, featuring a ruined church dating from 1629 and the remains of 16th-century Dunskey Castle.

🌸 Logan Botanic Garden
Near Port Logan, Stranraer. **Tel** (01776) 860231. ◻ 10am–5pm daily (to 6pm Apr–Sep). 🏵 ♿

GALLOWAY FOREST PARK WALK

This walk gives a taste of wild hill-country and remote, high-level lochs. Adequate footwear, waterproof clothing and a map are recommended. From the car park, descend towards the house, cross a bridge, and take a path northeast through a field. Follow the valley of the Gairland Burn for about 1.5 km (1 mile) to find Loch Valley. A few minutes further north, the path reaches lonely Loch Neldricken, from where you can return by the same route. This area is a combination of glaciated hills and small hill lochs, set in hollows scraped out by the ice thousands of years ago. If time is short, or the weather poor, there are shorter walks around Loch Trool.

KEY

-- Footpath

= Access road

☀ Viewpoint

🅿 Parking

TIPS FOR WALKERS

Starting point: Bruce's Stone car park, north side of Loch Trool.
Length: 10 km (6 miles).
Getting there: By car: off the A714, about 14 km (9 miles) north of Newton Stewart, along an access road for 8 km (5 miles).

Loch Enoch

Loch Aaron

Loch Neldricken

Loch Valley

Long Loch of Glenhead

Round Loch of Glenhead

Loch Trool

0 kilometres   2

0 miles   1

Culzean Castle ㉑

Robert Adam by George Willison

Standing on a cliff's edge in an extensive parkland estate, the 15th-century keep of Culzean (pronounced Cullayn), home of the Earls of Cassillis, was remodelled between 1777 and 1792 by the Neo-Classical architect Robert Adam. Restored in the 1970s, it is now a major showcase of Adam's later style of work. The grounds became Scotland's first public country park in 1969 and, with farming flourishing alongside ornamental gardens, they reflect both the leisure and everyday activities of life on a great country estate.

View of Culzean Castle (c.1815), by Nasmyth

The State Bedroom and Dressing Rooms contain typical mid-18th-century furnishings, including a gentleman's wardrobe of the 1740s.

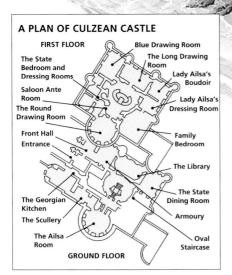

A PLAN OF CULZEAN CASTLE

FIRST FLOOR

- Blue Drawing Room
- The Long Drawing Room
- Lady Ailsa's Boudoir
- The State Bedroom and Dressing Rooms
- Lady Ailsa's Dressing Room
- Saloon Ante Room
- The Round Drawing Room
- Front Hall Entrance
- Family Bedroom
- The Library
- The Georgian Kitchen
- The State Dining Room
- The Scullery
- Armoury
- The Ailsa Room
- Oval Staircase

GROUND FLOOR

The Clock Tower, fronted by the circular carriageway, was originally the family coach house and stables. The clock was added in the 19th century, and today the buildings house a café, a shop and an education room.

STAR FEATURES

★ The Circular Saloon

★ Oval Staircase

For hotels and restaurants in this region see pp172–3 and pp188–90

Armoury
On the walls are the bayonet blades and flintlock pistols issued to the West Lowland Fencible Regiment when Napoleon threatened to invade in the early 1800s.

VISITORS' CHECKLIST

(NTS) 6 km (4 miles) west of Maybole, Ayrshire. **Tel** *(01655) 884455.* 🚆 *Ayr, then bus.* **Castle** ☐ *Apr–Oct: 10:30am–5pm (last entry 4pm).* **Grounds** ☐ *9am until dusk.* 🅿️ 🐾 ✔️ 🍴 🛍️ ⛪
www.culzeanexperience.org

The Eisenhower Apartment, on the top floor of Culzean, was where the General was granted lifetime tenancy in gratitude for his role in World War II.

Fountain Court
This sunken garden is a good place to begin a tour of the grounds to the east.

Carriageway

★ The Circular Saloon
With its restored 18th-century colour scheme and Louis XVI chairs, this elegant saloon perches on the cliff's edge 46 m (150 ft) above the Firth of Clyde. The carpet is a copy of one designed by Adam.

★ Oval Staircase
Illuminated by an overarching skylight, the staircase, with its Ionic and Corinthian pillars, is considered one of Adam's finest design achievements.

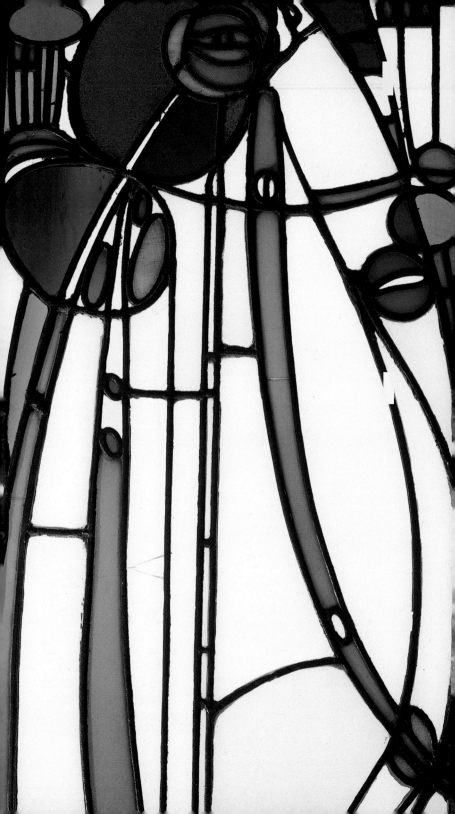

GLASGOW

Glasgow displays audacity in everything, from the profile of its contemporary buildings, such as the titanium-clad structures and tower of the Science Centre, to the presence of designer clothes shops and the wit of its people. As recently as the 1970s, this was a city with a fading industrial history and little sense of direction, but much has changed since then.

Glasgow's city centre, on the north bank of the River Clyde, has been occupied since ancient times. The Romans already had a presence in the area some 2,000 years ago, and there was a religious community here from the 6th century. Records show Glasgow's growing importance as a merchant town from the 12th century onwards.

Historic buildings such as Provand's Lordship, a 15th-century townhouse, remind visitors of its pre-industrial roots, but modern Glasgow grew from the riches of the British Empire and the Industrial Revolution. In the 18th century the city imported rum, sugar and tobacco from the colonies, while in the 19th century it reinvented itself as a cotton manufacturing centre. It then became a site for shipbuilding and for heavy engineering, attracting many incomers from poverty-stricken districts in the Scottish Highlands and islands, and in Ireland, in the process. Between the 1780s and the 1880s the population exploded from around 40,000 to over 500,000. The city boundaries expanded, and, despite an economic slump between the two World Wars, Glasgow clung to its status as an industrial giant until the 1970s, when its traditional skills were no longer needed. This was a bad time, but the city has since bounced back; it was named European Capital of Sport in 2003 and will host the 2014 Commonwealth Games. A £500 million project at Glasgow Harbour has reclaimed the city's old shipyards and dockland for commercial, residential and leisure usage.

Fashionable brasseries in the rejuvenated Merchant City area of Glasgow

◁ Stained glass by architect and designer Charles Rennie Mackintosh, whose work can be seen all over the city

Exploring Glasgow

Glasgow city centre is a neat grid of streets running east to west and north to south on the north bank of the River Clyde. This small area includes the main train stations, the principal shopping facilities and, at George Square, the tourist information office. Outside the centre, Byres Road to the west of Kelvingrove Park is the focus of the district known as "the West End", with its bars and restaurants near the University. Pollok Country Park, in the southwest, is home to the wonderful Burrell Collection.

Detail of St Mungo Museum's modern façade

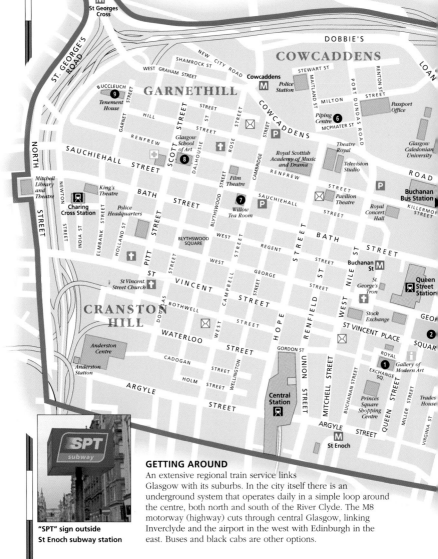

GETTING AROUND

An extensive regional train service links Glasgow with its suburbs. In the city itself there is an underground system that operates daily in a simple loop around the centre, both north and south of the River Clyde. The M8 motorway (highway) cuts through central Glasgow, linking Inverclyde and the airport in the west with Edinburgh in the east. Buses and black cabs are other options.

"SPT" sign outside St Enoch subway station

SIGHTS AT A GLANCE

Historic Streets and Buildings
George Square **2**
Glasgow Cathedral
 and Necropolis **5**
Pollok House **18**
Willow Tea Room **7**

Museums and Galleries
Burrell Collection pp104–5 **19**
Gallery of Modern Art **1**
Glasgow Science Centre **10**
Hunterian Art Gallery **14**
Kelvingrove Art Gallery
 and Museum **12**

People's Palace **16**
Provand's Lordship **3**
Riverside Museum **11**
Scotland Street School
 Museum **13**
St Mungo Museum of
 Religious Life and Art **4**
Tenement House **9**

Parks and Gardens
Botanic Gardens **15**

Arts Centres
Glasgow School of Art **8**
House for an Art Lover **17**
Piping Centre **6**

**Sauchiehall Street, the heart of
the city's busy shopping district**

SEE ALSO

• *Where to Stay* pp173–5

• *Where to Eat* pp190–92

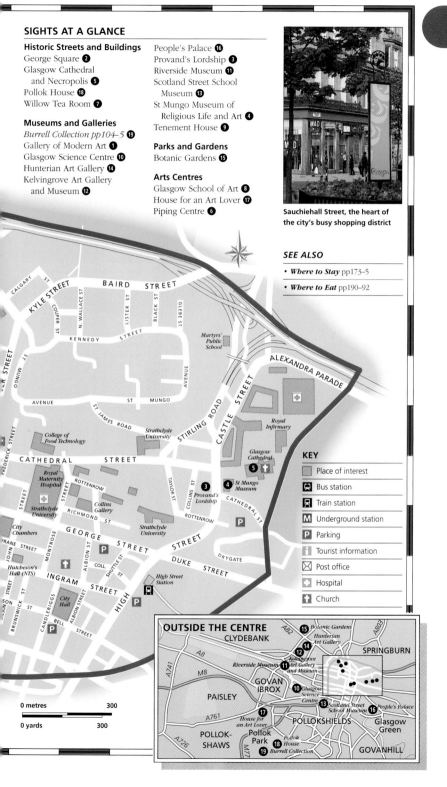

KEY

- ▢ Place of interest
- 🚌 Bus station
- 🚆 Train station
- Ⓜ Underground station
- 🅿 Parking
- ℹ Tourist information
- ⊠ Post office
- ✚ Hospital
- ⛪ Church

OUTSIDE THE CENTRE

CLYDEBANK
SPRINGBURN
GOVAN
IBROX
PAISLEY
POLLOKSHIELDS
POLLOK-SHAWS
GOVANHILL
Glasgow Green

A82 Botanic Gardens **15**
Hunterian Art Gallery **14**
Kelvingrove Art Gallery and Museum **12**
Riverside Museum **11**
Glasgow Science Centre **10**
Scotland Street School Museum **13**
People's Palace **16**
House for an Art Lover **17**
Pollok House **18**
Burrell Collection **19**
A803
A8
M8
A741
A761
A726
M77
Pollok Park

0 metres 300
0 yards 300

The imposing City Chambers in George Square, where a statue of Sir Walter Scott stands atop the central column

Gallery of Modern Art ❶

Royal Exchange Sq.
Tel (0141) 287 3050. ◯ *10am–5pm Mon–Wed & Sat, 10am–8pm Thu, 11am–5pm Fri & Sun.* ♿ ▣
www.glasgowlife.org.uk/museums

Once the home of Glasgow's Royal Exchange (the city's centre for trade), this building dates from 1829 and also incorporates a late 18th-century mansion that formerly occupied the site. The local authority took over the Exchange just after World War II, and for many years it served as a library. It finally opened its doors as the Gallery of Modern Art in 1996. One of the largest

Ornate tower of the Gallery of Modern Art

contemporary art galleries outside London, the GoMA is constantly building on its collection of work by Glasgow based artists. Accordingly, most of the gallery is home to a lively and thought-provoking programme of temporary exhibitions featuring work by Scottish and international artists. Many of these focus on contemporary and social issues, often featuring groups that are marginalized in today's society.

George Square ❷

City centre. **City Chambers** *Tel (0141) 287 2000.* ◯ *Mon–Fri, 10:30am & 2:30pm for guided tours.* ♿ ▢ **Merchant House** *Tel (0141) 221 8272.* ▢ *by appt.*

George Square was laid out in the late 18th century as a residental area, but redevelopment during Victorian times conferred its enduring status as the city's focal point. The only building not to be affected by the later 19th-century makeover is the Millennium Hotel (1807) on the north side of the Square.

The 1870s saw a building boom, with the construction of the former Post Office (1876) at the southeast corner, and the **Merchant House** (1877) to the west side. The latter is home to Glasgow's Chamber of Commerce. Founded in 1781, it is the oldest organization of its kind in the UK. The most dominant structure in George Square, however, is the **City Chambers** on the east side. Designed by William Young in an Italian Renaissance

style, the imposing building was opened in 1888 by Queen Victoria. With the elegant proportions of the interior decorated in marble and mosaic, the opulence of this building makes it the most impressive of its type in Scotland.

Provand's Lordship ❸

3 Castle St. ☎ *(0141) 552 8819.* ◯ *10am–5pm Mon–Thu & Sat, 11am–5pm Fri & Sun.*

Provand's Lordship was originally built as a canon's house in 1471, and is now Glasgow's oldest surviving house, as well as a museum. Its low ceilings and wooden furnishings create a vivid impression of life in a wealthy 15th-century household. Mary, Queen of Scots *(see p44)* may have stayed here when she visited Glasgow in 1566 to see her cousin, and husband, Lord Darnley.

Provand's Lordship, Glasgow's only medieval house

St Mungo Museum of Religious Life and Art ❹

2 Castle St. **Tel** (0141) 276 1625.
🕐 10am–5pm Tue–Thu & Sat,
11am–5pm Fri & Sun. 👤 📷 by
appointment. 🖥 📷
www.glasgowlife.org.uk/museums

Glasgow has strong religious roots, and the settlement that grew to become today's city started with a monastery founded in the 6th century AD by a priest called Mungo. He died in the early years of the 7th century, and his body lies buried underneath Glasgow Cathedral. The building itself dates from the 12th century, and stands on ground blessed by St Ninian as long ago as AD 397. The ever-growing numbers of visitors to the cathedral eventually prompted plans for an interpretive centre. Despite the efforts of the Society of Friends of Glasgow Cathedral, however, sufficient funds could not be raised. The local

Detail from the St Mungo Museum

authority decided to step in with money, and with the idea for a more extensive project – a museum of religious life and art. The site chosen was adjacent to the cathedral, where the 13th-century Castle of the Bishops of Glasgow once stood. The museum has the appearance of a centuries-old fortified house, despite the fact that it was completed in 1993.

The top floor describes the story of the country's religion from a non-denominational perspective. Both Protestant and Catholic versions of Christianity are represented, as well as the other faiths of modern Scotland. The many, varied displays touch on the lives of communities as extensive as Glasgow's Muslims, who have had their own Mosque in the city since 1984, as well as local converts to the Baha'i faith. The other floors are given over to works of art – among them is Craigie Aitchison's *Crucifixion VII*, which sits alongside religious artifacts and artworks, such as burial discs from Neolithic China (2,000 BC), contemporary paintings by Aboriginal Australians, and some excellent Scottish stained glass from the early part of the 20th century. Further displays in the museum examine issues of fundamental concern to people of all religions – war, persecution, death and the afterlife – and from cultures as far afield as West Africa and Mexico. In the grounds surrounding the building, there is a permanent Zen Garden, created by Yasutaro Tanaka. Such gardens have been a traditional aid to contemplation in Japanese Buddhist temples since the beginning of the 16th century.

An impressive stained-glass window at the St Mungo Museum of Religious Life and Art

Glasgow's medieval cathedral viewed from the southwest

Glasgow Cathedral and Necropolis ❺

Cathedral Square. **Cathedral Tel** (0141) 552 6891. 🕐 Apr–Sep: 9:30am–5:30pm Mon–Sat, 1–5:30pm Sun; Oct–Mar: 9:30am–4pm Mon–Sat, 1–4pm Sun. 👤 **Necropolis** 🕐 24hrs daily. **www**.glasgowcathedral.org.uk

As one of the few churches to escape destruction during the Scottish Reformation *(see p44)* by adapting itself to Protestant worship, this cathedral is a rare example of an almost complete original 13th-century church.

It was built on the site of a chapel founded by the city's patron saint, St Mungo, a 6th-century bishop of Strathclyde. According to legend, Mungo placed the body of a holy man, named Fergus, on a cart yoked to two wild bulls, telling them to take it to the place ordained by God. In the "dear green place" at which the bulls stopped, he built his church.

Because of its sloping site, the cathedral is built on two levels. The crypt contains the tomb of St Mungo, surrounded by an intricate forest of columns springing up to end in delicately carved rib-vaulting. The Blacader Aisle is reputed to have been built over a cemetery blessed by St Ninian.

Behind the cathedral, a likeness of Protestant reformer John Knox *(see p44)* surveys the city from his Doric pillar, overlooking a Victorian cemetery. The necropolis is filled with crumbling monuments to the dead of Glasgow's wealthy merchant families.

Piping Centre ❻

30–34 McPhater St. **Tel** (0141) 353 0220. ◯ 10am–4:30pm daily. 🅿 🍴 ♿ www.thepipingcentre.co.uk

The Piping Centre, which opened its doors in a refurbished church in 1996, aims to promote the study and history of piping in Scotland. It offers tuition at all levels, and houses the **National Museum of Piping**, which traces the development of the instrument. Displays show that bagpipes were first introduced to Scotland as early as the 14th century, although the golden age of piping was the 17th and 18th centuries. This was the era of the MacCrimmons of Skye (hereditary pipers to the chiefs of Clan MacLeod), when complex, extended tunes (ceol mor, or "the big music") were written for clan gatherings, battles and in the form of laments.

Traditional bagpipes with brass drones

Willow Tea Room ❼

217 Sauchiehall St. **Tel** (0141) 332 0521. ◯ 9am–5pm Mon–Sat, 11am–4:15pm Sun. ♿ www.willowtearooms.co.uk

This is the sole survivor of a series of delightfully frivolous tea rooms created by the designer Charles Rennie

The Mackintosh-designed interior of the Willow Tea Room

Mackintosh (see opposite page) at the turn of the century for the celebrated restaurateur Kate Cranston. Everything in the tearoom, from the high-backed chairs to the tables and cutlery, was of Mackintosh's own design. The 1904 **Room de Luxe** sparkles with eccentricity: striking mauve and silver furniture, coloured glass and a flamboyant leaded door create a remarkable venue.

The exterior of the Glasgow School of Art, Mackintosh's masterpiece

Glasgow School of Art ❽

167 Renfrew St. **Tel** (0141) 353 4500. ◯ Mon–Sat (by appointment). 🅿 🍴 ♿ limited. www.gsa.ac.uk

Widely considered to be the greatest architectural work in the illustrious career of Charles Rennie Mackintosh, the Glasgow School of Art was built between 1897 and 1909 to a design he submitted in a competition. Due to financial constraints, it was built in two stages. The earlier eastern half displays a severity of style, likened by a contemporary critic to a prison. The later western half is characterized by a softer architectural style.

An art student will guide you through the building to the Furniture Gallery, Board Room and the Library, the latter being a masterpiece of spatial composition. Each room is an exercise in contrasts between

height, light and shade, with innovative details echoing the architectural themes of the structure. How much of the school can be viewed depends on curricular requirements at the time of visiting, as it still functions as an active and highly successful art college.

Tenement House ❾

(NTS) 145 Buccleuch St. **Tel** (0141) 333 0183. ◯ Mar–Oct: 1–5pm daily. 🅿 📷 by appointment.

More a time capsule than a museum, the Tenement House is an almost undisturbed record of life as it was in a modest Glasgow flat on a tenement estate in the early 20th century. Glasgow owed much of its vitality and neighbourliness to tenement life, though in later years many of these Victorian and Edwardian apartments were to earn a bad name for poverty and overcrowding, and many of them have been pulled down.

The Tenement House was the home of Miss Agnes Toward, who lived here from 1911 until 1965. It remained largely unaltered during that time and, since Agnes threw very little away, the house has become a treasure-trove of social history. In the parlour, which would have been used only on formal occasions, afternoon tea is laid out on a white lace cloth. The kitchen, with its coal-fired range and box bed, is filled with the tools of a vanished era, such as a goffering-iron for ironing lace, a washboard and a stone hot-water bottle.

Agnes's lavender water and medicines are still arranged in the bathroom, and it feels almost as though she stepped out of the house 70 years ago and simply forgot to return.

The preserved Edwardian kitchen of the Tenement House

Glasgow Artists

The late 19th century was a time of great artistic activity in Glasgow, with painters such as Sir James Guthrie, Robert McGregor and others rising to prominence. But snobbery on the part of the Edinburgh-based arts establishment often led these men to seek recognition outside Scotland. The term "Glasgow School" was coined after an 1890 London exhibition, but the artists generally called themselves "Glasgow Boys". Art Nouveau designer Charles Rennie Mackintosh contributed his genius to the creative life of the city as well as to a new Glasgow School of Art, completed in two stages – 1899 and 1909. More recently, the term Glasgow Boys has been used to describe the generation of artists who attended the School of Art in the 1970s and '80s. Contemporary Glasgow artists include Ken Currie and Peter Howson.

Detail from House for an Art Lover

Stirling Station, by William Kennedy *(1859–1918), depicts the crowded platform with people waiting for a train. The rich colours, and steam from the trains, contribute to the atmosphere of this bustling station.*

A Star (1891) by Sir John Lavery *is indicative of the artist's dashing, fluid, style as a portraitist. Born in Belfast, Lavery studied at Glasgow and was part of the Whistler- and Impressionist-influenced Glasgow School.*

In The Wayfarer, *by Edward Arthur Walton (1860–1922), the winding path leads the viewer into the distance, in the direction of the wayfarer's gaze.*

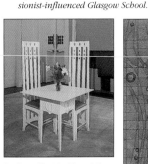

Designed by Mackintosh in 1901, *the House for an Art Lover (see p103) was finally built in 1996. The design of the building and all of the furniture remains true to the original plans.*

Mackintosh's stylized tulips *on a checkered background provide a striking example of Art Nouveau decoration, juxtaposing the organic with the geometric.*

Mackintosh's unique fluidity of form *is seen in this detail from a stained-glass door in the House for an Art Lover.*

CHARLES RENNIE MACKINTOSH
Glasgow's most celebrated designer (1868–1928) entered Glasgow School of Art at the age of 16. After his success with the Willow Tea Room, he became a leading figure in the Art Nouveau movement. His characteristic straight lines and flowing detail are the hallmark of early 20th-century style.

Glasgow Science Centre ❿

50 Pacific Quay. *Tel (0141) 420 5000.* ☐ *10am–5pm daily.* 📷 ♿
www.glasgowsciencecentre.org

The impressive gleaming tower of this science park is an unmistakable landmark on the city's skyline.

A three-storey science mall introduces the world of popular, everyday science through a range of dynamic interactive exhibits, laboratories and multimedia. Scotland's only IMAX Theatre stands next door, projecting breathtaking images from the natural and scientific world onto its 24-m (80-ft) by 18-m (60-ft) screen. Other notable exhibits include a lab where you can examine your hair and skin. The 127-m (416-ft) rotating tower is Scotland's tallest freestanding structure.

Riverside Museum ⓫

100 Pointhouse Place. *Tel (0141) 287 2729.* ☐ *10am–5pm Mon–Thu & Sat, 11am–5pm Fri & Sun.* ♿ 🖼
www.glasgowlife.org.uk/museums

This landmark attraction sits on the Clyde in a dramatic zinc-panelled building designed by architect Zaha Hadid. Focused on transport, it is crammed with locomotives, trams, cars and bikes of all styles and vintages. It also explores the social impact of transport on the city, with interactive and audio-visual features to bring the past to life.

George Henry's *Japanese Lady with a Fan* **(1894), at Kelvingrove**

Kelvingrove Art Gallery and Museum ⓬

Argyle St, Kelvingrove. *Tel (0141) 276 9599.* ☐ *10am–5pm Mon–Thu & Sat, 11am–5pm Fri & Sun.* 🍴 🖼
www.glasgowlife.org.uk/museums

An imposing red sandstone building, Kelvingrove is Scotland's most popular gallery, housing a magnificent art collection. Exhibits are grouped to reflect different aspects of the main collection. Among these are 19th-century British artists including Turner and Constable and French Impressionist and Dutch Renaissance painters. Scottish art and design is well represented with rooms dedicated to the Scottish Colourists and the Glasgow Style *(see p101)*. Included here are two works by Charles Rennie Macintosh – a fine gesso panel and a 1904

writing cabinet. LS Lowry's painting *VE Day* hangs here again after it was cut from its frame and stolen in 1992. You can also see Salvador Dalí's *Christ of St John of the Cross*. There is a vast natural history collection too, with displays on Scotland's wildlife.

Scotland Street School Museum ⓭

225 Scotland Street, Glasgow. *Tel (0141) 287 0500.* ☐ *10am–5pm Tue–Thu & Sat, 11am–5pm Fri & Sun.* ♿ 🖼 🖼 www.glasgowlife.org.uk/museums

This museum is housed in a former school designed by Charles Rennie Mackintosh between 1903 and 1906. It uses displays, audio-visual exhibits and reconstructed and restored classrooms to tell the story of the developments in education in Scotland from the Victorian era to the 1960s. You can read and listen to recollections of former pupils, decade by decade, covering topics such as classroom discipline, evacuation and World War II, school attire and playground games.

Hunterian Art Gallery ⓮

82 Hillhead St. *Tel (0141) 330 5431.* ☐ *9:30am–5pm Mon–Sat.* 🔴 *24 Dec– 4 Jan.* www.hunterian.gla.ac.uk

Built to house a number of paintings bequeathed to Glasgow University by an ex-student and physician, Dr William Hunter (1718–83), the Hunterian Art Gallery contains Scotland's largest print collection. There are also works by many major European artists, dating from the 16th century. A collection of work by the designer Charles Rennie Mackintosh *(see p101)* is supplemented by a complete reconstruction of No. 6 Florentine Terrace, where he lived from

Kelvingrove Art Gallery and the Glasgow University buildings, seen from the south

For hotels and restaurants in this region see pp173–5 and pp190–92

1906 to 1914. There is a major collection of 19th- and 20th-century Scottish art, but by far the most famous collection is of work by the Paris-trained American painter, James McNeill Whistler (1834–1903), who influenced so many of the Glasgow School painters.

Whistler's *Sketch for Annabel Lee* (c.1869), Hunterian Art Gallery

Botanic Gardens ⑮

Great Western Rd. **Tel** *(0141) 334 2422.* ⬤ *7am–dusk.* ♿ 🎫 *by appt.*

These gardens form a peaceful space in the heart of the city's West End, by the River Kelvin. Originally founded at another site in 1817, they were moved to the current location in 1839 and opened to the public three years later. Aside from the main range of greenhouses, with assorted displays including palm trees and an area of tropical crops, one of the

most interesting features is the **Kibble Palace**. Built at Loch Long in the Highlands by John Kibble, the glass palace was moved to its present site in the early 1870s. It houses a collection of carnivorous plants and tropical orchids and the national collection of tree ferns.

People's Palace ⑯

Glasgow Green. **Tel** *(0141) 271 2951.* ⬤ *10am–5pm Tue–Thu & Sat, 11am–5pm Fri & Sun.* ♿ 🖥

This Victorian sandstone structure was purpose-built in 1898 as a cultural museum for the people of Glasgow's East End. It houses everything from temperance tracts to trade-union banners, suffragette posters to the comedian Billy Connolly's banana-shaped boots, and thus provides a social history of the city from the 12th to the 20th century. A superb conservatory contains an exotic winter garden.

House for an Art Lover ⑰

Bellahouston Park, Dumbreck Rd. **Tel** *(0141) 353 4770.* ⬤ *10am–4pm Mon–Wed, 10am–1pm Thu–Sun.* 🖥 *Fri and during functions.* 🎫 ♿ 🎫 *by appt.* 🖥 **www**.houseforanartlover.co.uk

Plans for the House for an Art Lover were submitted by Charles Rennie Mackintosh and his partner Margaret

Distinctive Mackintosh piano in the Music Room, House for an Art Lover

Macdonald in response to a competition in a German magazine in the summer of 1900. The competition brief was to create a country retreat for someone of elegance and taste who loved the arts. As it was a theoretical exercise, the couple were unrestrained by logistics or budget and won a special prize for their efforts.

The plans lay unused for over 80 years until consulting engineer Graham Roxburgh, who had worked on the refurbishment of other Mackintosh interiors in Glasgow, decided to build the House for an Art Lover. Work began in 1989 and was completed in 1996. The House is host to a digital design studio and postgraduate study centre for students at the Glasgow School of Art.

The rooms on the main floor give a real insight into the vision of Mackintosh and the artistic talent of Macdonald. The Oval Room is a beautifully proportioned space in a single light colour, meant as a tranquil retreat for ladies, while the Music Room and its centrepiece piano that is played to add to the atmosphere is also bright and inspiring.

The Main Hall leads into the Dining Room, with its long table, sideboard and relief stone fireplace. The great attention to detail shown throughout the House, in the panelling, light fixtures and other elements, is enormously impressive. The exterior of the building is also an extraordinary achievement in art and design.

One of the greenhouses in Glasgow's peaceful Botanic Gardens

The Georgian Pollok House, viewed from the south

Pollok House ⑱

(NTS) 2060 Pollokshaws Rd. *Tel* (0141) 616 6410. ◯ 10am–5pm daily. Apr–Oct only.

Pollok House is Glasgow's finest 18th-century domestic building and contains one of Britain's best collections of Spanish paintings. The Neo-Classical central block was finished in 1750, the sobriety of its exterior contrasting with the exuberant plasterwork within. The Maxwells have lived at Pollok since the mid-13th century, but the male line ended with Sir John Maxwell, who added the grand entrance hall in the 1890s and designed most of the terraced gardens and parkland beyond.

Hanging above the family silver, porcelain, hand-painted Chinese wallpaper and Jacobean glass, the Stirling Pollok paintings are strong on British and Dutch schools, including William Blake's *Sir Geoffrey Chaucer and the Nine and Twenty Pilgrims* (1745) as well as William Hogarth's portrait of James Thomson, who wrote the words to *Rule Britannia*.

Spanish 16th- to 19th-century art predominates: El Greco's *Lady in a Fur Wrap* (1541) hangs in the library, while the drawing room contains works by Francisco de Goya and Esteban Murillo. In 1966 Anne Maxwell Macdonald gave the house and 146 ha (361 acres) of parkland to the City of Glasgow. The park provides the site for the city's fascinating Burrell Collection.

Burrell Collection ⑲

Given to the city in 1944 by Sir William Burrell (1861–1958), a wealthy shipping owner, this internationally acclaimed collection is the gem in Glasgow's crown, with objects of major importance in numerous fields of interest. The building housing these pieces was purpose-built in 1983. When the sun shines in, the stained glass blazes with colour, while the shaded tapestries seem a part of the surrounding woodland.

Figure of a Luohan
This sculpture of Buddha's disciple dates from the Ming Dynasty (1484).

Hutton Castle Drawing Room
This is a reconstruction of the Drawing Room at Burrell's own home – the 16th-century Hutton Castle, near Berwick-upon-Tweed. The Hall and Dining Room can also be seen nearby.

Bull's Head
Dating from the 7th century BC, this bronze head from Turkey was once part of a cauldron handle.

Hornby Portal
This detail shows the arch's heraldic display. The 14th-century portal comes from Hornby Castle in Yorkshire.

Main entrance

STAR EXHIBITS

★ Stained Glass

★ Tapestries

Rembrandt van Rijn
This self-portrait, signed and dated 1632, has pride of place among the paintings hanging in the 16th- and 17th-century room.

Mezzanine floor

GALLERY GUIDE
Except for a mezzanine-floor display of paintings, the exhibitions are on the ground floor. Right of the entrance hall, rooms are devoted to tapestries, stained glass and sculpture, while ancient civilizations, Oriental art and the period galleries are ahead.

KEY TO FLOORPLAN

⬜	Ancient civilizations
⬜	Oriental art
⬜	Medieval and post-medieval European art, stained glass and tapestries
⬜	Period galleries
⬜	Hutton Castle Rooms
⬜	Paintings and drawings
⬜	Temporary exhibition area

Matthijs Maris
This popular Dutch painter's ethereal style appealed to late 19th-century tastes. The Sisters (1875) is one of over 50 Maris works acquired by Burrell.

Ground floor

Lecture theatre

★ Stained Glass
A man warming himself before a fire is one of many secular themes illustrated in the stained-glass display. This 15th-century piece once decorated a church in Suffolk.

★ Tapestries
Scenes from the Life of the Virgin (c.1450), a Swiss work in wool and linen, is one of many tapestries on show.

SHOPPING IN GLASGOW

While Glasgow itself is home to some 570,000 people, as the focal point of a great conurbation in west central Scotland it provides the main shopping centre for almost half of the country's population. The large number of potential customers is allied to Glasgow's reputation as Scotland's

Ortak brooch

most fashion-conscious city: the best alternative fashion and design boutiques are in the West End, around Byres Road. A trip to the colourful Barras street market, which is held every weekend, offers a much more traditional, if somewhat anarchic, Glaswegian shopping experience.

St Enoch Centre, one of the city's malls

DEPARTMENT STORES AND MALLS

The impressive Buchanan Galleries has many well-known shops including a **John Lewis** department store. The **Italian Centre**, in the Merchant City area and **Princes Square**, houses designer boutiques. The St Enoch Centre houses a **Debenhams** department store. **House of Fraser** is one of the longest established department stores.

MARKETS

No visit to Glasgow is complete without a trip to **The Barras**, a weekend market in the east end of the city centre. The name is a dialect version of "The Barrows", and dates from a time when goods were sold from barrows.

The current site, between the Gallowgate and London Road, has been an official market since the 1920s. Every

Saturday and Sunday, thousands of bargain hunters descend on stalls that sell virtually everything from old junk to cheap clothes and CDs.

FASHION

Many fashion stores are housed in the malls in the city centre. Outside the malls, **Cruise** sells well-known designer names for men and women, while streetwise **Diesel** has an outlet on Buchanan Street. Further along this street, **Karen Millen** is the store for the chic professional woman. **Schuh** sells a range of fashionable footwear for both men and women; **Pied à Terre** has smart shoes for women. For special occasions, **Ella Bulloch** is the best place to buy or hire a lady's hat. For a luxurious range of underwear, try **Pampas Lingerie**. Second-hand clothes stores abound. **Mr Ben** offers 1950s American

chic, while **Starry Starry Night** is more classic and traditional in style. **Graham Tiso** is great for clothing and equipment for the outdoors. Tartan fans should seek out **Hector Russell**, a Highland outfitter that makes made-to-measure kilts. The West End is home to many small boutiques, such as **Pink Poodle**, which sells funky clothes and accessories.

FOOD AND DRINK

Glasgow's finest independent delicatessen is **Fratelli Sarti**, a traditional Italian food store also offering a good selection of wines. **Peckham's**, a chain of delis, has an excellent branch on Glassford Street, and its scope goes far beyond Italy. A man once described as the UK's top cheese-monger, **Iain Mellis**, opened an outlet in Glasgow in 1995. It is the best place in the entire west of Scotland for artisan

Glenlivet whisky

Traditional, "barrow-style" fruit stall in Glasgow's Barras Market

For hotels and restaurants in this region see pp173–5 and pp190–92

cheeses made from unpast-
eurized milk. **Roots and Fruits**
is Glasgow's leading fruit and
vegetable store, and **Grass
Roots** does superb breads.
Aside from national chains
selling beer, wine and spirits,
such as **Oddbins**, there is **The
Whisky Shop** in the city centre
and the **Ubiquitous Chip Wine
Shop** in the west end.

BOOK STORES

Glasgow is fairly well served
by bookshops. **Waterstone's**
on Sauchiehall Street is a
multi-floor chain store
complete with a coffee shop.
In the West End, **Caledonia
Books** and **Voltaire & Rousseau**
sell a variety of second-hand
and antiquarian books on a
wide range of subjects and
are well worth a visit.

Shopping on Argyle Street, with its profusion of high-street stores

ART AND DESIGN

There are a number of small
galleries concentrated in the
streets behind the Tron
Theatre, such as the **Glasgow
Print Studio** and **Art Exposure**.
The **Redcoat Gallery** is another
great place to pick up affordable and exciting work. The

Glasgow Art Fair, held at the
end of April, also provides an
opportunity to buy contemporary art. Fans of antiques
should try the extensive
Heritage House at Yorkhill
Quay beside the River Clyde.
For furniture and interior
design ideas, visit **Designworks** or **Dallas and Dallas**.

DIRECTORY

DEPARTMENT STORES AND MALLS

Debenhams
97 Argyll St, G2 8AR.
Tel (0141) 221 0088.

House of Fraser
45 Buchanan St,
G1 3HR.
Tel (0141) 221 3880.

Italian Centre
7 John St, G1 1HP.
Tel (0141) 552 6368.

John Lewis
Buchanan Galleries,
G1 2GF.
Tel (0141) 353 6677.

Princes Square
48 Buchanan St, G1 3JX.
Tel (0141) 221 0324.

FASHION

Cruise
180 Ingram St, G1 1DN.
Tel (0141) 572 3232.

Diesel
116–120 Buchanan St,
G1 2JW.
Tel (0141) 221 5255.

Ella Bulloch
461 Clarkston Rd,
G44 2LW.
Tel (0141) 633 0078.

Graham Tiso
129 Buchanan St,
G1 2JA.
Tel (0141) 248 4877.

Hector Russell
110 Buchanan St,
G1 2JN.
Tel (0141) 221 0217.

Karen Millen
36 Buchanan St, G1 3JX.
Tel (0141) 243 2136.

Mr Ben
Studio 6, 101 King St,
G1 5RB.
Tel (0141) 553 1936.

Pampas Lingerie
74 Hyndland Rd,
G12 9UT.
Tel (0141) 357 2383.

Pied à Terre
45 Buchanan St, G1 3JN.
Tel (0141) 221 3880.

Pink Poodle
181 Byres Road, G12 8TS.
Tel (0141) 357 3344.

Schuh
112–114 Argyle St,
G2 8BH.
Tel (0141) 248 7331.

Starry Starry Night
19–21 Dowanside Lane,
G12 9BZ.
Tel (0141) 337 1837.

FOOD AND DRINK

Fratelli Sarti
133 Wellington St, G2 2XD.
Tel (0141) 248 2228.

Grass Roots
20 Woodlands Road,
G3 6UR.
Tel (0141) 353 3278.

Iain Mellis
492 Great Western Rd,
G12 8EW.
Tel (0141) 339 8998.

Oddbins
132 Woodlands Rd, G3
6LF. *Tel (0141) 332 1663.*

Peckham's
61–65 Glassford St, G1
1UG. *Tel (0141) 553 0666.*

Roots & Fruits
351 Byres Rd, G12 8AU.
Tel (0141) 339 5164.

**Ubiquitous Chip
Wine Shop**
12 Ashton Lane, G12 8SJ.
Tel (0141) 334 5007.

The Whisky Shop
220 Buchanan St, G1 2GF.
Tel (0141) 331 0022.

BOOK STORES

Caledonia Books
483 Great Western Rd, G12
8HL. *Tel (0141) 334 9663.*

Voltaire & Rousseau
18 Otago Lane, G12 8PB.
Tel (0141) 339 1811.

Waterstone's
153–157 Sauchiehall St,
G2 3EW.
Tel (0141) 332 9105.

ART AND DESIGN

Art Exposure
19 Parnie St, G1 5RJ.
Tel (0141) 552 7779.

Dallas and Dallas
18 Montrose St, G1 1RE.
Tel (0141) 552 2939.

Designworks
38 Gibson St, G12 8NX.
Tel (0141) 339 9520.

Glasgow Art Fair
Tel (0141) 204 4400.

**Glasgow Print
Studio**
22 King St, G1 5QP.
Tel (0141) 552 0704.

Heritage House
3b Yorkhill Quay Estate,
G3 8QE.
Tel (0141) 334 4924.

Redcoat Gallery
323 North Woodside Rd,
G20 6RY.
Tel (0141) 341 0069.

ENTERTAINMENT IN GLASGOW

The dance music that emerged during the 1990s found a natural home in Glasgow, which has possibly the most exuberant nightlife in Scotland. With the Scottish Exhibition and Conference Centre housing two major rock venues, and Barrowlands still a fixture on the concert circuit, popular music is very prominent. There are a number of mainstream cinemas in the city,

A flag celebrating Glasgow as
"the friendly city"

as well as the Glasgow Film Theatre, a centre for arthouse releases. The annual Celtic Connections Festival in January is an international folk music event and there is plenty of culture in the city as a whole. Some major orchestras, the Scottish Ballet and Scottish Opera are based here. The Citizens' is a highly-acclaimed theatre and the Tramway and the Arches both stage large, innovative productions.

Scottish Opera performing *Eugene Onegin* on stage at the Theatre Royal

SOURCES OF INFORMATION

The twice-monthly arts and entertainment magazine *The List* covers all events in Glasgow and Edinburgh, as does *The Skinny* (www. skinnymag.co.uk).

CLASSICAL MUSIC AND OPERA

Scotland's national opera company, Scottish Opera, is based at the **Theatre Royal** and stages some eight productions each season.
   Glasgow Royal Concert Hall is the main venue for the Royal Scottish National Orchestra; it also hosts visits from major international orchestras. The RSNO's annual concert series runs from October to April. Family classical concerts are performed all year.
   For more intimate shows, the **Royal Scottish Academy of Music and Drama** has two smaller halls, while many venues across the city host recitals and concerts.

ROCK, JAZZ AND WORLD MUSIC

Rock bands have a choice of venues. There is the main auditorium at the **Scottish Exhibition and Conference Centre**, and the **Armadillo** in the same centre. It is **Barrowlands**, however, that remains the city's principal rock venue. There is also **King Tut's Wah Wah Hut**, where Oasis were

Musicians outside City Chambers
during a Festival of Jazz

discovered, and the **O2 Academy**. Jazz sessions take place at **Cottier's** and the **O2 ABC**. The Royal Concert Hall holds a Celtic Connections Festival. It also hosts international music, as does the **Old Fruitmarket**.

CINEMA

There are 18 screens at the **Cineworld**, while the **Odeon at the Quay** has 12. The **Glasgow Film Theatre**, or GFT, shows arthouse and foreign-language movies. Glasgow's new **IMAX Theatre** is also well worth a visit.

The stylish café-bar at the Tron
Theatre in the city centre

THEATRE AND DANCE

The Scottish ballet stages its Glasgow performances at the Theatre Royal (*see Classical Music and Opera*). Visiting dance companies, from classical to contemporary, also perform here and it is a noted stop on the touring circuit for major theatre companies from the rest of the UK and overseas.
   The **Citizens' Theatre** is the main venue for serious drama, from Greek tragedies to modern pieces, and it rightly claims to be Scotland's best.

For hotels and restaurants in this region see pp173–5 and pp190–92

Both the **Tramway** and the **Arches** are acclaimed for their experimental works. Smaller-scale productions can be seen at the **Tron** and Cottier's Theatre (see Rock, Jazz and World Music). Commercial productions, such as musicals and pantomimes, are a staple at the popular **King's**.

BARS AND CLUBS

Visitors can choose from traditional pubs, which give a flavour of the old city, or fashionable bars with a contemporary atmosphere. Old-fashioned pubs such as the **Horseshoe**, the **Griffin** and the **Halt**, have long been popular in Glasgow. Modern venues include **Home** and

Original road sign for the West End

Bar 91, both in the Merchant City, and the first-floor bar at the **Radio** in the West End continue to thrive. **Bar Soba** is another popular cocktail bar. The city's club culture is one of the best in the UK. Each venue has different styles of music on different nights, including house, hip-hop, techno or drum-and-bass. The Arches (see Theatre and Dance), **The Sub Club**, **The Tunnel**, **The Soundhaus** and **Artá** are among the best.

SPORTS

Glasgow is home to the country's most successful football (soccer) clubs, **Celtic** and **Glasgow Rangers**, and each has a large, impressive stadium. The football season runs from August to May, and there is usually a game at least once a week during the time. Scotland's refurbished **Hampden National Stadium** hosts the finals of domestic cup competitions in November and May each year, and major international games.

Celtic fans cheering on their football (soccer) team from the stands

DIRECTORY

CLASSICAL MUSIC AND OPERA

Glasgow Royal Concert Hall
2 Sauchiehall St, G2 3NY.
Tel (0141) 353 8000.
www.glasgowconcert
halls.com

Royal Scottish Academy of Music and Drama
100 Renfrew St, G2 3DB.
Tel (0141) 332 5057.

Theatre Royal
282 Hope St, G2 3QA.
Tel (0844) 871 7647.

ROCK, JAZZ AND WORLD MUSIC

Barrowlands
244 Gallowgate, G4 0TT.
Tel (0141) 552 4601.

Cottier's
93 Hyndland St, G11 5PX.
Tel (0141) 357 5825.

King Tut's Wah Wah Hut
272a St Vincent St, G2 5RL. **Tel** (0141) 221 5279.

O2 ABC
300 Sauchiehall St, G2 3JA. **Tel** (0844) 477 2000.

O2 Academy
121 Eglington St, G5 9NT.
Tel (0141) 418 3000.

Old Fruitmarket
Albion St, G1 1NQ.
Tel (0141) 353 8000.

Scottish Exhibition and Conference Centre/Armadillo
Finnieston, G3 8YW.
Tel (0141) 248 3000.
www.secc.co.uk

CINEMA

Cineworld
7 Renfrew St, G1 2LR.
Tel (0871) 200 2000.

Glasgow Film Theatre
12 Rose St, G3 6RB.
Tel (0141) 332 6535.

IMAX Theatre
50 Pacific Quay, G51 1EA.
Tel (0141) 420 5000.

Odeon at the Quay
Paisley Road West,
G5 8NP.
Tel (0871) 224 4007.

THEATRE AND DANCE

Arches
253 Argyll St, G2 8DL.
Tel (0870) 240 7528.

Citizens' Theatre
119 Gorbals St, G5 9DS.
Tel (0141) 429 0022.

King's
297 Bath St, G2 4JN.
Tel (0844) 871 7648.

Tramway
25 Albert Drive, G41 2PE.
Tel (0845) 330 3501.

Tron
63 Trongate, G1 5HB.
Tel (0141) 552 4267.

BARS AND CLUBS

Artá
13 Walls St, G1 1DA.
Tel (0845) 166 6018.

Bar 91
91 Candleriggs, G1 1NP.
Tel (0141) 552 5211.

Bar Soba
11 Mitchell Lane, G1 3NU.
Tel (0141) 204 2404.

Chinaskis
239 North St, G3 7DL.
Tel (0141) 221 0061.

Griffin
266 Bath St, G2 4JP.
Tel (0141) 331 5171.

Halt
160 Woodlands Rd, G3 6LF. **Tel** (0141) 352 9996.

Home
80 Albion St, G1 1NY.
Tel (0141) 552 1734.

Horseshoe
17 Drury St, G2 5AE.
Tel (0141) 229 5711.

Radio
44–46 Ashton Lane, G12 8SJ. **Tel** (0141) 334 6688.

The Soundhaus
47 Hyde Park St, G3 8BW.
Tel (0141) 221 4659.

The Sub Club
22 Jamaica St, G1 4QD.
Tel (0141) 248 4600.

The Tunnel
84 Mitchell St, G1 3NA.
Tel (0141) 204 1000.

SPORTS

Celtic
Celtic Park,
95 Kerrydale St, G40 3RE.
Tel (0870) 161 1888.

Glasgow Rangers
Ibrox Stadium, G51 2YX.
Tel (0870) 600 1993.

Hampden National Stadium
Hampden Park,
Letherby Drive, G42 9BA.
Tel (0141) 620 4000.

CENTRAL SCOTLAND

*C*entral Scotland is a contrast of picturesque countryside and major urban centres, where a modern industrialized country meets an older and wilder landscape. Historically, it was here that the English-speaking Lowlands bordered the Gaelic Highlands, and there is still a strong sense of transition for anyone travelling north.

The Highland Boundary Fault is a geological feature running through Central Scotland from Arran in the southwest to Stonehaven on the northeast coast. The Fault divides the Highlands from the Lowlands, making Central Scotland an area of contrasts, with both mountainous areas and green farmland. For hundreds of years, this line was also a meeting place, or border, between two very different cultures. To the north and west was a Gaelic-speaking people, who felt loyalty to their local clan chiefs. This way of life began to be marginalized in the late 18th century, as the more Anglicized Lowlands established their dominance.

In the Lowlands, Scotland's industry developed, drawing on coal reserves in districts such as Lanarkshire and the Lothians, while the Highlands were depopulated and eventually set aside for sporting estates and sheep farming.

Because Central Scotland is so compact, the opposing characteristics of Highland and Lowland, industrial and pre-industrial, exist side by side. Stirling Castle, parts of which date from the 16th century, is sited close to the petro-chemical plants and power plants on the upper reaches of the Forth. The tranquillity of the Trossachs and the hills of Arran are easily accessible from Glasgow, Scotland's largest, and largely industrial, city. The country's first coal-run ironworks was built at Carron in 1759, very close to Falkirk, where Bonnie Prince Charlie had enjoyed one of his last military successes as claimant to the British throne 13 years earlier. Perth and Dundee are important centres of commerce just a short distance from the relative wildness of the southern Highlands. From gritty cities to the great outdoors, the region displays huge contrasts.

The view from Goatfell Ridge, near Brodick, across to the spectacular mountains of Arran

◁ A golfer in the grounds of a stately home, one of a number in Central Scotland providing golfing facilities

Exploring Central Scotland

Central Scotland has a huge variety of landscapes. The Goatfell ridge on the Isle of Arran, off the west coast, has one of the most inspiring island hill walks in the entire country while, just to the north, the Isle of Bute is a more placid tourist destination. On the mainland, the Trossachs, near Callander, is an area of outstanding mountain beauty, very different from the lowlands of the Forth Valley futher east. Stirling Castle stands at the head of the Forth under the shadow of the Ochil Hills, while Perth occupies a similar position on the Tay. The Firth of Tay, with its open views, is home to Dundee, Scotland's fourth city.

Loch Katrine in the Trossachs

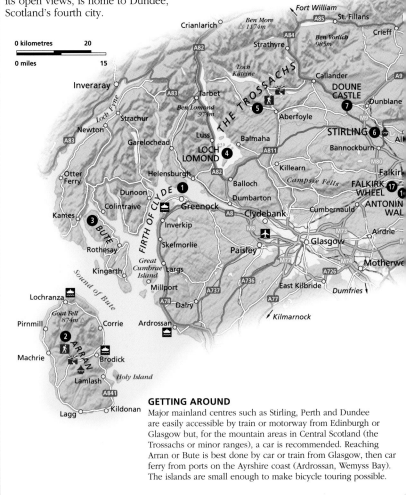

0 kilometres   20

0 miles   15

GETTING AROUND

Major mainland centres such as Stirling, Perth and Dundee are easily accessible by train or motorway from Edinburgh or Glasgow but, for the mountain areas in Central Scotland (the Trossachs or minor ranges), a car is recommended. Reaching Arran or Bute is best done by car or train from Glasgow, then car ferry from ports on the Ayrshire coast (Ardrossan, Wemyss Bay). The islands are small enough to make bicycle touring possible.

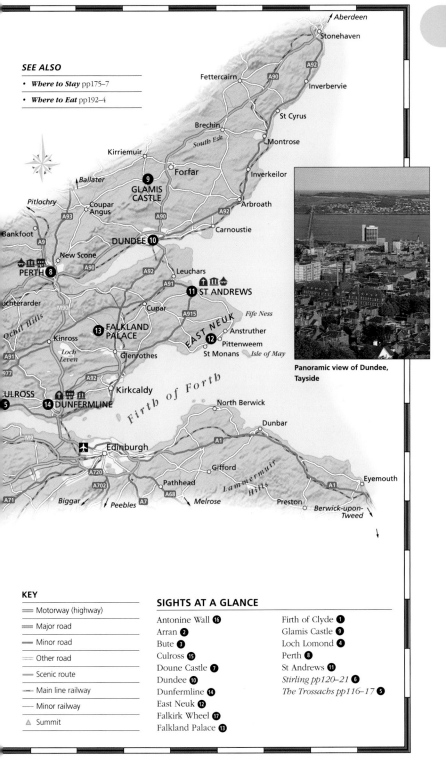

SEE ALSO
- **Where to Stay** pp175–7
- **Where to Eat** pp192–4

Panoramic view of Dundee, Tayside

KEY

▬▬	Motorway (highway)
▬▬	Major road
▬▬	Minor road
═══	Other road
▬▬	Scenic route
▬•▬	Main line railway
▬▬	Minor railway
△	Summit

SIGHTS AT A GLANCE

Antonine Wall ⑯
Arran ❷
Bute ❸
Culross ⑮
Doune Castle ❼
Dundee ❿
Dunfermline ⑭
East Neuk ⑫
Falkland Palace ⑬

Firth of Clyde ❶
Glamis Castle ❾
Loch Lomond ❹
Perth ❽
St Andrews ⓫
Stirling pp120–21 ❻
The Trossachs pp116–17 ❺

Falkirk Wheel ⑰

Firth of Clyde ❶

Numerous counties west of Glasgow.
🚆 *Helensburgh and Dumbarton in
the north; Troon and Ayr in the south.*
🚢 *from Largs to Great Cumbrae;
from Gourock to Dunoon.*
ℹ️ *Largs (0845) 2255121;
Dumbarton (01389) 742306.*

As might be expected of a
waterway that leads from
Glasgow, a former economic
powerhouse of the British Empire *(see p46)*, to the Irish Sea
and the Atlantic, the Firth of
Clyde has many reminders of
its industrial past. **Greenock**,
some 40 km (25 miles) west
of Glasgow, was once a shipbuilding centre. Few visit for
the town's beauty, but the
**McLean Museum and Art
Gallery**, with its exhibits and
information on the engineer
James Watt *(see p24)*, a native
of Greenock, is worth a visit.
Princes Pier is a departure
point for cruises along the
Clyde. **Dumbarton**, 24 km
(15 miles) from Glasgow on
the northern bank, dates from
the 5th century AD. Its ancient
castle perches on a rock overlooking the rest of the town.

The Firth itself is L-shaped,
heading northwest as it opens
up beyond the Erskine Bridge.
On reaching Gourock, just
west of Greenock, the Firth
branches south to more open
water. Kip Marina at nearby
Inverkip is a major yachting
centre, while many towns on
the Ayrshire coast have served
as holiday resorts for Glasgow
since Victorian times. **Largs**,
site of the clash between Scots
and Vikings in 1263, has a
multimedia centre about the
Vikings in Scotland, as well

The old harbour at Brodick, with
Goatfell ridge in the distance

as a modern monument
to the 1263 battle. A ferry
service is offered to **Great
Cumbrae Island**, which lies
just off the coast. The main
town on the island is
Millport, which is built
around a picturesque bay.
The western side of the
Firth of Clyde is much
less developed, bor-
dered by the Cowal
Peninsula with its
hills and lochs. The
only town of note in this
wild country is **Dunoon**.
Again once a Victorian
holiday resort, it still relies
on tourism for its income.
For many years there
was a strong American
influence in Dunoon
due to the US nuclear
submarine base at Holy
Loch that is now closed.

🏛 **McLean Museum and Art
Gallery**
15 Kelly St, Greenock. **Tel** (01475)
715624. ⏰ *10am–5pm Mon–Sat.*

Arran ❷

North Ayrshire. 🏔 *4,500.* 🚢 *from
Ardrossan to Brodick; from Claonaig
(Isle of Mull) to Lochranza (Apr–Oct
only).* ℹ️ *Ayr (0845) 2255121.*
www.ayrshire-arran.com

Arran is thought to have been
populated as long ago as the
end of the last Ice Age. The
island's neolithic chambered
burial tombs, such as the one
at **Torrylinn** near Lagg in the
south, indicate this. Bronze
Age stone circles can also be
seen around **Machrie** on the
west coast. Vikings arrived
from about AD 800 and
exerted an influence for more
than four centuries. After the
Battle of Largs in 1263, when
Alexander III defeated the
Norsemen, Scotland bought
Arran from the Vikings in 1266.

Today, visitors tend to
come to Arran for
outdoor pursuits. Golf
is especially popular,
with 18-hole courses at
Brodick, Whiting Bay
and Lamlash. Fishing
is also popular.
Brodick is the
island's only real
town. The more
mountainous parts
offer some of the
most spectacular
hillwalking in
Central Scotland.
The Goatfell ridge
to the east of Glen
Rosa and **Beinn
Tarsuinn** to the west

*Golfer on the
island of Arran*

have a particular rugged beauty.
Robert the Bruce stayed on
Arran on his return to Scotland in 1307. His followers
had already been harassing
the garrison at **Brodick Castle**,
then occupied by supporters
of the King of England. Legend
states that it was from Arran
that Bruce saw a signal fire
on the Ayrshire coast that told
him it was safe to return to
the mainland and launch the
campaign against the English
(see p43). Parts of the Castle
still date from the 13th
century, though it has had
many later additions.

⚓ **Brodick Castle**
(NTS) Brodick. **Tel** (01770) 302202.
Castle ⏰ *Apr–Sep: 11am–4pm (to
3pm Oct).* **Gardens** ⏰ *daily.* 🏠 ♿

Largs seafront, the departure point for ferries to Great Cumbrae Island

For hotels and restaurants in this region see pp175–7 and pp192–4

The snowy peak of Ben Lomond rising majestically over Loch Lomond, part of the West Highland Way

Bute ❸

Argyll & Bute. 🏔 *7,000.* 🚢 *from Wemyss Bay to Rothesay; from Colintraive to Rhubodach.* 🚌 *from Dunoon.* ℹ️ *Rothesay (01700) 502151.*

Bute is almost an extension of the Cowal Peninsula, and the small ferry from Colintraive takes only five minutes to cross the Kyles of Bute to Rhubodach on the island. This route is a long drive from Glasgow, however, and most people choose to travel via Wemyss Bay on the Firth of Clyde across to the island's main town, Rothesay.

Just 25 km (16 miles) long by 8 km (5 miles) at its widest point, Bute has been occupied since at least the Bronze Age. The remains of the chapel at St Ninian's Point on the west coast date from around the 6th century, while **Rothesay Castle**, now ruined, is mostly

a 12th-century structure and was the site of struggles between islanders and Vikings in the 13th century. Over the last 120 years or so, Bute has played a more placid role as a popular holiday resort.

One of Bute's attractions is **Mount Stuart House**, 5 km (3 miles) south of Rothesay. This aristocratic house, built in 1877 by the third Marquess of Bute, is set in 18th-century gardens. The features of this Gothic edifice reflect the Marquess's interests in mythology, religion and astronomy.

⚓ **Rothesay Castle**
Castle Hill St, Rothesay. **Tel** (01700) 502691. ⏲ *Apr–Sep: 9:30am–5:30pm; Oct–Mar: 9:30am–4:30pm Sat–Wed (also Thu in Oct).* 📷

⚓ **Mount Stuart House**
Mount St. **Tel** (01700) 503877.
⏲ *Mar–mid-Apr: Wed–Sun; mid-Apr–Oct: daily.* 📷 🛍 ♿ 📺
www.mountstuart.com

Loch Lomond ❹

West Dunbartonshire, Argyll & Bute, Trossachs. 🚆 *Balloch, Tarbet.* 🚌 *Balloch, Balmaha.* ℹ️ *Balloch (08707) 200 607*

Of Scotland's many lochs, Lomond is perhaps the most popular and best loved. Lying just 30 km (19 miles) northwest of Glasgow, its accessibility has helped its rise to prominence. The loch is the largest body of fresh water in the British Isles, 35 km (22 miles) long and 8 km (5 miles) at its widest point in the south, where there is a scattering of over 30 islands, some with ancient ruins. Duncryne, a small hill some 5 km (3 miles) northeast of **Balloch** on the southern shore, gives an excellent view of the Loch. Much of the area became Scotland's first national park in 2002, fronted by the **Loch Lomond Shores** visitor centre complex in Balloch.

In general, the western shore is the more developed, with villages such as **Luss** and **Tarbet** attracting large numbers of visitors. The contrast between the Loch and **Ben Lomond**, 974 m (3,196 ft), high above its eastern shore adds to the spectacle. Many walkers pass this way since Scotland's most popular long-distance footpath, the West Highland Way (*see p207*) from Glasgow to Fort William, skirts the eastern shore. Boat trips around the loch operate regularly from Balloch Pier. The area is also good for watersports enthusiasts – speed boats, kayaks and jet skis can all be rented.

View of Bute with 14th-century Kames Castle, at the head of Kames Bay

The Trossachs

Combining the ruggedness of the Grampians with the pastoral tranquillity of the Borders, this beautiful region of craggy hills and sparkling lochs is the colourful meeting place of the Lowlands and Highlands. Home to a wide variety of wildlife, including the golden eagle, peregrine falcon, red deer and the wildcat, the Trossachs and their inhabitants have inspired numerous writers,

Golden eagle

including Sir Walter Scott (*see p86*) who made the area the setting for several of his novels. In 2002, a large part of the area was designated as Loch Lomond and The Trossachs National Park, the first national park in Scotland.

Loch Katrine
The setting of Sir Walter Scott's Lady of the Lake (1810), this freshwater loch can be explored on the Victorian steamer Sir Walter Scott, which cruises from the Trossachs Pier.

Loch Lomond
Britain's largest freshwater lake was immortalized in a ballad composed by a local Jacobite soldier, dying far from home. He laments that though he will return home before his companions who travel on "the high road", he will be doing so on "the low road" (of death).

The West Highland Way provides a good footpath through the area.

Luss
With its exceptionally picturesque cottages, Luss is one of the prettiest villages in Central Scotland. Surrounded by grassy hills, it occupies one of the most scenic parts of Loch Lomond's western shore.

Map labels: FORT WILLIAM, Inveruglas, LOCH ARKLET, Tarbet, BEN LOMOND 974 m (3,195 ft), Kinlochard, BEN UIRD 596 m (1,955 ft), Luss, LOCH LOMOND, Balmaha, Balloch, GLASGOW

KEY

ⓘ	Tourist information
▬	Major road
═	Minor road
=	Narrow lane
- -	Footpath
☀	Viewpoint

0 kilometres 5

0 miles 5

Inchmahome Priory
Mary, Queen of Scots was hidden in this island priory to escape the armies of King Henry VIII, before fleeing for France.

VISITORS' CHECKLIST

Central. 🚋 Stirling.
🚌 Callander. 🛈 Ancaster Sq,
Callander (08707) 200631.
⭕ daily. **Inchmahome Priory,**
off A81, near Aberfoyle.
Tel (0131) 668 8800. ⭕ Apr–
Sep: daily. 📷 ♿ limited. **Sir
Walter Scott Steamer,** Katrine
Pier. **Tel** (01877) 332 000.

Balquhidder 🏛   PERTH

LOCH VOIL

Rob Roy's grave

A84

TROSSACHS   LOCH LUBNAIG

BEN LEDI
▲
878 m
(2,881 ft)   A84

BEN VENUE
▲
727 m
(2,385 ft)

Brig O'Turk   Callander 🛈

LOCH VENNACHAR   A821

A81

B829

MENTEITH HILLS

Aberfoyle   A81   A873   B822

CH ARD

B8034   Goodie Water   STIRLING

LAKE OF MENTEITH

A811   STIRLING

A811   Arnprior

rymen   Balfron

B875

Killearn

Callander
With its Rob Roy and Trossachs Visitor Centre, Callander is the most popular town from which to explore the Trossachs.

The Duke's Pass, between Callander and Aberfoyle, affords some of the finest views in the area.

ROB ROY (1671–1734)

Robert MacGregor, known as Rob Roy (Red Robert) from the colour of his hair, grew up as a herdsman near Loch Arklet. After a series of harsh winters, he took to raiding richer Lowland properties to feed his clan, and was declared an outlaw by the Duke of Montrose who burned his house to the ground. After this, Rob Roy's Jacobite sympathies became inflamed by his desire to avenge the crime. Plundering the duke's lands and repeatedly escaping from prison earned him a reputation similar to that of England's Robin Hood. He was pardoned in 1725 and spent his last years freely in Balquhidder, where he is buried.

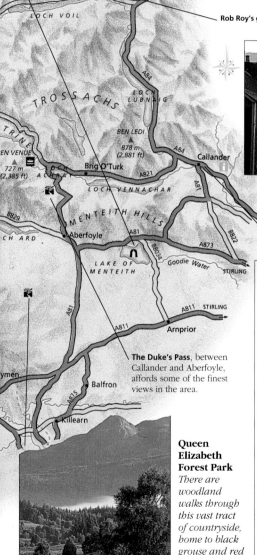

Queen Elizabeth Forest Park
There are woodland walks through this vast tract of countryside, home to black grouse and red deer, between Loch Lomond and Aberfoyle.

The 17th-century town house of the Dukes of Argyll

Stirling ❻

Central. 🏠 28,000. 🚉 🚌
ℹ 41 Dunbarton Rd (01786) 475019.
www.visitstirling.org

Situated between the Ochil Hills and the Campsie Fells, the town of Stirling grew up around its castle, historically one of Scotland's most important fortresses. Below the castle the Old Town is still protected by the original walls, built in the 16th century to keep Mary, Queen of Scots safe from Henry VIII. The medieval **Church of the Holy Rude**, on Castle Wynd, where the infant James VI was crowned in 1567, has one of Scotland's few surviving hammerbeam oak roofs. In front of the church, the ornate façade of **Mar's Wark** is all that remains of a grand palace which, though never completed, was commissioned in 1570 by the first Earl of Mar. It was destroyed by the Jacobites in 1746.

Environs
Three kilometres (2 miles) south of Stirling, the **Bannockburn Heritage Centre** stands by the field where Robert the Bruce defeated the English in 1314 (see p43). After the battle, he dismantled the castle so it would not fall back into English hands. A bronze equestrian statue commemorates the man who became an icon of Scottish independence.

ℹ **Bannockburn Heritage Centre**
(NTS) Glasgow Rd. **Tel** (01786) 812664. ⬜ Mar–Oct: 10am–5:30pm daily. ⬛ 24 Dec–Feb. 📷 ♿ 📷

Stirling Castle

Rising high on a rocky crag, this magnificent castle, which dominated Scottish history for centuries, now remains one of the finest examples of Renaissance architecture in Scotland. Legend says that King Arthur wrested the original castle from the Saxons; however, the first written evidence of a castle is from 1100. The present building dates from the 15th and 16th centuries and was last defended, against the Jacobites, in 1746. From 1881 to 1964 it was used as a depot for recruits into the Argyll and Sutherland Highlanders, though it now serves no military function.

Gargoyle on castle wall

Robert the Bruce
In the esplanade, this modern statue shows Robert the Bruce sheathing his sword after the Battle of Bannockburn in 1314.

Prince's Tower

Forework

Entrance

Stirling Castle in the Time of the Stuarts, painted by Johannes Vorsterman (1643–99)

◁ **Loch Ard, near Stirling, in the Trossachs**

★ Palace
The sumptuous interiors of the royal apartments contain the carved, wooden Stirling Heads. The rooms have been restored to their mid-16th-century appearance.

VISITORS' CHECKLIST

Castle Wynd, Stirling. *Tel* (01786) 450000. ☐ Apr–Sep: 9:30am–6pm daily; Oct–Mar: 9:30am–5pm daily. 🎫 🚻 museum. 🦽 limited. 📷 🍴 🚻 📖 🏪
www.historic-scotland.gov.uk

The King's Old Building houses the Regimental Museum of the Argyll and Sutherland Highlanders.

★ Chapel Royal
Seventeenth-century frescoes by Valentine Jenkins adorn the chapel, built in 1594.

Nether Bailey

STAR FEATURES

★ Palace

★ Chapel Royal

The Great Hall, built in 1500, has a roof similar to that of Edinburgh Castle (see pp60–61).

The Elphinstone Tower was originally home to the constable of the castle.

Grand Battery
Following the unrest after the deposition of the Stuarts (see p45), this parapet was built in 1708, to strengthen the castle's defences.

STIRLING BATTLES

At the highest navigable point of the Forth and holding the pass to the Highlands, Stirling occupied a key position in Scotland's struggles for independence. Seven battlefields can be seen from the castle; the 67-m (220-ft) Wallace Monument at Abbey Craig recalls William Wallace's defeat of the English at Stirling Bridge in 1297, foreshadowing Bruce's victory in 1314.

The Victorian Wallace Monument

Perth seen from the east across the Tay

Doune Castle ❼

Doune, Central. **Tel** *(01786) 841742.*
🚆 🚌 *Stirling then bus.* ⭕ *Apr–Sep:
9:30am–5:30pm daily; Oct–Mar:
9:30am–4:30pm (closed Thu
Nov–Mar).* 🎫 ♿ *limited.*
www.historic-scotland.gov.uk

Built as the residence of
Robert, Duke of Albany, in the
late 1300s, Doune Castle was
a Stuart stronghold until it fell
into ruin in the 18th century.
Now fully restored, it offers
a unique view into the life of
the medieval royal household.
    The Gatehouse leads through
to the central courtyard, from
which the Great Hall can be
entered. Complete with its
open-timber roof, minstrels'
gallery and central fireplace,
the Hall adjoins the Lord's Hall
and Private Room with its
original privy and well-hatch.
A number of private stairs and
narrow passages illustrate the
ingenious means by which
the royal family protected

itself during times of danger.
The film *Monty Python and
the Holy Grail* was shot here,
making the castle a popular
destination for Python fans.

Perth ❽

Perthshire. 🏛 *45,000.* 🚆 🚌
🛈 *Lower City Mills, West Mills St.*
Tel *(01738) 450600.*
www.perthshire.co.uk

Once the capital of medieval
Scotland, Perth has a rich
heritage that is reflected in
many of its buildings. It was
in the **Church of St John**,
founded in 1126, that the
preacher John Knox delivered
the fiery sermons that led to
the destruction of many local
monasteries. The Victorianized
Fair Maid's House (c.1600),
on North Port, is one of the
oldest houses in town and
was the fictional home of the
heroine of Sir Walter Scott's
The Fair Maid of Perth (1828).

In **Balhousie Castle**, the
Museum of the Black
Watch commemorates the
first ever Highland regiment,
while the **Museum and Art
Gallery** has displays on local
industry and exhibitions of
Scottish painting.

Environs: Three km (2 miles)
north of Perth, Gothic **Scone
Palace** stands on the site of
an abbey destroyed by John
Knox's followers in 1559.
Between the 9th and 13th
centuries, Scone guarded the
sacred Stone of Destiny,
now in Edinburgh Castle
(*see pp60–61*).

⛪ **Balhousie Castle**
RHQ Black Watch, Hay St. **Tel**
(0131) 310 8530. ⭕ May–Sep:
10am–4:30pm Mon–Sat; Oct–Apr:
10am–3:30pm Mon–Fri.
⬤ 23 Dec–18 Mar.

🏛 **Museum and Art Gallery**
78 George St. **Tel** (01738) 632488.
⭕ Mon–Sat. ♿

⛪ **Scone Palace**
A93 to Braemar. **Tel** (01738) 552300.
⭕ Easter–Oct: daily. 🎫 ♿

Glamis Castle ❾

Glamis, outside Forfar, Tayside.
Tel *(01307) 840393.* 🚆 🚌 *Dundee
then bus.* ⭕ *Apr–Oct: 10am–6pm;
Nov–Dec: 10:30am–4:30pm.* 🎫 📷
♿ *grounds.*

With the pinnacled outline of
a Loire chateau, the imposing
medieval towerhouse of **Glamis**

Glamis Castle with statues of James VI (left) and Charles I (right)

Castle began as a royal hunting lodge in the 11th century but underwent reconstruction in the 17th century. It was the childhood home of the late Queen Elizabeth the Queen Mother, and her former bedroom can be seen with a youthful portrait by Henri de Laszlo (1878–1956).

Many rooms are open to the public, including Duncan's Hall, the oldest in the castle and Shakespeare's setting for the king's murder in *Macbeth*. Together, the rooms present an array of china, paintings, tapestries and furniture spanning 500 years. In the grounds stand a pair of wrought-iron gates made for the Queen Mother on her 80th birthday in 1980.

Dundee ⓾

Tayside. 🏘 *150,000.* ✈ 🚆 🚌
ℹ *Discovery Point (01382) 527527.*
🗓 *Tue, Fri–Sun.*
www.angusanddundee.co.uk

Famous for its fruit cake and marmalade, the city of **Dundee** was also a major ship-building centre in the 18th and 19th centuries, a period which is recreated at the Victoria Docks.

HMS Unicorn, built in 1824, is the oldest British-built warship still afloat and is fitted as it was on its last voyage. Berthed at Riverside is the royal research ship **Discovery**. Built here in 1901 for the first of Captain Scott's voyages to the Antarctic, the *Discovery* was one of the last sailing ships to be made in Britain. Housed in

View of St Andrews over the ruins of the cathedral

a Victorian Gothic building, the **McManus Galleries** provide a glimpse of Dundee's industrial heritage, with exhibitions of archaeology and Victorian art.

Environs
Along the coast, **Arbroath** is famed for its red stonework, ancient Abbey and "Arbroath Smokies" (smoked haddock). Arbroath Abbey displays a copy of *The Declaration of Arbroath*, attesting Scotland's independence.

🏛 **HMS Unicorn**
Victoria Docks, *Tel (01382) 200900.*
☐ *Easter–Oct: 10am–5pm;
Nov–Mar: noon–4pm Wed–Fri (from 10am Sat & Sun).* 🚫 🚹 *limited.*

🏛 **Discovery**
Discovery Point. *Tel (01382)
309 060.* ☐ *daily.* 🚫 🚹 ☐
📷 *by appt.*

🏛 **McManus Galleries**
Albert Institute, Albert Square.
Tel (01382) 432350. ☐ *daily.*

St Andrews ⓫

Fife. 🏘 *14,000.* 🚆 *Leuchars.* 🚌
ℹ *70 Market St (01334) 472021.*
www.standrews.co.uk

Scotland's oldest university town and one-time ecclesiastical capital, **St Andrews** is now a shrine to golfers from all over the world. Its main streets and cobbled alleys, full of crooked housefronts, dignified university buildings and medieval churches, converge on the venerable ruins of the 12th-century **cathedral**. Once the largest cathedral in Scotland, it was later pillaged for its stones, which were used to build the town. **St Andrew's Castle** was built for the town's bishops in the year 1200 and the dungeon can still be seen. St Andrews' golf courses occupy the land to the west of the city, and each is open for a modest fee.

The **British Golf Museum**, which tells how the city's Royal and Ancient Golf Club became the ruling arbiter of the game, will delight golf enthusiasts.

One of the chief pleasures of a visit here is a walk along the sands, immortalized in the film, *Chariots of Fire*.

⛴ **St Andrew's Castle**
The Scores. *Tel (01334) 477196.*
☐ *daily.* 🚫 🚹 📷

🏛 **British Golf Museum**
Bruce Embankment.
Tel (01334) 4600046.
☐ *daily.* 🚫 🚹

THE BIRTHPLACE OF GOLF

Scotland's national game *(see pp202–5)* was pioneered on the sandy links around St Andrews. The earliest record of the game being played dates from 1457, when golf was banned by James II because it was interfering with his subjects' archery practice. Mary, Queen of Scots was berated in 1568 for playing immediately after her husband, Darnley, had been murdered.

Mary, Queen of Scots at St Andrews in 1563

The central courtyard of Falkland Palace, bordered by rose bushes

East Neuk ⓬

Fife. 🚃 *Leuchars*. 🚌 *Glenrothes & Leuchars*. 🛈 *St Andrews (01334) 472021.* www.eastneukwide.co.uk

A string of pretty fishing villages peppers the shoreline of the **East Neuk** (the eastern "corner") of Fife, stretching from Earlsferry to Fife Ness. Much of Scotland's medieval trade with Europe passed through these ports, a connection reflected in the Flemish-inspired crow-stepped gables of many of the cottages. Although the herring industry has declined and the area is now a peaceful holiday centre, the sea still dominates village life. The harbour is the heart of St Monans, a charming town of narrow twisting streets, while Pittenweem is the base for the East Neuk fishing fleet.

The town is also known for **St Fillan's Cave**, the retreat of a 9th-century hermit whose relic was used to bless the army of Robert the Bruce before the Battle of Bannockburn. A church stands among the cobbled lanes and colourful cottages of Crail; legend goes that the stone by the church gate was hurled across to the mainland from the Isle of May by the Devil.

A number of 16th- to 19th-century buildings in the village of Anstruther contain the **Scottish Fisheries Museum**, which tells the area's history with the aid of cottage interiors, boats and displays on whaling. From the village you can also embark for the nature reserve on the **Isle of May**, which teems with seabirds and a colony of grey seals. The statue of Alexander Selkirk in Lower Largo recalls the local boy whose seafaring adventures inspired Daniel Defoe's novel *Robinson Crusoe* (1719). After disagreeing with his captain, he was put ashore on an uninhabited island where he survived for four years.

🏛 Scottish Fisheries Museum
St Ayles, Harbour Head, Anstruther. *Tel (01333) 310628.* ◯ *daily.* 🖼 🗷 🖾 🖾 🖾

THE PALACE KEEPER

Due to the size of the royal household and the necessity for the king to be itinerant, the office of Keeper was created by the medieval kings who required custodians to maintain and replenish the resources of their many palaces while they were away. Now redundant, it was a hereditary title and gave the custodian permanent and often luxurious lodgings.

James VI's bed in the Keeper's Bedroom at Falkland Palace

Falkland Palace ⓭

(NTS) Falkland, Fife. *Tel (0844) 4932 186.* 🚃 🚌 *Ladybank, Kirkcaldy, then bus.* ◯ *Mar–Oct: 10am–5pm daily, 1–5pm Sun.* 🖼 🖾 www.nts.org.uk

This stunning Renaissance palace was designed as a hunting lodge for the Stuart kings. Although its construction was begun by James IV in 1500, most of the work was carried out by his son, James V, in the 1530s. Under the influence of his two French wives, he employed French workmen to redecorate the façade of the East Range with dormers, buttresses and medallions, and to build the beautifully proportioned South Range. The palace fell into ruin during the years of the Commonwealth and was occupied briefly by Rob Roy *(see p117)* in 1715.

After buying the estates in 1887, the third Marquess of Bute became the Palace Keeper and subsequently restored the building. The richly panelled interiors are filled with superb furniture and contemporary portraits of the Stuart monarchs. The royal tennis court, built in 1539 for King James V, is the oldest in Britain.

Dunfermline ⓮

Fife. 🏠 *45,000.* 🚃 🖾 🛈 *1 High St (01383) 720999.*

Scotland's capital until 1603, Dunfermline is dominated by the ruins of the 12th-century abbey and palace, which recall its royal past. The town first came to prominence in the 11th century as the seat of King Malcolm III, who founded a priory on the present site of the **Abbey Church**. With its Norman nave and 19th-century choir, the abbey church contains the tombs of 22 Scottish kings and queens, including that of the renowned Robert the Bruce.

The ruins of the **palace** soar over the beautiful gardens of Pittencrieff Park. Dunfermline's most famous son, the philanthropist Andrew Carnegie (1835–1919), had been forbidden entrance to the park as a boy. After making his fortune, he bought the entire Pittencrieff estate and gave it to the people of Dunfermline. Carnegie emigrated to Pennsylvania in his teens and through iron and steel, became one of the wealthiest men in the world. He donated some $350 million for the benefit of mankind. The town's **Carnegie Birthplace Museum** tells his story.

🏛 **Carnegie Birthplace Museum**
Moodie St. *Tel (01383) 724302.* ◯ Apr–Oct: daily (Sun pm only). 🖼 🔧

The 12th-century Norman nave of Dunfermline Abbey Church

Culross ⑮

Fife. 🏘 450. 🚉 Dunfermline. ◻ Dunfermline. 🚶 National Trust, The Palace (01383) 880359. ◯ Easter–Sep: daily. 🖼 🔧 limited.

An important religious centre in the 6th century, the town of Culross is reputed to have been the birthplace of St Mungo in 514. Now a beautifully

preserved 16th- and 17th-century village, Culross prospered in the 16th century due to the growth of its coal and salt industries, most notably under the genius of Sir George Bruce. Descended from the family of Robert the Bruce, Sir George took charge of the Culross colliery in 1575 and created a drainage system called the "Egyptian Wheel" which cleared a mine 1.5 km (1 mile) long, running underneath the River Forth.

The National Trust for Scotland began restoring the town in 1932 and now provides a guided tour. This starts at the **Visitors' Centre**, housed in the one-time village prison.

Built in 1577, Bruce's **palace** has the crow-stepped gables, decorated windows and red pantiles typical of the period. The interior retains its original early 17th-century painted ceilings, which are among the finest in Scotland. Crossing the square past the **Oldest House**, dating from 1577, head for the **Town House** to the west. Behind it, a cobbled street known as the Back Causeway leads to the turreted **Study**, built in 1610 as a house for the Bishop of Dunblane. The main room is open to visitors and should be seen for its original Norwegian ceiling. Continuing northwards to the ruined abbey, fine church and Abbey House, don't miss the Dutch-gabled **House with the Evil Eyes**.

The 16th-century palace of industrialist George Bruce, at Culross

Antonine Wall ⑯

Falkirk. 🚶 2–4 Glebe St (01324) 620244. 🚉 Falkirk. ◯ Mon–Sat.

The Romans invaded Scotland for a second time around AD 140, in the reign of Emperor Antonius and built a 60 km (37 mile) earth rampart across Central Scotland from the Firth of Clyde to the Firth of Forth. The rampart was further defended by ditches and forts at strategic points. One of the best preserved sections of the fortifications can be seen at Rough Castle, west of Falkirk.

Falkirk Wheel ⑰

Lime Rd, Tamfourhill, Falkirk. *Tel (01324) 619888; booking line: (08700) 500208.* 🚉 Falkirk. ◯ 9:30am–6pm daily. 🖼 for boat trip. 📧 📱 www.thefalkirkwheel.co.uk

This impressive, elegant boat lift is the first ever to revolve and the centrepiece of Scotland's ambitious canal regeneration scheme. Once important for commercial transport, the Union and the Forth and Clyde canals were blocked by numerous roads during the 1960s. Now the Falkirk Wheel gently swings boats between the two waterways creating an uninterrupted link between Glasgow and Edinburgh. This huge, moving sculpture rotates continuously, lifting boats 35m, a height equivalent to 11 traditional locks, in just 15 minutes. Visitors can ride the wheel on one of the boats that leave the visitor centre every half hour.

The rotating Falkirk Wheel boat lift

THE HIGHLANDS AND ISLANDS

Most of the stock images of Scottishness – clans and tartans, whisky and porridge, bagpipes and heather – originate in the Highlands, and enrich the popular picture of Scotland as a whole. But for many centuries the Gaelic-speaking, cattle-raising Highlanders had little in common with their southern neighbours.

Clues to the non-Celtic ancestors of the Highlanders lie scattered across the Highlands and islands in the form of stone circles, brochs and cairns spanning over 5,000 years. By the end of the 6th century, the Gaelic-speaking Celts had arrived from Ireland, as had St Columba, who taught Christianity to the monastic community he established on the island of Iona. The later fusion of Christianity with Viking culture in the 8th and 9th centuries produced the beautiful St Magnus Cathedral in the Orkney Islands.

For over 1,000 years, Celtic Highland society was founded on a clan system, built on family ties to create loyal groups dependent on a feudal chief. However, the clans were systematically broken up by England after 1746, following the defeat of the Jacobite attempt on the British crown led by Bonnie Prince Charlie *(see p153)*. A more romantic vision of the Highlands began to emerge in the early 19th century, largely due to Sir Walter Scott's novels and poetry depicting the majesty and grandeur of a country previously considered merely poverty-stricken and barbaric. Another great popularizer was Queen Victoria, whose passion for Balmoral Castle helped establish the trend for acquiring Highland sporting estates. But behind the senti-mentality lay harsh economic realities that drove generations of Highland farmers to seek a new life overseas.

Today, over half the inhabitants of the Highlands and islands still live in communities of less than 1,000 people. But thriving oil and tourist industries now supplement fishing and whisky, and population figures are rising.

A group of puffins congregating on the rocks, a common sight on Scottish islands

◁ The castle of Eilean Donan, Loch Duich in Glen Shiel

Exploring the Highlands and Islands

To the north and west of Stirling, the historic gateway to the Highlands, lie the magnificent mountains and glens, fretted coastlines and lonely isles that are the epitome of Scottish scenery. Inverness, the Highland capital, makes a good starting point for exploring Loch Ness and the Cairngorms, while Fort William holds the key to Ben Nevis. Inland from Aberdeen lie Royal Deeside and the Spey Valley whisky heartland. The romantic Hebridean Islands are a ferry-ride from Oban, Mallaig or Ullapool.

0 kilometres   25

0 miles   25

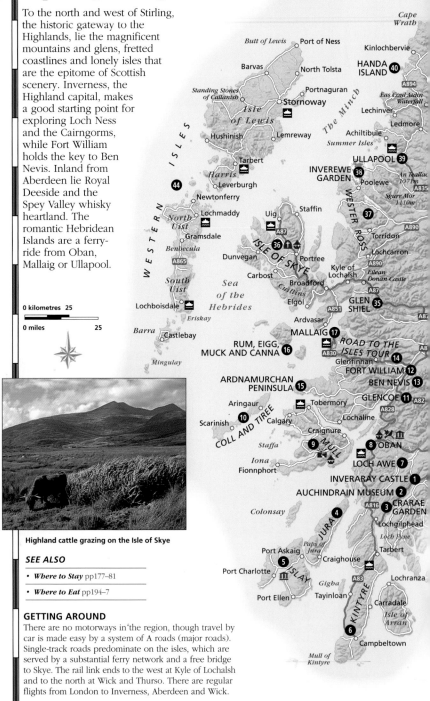

Highland cattle grazing on the Isle of Skye

GETTING AROUND

There are no motorways in the region, though travel by car is made easy by a system of A roads (major roads). Single-track roads predominate on the isles, which are served by a substantial ferry network and a free bridge to Skye. The rail link ends to the west at Kyle of Lochalsh and to the north at Wick and Thurso. There are regular flights from London to Inverness, Aberdeen and Wick.

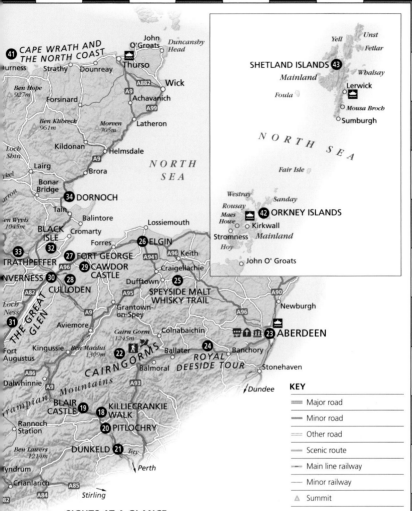

KEY

Major road
Minor road
Other road
Scenic route
Main line railway
Minor railway
△ Summit

SIGHTS AT A GLANCE

Aberdeen pp142–3 23	Fort William 12	Orkney Islands 42
Ardnamurchan Peninsula 15	Glen Shiel 35	Pitlochry 20
Auchindrain Museum 2	Glencoe 11	Rum, Eigg, Muck
Ben Nevis 13	*The Great Glen*	and Canna 16
Black Isle 32	*pp148–9* 31	Shetland Islands 43
Blair Castle 19	Handa Island 40	Speyside Malt Whisky
The Cairngorms pp140–41 22	Inveraray Castle 1	Trail 25
Cape Wrath and	Inverewe Garden 38	Strathpeffer 33
the North Coast 41	Inverness 30	Ullapool 39
Cawdor Castle 29	Islay 5	Wester Ross 37
Coll and Tiree 10	*Isle of Skye pp152–3* 36	Western Isles 44
Crarae Gardens 3	Jura 4	
Culloden 28	Kintyre 6	**Walks and Tours**
Dornoch 34	Loch Awe 7	Killiecrankie Walk 18
Dunkeld 21	Mallaig 17	Road to the Isles Tour 14
Elgin 26	Mull 9	Royal Deeside Tour 24
Fort George 27	Oban 8	

Inveraray Castle ❶

Inveraray, Argyll & Bute. 🚊 *Arrochar, then bus.* **Tel** *(01499) 302203.* ⬤ *Apr–Oct: 10am–5:45pm daily.* ⬤ *Apr, May, Oct: Fri.* 🖼 📷 🚻 &
www.inveraray-castle.com

This multi-turreted mock Gothic palace is the family home of the powerful Clan Campbell, who have been the Dukes of Argyll since 1701. It was built in 1745 by architects Roger Morris and William Adam on ruins of a 15th-century castle. The conical towers were added later, after a fire in 1877.

The pinnacled Gothic exterior of Inveraray Castle

The magnificent interiors, designed by Robert Mylne in the 1770s, form a backdrop to such treasures as Regency furniture, a huge collection of Oriental and European porcelain and portraits by Ramsay, Gainsborough and Raeburn. The Armoury Hall contains early weaponry collected by the Campbells to fight the Jacobite rebels. The Combined Operations Museum commemorates the 250,000 allied troops who trained at Inveraray during World War II.

Auchindrain Museum ❷

Inveraray, Argyll & Bute. **Tel** *(01499) 500235.* 🚌 *Inveraray, then bus.* ⬤ *May–Oct: 10am–5pm daily.* 🖼 & *limited.* **www**.auchindrain museum.org.uk

The first open-air museum in Scotland, Auchindrain illuminates the working lives of the kind of farming community typical of the Highlands until the late 19th century. Constituting a township of some 20 thatched cottages, the site was communally farmed by its tenants until the last one retired in 1962. Visitors can wander through the houses, most of which combine living space,

kitchen and a cattle shed all under one roof. They are furnished with box beds and rush lamps, and edged by herb gardens. Auchindrain is a fascinating memorial to a time before the Highland farmers made the transition from subsistence to commercial farming.

A traditional crofter's plough at the Auchindrain Museum

Crarae Gardens ❸

Crarae, Argyll & Bute. **Tel** *(0844) 493 2210.* 🚌 *Inveraray, then bus.* ⬤ *Apr–Oct: 9:30am–sunset daily.* 🖼 & 📷 *by appointment.* **www**.nts.org.uk

Considered the most beguiling of the many gardens of the West Highlands, the Crarae Gardens *(see also pp22–3)* were created in the 1920s by Lady Grace Campbell. She was the aunt of explorer Reginald Farrer, whose specimens from Tibet were the beginnings of a collection of exotic plants.

The gardens now resemble a Himalayan ravine, nourished by the warmth of the Gulf Stream and the high rainfall of the region. Although unusual Himalayan rhododendrons flourish here, the gardens are also home to exotic plants from Tasmania, New Zealand and the US. Great plant collectors still contribute to the gardens, which thrive in late spring.

Jura ❹

Argyll & Bute. 🚶 *250.* 🚢 *from Kennacraig to Islay, Islay to Jura.* ℹ *Bowmore (01496) 810254.*

Barren, mountainous and overrun by red deer, the Isle of Jura has only one road, which connects the single village of Craighouse to the Islay ferry. Though walking is restricted from August to October during the stalking (deer-hunting) season, Jura offers superb hill-walking, especially on the slopes of the three main peaks known as the Paps of Jura. The tallest of these is Beinn An Oir at 784 m (2,572 ft). Beyond the northern tip of the isle are the notorious whirlpools of Corryvreckan. The author George Orwell, who came to the island to write his final novel, *1984*, nearly lost his life here in 1946 when he fell into the water. A legend tells of Prince Breackan who was

Lagavulin distillery, producer of one of Scotland's finest malts, on Islay

For hotels and restaurants in this region see pp177–81 and pp194–7

Mist crowning the Paps of Jura, seen at sunset across the Sound of Islay

drowned in his attempt to win the hand of a princess. He tried to keep his boat anchored in the whirlpool for three days, held by ropes made of hemp, wool and maidens' hair, until one rope, containing the hair of an unfaithful girl, finally broke.

Islay ❺

Argyll & Bute. 🏠 3,500. 🚢 from Kennacraig. 🚉 Bowmore (08707) 200617. **www**.islayinfo.com

The most southerly of the Western Isles, Islay (pronounced "Eyeluh") is the home of such respected Highland single malt whiskies (*see p32*) as Lagavulin and Laphroaig. Most of the island's distilleries produce heavily peated malts with a distinctive tang of the sea. The Georgian village of Bowmore has the island's oldest distillery and a circular church designed to minimize the Devil's possible lurking-places. The **Museum of Islay Life** in Port Charlotte contains a wealth of fascinating information concerning the island's social and natural history. Eleven kilometres (7 miles) east of Port Ellen stands the Kildalton Cross. A block of local green stone adorned with Old Testament scenes, it is one of the most impressive 8th-century

Celtic crosses in Britain. Worth a visit for its archaeological and historical interest is the medieval stronghold of the Lords of the Isles, **Finlaggan**, which is under excavation. Islay's superb beaches support a variety of bird life, some of which can be seen at the Royal Society for the Protection of Birds (RSPB) reserve at Gruinart.

🏛 Museum of Islay Life
Port Charlotte. **Tel** (01496) 850358. ◻ Easter–Oct: daily (Sun pm). 🎦 🔥

Kintyre ❻

Argyll & Bute. 🏠 8,000. 🚢 Oban. 🚍 Campbeltown. 🚉 Campbeltown (08707) 200609. **www**.visitscottishheartlands.com

A long, narrow peninsula stretching far south of Glasgow, Kintyre has superb views across to the islands of Gigha, Islay and Jura. The 14 km (9 mile) Crinan Canal,

which opened in 1801 and has a total of 15 locks, bustles with pleasure craft in the summer. The town of Tarbert (meaning "isthmus" in Gaelic) takes its name from the neck on which it stands, which is narrow enough to drag a boat across, between the waters of Loch Fyne and West Loch Tarbert. This feat was first achieved by the Viking King Magnus Barfud who, in 1198, was granted by treaty as much land as he could sail around.

Travelling further south past Campbeltown, the B842 road ends at the headland known as the Mull of Kintyre, which was made famous when former Beatle Paul McCartney commercialized a traditional pipe tune of the same name. Westward from Kintyre lies the isle of Rathlin. It is here that Robert the Bruce learned patience in his constant struggles against the English by observing a spider weaving an elaborate web in a cave.

Sailing boats moored at Tarbert harbour, Kintyre

Loch Awe ❼

Argyll. ⬆ 🚂 *Dalmally.* ℹ *Inveraray (01499) 302063.* **www**.loch-awe.com

One of the longest freshwater lochs in Scotland, Loch Awe stretches 40 km (25 miles) across a glen in the south-western Highlands. A short drive east from the town of Lochawe are the remains of **Kilchurn Castle**, abandoned after being struck by lightning in the 18th century. Dwarfing the castle is Ben Cruachan. The huge summit of 1,125 m (3,695 ft) can be reached by the narrow Pass of Brander, where Robert the Bruce fought the Clan MacDougal in 1308. Near the village of Taynuilt, the preserved Lorn Furnace at Bonawe is a reminder of the iron-smelting industry that destroyed much of the area's woodland in the last centuries.

On the A816, to the south of the loch, is **Kilmartin House**. The museum here displays artifacts from local prehistoric sites, as well as reconstructions of boats, utensils and jewellery, providing a vivid glimpse of life in prehistoric Scotland.

🏛 **Kilmartin House**
Kilmartin. *Tel (01546) 510278.* ⬭ *daily.* 📷 ♿ 🖥 www.kilmartin.org

McCaig's Tower looming over the houses and fishing boats of Oban

Oban ❽

Argyll. 👥 *8,500.* ⬆ 🚂 🚌 ⛴
ℹ *Argyll Square (01631) 563122.* **www**.oban.org.uk

Known as the "Gateway to the Isles", this bustling port on the Firth of Lorne commands fine views of the Argyll coast. Shops crowd the seafront around the "little bay" which gives Oban its name, and fresh fish is always for sale on the busy pier. Regular ferries leave for Mull, Coll, Tiree, Barra, South Uist, Islay, Colonsay and Lismore, making Oban one of the most visited

places on the west coast. Built on a steep hill, the town is dominated by the immense **McCaig's Tower**, an eccentric Colosseum-like structure built in the 1800s. Other major landmarks are the pink granite cathedral and the 600-year-old ruined keep, **Dunollie Castle**, once the northern outpost of the Dalriadic Scots. Among Oban's other attractions are working centres for glass and pottery, and Oban Distillery, producers of fine malt whisky.

Early in August yachts converge on the town for West Highland Week, while at the end of the month, Oban's Highland Games take place. Nearby Kilmore, Taynuilt and Tobermory, on Mull, also host summer Highland Games.

Environs
A few miles north of Oban, off the A85, is the 13th-century **Dunstaffnage Castle** where Flora MacDonald was briefly imprisoned for helping Bonnie Prince Charlie escape in 1746. Further north at Barcaldine is the **Scottish Sealife Sanctuary**. This centre combines looking after injured and orphaned seals, with displays of underwater life. The **Rare Breeds Park**, situated 3 km (2 miles) south of Oban, has unusual breeds of farm animals such as Soay and Jacobs sheep. The Isle of Seil is reached via the 18th century "Bridge over the Atlantic". The **Island Folk Museum** on the small island off Easdale describes the history of slate mining in the area. To the south is **Arduaine Garden**, noted for its varieties of spring blooming rhododendrons and azaleas.

⚓ **Dunstaffnage Castle**
Connel. *Tel (01631) 562465.* ⬭ *daily.* ⬤ *Oct–Mar: Thu pm & Fri.* 📷 🖥
🐾 **Scottish Sealife Sanctuary**
Barcaldine, near Connel. *Tel (01631) 720386.* ⬭ *daily.* 📷 ♿
🐾 **Rare Breeds Park**
New Barren. *Tel (01320) 366433.* ⬭ *Easter–Oct: daily.* 📷 ♿
🏛 **Island Folk Museum**
Easdale. *Tel (01852) 300173.* ⬭ *Apr–Oct: daily.*
🌷 **Arduaine Garden**
(NTS) Kilmelford. *Tel (01852) 200366.* ⬭ *daily.* 📷 ♿ 🖥 *by appointment.*

The ruins of Kilchurn Castle on the shore of Loch Awe

For hotels and restaurants in this region see pp177–81 and pp194–7

The picturesque kaleidoscope of houses in Tobermory, one of Mull's most favoured tourist stops

Mull ❾

Argyll. 2,800. from Oban,
Lochaline and Kilchoan; from
Fionnphort, on Mull, to Iona.
Tobermory (08707) 200 625;
Craignure (08707) 200 610.

The largest of the Inner
Hebridean islands, Mull
features rough moorlands, the
rocky peak of Ben More and
a splendid beach at Calgary.
Most roads follow the coastline, affording wonderful sea-
views. From Craignure, the
Mull and West Highland Railway offers a short trip to the
baronial **Torosay Castle**. The
gardens are lined with statues,
and inside is a wealth of 19th-
century paintings and furniture.
On a promontory to the east
lies the 13th-century **Duart
Castle**, home of the chief of
Clan Maclean. You can visit the
Banqueting Hall, State Rooms
and the dungeons that once
held prisoners from a Spanish
Armada galleon, sunk in 1588
by one Donald Maclean. At the
northern end of Mull is the
town of **Tobermory**, with its
brightly coloured buildings
along the seafront. Built as a
fishing village in 1788, it is now
a popular harbour for yachts.

Environs
The small and very beautiful
island of **Iona** is one of the
biggest attractions on Scotland's
west coast. A restored abbey
stands on the site where Irish
missionary St Columba began
his crusade in 563 and made
Iona the home of Christianity
in Europe. In the abbey graveyard, 48 Scottish kings are

said to be buried. During the
summer months the abbey
has a large influx of visitors.
If the weather is fine, make
a trip to **Fingal's Cave** on the
Isle of Staffa *(see p17)*. One of
Scotland's natural wonders,
the cave is surrounded by
"organ pipes" of basalt, the
inspiration for Mendelssohn's
Hebrides Overture. Boat trips
run there from Fionnphort
and Ulva, and to the seven
Treshnish Isles. These
uninhabited isles are a sanctuary for thousands of seabirds,
including puffins, razorbills,
kittiwakes and skuas. Lunga is
the main stop for tour boats.

🏰 **Torosay Castle**
Near Craignure. *Tel* (01680) 812421.
Castle Easter–end-Oct: daily.
Gardens daily. 🔲 🔲 gardens
🏰 **Duart Castle**
Off A849, near Craignure. *Tel* (01680)
812309. May–mid-Oct: daily.
🔲 🔲
🦜 **Fingal's Cave and
Treshnish Isles**
Easter–Oct. *Tel* (01688) 400242.
Timetable varies, call for details.

Coll and Tiree ❿

Argyll. 950. from Oban.
from Glasgow to Tiree only.
Oban (01631) 563122.
www.guide.visitscotland.com

Despite frequent notices of
winter gale warnings, these
islands, the most westerly in the
Inner Hebrides, record more
hours of sunshine than the rest
of Britain. They offer beautiful
beaches and impressive surf.
Tiree's soil is 60 per cent shell
sand, so no trees can grow. As
a result, it is perhaps the wind-
iest place in Scotland. Wild
flowers flourish here in spring.
Breacachadh Castle, the
15th-century home of Clan
Maclean until 1750, overlooks
a bay in south Coll but is not
open to the public. Tiree has
two free museums, the **Sandaig
Thatched House Museum**,
with items from the late
19th and early 20th centuries,
and the **Skerryvore Lighthouse
Museum** in Hynish – the
lighthouse stands 20 km
(12 miles) offshore.

A traditional croft building on the island of Coll

The Three Sisters, Glencoe, rising majestically in the late autumn sunshine

Glencoe ⓫

Lochaber. ⚡ *Fort William.*
📷 *Glencoe.* 🛈 *NTS Visitor Centre,*
Ballachulish (0844) 493 2222.
⭘ *Apr–Oct: 9:30am–5:30pm daily;*
Nov–Mar: 10am–4pm Thu–Sun. 🖼
📷 ♿ www.glencoe-nts.org.uk

Renowned for its awesome
scenery and savage history,
Glencoe was compared by
Dickens to "a burial ground of
a race of giants". The precip-
itous cliffs of Buachaille Etive
Mor and the knife-edged ridge
of Aonach Eagach present a
formidable challenge even to
experienced mountaineers.
Against a backdrop of craggy
peaks and the tumbling River
Coe, the Glen offers superb
hill-walking. Stout footwear,
waterproofs and attention to
safety warnings are essential.
Details of routes, ranging from
an easy walk in the vicinity of
Signal Rock (from which the
signal was given to commence
the massacre) to a stiff 10-km
(6-mile) haul up the Devil's
Staircase can be had from the
Visitor Centre. Guided walks
are offered in summer by the
NTS Ranger Service. East of
Glencoe lies Rannoch Moor,
one of the emptiest areas in
Britain. A dramatic way to
view it is from the chairlift
at the **Glencoe Ski Centre**.

To the southwest, a minor
road leads down beautiful
Glen Etive to the head of
Loch Etive. This impressive
sea loch eventually emerges
on the coast at the Connel
Bridge north of Oban.

At the Ballachulish Bridge a
side road branches to Kinloch-
leven. This village, at the head
of a long attractive loch, combines two contrasting images
of dramatic mountains and
an austere aluminium works.

🎿 Glencoe Ski Centre
Kingshouse, Glencoe. ***Tel*** *(01855)*
851226. ⭘ *daily.* 🖼 ♿ *limited.*

THE MASSACRE OF GLENCOE

In 1692, the chief of the Glencoe MacDonalds was five
days late in registering an oath of submission to William III,
giving the government an excuse to root out a nest of
Jacobite supporters. For ten days 130 soldiers, captained
by Robert Campbell, were hospitably entertained by the
unsuspecting MacDonalds. At dawn on 13 February, in a
terrible breach of trust, the soldiers fell on their hosts, kill-
ing some 38 MacDonalds. Many more died in their wintry
mountain hideouts. The mas-
sacre, unsurprisingly, became
a political scandal, though
there were to be no
official reprimands
for three years.

Detail of *The*
Massacre of Glencoe
by James Hamilton

Fort William ⓬

Lochaber. 👥 *11,000.* ⚡ 📷
🛈 *(01845) 2255121.*
www.visithighlands.com

Fort William, one of the
major towns on the west
coast, is noted not for its looks
but for its location at the foot
of Ben Nevis. The **Jacobite**
Steam Train runs the magical
route from here to Mallaig *(see*
p137), as do ordinary trains.

🚂 Jacobite Steam Train
⚡ *Fort William.* ***Tel*** *(01524) 732100.*
Departs late May–mid-Oct: 10:20am
Mon–Fri; Jul & Aug: Sat & Sun.

For hotels and restaurants in this region see pp177–81 and pp194–7

Ben Nevis ⑬

Lochaber. 🚆 *Fort William.* 🚌 *Glen Nevis.* 🛈 *Glen Nevis Visitor Centre, Glen Nevis (01397) 705922.* ⬜ *9am–5pm daily (to 3pm Nov–Mar).* ♿

With its summit in cloud for about nine days out of ten, and capable of developing blizzard conditions at any time of the year, Britain's highest mountain is a mishmash of metamorphic and volcanic rocks. The sheer northeastern face poses a technical challenge to experienced rock climbers. By contrast, thousands of visitors each year make their way to the peak via a relatively gentle, but long and stony, western path. Motorbikes, even cars, have ascended via this path, and runners pound up and down it during the annual Ben Nevis

Ben Nevis as seen from the northwest

Race. On one of the rare fine days, visitors who make their way to the summit will be rewarded with breathtaking views. On a cloudy day, a walk through the lush landscape of

Glen Nevis may be more rewarding than making an ascent, which will reveal little more at the summit than a ruined observatory and memorials testifying to the tragic deaths of walkers and climbers.

To the north of Ben Nevis, the **Nevis Range Gondola** provides access to a ski centre, restaurant and other tourist facilities, all situated at 650 m (2,130 ft).

🚠 Nevis Range Gondola
Off A82, Torlundy. **Tel** (01397) 705825. ⬜ 10am–5pm daily (weather permitting).

CLIMBING BEN NEVIS

The main path up Ben Nevis, called the Old Bridle Path, starts in Glen Nevis. Numerous visitors each year are lulled into a false sense of security by mild weather conditions in the Glen, occasionally with fatal results. You must wear stout footwear (not trainers) and take hat and gloves and enough layers of clothing to allow for sub-zero temperatures at the top, even on a summer day. Also take plenty of food and drink and an Ordnance Survey map and compass, even if you think you won't need them. It is very easy to lose the path in cloudy or snowy conditions, especially when starting the descent.

TIPS FOR WALKERS

Starting Point ①: Visitor Centre.
Starting Point ②: Achintee.
Starting Point ③: 400 m (440 yds) beyond campsite (very limited parking).
Length: 16 km (10 miles); 6–8 hours average for round trip.
Weather Information: Western Highlands (09068) 500442.
Level: moderate difficulty on a dry day with broken cloud, but prone to rapid weather change; extremely difficult in snow.

To Fort William

Achintee House

To northeast face

Loch Meall

P ①
i
P ②

⌂

Glen Nevis House ③

G L E N   N E V I S

River Nevis

N E V I S
F O R E S T

BEN NEVIS
▲
1,344 m
(4,406 ft)

↓ *To Glen Nevis walk*

KEY

▪▪ Old Bridle Path
═ Minor road
⌂ Camping
※ Viewpoint
P Parking
🛈 Visitor centre

0 metres 1,000
0 yards 1,000

Road to the Isles Tour ⑭

This scenic route goes past vast mountain corridors, breathtaking beaches of white sand and tiny villages to the town of Mallaig, one of the ferry ports for the isles of Skye, Rum, Eigg, Muck and Canna. In addition to stunning scenery, the area is steeped in Jacobite history (see p147).

SKYE ⑦

A830

Arisaig

LOCH MORAR

TIPS FOR DRIVERS

Tour length: 72 km (45 miles).
Stopping-off points: Glenfinnan NTS Visitors' Centre (01397 722 250) explains the Jacobite risings and serves refreshments; the Old Library Lodge in Arisaig serves excellent Scottish food.

A830

⑤

LOCH NAN UAMH

ARDNISH

LOCH AILORT

LOCH EILT

Mallaig ⑦
The Road to the Isles ends at Mallaig, an active little fishing port with a very good harbour and one of the ferry links to Skye (see pp152–3) and the Small Isles.

Morar ⑥
The road continues through Morar, renowned for its white sands, and Loch Morar, rumoured to be the home of a 12-m (40-ft) monster known as Morag.

Prince's Cairn ⑤
The road crosses the Ardnish Peninsula to Loch Nan Uamh, where a cairn marks the spot from which Bonnie Prince Charlie left for France in 1746.

Ardnamurchan Peninsula ⑮

Argyll. 🚢 Corran Ferry on A82 from Glencoe to Fort William, or Fishnish (Mull) to Kilchoan. ℹ️ (08452) 255121.

This peninsula and the adjacent areas of Moidart and Morvern are some of the west coast's best-kept secrets. They are characterized by a sinuous coastline, rocky mountains and beaches. Some of the best beaches are found at the tip of the peninsula, the most westerly point of mainland Britain.
    The **Ardnamurchan Point Visitor Centre** at Kilchoan explores the history of lighthouses and light-keeping. The 1846 lighthouse was designed by Alan Stevenson, uncle of author Robert Louis Stevenson. It is one of many built by the Stevenson family throughout Britain.
    The award-winning **Ardnamurchan Natural History Centre** at Glenmore has encouraged wildlife to

A view from Roshven, near Arisaig, across to the islands of Eigg and Rum

inhabit its "living building", and wild red deer can even graze on its turf roof. An enchanting wooded road runs from Salen to Strontian, or you can go north to Acharacle.

ℹ️ **Ardnamurchan Point Visitor Centre**
Kilchoan. **Tel** (01972) 510210.
🕐 Apr–Oct: daily. 🎟️ ♿

🏛️ **Ardnamurchan Natural History Centre**
Glenmore. **Tel** (01972) 500209. 🕐
Easter–Oct: daily. 🎟️ exhibition only. ♿

Rum, Eigg, Muck and Canna ⑯

Small Isles. 🚶 150. 🚢 from Mallaig or Arisaig. 🚢 Canna only.
ℹ️ (08452) 255121.

Each of the four "Small Isles" has an individual character and atmosphere, but shares a sense of tranquillity. Canna is a narrow island surrounded by cliffs and has a scattering of unworked archaeological sites.

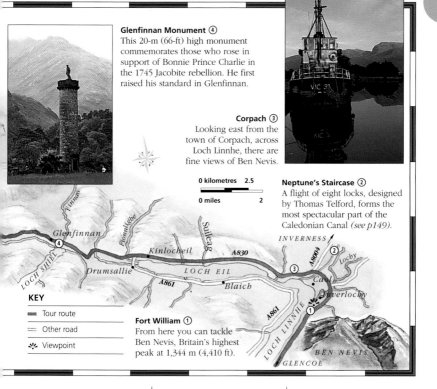

Glenfinnan Monument ④
This 20-m (66-ft) high monument
commemorates those who rose in
support of Bonnie Prince Charlie in
the 1745 Jacobite rebellion. He first
raised his standard in Glenfinnan.

Corpach ③
Looking east from the
town of Corpach, across
Loch Linnhe, there are
fine views of Ben Nevis.

Neptune's Staircase ②
A flight of eight locks, designed
by Thomas Telford, forms the
most spectacular part of the
Caledonian Canal (see p149).

0 kilometres 2.5

0 miles 2

KEY

▬▬ Tour route

═══ Other road

✸ Viewpoint

Fort William ①
From here you can tackle
Ben Nevis, Britain's highest
peak at 1,344 m (4,410 ft).

Once owned by Gaelic scholar
John Lorne Campbell, it now
belongs to the National Trust
for Scotland. It has few inhabitants and little accommodation.

Eigg is the most varied of the
four islands. Dominated by the
distinctive sugarloaf hill, the
Sgurr of Eigg, it has a glorious
beach with "singing sands" that
make odd noises when moved
by feet or by the wind. Here
the islanders sym-
bolize the spirit of
community land
ownership, having
successfully led a
high-profile cam-
paign to buy their
island from their
landlord.

Muck takes its
name from the
Gaelic for "pig",
which it is said to
resemble in shape.
The smallest of
the islands, but no
less charming, it is
owned by a family
who live and farm
on the island. Rum

is the largest and most magnificent island, with scabrous
peaks that bear Norse names
and are home to an unusual
colony of Manx shearwater
birds. The island's rough tracks
make it best suited to the active
visitor. Now owned by Scottish
Natural Heritage and a centre
for red deer research, it
previously belonged to the
wealthy Bullough family.

Colourful fishing boats in Mallaig harbour

They built the lavish **Kinloch
Castle** whose design and furnishings were revolutionary at
the time. Visitors to the castle
can stay at the on-site hostel.

⚓ **Kinloch Castle, Rum**
Tel (01687) 462037. ☐ Apr–Oct: daily;
Nov–Mar: call for details. ▨ ♿ ☑

Mallaig ⑰

Lochaber. ⌂ 980. 🚉 🚌 🚢 from
Ardvasar (Skye). ℹ (08452) 255121.

The heart of Mallaig is its
harbour, which has an active
fishing fleet and ferries that
serve the "small isles" and
Skye. The atmosphere is
rather more commercial than
leisurely, but it is set in an
area of outstanding beauty.
The **Mallaig Heritage Centre**
is a local history museum
covering fishing, railways,
steamers and ferries.

⚒ **Mallaig Heritage Centre**
Tel (01687) 4620851.
☐ 11am–4pm Mon–Sat. ▨
☑ by appointment.

Killiecrankie Walk ⑱

In an area famous for its scenery and historical connections, this circular walk offers views that are typical of the Highlands. The route is fairly flat, though ringed by mountains, and meanders through a wooded gorge, passing the Soldier's Leap and a Victorian viaduct.

There are ideal picnic spots along the way, and the shores of man-made Loch Faskally are lined with beautiful trees. Returning along the River Tummel, the route crosses one of Queen Victoria's favourite Highland areas before it doubles back to complete the circuit.

Killiecrankie ①
A visitor centre provides information on the Battle of Killiecrankie, fought in 1689.

BLAIR ATHOLL

Linn of Tummel ⑦
The path passes a pool beneath the Falls of Tummel and continues through a beautiful forest.

Coronation Bridge ⑥
Spanning the River Tummel, this footbridge was built in 1860 in honour of George IV.

Garry Bridge

Faskally House

Soldier's Leap ②
A soldier named Donald MacBean leapt over the river here to avoid capture by Jacobites during the battle of 1689.

TUMMEL FOREST PARK

Killiecrankie Pass ③
This military road, built by General Wade in the 1600s, follows the gorge.

Memorial Arch ⑤
Workers killed in the construction of the Clunie Dam are commemorated here.

LOCH FASKALLY

PITLOCHRY

KEY

- -	Route
▬	Major road
=	Minor road
=	Narrow lane
⚘	Viewpoint
P	Parking
i	Visitor centre

Clunie Foot Bridge ④
This bridge crosses the artificial Loch Faskally, created by the damming of the River Tummel for hydroelectric power in the 1950s.

0 kilometres | 1
0 miles | 0.5

TIPS FOR WALKERS

Starting point: *NTS Visitor Centre Killiecrankie. Tel (01796) 473233.*
Getting there: *Bus from Pitlochry or Aberfeldy.*
Length: *13 km (8 miles).*
Level: *Very easy.*

The distinctive white turrets and façade of the ducal Blair Castle

One of Scotland's most famous stages, the **Festival Theatre**, is located in Port-na-Craig. It operates a year-round programme with performances changing daily.

Blair Athol Distillery
Perth Rd. **Tel** (01796) 482003.
☐ Easter–Sep: daily (Sun: pm); Oct–Easter: Mon–Fri. 🖼 🚗 🚻 limited.

Festival Theatre
Port-na-Craig. **Tel** (01796) 484626.
☐ mid-May–Oct: daily. 🖼 for plays. 🚻 🚗 🖳

Power Station Visitor Centre
Port-na-Craig. **Tel** (01796) 473152.
☐ Apr–Oct: daily. 🖼 🚗

Blair Castle ⓳

Blair Atholl, Perthshire. **Tel** (01796) 481207. 🚆 Blair Atholl. ☐ 9:30am–5:30pm daily (Nov–Mar: 9:30am–2pm Tue & Sat). 🍴 🖼 🚗 🚻 limited. **www**.blair-castle.co.uk

This rambling, turreted castle has been altered and extended so often in its 700-year history that it now provides a unique insight into the history and changing tastes of aristocratic life in the Highlands.

The elegant 18th-century wing, with its draughty passages hung with antlers, has a display that includes the gloves and pipe of Bonnie Prince Charlie (see p153), who spent two days here gathering support for a Jacobite uprising (see p147). Family portraits span 300 years and include paintings by such masters as Johann Zoffany and Sir Peter Lely. Sir Edwin Landseer's *Death of a Hart in Glen Tilt* (1850) hangs in the ballroom.

Queen Victoria visited the castle in 1844 and conferred on its owners, the Dukes of Atholl, the distinction of being allowed to maintain a private army. The Atholl Highlanders are still in existence today.

Pitlochry ⓴

Perthshire. 🚶 2,500. 🚆 🚌
🛈 22 Atholl Rd (01796) 472215.
www.perthshire.co.uk

Surrounded by the pine-forested hills of the central Highlands, Pitlochry became a famous town after Queen Victoria described it as one of the finest resorts in Europe.

In early summer, wild salmon leap up the ladder built into the Power Station Dam on their way to spawning grounds further up the river. The **Power Station Visitor Centre** outlines the hydro-electric scheme, which harnesses the waters of the River Tummel.

Blair Athol Distillery, the home of Bell's whisky, offers guided tours in the art of whisky making (see pp32–3).

Salmon ladder at the Power Station Dam in Pitlochry

The ruins of Dunkeld Cathedral

Dunkeld ⓴

Tayside. 🚶 2,200. 🚆 Birnam. 🚌
🛈 The Cross (01350) 727688.

Situated by the River Tay, this ancient and charming village was all but destroyed in the Battle of Dunkeld, a Jacobite defeat, in 1689. The **Little Houses** lining Cathedral Street were the first to be re-built, and remain fine examples of an imaginative restoration.

The partly ruined 14th-century **cathedral** enjoys an idyllic setting on shady lawns beside the Tay, against a backdrop of steep and wooded hills. The choir is used as the parish church, and its north wall contains a Leper's Squint (a little hole through which lepers could see the altar during mass). It was while on holiday in the countryside around Dunkeld that the children's author Beatrix Potter found the inspiration for her Peter Rabbit stories.

The Cairngorms ㉒

Wild goat

Rising to a height of 1,309 m (4,296 ft), the Cairngorm mountains form the highest landmass in Britain. Cairn Gorm itself is the site of one of Britain's first ski centres. A weather station at the summit provides regular reports, essential in an area known for sudden changes of weather. Walkers should be sure to follow the mountain code without fail. During the summer a funicular railway climbs Cairn Gorm affording superb views over the Spey Valley. Many estates in the valley have centres which introduce the visitor to Highland land use.

Strathspey Steam Railway
This track between Aviemore and Broomhill dates from 1863.

Aviemore, the commercial centre of the Cairngorms, provides buses to the ski area 13 km (8 miles) away.

Kincraig Highland Wildlife Park
Driving through this park, the visitor can see bison alongside bears, wolves and wild boar. All of these animals were once common in the Highlands.

INVERNESS NAIRN
A 938 Carrbridge
B9153
Boat of Garten
Aviemore
Coylumbr
Beanaidh
A9 B9152 Spey LOCH AN EILEIN
Kincraig
LOCH INSH
Feshie
Kingussie
NEWTONMORE B970
PERTH
Tolvah
BRAERIACH
▲ 1,295 m (4,248 ft)
LOCH EINICH

0 kilometres 5
0 miles 5

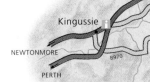

The Cairngorms by Aviemore

Rothiemurchus Estate
Highland cattle can be seen among many other creatures at Rothiemurchus. A visitor centre provides guided walks and illustrates life on a Highland estate.

For hotels and restaurants in this region see pp177–81 and pp194–7

Loch Garten Nature Reserve

Ospreys now thrive in this reserve, which was established in 1959 to protect the first pair seen in Britain for 50 years.

GRANTOWN-ON-SPEY

Broomhill

A 95

B970

Nethy Bridge

The Cairngorm Reindeer Centre provides walks in the hills among Britain's only herd of reindeer.

Nethy

Skiing

During the winter, chairlifts and tows provide access to more than 28 ski runs on Cairn Gorm's northern flanks.

CAIRN GORM
1,245 m
(4,084 ft)

BEN MACDHUI
1,309 m
(4,296 ft)

CAIRNGORM
MOUNTAINS

Ben MacDhui is Britain's second highest peak, after Ben Nevis.

FLORA OF THE CAIRNGORMS

With mixed woodland at their base and the summits forming a sub-polar plateau, the Cairngorms present a huge variety of flora. Ancient Caledonian pines (once common in the area) survive in Abernethy Forest, while arctic flowers flourish in the heights.

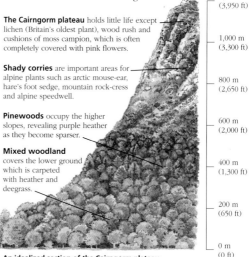

The Cairngorm plateau holds little life except lichen (Britain's oldest plant), wood rush and cushions of moss campion, which is often completely covered with pink flowers.

Shady corries are important areas for alpine plants such as arctic mouse-ear, hare's foot sedge, mountain rock-cress and alpine speedwell.

Pinewoods occupy the higher slopes, revealing purple heather as they become sparser.

Mixed woodland covers the lower ground which is carpeted with heather and deergrass.

1,200 m (3,950 ft)

1,000 m (3,300 ft)

800 m (2,650 ft)

600 m (2,000 ft)

400 m (1,300 ft)

200 m (650 ft)

0 m (0 ft)

An idealized section of the Cairngorm plateau

KEY

	Tourist information
	Major road
	Minor road
	Narrow lane
	Footpath
	Viewpoint

Aberdeen ㉓

Scotland's third-largest city and Europe's offshore oil capital, Aberdeen has prospered since the discovery of oil in the North Sea in the early 1970s. The sea bed has now yielded 50 oilfields. Widely known as the Granite City, its forbidding and rugged outlines are softened by year-round floral displays in the public parks and gardens, the Duthie Park Winter Gardens being the largest indoor gardens in Europe. Aberdeen's busy harbour can be observed from the picturesque village of Footdee at the southern end of the city's 2 mile (3 km) sandy beach.

The spires of Aberdeen, rising behind the city harbour

Exploring Aberdeen

The city centre flanks the 1.5-km- (1-mile-) long Union Street, ending at the Mercat Cross. The cross stands by Castlegate, the one-time site of the city castle, and now only a marketplace. From here, the cobbled Shiprow meanders southwest and passes Provost Ross's House on its way to the harbour. A bus can be taken 1.5 km (1 mile) north of the centre to Old Aberdeen, which, with its medieval streets and wynds (narrow, winding lanes), has the peaceful character of a separate village. Driving is restricted in some streets.

🏫 King's College
College Bounds, Old Aberdeen. **Tel** (01224) 272000. ⬛ daily. ♿
Founded in 1495, King's College was the city's first university. The visitor centre gives background on its long history. The interdenominational chapel, consecutively Catholic and Protestant in the past, has a distinctive lantern tower, rebuilt in 1633. Douglas Strachan's stained-glass windows add a modern touch to the interior, which contains a 1540 pulpit, later carved with heads of Stuart monarchs.

🔒 St Andrew's Cathedral
King St. **Tel** (01224) 640119. ⬛ May–Sep: 11am–4pm Tue–Fri; Oct–Apr: 10:30am–1pm Sat. ♿ 📷 by arrangement.
The Mother Church of the Episcopal Church in the United States, St Andrew's has a memorial to Samuel Seabury, the first Episcopalian bishop in the US, who was consecrated in Aberdeen in 1784. A series of coats of arms contrast colourfully with the white walls and pillars. They represent the American states and the Jacobite families of Aberdeenshire.

The elegant lantern tower of the chapel at King's College

🏛 Art Gallery
Schoolhill. **Tel** (01224) 523700. ⬛ 10am–5pm Tue–Sat, 2–5pm Sun. ♿ ⬛ www.aagm.co.uk
Housed in a Neo-Classical building, the Art Gallery has a wide range of exhibitions, with an emphasis on modern works. A collection of Aberdonian silver is included among the decorative arts on the ground floor. A permanent collection of 18th- to 20th-century art features such names as Toulouse-Lautrec, Raeburn and Reynolds. Local granite merchant Alex Macdonald bequeathed a number of the works on display.

🔒 St Nicholas Kirk
Union St. **Tel** (01224) 643494. ⬛ May–Sep: noon–4pm Mon–Fri, 9:30am–1pm Sun; Oct–Apr: Mon–Fri am only. ♿ www.kirk-of-st-nicholas.org.uk
Founded in the 12th century, St Nicholas is Scotland's largest parish church. Though the present structure dates from 1752, many earlier relics can be seen inside. After damage during the Reformation, the interior was divided into two. A chapel in the East Church holds iron rings used to secure witches in the 17th century, while in the West Church there are embroidered panels attributed to Mary Jameson (1597–1644).

🏛 Maritime Museum
Shiprow. **Tel** (01224) 337700. ⬛ 10am–5pm Tue–Sat, noon–3pm Sun. ♿ ⬛ www.aagm.co.uk
Overlooking the harbour is the Provost Ross's House, dating back to 1593. It now houses the Maritime Museum, which traces the history of Aberdeen's seafaring tradition. The exhibitions cover numerous topics from shipwrecks, rescues and shipbuilding to models that illustrate the workings of the many oil installations situated off the east coast of Scotland.

🔒 St Machar's Cathedral
The Chanonry. **Tel** (01224) 485988. ⬛ Apr–Oct: 9am–5pm daily; Nov–Mar: 10am–4pm daily. ♿ www.stmachar.com
This 15th-century cathedral is the city's oldest granite building. One of its arches dates back to the 14th century. The nave is a parish church and its ceiling is adorned with coats of arms of popes and emperors.

PROVOST SKENE'S HOUSE

Guestrow. *Tel* (01224) 641086. ☐ 10am–5pm Mon–Sat. 🖼 👤 limited.

Once the home of Sir George Skene, a 17th-century provost (mayor) of Aberdeen, the house was built in 1545 and remains one of the oldest houses in the city. Inside, period rooms span 200 years of design. The Duke of Cumberland stayed here during the weeks preceding the Battle of Culloden *(see p146).*

VISITORS' CHECKLIST

Grampian. 🏛 212,000.
✈ 13 km (8 miles) NW Aberdeen.
🚉 🚌 Guild St. 🛈 Union St
(01224) 288828. 🎭 Fri, Sat.

The 18th-century Parlour, with its walnut harpsichord and covered fire-side chairs, was the informal room in which the family would have tea.

The Regency Room typifies early 19th-century elegance. A harp dating from 1820 stands by a Grecian-style sofa and a French writing table.

The Painted Gallery has one of Scotland's most important cycles of religious art. The panels are early 17th century, though the artist is unknown.

The 17th-century Great Hall contains heavy oak dining furniture. Provost Skene's wood-carved coat of arms hangs above the fireplace.

The Georgian Dining Room, with its Classical design, was the main formal room in the 16th century and still has its original flagstone floor.

Entrance

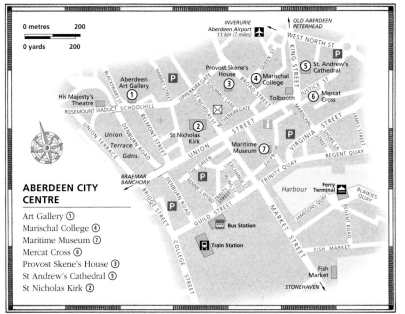

ABERDEEN CITY CENTRE

Art Gallery ①
Marischal College ④
Maritime Museum ⑦
Mercat Cross ⑥
Provost Skene's House ③
St Andrew's Cathedral ⑤
St Nicholas Kirk ②

Royal Deeside Tour

Since Queen Victoria's purchase of the Balmoral Estate in 1852, Deeside has been best known as the summer home of the British Royal Family, though it has been associated with royalty since the time of Robert the Bruce in the 1300s. This route follows the Dee, one of the world's most prolific salmon rivers, through some magnificent Grampian scenery.

Muir of Dinnet Nature Reserve ④
An information centre on the A97 provides an excellent place from which to explore this beautiful mixed woodland area, formed by the retreating glaciers of the last Ice Age.

Balmoral ⑥
Bought by Queen Victoria for 30,000 guineas in 1852, after its owner choked to death on a fishbone, the castle was rebuilt in the Scottish Baronial style at Prince Albert's request.

Ballater ⑤
The old railway town of Ballater has royal warrants on many of its shop fronts. It grew as a 19th-century spa town, its waters reputedly providing a cure for tuberculosis.

Speyside Malt Whisky Trail ㉕

Moray. ℹ *Elgin (01343) 562608.*
www.maltwhiskytrail.com

Such are the climate and geology of the Grampian mountains and glens bordering the River Spey that half of Scotland's whisky distilleries are found on Speyside. They span a large area so a car is required. The signposted "Malt Whisky Trail" takes you to seven distilleries and one cooperage (a place where barrels are made), all with excellent visitor centres and tours of their premises.

There is no secret to whisky distilling *(see pp32–3)*: essentially barley is steeped in water and allowed to grow, a process called "malting"; the grains are then dried with peat smoke, milled, mixed with water and allowed to ferment; the frothy liquid goes through a double process of distillation.

Oak casks, in which the maturing whisky is stored at the distilleries

The final result is a raw, rough whisky that is then stored in old oak sherry casks for 3 to 16 years, during which time it mellows. Worldwide, an average of 30 bottles of Scotch whisky are sold every second.

The visitor centres at each Whisky Trail distillery provide similar, and equally good, guided tours of the workings and audio-visual displays of their individual histories. Their entry charges are usually redeemable against the purchase of a bottle of whisky. A different slant on the process is given at the **Speyside Cooperage**. Here the visitor can learn about the making of the wooden casks that are eventually used to store the whisky.

TIPS FOR DRIVERS

Length: 111 km (69 miles).
Stopping-off points: Crathes
Castle café. ☐ May–Sep: daily;
Station Restaurant, Ballater
serves traditional meals all day.

Banchory ③
Just south of the town is the
18th-century Brig o' Feugh,
where salmon leap.

Drum Castle ①
This 13th-century keep was granted
by Robert the Bruce to his standard
bearer William de Irwyn in 1323,
in gratitude for his services.

PETERHEAD

A96

A93

A980

Peterculter

Dee

Crathes

B9077

STONEHAVEN

A93

A90

Crathes Castle and Gardens ②
This is the family home
of the Burnetts, who were
made Royal Foresters of
Drum by Robert the Bruce.
Along with the title, he
gave Alexander Burnett
the ivory Horn of Leys,
which is still on display.

0 kilometres 5

0 miles 4

KEY
▬ Tour route
▬ Other road
☆ Viewpoint

Benromach Distillery
Forres. **Tel** (01309) 675968.
☐ Oct–Apr: Mon–Fri; May–Sep:
Mon–Sat; Jun–Aug: Sun. ⏰ & ✉

Cardhu Distillery
Knockando. **Tel** (01340) 872555.
☐ Jan–Jun: Mon–Fri; Jul–Sep:
Mon–Sun; Oct–Dec: Mon–Fri. ⏰ &

Dallas Dhu Distillery
Forres. **Tel** (01309) 676548. ☐ Jan–
Mar: Mon–Thu, Sat, Sun; Apr–Sep: daily;
Oct–Mar: Mon–Wed, Sat, Sun. ⏰ &

Glenfiddich Distillery
Dufftown. **Tel** (01340) 820373.
☐ Easter–mid-Oct: daily; mid-
Oct–Easter: Mon–Fri. & ✉

Glen Grant Distillery
Rothes. **Tel** (01340) 832118.
☐ Apr–Oct: daily. ⏰ ✉ & limited.

The Glenlivet Distillery
Glenlivet. **Tel** (01340) 821720.
☐ Easter–Oct: daily.
⏰ ✉ & limited.

Speyside Cooperage
Craigellachie. **Tel** (01340) 871108.
☐ 9am–4pm Mon–Fri.
⏰ ✉ & limited. ☐

Strathisla Distillery
Keith. **Tel** (01542) 783044.
☐ Easter–Oct. ⏰ & limited.

Elgin ㉖

Moray. 🏛 25,000. 🚌 ✈ 🚉 🛈 17
High St (01343) 542666. 🕾 Sat.

With its cobbled marketplace
and crooked lanes, Elgin
retains much of its medieval
layout. The 13th-century
cathedral ruins are all that
remain of one of Scotland's
architectural triumphs. Once
known as the Lantern of the
North, the cathedral was
severely damaged in 1390 by
the Wolf of Badenoch (the son
of Robert II) in revenge for
his excommunication by the
Bishop of Moray. Further
damage came in 1576 when
the Regent Moray ordered the
lead roofing to be stripped.
Among the remains is a Pictish
cross-slab in the nave and a
basin where one of the town's
benefactors, Andrew Anderson,
was kept as a baby by his
homeless mother. The **Elgin
Museum** has anthropological
and geological displays, while

the **Moray Motor Museum** has
over 40 cars and motorbikes,
dating back to 1904.

Elgin Museum
1 High St. **Tel** (01343) 543675.
☐ Apr–Oct: 10am–5pm Mon–Sat,
11am–4pm Sun. ⏰ & ✉

Moray Motor Museum
Bridge St. **Tel** (01343) 544933. ☐
Easter–Oct: 11am–5pm daily. ⏰ &

**Details of the central tower of
the 13th-century Elgin Cathedral**

An aerial picture of Fort George, illustrating its imposing position

Fort George 27

Inverness. **Tel** (01667) 460232. ⛴
🚆 Inverness, Nairn. ⏱ Apr–Sep:
9:30am–5:30pm daily; Oct–Mar:
9:30am–4:30pm daily. 🅿 🛅 ♿ ▢
www.historic-scotland.gov.uk

One of the finest examples of European military architecture, Fort George holds a commanding position on the Moray Firth, ideally located to suppress the Highlands. Completed in 1769, the fort was built after the Jacobite risings to discourage further rebellion, and has remained a military garrison ever since.

The **Regimental Museum** of the Highlanders Regiment is housed in the Fort. Some of the barrack rooms have been reconstructed to show the conditions of the common soldiers stationed here more than 200 years ago. The **Grand Magazine** contains an outstanding collection of arms and military equipment. Fort George's battlements also make an excellent place from which to watch dolphins playing in the waters of the Moray Firth.

Culloden 28

(NTS) Inverness. ⛴ 🚆 Inverness.

The desolate battlefield of Culloden looks much as it did on 16 April 1746, the date of the last battle to be fought on British soil *(see p45)*. Here the Jacobite cause, with the help of Bonnie Prince Charlie's

leadership *(see p153)*, perished under the onslaught of nearly 9,000 troops, led by the Duke of Cumberland. Visitors can roam the battlefield, visit the clan graves and experience the audio-visual displays at the **NTS Visitor Centre**.

Environs
Roughly 1.5 km (1 mile) east of Culloden are the outstanding Neolithic burial sites at **Clava Cairns**.

🄝 **NTS Visitor Centre**
On the B9006 east of Inverness.
Tel (0844) 493 2159. ⏱ daily. 🅿
♿ 🍴 ▢ **www**.nts.org.uk

Cawdor Castle 29

On B9090 (off A96). **Tel** (01667) 404
401. ⛴ Nairn, then bus or taxi.
🚌 from Inverness. ⏱ May–Sep:
10am–5:30pm daily (last entry 5pm).
🍴 🅿 ♿ gardens and ground floor
only. **www**.cawdorcastle.com

With its turreted central tower, moat and drawbridge, Cawdor Castle is one of the most romantic stately homes in the Highlands. Though the castle is famed for being the 11th-century home of Shakespeare's tragic character Macbeth, and the scene of his murder of King Duncan, it is historically unproven that either figure came here.

An ancient holly tree preserved in the vaults is said to be the one under which, in 1372, Thane William's donkey stopped for a rest during its master's search for a place to build a fortress. According to legend, this was how the site for the castle was chosen. Now, after 600 years of

continuous occupation (it is still the home of the Thanes of Cawdor) the house contains a number of rare tapestries and portraits by the 18th-century painters Joshua Reynolds (1723–92) and George Romney (1734–1802). Furniture in the Pink Bedroom and Woodcock Room includes work by the 18th-century designers Chippendale and Sheraton. In the Old Kitchen, the huge Victorian cooking range stands as a shrine to below-stairs drudgery. The castle's grounds provide beautiful nature trails, as well as a nine-hole golf course.

The drawbridge on the eastern side of Cawdor Castle

Inverness 30

Highland. 🏘 60,000. ⛴ 🚌
🄝 Castle Wynd (01463) 234353.
www.visithighlands.com

In the Highlands, all roads lead to the region's "capital", Inverness, the centre of communication, commerce and administration for six million outlying acres and their scattered populations. Despite

A contemporary picture, *The Battle of Culloden* (1746), by D Campbell

For hotels and restaurants in this region see pp177–81 and pp194–7

The red sandstone exterior of Inverness Castle, high above the city centre, in the light of the setting sun

being the largest city in the north, it is more like a town in its atmosphere, with a compact and easily accessible centre. Although sadly defaced by modern architecture, Inverness earns a worthy reputation for its floral displays in summer, and for the River Ness, which flows through the centre and adds considerable charm. The river is frequented by salmon fishermen during the summer, even where it runs through the city centre. Holding the high ground above the river is **Inverness Castle**, a Victorian building of red sandstone, now used as the court house. Just below the castle, next to the tourist information office, is **Inverness Museum and Art Gallery**, which houses permanent and touring exhibitions and runs workshops for children. The main shopping area fans out in three directions from here and includes a lively pedestrian precinct where pipers and other musicians can be found busking.

Just across the river is the **Scottish Kiltmaker Visitor Centre**, part of the Highland House of Fraser Group. Here visitors will get an insight into the history, culture and tradition of the kilt, with audio-visual and workshop presentations of kiltmaking. On the banks of the Ness, stands **Eden Court Theatre**, which

Kilt maker with Royal Stuart tartan

has a varied programme of local and international performers. Following the tree-lined banks of the river further upstream leads to the **Island Walks**, accessed by a pedestrian suspension bridge. Beyond this, further upstream still, is **Inverness Sports Centre and Aquadome**, which offers swimming pools, spas and a variety of wild, spiralling flumes. Thomas Telford's Caledonian Canal *(see pp148–9)*, constructed between 1804 and 1822, is still in constant use and can be viewed at Tomnahurich Bridge. From here, **Jacobite Cruises** runs summer cruises along the length of Loch Ness – an excellent way to spend a sunny afternoon. Inverness is

an ideal base for touring the rest of the Highlands, as it lies within easy reach of most of the region's best-known attractions, including the battle-site of Culloden, 8 km (5 miles) to the east *(see opposite)*.

🏛 **Inverness Museum and Art Gallery**
Castle Wynd. **Tel** (01463) 237114.
◯ 10am–5pm Mon–Sat. ♿
www.inverness.highland.museum.com

🏛 **Scottish Kiltmaker Visitor Centre**
4–9 Huntly St. **Tel** (01463) 222781.
◯ daily (Oct–May: Mon–Sat). 📷

🎭 **Eden Court Theatre**
Bishop's Rd. **Tel** (01463) 234234.
📷 🅿 ♿ www.eden-court.co.uk

🏊 **Inverness Sports Centre and Aquadome**
Bught Park. **Tel** (01463) 667500.
◯ daily. 📷 ♿

⛴ **Jacobite Cruises**
Tomnahurich Bridge, Glenurquhart.
Tel (01463) 233999. 📷 ♿

THE JACOBITE MOVEMENT

The first Jacobites (mainly Catholic Highlanders) were the supporters of James VII of Scotland (James II of England) who was deposed by his Parliament in the "Glorious Revolution" of 1688. With the Protestant William of Orange on the throne, the Jacobites' desire to restore the Stuart monarchy led to the uprisings of 1715 and 1745. The first, in support of James VIII, the "Old Pretender", ended at the Battle of Sheriffmuir (1715). The failure of the second uprising, with the defeat at Culloden, saw the end of Jacobite hopes and led to the demise of the clan system and the suppression of Highland culture for more than a century.

James II, by Samuel Cooper (1609–72)

The Great Glen ❸

Following the path of a geological fault, the Great Glen forms a scenic route from Inverness on the east coast to Fort William on the west. The glacial rift valley was created when the landmass split and moved 400 million years ago. A series of four lochs includes the famous Loch Ness, home of the elusive monster. The Caledonian Canal, built by Thomas Telford, provides a link between the lochs, and has been a shipping channel as well as a popular tourist route since 1822. Hiring a boat or taking a leisurely drive are ideal ways to view the Glen.

Common redpoll

THE GREAT GLEN

Spean Bridge is home to a Woollen Mill selling traditional knitwear and tweeds. Close to the village is the impressive Memorial to all the Commandos who lost their lives in World War II. The surrounding rugged terrain was their training ground.

Loch Lochy
Lochy is one of the four beautiful lochs of the Great Glen, formed by a fissure in the earth and erosion by glaciers. There are caves nearby where Bonnie Prince Charlie is said to have hidden after the Battle of Culloden.

STAR SIGHTS

★ Loch Ness

★ Caledonian Canal

Loch Mullardoch

Kinlochourn

Loch Quoich

Loch Arkaig

Invergarry
South Laggan

Lochailort

Loch Lochy

A830

Spean

Loch Shiel

FORT WILLIAM

Ben Nevis

Corran

A861   A82

Strontian

Ardgour

A861   Onich   Glencoe

A884

Ballachulish

Loch Linnhe

Duror

A828

Port Appin

Steall Waterfall
Located at the foot of the magnificent Ben Nevis, this impressive waterfall tumbles down into a valley of wild flowers. The walk takes 45 minutes and passes through a dramatic gorge. It's the perfect place to picnic.

0 kilometres   10

0 miles   10

Ben Nevis *(see p135)* is Britain's highest mountain at 1,343 m (4,406 ft), but its broad, indefinable shape belies its immense size.

For hotels and restaurants in this region see pp177–81 and pp194–7

Fort Augustus is a pretty village situated at the southwestern end of Loch Ness. The base for boat cruises around the loch, it is also the site of a Benedictine Abbey.

VISITORS' CHECKLIST

Highland. Castle Wynd, Inverness (01463) 234353, (01397) 703781. www.visitscotland.com
The Loch Ness Centre and Exhibition Tel (01456) 450573. ☐ daily. 🄯 ☒ **Urquhart Castle Tel** (01456) 450551. ☐ daily. 🄯

★ Loch Ness

Scotland's most famous loch, the 37 km (23 miles) of Loch Ness provide a beautiful route through the Glen. Urquhart Castle rises imposingly over the water.

Falls of Foyers nestle among the trees above Loch Ness; a winding path yields spectacular views.

KEY

━━	Main route through the Glen
━━	Major road
═══	Minor road
🚶	Good walking area
☀	Viewpoint
ℹ	Tourist information
⛴	Car ferry
🛥	Boating and watersports centre

THE LOCH NESS MONSTER

First sighted by St Columba in the 6th century, "Nessie" has attracted attention since photographs – later revealed to be faked – were taken in the 1930s. Though serious investigation is often undermined by hoaxers, sonar techniques continue to yield enigmatic results: plesiosaurs, giant eels and too much whisky are the most popular explanations. The Loch Ness Centre, at Drumnadrochit, presents the photographic evidence and wide variety of scientific explanations proffered over the years.

★ Caledonian Canal

This splendid canal provides a base from which to view the Glen's beautiful surroundings. From Inverness, the canal travels via Fort Augustus to the eight locks at Neptune's Staircase – a feat of engineering.

The shores of the Black Isle in the Moray Firth

Black Isle 32

Ross & Cromarty. 🏠 *10,600.* 🚉 🔲 Inverness. 🛈 www.visitscotland.com *(01463) 731505.*

Though the drilling platforms in the Cromarty Firth recall how oil has changed the local economy, the broad peninsula of the Black Isle is still largely composed of farmland and fishing villages. The town of **Cromarty** was an important 18th-century port with rope and lace industries. Many of its merchant houses still stand. The award-winning museum in the **Cromarty Courthouse** provides heritage tours of the town. The thatched **Hugh Miller Museum** celebrates the life of theologian and geologist Hugh Miller (1802–56), who was born in Cromarty. **Fortrose** boasts a ruined

14th-century cathedral, while a stone on Chanonry Point commemorates the Brahan Seer, a 17th-century prophet. He was burnt alive in a barrel of tar by the Countess of Seaforth after he foresaw her husband's infidelity. For local archaeology, the **Groam House Museum** in the town of Rosemarkie is worth a visit.

🏛 Cromarty Courthouse
Church St, Cromarty. **Tel** (01381) 600418. ◯ May–Sep: 11am–4pm Sun–Thu; Oct–Apr: by appointment. ⬤ 23 Dec–Feb. 🈶

🏠 Hugh Miller Museum
(NTS) Church St, Cromarty. **Tel** (01381) 600245. ◯ Mar–Sep: 1–5pm daily. 🈶 🛂 limited.

🏛 Groam House Museum
High St, Rosemarkie. **Tel** (01381) 620961. ◯ Easter week: pm only; May–Sep: daily (Sun: pm); Oct–Apr: Sat & Sun (pm). 🈶 🛂 ground floor only.

THE HIGHLAND CLEARANCES

During the heyday of the clan system *(see pp28–9)*, tenants paid their land-holding chieftains rent in the form of military service. However, with the destruction of the clan system after the Battle of Culloden *(see p146)*, landowners began to demand a financial rent, which their tenants were unable to afford, and the land was gradually bought up by Lowland and English farmers. In what became known as "the year of the sheep" (1792), thousands of tenants were evicted, sometimes forcibly, to make way for livestock. Many emigrated to Australia, America and Canada. The ruins of their crofts can still be seen, especially in Sutherland and the Wester Ross.

The Last of the Clan **(1865) by Thomas Faed**

Strathpeffer 33

Ross & Cromarty. 🏠 *1,400.* 🚉 Dingwall. 🚌 Inverness. 🛈 www. visitscotland.com *(01463) 731505.*

Standing 8 km (5 miles) east of the Falls of Rogie, the holiday centre of Strathpeffer still retains the refined charm that made it well-known as a Victorian spa and health resort. The town's huge hotels and gracious layout recall the days when European royalty and lesser mortals flocked to the chalybeate- and sulphur-laden springs, believed to alleviate tuberculosis. It is still possible to sample the water at the unmanned **Water Tasting Pavilion** in the town centre.

🎪 Water Tasting Pavilion
The Square. ◯ Easter–Oct: daily.

Dornoch 34

Sutherland. 🏠 *2,200.* 🚉 Golspie, Tain. 🚌 Inverness, Tain. 🛈 The Square *(01463) 731505.* www.visithighlands.com

With its first-class golf course and extensive sandy beaches, Dornoch is a popular holiday resort, but it has retained a peaceful atmosphere. The medieval cathedral (now the parish church) was all but destroyed in a clan dispute in 1570; it was finally restored in the 1920s for its 700th anniversary. More recently, the pop star Madonna chose the cathedral for the christening of her child.

A stone at the beach end of River Street marks the place where Janet Horne, the last woman to be tried for witchcraft in Scotland, was executed in 1722.

Environs
Nineteen kilometres (12 miles) northeast of the resort is the stately, Victorianized pile of **Dunrobin Castle**, magnificently situated in a great park with formal gardens overlooking the sea. Since the 13th century this has been the seat of the Earls of Sutherland. Many of its rooms are open to visitors.
The peaceful town of **Tain** to the south became an

THE HIGHLANDS AND ISLANDS

administrative centre for the Highland Clearances, when the tolbooth was used as a jail. All is explained in the heritage centre, **Tain Through Time**.

♣ **Dunrobin Castle**
Near Golspie. **Tel** (01408) 633177.
◌ Apr–mid-Oct: daily. 🏛️ 🎦 🖥️

🏛 **Tain Through Time**
Tower St. **Tel** (01862) 894089.
◌ Apr–Oct: 10am–5pm Mon–Sat;
Nov–Mar: by appt. 🏛️ 🖥️

The serene cathedral precinct in the town of Dornoch

Glen Shiel ㉟

Skye & Lochalsh. 🚋 Kyle of Lochalsh.
🚌 Glen Shiel. 🛈 Bayfield House,
Bayfield Road (01478) 612137.

Dominating one of Scotland's most haunting regions, the awesome summits of the Five Sisters of Kintail rear into view at the northern end of Loch Cluanie as the A87 enters Glen Shiel. The **visitor**

centre at Morvich offers ranger-led excursions in the summer. Further west, the road passes the romantic **Eilean Donan Castle**, connected to the land by a causeway. After becoming a Jacobite (see p147) stronghold, it was destroyed in 1719 by English warships. In the 19th century it was restored, and it now contains a number of relics of the Jacobite cause.

♣ **Eilean Donan Castle**
Off A87, near Dornie. **Tel** (01599) 555202. ◌ Apr–Oct: daily. 🏛️ 🖥️

Isle of Skye ㊱

See pp152–3.

Wester Ross ㊲

Ross & Cromarty. 🚋 Achnasheen, Strathcarron. 🚌 Gairloch. 🛈 **www. visitscotland.com**, (01445) 712130.

Leaving Loch Carron to the south, the A890 suddenly enters the northern Highlands and the great wilderness of Wester Ross. The Torridon Estate, sprawling on either side of Glen Torridon, includes some of the oldest mountains on earth (Torridonian rock is over 600 million years old), and is home to red deer, wild cats and wild goats. Peregrine falcons and golden eagles nest in the towering sandstone mass of Beinn Eighe, above the village of Torridon, with its breathtaking views over Applecross towards Skye. The **Torridon**

Typical Torridonian mountain scenery in the Wester Ross

Countryside Centre offers guided walks in season, and essential information on the natural history of the region.
Further north, the A832 cuts through the **Beinn Eighe National Nature Reserve**, Britain's oldest wildlife sanctuary. Remnants of the ancient Caledonian pine forest still stand on the banks and isles of Loch Maree, providing shelter for pine martens and wildcats. Buzzards and golden eagles nest on the alpine slopes. **Beinn Eighe Visitor Centre** has information on the reserve.
Along the coast, a series of exotic gardens thrive in the warming influence of the Gulf Stream. The most impressive is Inverewe Gardens (see p156).

🏛 **Torridon Countryside Centre**
(NTS) Torridon. **Tel** (01445) 791221.
◌ Easter–Sep: daily. 🏛️ 🎦 🖥️

🛝 **Beinn Eighe Visitor Centre**
Near Kinlochewe, on A832. **Tel** (01445) 760258. ◌ Easter–Oct: daily. 🖥️

The western side of the Five Sisters of Kintail, seen from a viewpoint above Ratagan

Isle of Skye ③⑥

Otter by the coast at Kylerhea

The largest of the Inner Hebrides, Skye can be reached by the bridge linking Kyle of Lochalsh and Kyleakin. A turbulent geological history has given the island some of Britain's most varied and dramatic scenery. From the rugged volcanic plateau of northern Skye to the ice-sculpted peaks of the Cuillins, the island is divided by numerous sea lochs, leaving the traveller never more than 8 km (5 miles) from the sea. Limestone grasslands predominate in the south, where the hillsides, home of sheep and cattle, are scattered with the ruins of crofts abandoned during the Clearances *(see p150)*. Historically, Skye is best known for its association with Bonnie Prince Charlie.

Skeabost has the ruins of a chapel which is associated with St Columba. Medieval tombstones can be found in the graveyard.

Grave of Flora MacDonald

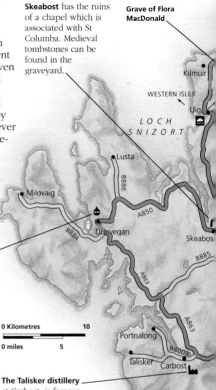

0 Kilometres	10
0 miles	5

Dunvegan Castle

For over seven centuries, Dunvegan Castle has been the seat of the chiefs of the Clan MacLeod. It contains the Fairy Flag, a piece of magical silk treasured for its protective powers.

The Talisker distillery at Carbost, is famous for its Highland malts, often described as "the lava of the Cuillins".

Cuillins

Britain's finest mountain range is within walking distance of Sligachan, and in summer a boat sails from Elgol to the desolate inner sanctuary of Loch Coruisk. As he fled across the surrounding moorland, Bonnie Prince Charlie is said to have claimed: "even the Devil shall not follow me here!"

KEY

ℹ	Tourist information
▬	Major road
▭	Minor road
━	Narrow lane
☼	Viewpoint

Quiraing

A series of landslides has exposed the roots of this volcanic plateau, revealing a fantastic terrain of spikes and towers. They are easily explored off the Uig to Staffin road.

VISITORS' CHECKLIST

The Highlands. 🚶 11,500. ✈ Kyle of Lochalsh. 🚌 Portree. ⛴ from Mallaig or Glenelg. 🛈 Bayfield House, Portree (01478) 612137. **Dunvegan Castle**, Dunvegan. **Tel** (01470) 521206. ⬜ Apr–mid-Oct: daily. 🎫 ♿ limited. **Armadale Castle**, Armadale. **Tel** (01471) 844227. ⬜ Apr–Oct: daily (gardens open all year). 🎫 ♿ **Talisker Distillery**, Carbost. **Tel** (01478) 614308. ⬜ daily. 🎫 ♿ limited. 🎫

Kilt Rock

The Storr

The erosion of this basalt plateau has created the Old Man of Storr, a monolith rising to 49 m (160 ft) by the Portree road.

Loch Coruisk

Luib has a beautiful thatched cottage, preserved as it was 100 years ago.

Portree

With its colourful harbour, Portree (meaning "port of the king") is Skye's metropolis. It received its name after a visit by James V in 1540.

Bridge to mainland

KYLE OF LOCHALSH

Otters can be seen from the haven in Kylerhea.

Armadale Castle Gardens and Museum of the Isles houses the Clan Donald visitor centre.

Kilchrist Church

This ruined pre-Reformation church's last service was held in 1843. It once served Skye's most populated areas, though the surrounding moors are now deserted.

BONNIE PRINCE CHARLIE

The last of the Stuart claimants to the Crown, Charles Edward Stuart (1720–88), came to Scotland from France in 1745 to win the throne. After marching as far as Derby, his army was driven back to Culloden where it was defeated. Hounded for five months through the Highlands, he escaped to Skye, disguised as the maidservant of a woman called Flora MacDonald, from Uist. From the mainland, he sailed to France in September 1746, and died in Rome. Flora was buried in 1790 at Kilmuir, on Skye, wrapped in a sheet taken from the bed of the "bonnie" (handsome) prince.

The prince, disguised as a maidservant

Inverewe Garden 38

On A832, near Poolewe, Ross-shire.
Tel (01445) 781200. ☐ daily. 🖼 🖒
🖒 🛈 www.nts.org.uk

Inverewe Garden attracts over
130,000 visitors a year and is
considered a national treasure.
The gardens contain an extraordinary variety of trees, shrubs
and flowers from around the
world, despite being at a latitude of 57.8° north.

Inverewe was started in 1862
by the 20-year-old Osgood
Mackenzie after being given
an estate of 4,860 ha (12,000
acres) of exposed, barren
land next to his family's holding. At that time there was
just one dwarf willow growing
there. Mackenzie began by
planting shelter trees and then
went on to create a walled
garden using imported soil.
He found that the west coast's
climate, warmed by the North
Atlantic Drift from the Gulf
Stream (see p23), encouraged
the growth of exotic species.

By 1922, the garden had
achieved international recognition as one of the great plant
collections. In 1952 it was donated to the National Trust for
Scotland. At Inverewe today
you can find Blue Nile lilies,
the tallest Australian gum trees

**Some of the many unusual plants
cultivated at Inverewe Garden**

growing in Britain and
fragrant rhododendrons from
China. Planting is designed to
provide colour all year, but
the gardens are at their best
between spring and autumn.

Ullapool 39

Highland. 🏘 1,800. 🚌 Inverness.
🚏 🚢 🛈 Argyle St (08452)
255121. **www**.ullapool.com

With its wide streets, white-
washed houses, palm trees
and street signs in Gaelic,
Ullapool is one of the prettiest
villages on the west coast.
Planned and built as a fishing
station in 1788, it occupies
a peninsula jutting into Loch

Broom. Fishing is no longer
important, except when East
European "klondyker" factory
ships moor in the loch in the
winter. The major activity is
now the ferry to Stornoway
on Lewis (see table, p229).
The **Ullapool Museum** offers
an insight into local history.

🏛 **Ullapool Museum**
7–8 West Argyle St. **Tel** (01854) 612
987. ☐ Apr–Sep daily. 🖼 🖒 🖒

Environs
The natural wonders of this
area include the rugged Assynt
Mountains to the north, and, to
the south, the deep and precipi-
tous Corrieshalloch Gorge.

At **Achiltibuie**, it is worth
visiting the **Hydroponicum**, a
"Garden of the Future", where
flowers grow without soil. The
town also has a **Smokehouse**
where the process of curing
salmon can be viewed. Tour
boats run from here, and from
Ullapool, to the **Summer Isles**
– a small, sparsely populated
group, once the home of
noted environmentalist, Fraser
Darling. Achiltibuie is worth a
visit for the scenic drive alone.

🌸 **Hydroponicum**
Achiltibuie. **Tel** (01854) 622202.
☐ Mar–Sep: daily. 🖼 🖒 limited.
⛰ **Smokehouse**
Achiltibuie. **Tel** (01854) 622353.
☐ Easter–end Sep: Mon–Sat.

A tranquil, late-evening view of Ullapool and Loch Broom on the northwestern coast of Scotland

For hotels and restaurants in this region see pp177–81 and pp194–7

Majestic cliffs on Handa Island, a welcome refuge for seabirds

Handa Island ⑩

Highland. 🚢 *from Tarbet, near Scourie, Apr–Aug.* 🛈 *Scottish Wildlife Trust, Edinburgh (0131) 312 7765.*

Located just offshore from Scourie on the west coast, this small island is an important breeding sanctuary for many species of seabirds.

In past centuries it was inhabited by a hardy people, who had their own queen and parliament. The last 60 inhabitants were evacuated in 1847 when their potato crop failed. The island was also used as a burial ground as it was safe from the wolves that inhabited the mainland.

The island is now managed by the Scottish Wildlife Trust. A walk takes visitors to the 100-m (328-ft) high northern cliffs. On the way you are liable to experience the intimidating antics of great and Arctic skuas (large migratory birds) swooping low over your head. Early in the year 11,000 pairs of razorbills can be found on Handa, and 66,000 pairs of guillemots.

Environs
The highest waterfall in Britain is **Eas Coul Aulin**, at 180 m (590 ft). It is best Seen after rainfall, from a tour boat based at Kylesku, 24 km (15 miles) to the south of Handa.

Cape Wrath and the North Coast ㊶

Highland. 🚗 📧 *May–Sep (01971) 511376.* 🛈 *John O'Groats (01955) 611373.*

The northern edge of mainland Scotland spans the full variety of Highland geography, from mountainous moorlands and dazzlingly white beaches to flat, green farmland.

Cape Wrath is alluring not only for its name but for its cliffs, constantly pounded by the Atlantic. There are many stacks rising out of the sea that swarm with seabirds. The lighthouse was among the last in Scotland to be automated in 1998. In summer, a minibus serves the 13-km (8-mile) road leading to Cape Wrath. In order to reach the bus, you must take the connecting **Cape Wrath Ferry** from the pier by the Cape Wrath Hotel, as the cape is cut off by the Kyle of Durness. At Durness is **Smoo Cave**, an awesome cavern hollowed out of limestone. **Smoo Innercave Tours** run trips there. Just outside Durness, a community of artists has established the **Balnakeil Craft Village**, displaying pottery, enamelwork, wood carving, printmaking and paintings.

A nesting kittiwake

Astonishingly white beaches follow one after the other along the coast, and the road then loops round Loch Eriboll – the deepest of the sea lochs and a base for Atlantic and Russian convoys during World War II.

The **Strathnaver Museum** in Bettyhill explains the notorious Sutherland "Clearances", the forced evictions of 15,000 people to make way for sheep. At Rossal, 16 km (10 miles) south of Bettyhill, is an archaeological walk around an excavated village, which provides important information on life in pre-Clearance days.

A gigantic white dome at **Dounreay** marks the nuclear reprocessing plant, where you can tour the works and visit the free exhibition centre in summer. The main town on the coast here is Thurso, a village of solid stone buildings. Once famous for its locally quarried stone slabs, Thurso's industry died with the advent of cement. Each September, Thurso hosts "Northlands", the Scottish Nordic Music Festival. **John O'Groats** is probably the most famous name on the map here, said to be the very northerly tip of the mainland, although this is in fact nearby **Dunnet Head**. Apart from a quaint harbour where day trips leave for Orkney, John O'Groats is a tourist trap. More rewarding are the cliffs at **Duncansby Head**, where you can enjoy the natural ferocity of the Pentland Firth.

🚢 **Smoo Innercave Tours**
38 Sango Mor, Durness. **Tel** *(01971) 511704.* ⬜ *Apr–Sep: daily.* 🖂

🏛 **Strathnaver Museum**
Clachan, Bettyhill. **Tel** *(01641) 521418.* ⬜ *Apr–Oct: Mon–Sat.* 🖂 ♿ *limited.*

Duncansby Head, Caithness, at the far northeast corner of Scotland

Orkney Islands ⑫

Beyond the Pentland Firth, less than 10 km (6 miles) off the Scottish mainland, the Orkney archipelago consists of some 70 islands and rocky skerries boasting the densest concentration of archaeological sites in Britain. Today, only about 16 of these islands are permanently inhabited. Orkney's way of life is predominantly agricultural – it's said that, whereas the Shetlanders are fishermen with crofts, the Orcadians are farmers with boats. The climate is tempered by the Gulf Stream, and the rich soils overlying old red sandstone produce lush green turf and summer crops of grain.

The delightfully frescoed Italian Chapel, in East Mainland

Kirkwall

The winding flagstoned streets of Orkney's capital are lined with period houses and craft shops. Opposite **St Magnus Cathedral**, an 870-year-old masterpiece of red and yellow stone, lie the ruins of the **Bishop's Palace**, dating mostly from the 16th century. Also nearby, in a former manse called Tankerness House, the excellent **Orkney Museum** illustrates the history of habitation on the islands. South of the town centre, the **Highland Park Distillery** dispenses a fine dram at the end of its guided tours.

Orcadian man on a bicycle

♠ St Magnus Cathedral
Tel (01856) 874894. ◯ Mon–Fri (daily in summer). 🖼

♛ Bishop's Palace
Tel (01856) 871918. ◯ Apr–Sep.

♛ Orkney Museum
Tel (01856) 873535. ◯ Mon–Sat (daily Apr–Oct).

🏭 Highland Park Distillery
Tel (01856) 874619. ◯ Mon–Fri (pm only Nov–Mar; daily May–Aug). 🖼 (includes tasting). 🖼 ♿

West Mainland

Many of the waterfront buildings in **Stromness**, the main town on Orkney's largest island, date from the 18th and 19th centuries. Among them, the **Pier Arts Centre** contains a fine collection of 20th-century works. The **Stromness Museum** traces Orkney's history as a trading port. West Mainland is renowned for its prehistoric sites. Said to date from around 2750 BC, **Maes Howe** is a chambered tomb aligned with the winter solstice. Vikings plundered it around 1150, leaving a fascinating legacy of runic graffiti on the walls. Nearby are the huge **Standing Stones of Stenness** and the **Ring of Brodgar**, a megalithic henge of 36 stones. The Neolithic village of **Skara Brae** was discovered when a storm stripped dunes from the site in 1850. Beneath the sands lay wonderfully preserved evidence of everyday life in the Stone Age, such as beds, fireplaces and shelves.

The cliffs of **Marwick Head**, overlooking Birsay Bay, are one of several RSPB reserves on West Mainland, home to thousands of nesting seabirds in early summer. A memorial commemorates Lord Kitchener

and the crew of HMS *Hampshire*, sunk off this headland by a German mine in 1916.

🏛 Pier Arts Centre
Tel (01856) 850209. ◯ 10:30am–5pm.

🏛 Stromness Museum
Tel (01856) 850025. ◯ Mon–Sat (daily May–Sep). 🖼 ♿

♠ Maes Howe
Tel (01856) 841815. ◯ daily. 🖼 ♿

♠ Standing Stones of Stennes and Ring of Brodgar
◯ daily. ♿

♠ Skara Brae
Tel (01856) 841001. ◯ daily. 🖼 ♿

East Mainland

East of Kirkwall, the road runs through quiet agricultural land over a series of causeways linking the southernmost islands to the mainland. The **Churchill Barriers** were built by Italian prisoners of war during the 1940s to protect the British fleet stationed in Scapa Flow. In their spare time, these POWs also constructed the remarkable **Italian Chapel**, whose beautiful frescoed interior is well worth seeing.

On South Ronaldsay, the 5,000-year-old **Tomb of the Eagles** was excavated by a local farmer. Some 340 burial sites were unearthed at this clifftop location, along with stone tools and the talons of many sea eagles.

♠ Italian Chapel
Tel (01856) 872856. ◯ daily (Mass: 1st Sun of mth). ♿

♠ Tomb of the Eagles
Tel (01856) 831339. ◯ Apr–Oct. 🖼 ♿ ▯ ▮

The rich-coloured exterior of St Magnus Cathedral

For hotels and restaurants in this region see pp177–81 and pp194–7

Hoy

Orkney's second-largest island takes its name from the Norse word for "high island", which refers to its spectacular cliff-lined terrain. Hoy is very different from the rest of the archipelago, and its northern hills make excellent walking and birdwatching country. The **Old Man of Hoy**, a 137-m (450-ft) vertical stack off the western coast, is the island's best-known landmark, a popular challenge to keen rock-climbers. Near Rackwick, the

The Old Man of Hoy, a majestic stone column off the coast of Hoy

5,000-year-old **Dwarfie Stane** is a unique chambered cairn cut from a single block of stone.

At Lyness, on the eastern side of Hoy, the **Scapa Flow Visitor Centre** contains a fascinating exhibition on this huge deep-water naval haven. It recounts the events of 16 June 1919, when the captured German fleet was scuttled on the orders of its commanding officer to prevent handover: 74 ships were sunk. Many of these have since been salvaged; others provide one of the world's great wreck-diving sites. Tours from Houton Pier, using a remote-controlled vehicle fitted with an underwater camera, give a glimpse of this eerie sub-aquatic graveyard.

🛈 Scapa Flow Visitor Centre
Tel (01856) 791300. ☐ summer: daily; winter: Mon–Fri. ♿
www.scapaflow.co.uk

The Northern Isles

Orkney's outlying islands are sparsely populated and mostly the preserve of seals and sea-birds. They include **Rousay**, known as the "Egypt of the

North" for its many archaeo-logical sites, and **Egilsay**, the scene of St Magnus's grisly murder in 1115. The 12th-century round-towered church dedicated to his memory is a rare example of Irish-Viking design. **Sanday** is the largest of the northern isles, its fertile farmland fringed by sandy beaches. **North Ronaldsay**, the northernmost of the Orkney Islands, is noted for its hardy, seaweed-eating sheep and rare migrant birds.

Day Trips to Remote Islands

There are flights from Kirkwall to a dozen outlying islands several times a week, as well as daily ferries. The two-minute hop between **Westray** and **Papa Westray** is the world's shortest scheduled air route. Inter-island transport is weather-dependent.

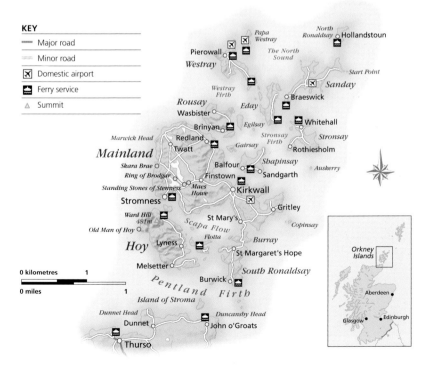

KEY

▬	Major road
═	Minor road
✕	Domestic airport
⛴	Ferry service
△	Summit

Shetland Islands

Shetland Pony

More than 100 rugged, cliff-hemmed islands form Scotland's most northerly domain. Nowhere in Shetland is further than 5 km (3 miles) from the sea. Fishing and salmon-farming are mainstays of the economy, boosted in recent decades by revenue from the North Sea oil industry. In winter the islands suffer severe gales and storms, but in high summer, the sun may shine for as long as 19 hours, and a twilight known as the "simmer dim" persists throughout the night.

The 17th-century Scalloway Castle, Central Mainland

Lerwick

Shetland's chief town is a pretty place of grey stone buildings and narrow, flag-stoned lanes. First established by Dutch fishermen in the 1600s, it grew to become wealthy from the whaling trade. The increase in North Sea oil traffic has made the harbour area very busy.

At the heart of the town is Commercial Street, its northern end guarded by **Fort Charlotte**, which affords fine views from its battlements. At the **Shetland Museum and Archive**, on Hay's Dock, you can admire a fine collection of historic boats, archaeological finds and Shetland textiles tracing the islands' history.

On Lerwick's outskirts lie the **Clickminin Broch**, a prehistoric fort dating from around 700 BC, and the 18th-century **Böd of Gremista**, birthplace of Arthur Anderson, co-founder of the P&O shipping company. The building now houses a maritime museum.

The fortified tower of Mousa Broch

🏛 Shetland Museum and Archive
Tel (01595) 695057. ⬜ *daily.* ♿ ▣

🏛 Böd of Gremista
Tel (01595) 696729. ⬜ *May–Sep: Wed–Sun.* ♿

Central Mainland

Sheltering Lerwick from the winter gales is **Bressay**, an island with fine walks and views.

Boats run from Lerwick to tiny **Noss**, off Bressay's east coast. This nature reserve is home to thousands of breeding seabirds, including gannets and great skuas (bonxies).

West of Lerwick is the quiet fishing port of **Scalloway**, Shetland's second town and the islands' former capital. **Scalloway Castle** is a fortified tower dating from 1600, while the **Scalloway Museum** contains an exhibition on the "Shetland Bus", a wartime resistance operation that used fishing boats to bring refugees from German-occupied Norway. North of Scalloway, near Weisdale, the fertile region

of **Tingwall** is a well-known angling centre. Connected by bridges to Central Mainland's west coast are the islands of **Burra** and **Trondra**, with lovely beaches and good walks.

🏛 Scalloway Museum
Tel (01595) 880783. ⬜ *May–Sep: Tue–Thu, Sat.*

🦌 Noss National Nature Reserve
Tel (01595) 693345. ⬜ *May–Aug: Tue, Wed, Fri–Sun.* ▣

South Mainland

This area offers two important archaeological sights. The ornate **Mousa Broch**, on an easterly islet reached by a summer ferry, is the best example of this type of ancient fortified tower in Britain. The dry-stone walls make ideal nestboxes for a colony of storm petrels. **Jarlshof**, in the far south, spans over 3,000 years of occupation from Neolithic to Viking times.

The impressive cliffs and lighthouse (an RSPB centre) at **Sumburgh Head** are also worth visiting. The island of **St Ninian's** is linked to South Mainland by a causeway of dazzling silver sand.

🏛 Mousa Broch
Tel (01950) 431367. ⬜ *Apr–Sep.* ▣ *included in boat fare.*

🏛 Jarlshof Prehistoric and Norse Settlement
Tel (01950) 460112. ⬜ *Mar–Sep: daily.* ▣ ♿ *limited.* ▣ *by request.*

🦌 Sumburgh Head Lighthouse (RSPB)
Tel (01950) 460800. ⬜ *daily.*

Early evening lights over Lerwick Harbour

For hotels and restaurants in this region see pp177–81 and pp194–7

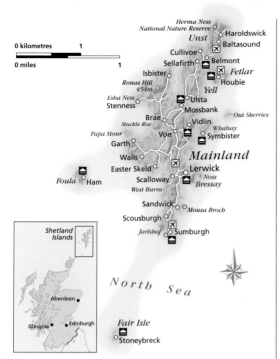

0 kilometres   1

0 miles   1

Herma Ness National Nature Reserve
Unst
Haroldswick
Baltasound
Cullivoe
Sellafirth
Belmont
Isbister
Fetlar
Houbie
Ronas Hill 454m
Yell
Esba Ness
Stenness
Ulsta
Mossbank   *Out Skerries*
Brae
Vidlin
Muckle Roe
Whalsay
Papa Stour
Voe
Symbister
Garth
Walls   **Mainland**
Easter Skeld
Lerwick
Scalloway   *Noss*
West Burra   *Bressay*
Sandwick
Scousburgh   *Mousa Broch*
Jarlsbof   Sumburgh

Shetland Islands

North Sea

Aberdeen

Glasgow   Edinburgh

Fair Isle
Stoneybreck

VISITORS' CHECKLIST

Shetland. 22,000.
from Aberdeen and Stromness
on mainland Orkney. Lerwick
(01595) 693434. Up Helly Aa
(Jan). www.visitshetland.org

Fetlar there's a chance of
glimpsing rare migrant birds,
like the red-necked phalarope
or the snowy owl. Unst has
the most varied scenery and
the richest flora and fauna,
plus an excellent visitor
centre at the **Herma Ness
National Nature Reserve**.
Beyond the lighthouse of
Muckle Flugga is **Out Stack**,
Britain's most northerly point.

West of Mainland, **Foula** has
dramatic sea cliffs, while **Fair
Isle**, midway between Orkney
and Shetland, is owned by the
National Trust for Scotland.

Herma Ness National Nature Reserve
Tel (01957) 711278.
daily (visitors' centre: Apr–Sep).

Day Trips to Remote Islands
There are regular, inexpensive
internal flights in Shetland
to Fair Isle, Foula and Papa
Stour, as well as lots of inter-
island ferries. Most routes
depart from Tingwall, on
the Central Mainland.

**An inquisitive otter, one of a large
population on the island of Yell**

KEY

== Minor road

Domestic airport

Ferry service

Summit

North Mainland
North of Lerwick, Shetland
rises to its highest point at
Ronas Hill (454 m/1,475 ft)
amid tracts of bleak, empty
moorland. The sheltered
sea loch of **Sullom Voe** is
dominated by the jetties and
support buildings of Europe's
biggest oil and gas terminal.
The west coast has spectacular natural scenery, notably
the red granite cliffs and
blow-holes at **Esha Ness**,
from where you can see the
wave-gnawed stacks of **The
Drongs** and a huge rock arch
called **Dore Holm**. Offshore,
the island of **Papa Stour** has
further startling formations
of volcanic rock.

Outlying Islands
The northern isles of **Yell**,
Fetlar and **Unst** have regular,
though weather-dependent,
boat connections to the
Mainland. Yell has a large
otter population, and on

**The red granite cliffs of Esha Ness,
North Mainland**

BIRDS ON ORKNEY AND SHETLAND
Millions of migrant and local birds
can be admired on these islands.
Over 20 species of seabirds regularly
breed here, and over 340 different
species have been recorded passing
through Fair Isle, one of the world's great
staging posts. Inaccessible cliffs provide
security at vulnerable nesting times for
huge colonies of gannets, guillemots, puffins, kittiwakes,
fulmars and razorbills. Species found in few other UK
locations include great skuas and storm petrels.

Puffin

Western Isles

Western Scotland ends with this remote chain of islands, made of some of the oldest rock on earth. Barren landscapes are divided by countless waterways, while the western, windward coasts are edged by white sandy beaches. For centuries, the eastern shores, composed largely of peat bogs, have provided islanders with fuel. Man has been here for 6,000 years, living off the sea and the thin turf, though abandoned monuments, including a Norwegian whaling station on Harris, attest to the difficulties faced in commercializing traditional local skills. Gaelic, part of an enduring culture, is widely spoken, and most signs are in both English and Gaelic.

The interior of a croft house at the Black House Museum

The monumental Standing Stones of Callanish in northern Lewis

Lewis and Harris

Forming the largest landmass of the Western Isles, Lewis and Harris are a single island, though Gaelic dialects differ between the two areas. From the administrative centre of **Stornoway**, with its bustling harbour and colourful house fronts, the ancient **Standing Stones of Callanish** are only 26 km (16 miles) to the west. Just off the road on the way to Callanish are the ruins of **Carloway Broch**, a Pictish *(see p41)* tower over 2,000 years old. The more recent past can be explored at Arnol's **Black House Museum** – a showcase of crofting life as it was until 50 years ago.

South of the rolling peat moors of Lewis, a range of mountains marks the border with Harris, which is entered by passing Aline Lodge at the head of Loch Seaforth. The mountains of Harris are a paradise for the hillwalker. From their summits on a clear day, the distant isle of St Kilda can be seen 80 km (50 miles) to the west.

The ferry port of Tarbert stands on a slim isthmus separating North and South Harris. The tourist office provides addresses for local weavers of the tough Harris Tweed. Some weavers still use indigenous plants to create the various dyes. From Leverburgh, on Harris' southern tip, a ferry sails to North Uist, linked by a causeway to Berneray.

🏛 Black House Museum & Visitor Centre
Tel *(01851) 710395.* ☐ *9:30am–5pm Mon–Sat.* 📷 ✉

The Uists and Benbecula

After the dramatic scenery of Harris, the lower-lying, largely waterlogged southern isles may seem an anticlimax, though they nurture secrets well worth discovering. Long, white, sandy beaches fringe the Atlantic coast, edged with one of Scotland's natural treasures: the lime-rich soil known as *machair*. During the summer months, the soil is covered with wild flowers, the unique fragrance of which can be detected far out to sea.

From **Lochmaddy**, North Uist's main village, the A867 crosses 5 km (3 miles) of causeway to **Benbecula**, the isle from which the brave Flora MacDonald smuggled Bonnie Prince Charlie to Skye *(see p153)*. Benbecula is a flat island covered by a mosaic of small lochs. Like its neighbours, it is known for good trout fishing. Here, and to the north, the Protestant religion holds sway, while Catholicism prevails in the southern islands. Benbecula's chief source of employment is the Army Rocket Range, which

The harbour at Stornoway, the principal town on Lewis and Harris

For hotels and restaurants in this region see pp177–81 and pp194–7

has its headquarters in the main village of Bailivanich. Another causeway leads to South Uist, with its golden beaches, which are renowned as a National Scenic Area.

Eriskay

One of the smallest and most enchanting of the Western Isles, Eriskay epitomizes their peace and beauty. The island is best known for the wrecking of the *SS Politician* in 1941, which inspired the book and film *Whisky Galore*. A bottle from its cargo and other relics can be seen in Eriskay's only bar. It was at the beautiful beach of Coilleag A'Phrionnsa (Prince's beach) that Bonnie Prince Charlie first set foot on Scotland at the start of his 1745 campaign. As a result, a rare convolvulus flower that grows here has become associated with him.

Blue waters off the coast of Barra, looking east to the Isle of Rum

Barra

The dramatic way to arrive on Barra is by plane – the airstrip is a beach and the timetable depends on the tide. Barra is a pretty island, with its central core of hills and circular road. The western side is almost all beaches. Over 1,000 species of flowers have been recorded.

The view over Castlebay from the Madonna and Child statue, on the top of Heaval hill, is particularly fine. The romantic **Kisimul Castle**, set on an island, is the 15th seat of the Clan MacNeil. It is currently being restored. Other attractions are the **Barra Heritage Centre** and also a golf course.

⚓ Kisimul Castle
Tel (01871) 810313. ☐ Apr–Sep: daily. 🎫 includes boat trip.

🛈 Barra Heritage Centre
Tel (01871) 810336. ☐ May–Sep: Mon–Sat. ♿

A group of St Kildan men with their catch of fulmar seabirds

St Kilda

These "Islands on the Edge of the World" were the most isolated habitation in Scotland until the ageing population requested to be evacuated in 1930. The St Kildans developed a unique lifestyle based on harvesting seabirds. The largest gannetry in the world (40,000 pairs) is now to be found here. There are three islands and three stacks of awesome beauty, each with soaring cliffs rising sheer to 425 m (1,400 ft) at their highest. Such is their isolation that separate sub-species of mouse and wren have evolved. Tours are run by **Westernedge Charters** and **Murdo Macdonald**. Volunteers can also pay to join summer work parties on the island, run by the **National Trust for Scotland**, which owns St Kilda.

🛈 Westernedge Charters
Linlithgow. *Tel* (01506) 204053.
🛈 Murdo Macdonald
1 Erista, Uig, Isle of Lewis. *Tel* (01851) 672381.
🛈 National Trust for Scotland
Balnain House, Inverness. *Tel* (01463) 232034.

CROFTING

Crofts are small parcels of agricultural land, worked in conjunction with another source of income as they are too small to provide total subsistence. They originated in the early 1800s when landlords made available units of poor land on the coast, clearing the people from the more fertile areas, and making them dependent on wages from either fishing or collecting kelp (seaweed used to make commercial alkali). When these sources of income diminished, crofters endured over 50 years of extreme hardship through famine, high rents, eviction and lack of security. Not until 1886 was an Act passed which gave crofters security and allowed families the right of inheritance (but not ownership). Today there are 17,000 registered crofts, almost all in the Highlands and islands. Governed by special regulations prohibiting the creation of new crofts, the crofters are eligible for special grants. Most crofters raise sheep, but recent trends are tree planting and providing habitats for rare birds. Crofting remains a vital part of Highland communities.

A traditional, thatched crofter's house on the island of North Uist

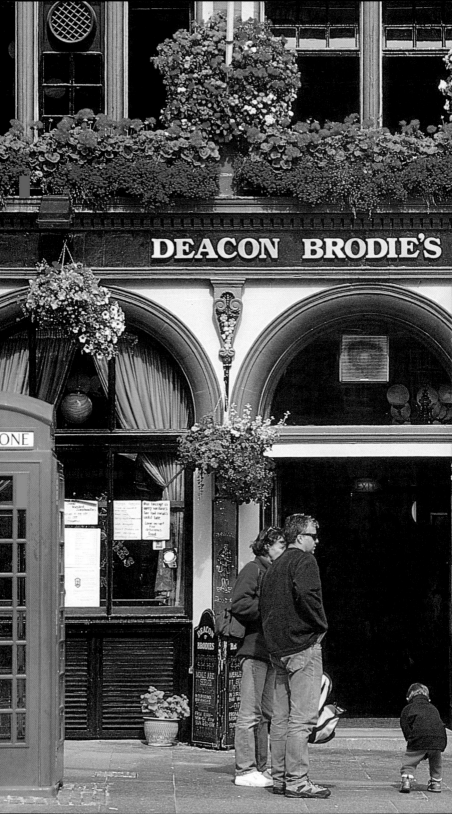

TRAVELLERS' NEEDS

WHERE TO STAY

The range of hotels and other accommodation available in Scotland is extensive, and whatever your budget, you should be able to find something to suit your needs. Different types of accommodation are described below, and the hotel listings section on pages 168–181 includes over 90 of the best places to stay, from luxurious country-house hotels and castles, to cosy bed-and-breakfasts and basic campsites. This selection represents both excellence and good value. Self-catering holidays are also growing in popularity. This type of accommodation is particularly well suited to those on a tight budget or families with young children, who may find hotels to be a little formal and inflexible. We have also added some useful introductory information on the campsites and caravan parks in Scotland, which provide an adventurous, reasonably priced alternative to hotels and guest houses.

Malmaison Hotel's distinctive sign

The refined, stately interior of a hotel in the Grampians

HOTEL CLASSIFICATIONS

The Quality Assurance Scheme run by VisitScotland is a useful guide when choosing holiday accommodation. Hotels, bed-and-breakfasts and self-catering are all covered in the scheme. A grade from "acceptable" to "exceptional" is awarded along with a classification of stars from one to five, indicating the facilities available.

PRICES, HIDDEN EXTRAS AND BOOKING

Hotel rates are normally quoted per room and include VAT (value-added tax) and service charge. Top-of-the-range hotels can cost over £200 and an average hotel in Edinburgh or Glasgow about £70–£150 for two people, including breakfast. Outside the city, expect to pay £50–£90 for a similar standard, or

£20–£50 for bed-and-breakfast. Tipping is not expected other than in very exclusive hotels. High rates are charged for telephone calls made from your room, so it may be worth buying a phonecard and using the lobby telephone instead.

Some hotels require a non-refundable deposit. If you cancel a room early on, you should not have to pay the full price. Tourist Information Centres offer a Book-a-Bed-Ahead scheme and, for a small fee, they will reserve a room.

COUNTRY HOUSE HOTELS AND CASTLES

The term "country house hotel" has been applied liberally by some hoteliers who think gas log-fires and reproduction furniture are sufficient to warrant the name on their brochures. The genuine article is not hard to spot, however, as the buildings are invariably of architectural value, filled with antiques and fine furnishings, and situated in extensive grounds. Converted castles offer visitors the chance to live and dine like a lord. The atmosphere is intimate yet refined, with cordon bleu cooking and a well-stocked wine cellar. Room tariffs are high, but the height of comfort and luxury is guaranteed.

COACHING INNS AND SHOOTING LODGES

Coaching inns can be found throughout Scotland. In former times they were staging points for people journeying by horse and carriage, where horses could rest and travellers could find food and lodging.

Generally attractive, historic buildings, inns are often the town's focal point. Some are cottage style with a thatched roof, others are Georgian or Victorian with sash windows and doorways framed with pillars and porticoes. They nearly always have traditional decor, and often a reliable restaurant serving regional, home-cooked food in a friendly and informal atmosphere.

The cosy dining area of a Scottish hotel

◁ **A colourful display of flowers outside Deacon Brodie's Tavern on the Royal Mile in Edinburgh**

In the more rural areas of Scotland, there are shooting lodges which also provide accommodation. These are often part of a large estate, and the property of a local landowner. They are comfortably furnished without being overly luxurious, which helps to keep down the price of a room. It is not obligatory to go shooting while staying at these lodges, but that may be a facility on offer, and fresh game will be served in the restaurant.

A traditional croft cottage, one of many self-catering properties in Scotland

A majestic hotel on the quayside in Leith, near Edinburgh

BED-AND-BREAKFASTS AND GUESTHOUSES

For inexpensive accommodation and a chance to meet local people, bed-and-breakfast is the ideal choice. Often family-owned, they are basic, no-frills establishments with a choice of a full, cooked breakfast or cereal and toast included in the price.

B&Bs, as they are commonly known, dominate the lower price range, and in the remote areas of Scotland can be the only form of accommodation available. The buildings are often cosy farmhouses with homely decor, and you are likely to receive a more personal, friendly welcome than at the larger, busier hotels.

Guesthouses also offer reasonably priced, basic accommodation. They usually contain a number of bedrooms, as well as a communal sitting or dining area. VisitScotland publishes the "Scotland: Bed-and-Breakfast" guide, which lists over 1,500 B&Bs and guesthouses.

SELF-CATERING

The freedom of self-catering accommodation (efficiency units) will appeal to those who prefer to stay in one place and be independent, or those with young children and a limited budget. There are many places all over Scotland, ranging from luxury apartments in the cities to converted barns or cottages in the country. Local tourist offices have the most comprehensive and up-to-date lists, and provide a booking service.

CAMPING AND CARAVANNING

A choice of campsites and caravan (recreational vehicle) parks, normally open from Easter to October, can be found all over Scotland. During the summer months parks fill up quickly, so book ahead. Road signs indicate where to find the campsites and caravan parks off the main roads.

Two clubs, the **Caravan Club** (01342 326944; www.caravan club.co.uk) and the **Camping and Caravanning Club** (0845 130 7631; www.campingand caravanningclub.co.uk), publish guides listing their parks, and it may be worthwhile becoming a member. A typical camping or caravan pitch (site) costs £6–£10 per night, making it an economical way to see Scotland.

YOUTH HOSTELS

There are around 80 hostels in Scotland, owned by the **Scottish Youth Hostels Association** or **SYHA** (01786 891400; www.syha.org.uk). Most offer central heating, hot showers and cheap evening meals. Accommodation is usually single-sex dormitories, but occasionally there are separate family rooms. You must be a member of the SYHA to stay, but anyone over the age of five can join upon arrival.

Invercoe campsite in the Highlands – basic facilities but wonderful views

Choosing a Hotel

The hotels featured in this guide have been selected across a wide price range for their excellent facilities and location. Many also have a recommended restaurant. The chart lists hotels by region, starting with Edinburgh, and in ascending price order. For restaurant listings, see pp185–97

PRICE DETAILS
For a standard double room per night, inclusive of service charge and any additional taxes such as VAT:

£ Under £65
££ £65–£100
£££ £100–£150
££££ £150–£200
£££££ Over £200

EDINBURGH

NEW TOWN St Bernard's Guest House £

22 St Bernard's Crescent, Edinburgh, EH4 1NS **Tel** *0131 332 2339* **Fax** *0131 332 8842* **Rooms** *8*

This two-star guesthouse is in a charming Victorian townhouse in the Stockbridge area. The area has a pleasant, village-like atmosphere but is also within easy walking distance of the city centre. Four of the eight rooms are en suite and there are tea and coffee-making facilities.

NEW TOWN Christopher North House Hotel ££

6 Gloucester Place, Edinburgh, EH3 6EF **Tel** *0131 225 2720* **Fax** *0131 220 4706* **Rooms** *30*

Ideally located within easy walking distance of the city centre and the more bohemian Stockbridge area, this elegantly refurbished boutique hotel offers a high standard of accommodation and service. Guests can enjoy skilfully prepared and presented local dishes at the highly commended restaurant. **www.christophernorth.co.uk**

NEW TOWN Channings £££

12–16 South Learmonth Gardens, Edinburgh, EH4 1EZ **Tel** *0131 274 7401* **Fax** *0131 332 9631* **Rooms** *42*

Channings is located close to the city centre. This smart yet homely hotel consists of five converted Edwardian houses on a quiet cobbled street overlooking private gardens. Rooms are individually decorated, but they all feature elegant furnishings. The hotel feels a bit like a Scottish country home. **www.channings.co.uk**

NEW TOWN The George Hotel £££

19–21 George Street, Edinburgh, EH2 2PB **Tel** *0131 225 1251* **Fax** *0131 220 3624* **Rooms** *195*

This long-established delightful hotel, the grand dame of George Street, offers a high standard of accommodation and facilities. Most remarkable is the restaurant and bar Tempus, which offers a stylish place for guests and locals to enjoy good bistro food, cocktails and very fine dining. **www.principal-hotels.com**

NEW TOWN Mount Royal Ramada Jarvis Hotel £££

53 Princes Street, Edinburgh, EH2 2DG **Tel** *0131 225 7161* **Fax** *0131 220 4671* **Rooms** *158*

This hotel is located, quite literally, in the heart of the city and has rooms with views of the castle, across the Princes Street gardens. Accommodation is comfortable, and the service friendly and welcoming. The hotel is comfortably appointed with a good range of facilities, including 24-hour room service. **www.ramadajarvis.co.uk**

NEW TOWN Parliament House £££

15 Calton Hill, Edinburgh, EH1 3BJ **Tel** *0131 478 4000* **Fax** *0131 478 4001* **Rooms** *53*

An original Georgian townhouse, Parliament House boasts an impressive, convenient location next to Calton Hill and just minutes from Princes Street. The helpful management offers a range of holiday packages, including golf, rugby and theatre breaks, as well as International Festival packages. **www.parliamenthouse-hotel.co.uk**

NEW TOWN 1 Royal Circus ££££

1 Royal Circus, Edinburgh, EH3 6TL **Tel** *0131 625 6669* **Rooms** *5*

A stylish B&B located in a grand Georgian terrace building. The interior was refurbished by the owner himself and features high ceilings, Philippe Starck furnishings, nostalgic French posters and gleaming parquet floors. Guests are welcome to play the baby grand piano. Breakfasts are concocted by a pastry chef.

NEW TOWN Caledonian Hilton Hotel ££££

Princes Street, Edinburgh, EH1 2AB **Tel** *0131 222 8888* **Fax** *0131 222 8889* **Rooms** *251*

A landmark in Edinburgh's skyline, the Caledonian Hilton dates back to 1903. Many rooms have stunning views of the castle. The hotel is ideally located for exploring the city and has excellent leisure facilities, as well as a range of lounges, bars and restaurants offering something to suit every taste and occasion. **www.hilton.co.uk/caledonian**

NEW TOWN Le Monde ££££

16 George Street, Edinburgh, EH2 2PF **Tel** *0131 270 3900* **Fax** *0131 270 3901* **Rooms** *18*

In the heart of the city, this is one of the first boutique hotels in Edinburgh. Featuring several bars and restaurants and a nightclub, this is a great place to enjoy all that the city has to offer – in style. Le Monde has already won a handful of design awards for the quality of the accommodation and the facilities. **www.lemondehotel.co.uk**

Key to Symbols *see back cover flap*

NEW TOWN The Scotsman
20 North Bridge, Edinburgh, EH1 1YT **Tel** *0131 556 5565* **Fax** *0131 652 3652* **Rooms** *69*

Housed in the converted offices of *The Scotsman* newspaper, this elegantly refurbished hotel offers great views of the city. The luxurious rooms and suites are decorated with authentic Scottish estate tweeds, and they feature modern amenities such as DVD and CD players and Internet access. **www.thescotsmanhotel.com**

NEW TOWN The Balmoral
1 Princes Street, Edinburgh, EH2 2EQ **Tel** *0131 556 2414* **Fax** *0131 557 3747* **Rooms** *188*

Boasting the best-known address in Edinburgh, The Balmoral caters for anyone accustomed to the very best in life. This elegant hotel has luxurious, tastefully furnished suites and rooms, all featuring Internet access, fax machine, TV and more. The hotel also has conference facilities and a spa. **www.thebalmoralhotel.com**

NEW TOWN The Bonham Hotel
35 Drumsheugh Gardens, Edinburgh, EH3 7RN **Tel** *0131 274 7400* **Fax** *0131 274 7405* **Rooms** *48*

The Bonham has some of the most stylish rooms in town: each is individually designed in a contemporary style using bold colours. The latest technology is also available for the modern traveller. The famous Restaurant at the Bonham offers European-inspired fare and a superb wine list. **www.thebonham.com**

NEW TOWN Sheraton Grand
1 Festival Square, Edinburgh, EH3 9SR **Tel** *0131 229 9131* **Fax** *0131 228 4510* **Rooms** *260*

Nestling in the shadow of the Castle, this is a superb hotel offering all that you would expect from the Sheraton name – and more. The air-conditioned rooms are sumptuously decorated. The hotel boasts several eating options, including the award-winning Grill Room. Superb spa facilities at the One Spa. **www.starwoodhotels.com**

OLD TOWN Bank Hotel
The Royal Mile, 1 South Bridge, Edinburgh, EH1 1LL **Tel** *0131 622 6800* **Fax** *0131 622 6822* **Rooms** *9*

Originally built as a bank in 1923, this comfortable hotel enjoys an enviable location, close to many shops and eating places. The rooms are tastefully furnished, with a wide range of amenities; some overlook Edinburgh Castle. There is no lift, so the Bank is not recommended for the elderly and disabled. **www.festival-inns.co.uk**

OLD TOWN Classic Guest House
50 Mayfield Road, Edinburgh, EH9 2NH **Tel** *0131 667 5847* **Fax** *0131 662 1016* **Rooms** *4*

All rooms at this elegant Victorian house near the city centre are en suite, comfortably furnished and attractively decorated. Parking is free on the street. The warm, welcoming hosts serve an excellent Scottish and continental breakfast that also includes vegetarian options. **www.classichouse.demon.co.uk**

OLD TOWN Jury's Inn Edinburgh
43 Jeffrey Street, Edinburgh, EH1 1DH **Tel** *0131 200 3300* **Fax** *0131 200 0400* **Rooms** *186*

With great views to Calton Hill, this hotel is conveniently situated close to the Royal Mile, Princes Street and Waverley Station. Part of a growing chain of hotels, the Jury's Edinburgh Inn offers a varied selection of amenities, including bars and restaurants, laundry service and five meeting rooms. **www.edinburghhotelsjurysinns.com**

OLD TOWN Best Western Edinburgh City Hotel
79 Lauriston Place, Edinburgh, EH3 9HZ **Tel** *0131 622 7979* **Fax** *0131 622 7900* **Rooms** *52*

Near the Grassmarket, the City Hotel is located in what was formerly the city's maternity hospital. It has been extensively refurbished in a modern and elegant style that complements the traditional aspects of the building. The in-house restaurant offers a wide range of traditional cooking. **www.bestwesternedinburghcity.co.uk**

OLD TOWN Holyrood Aparthotel
1 Netherbakehouse, Edinburgh, EH8 8PE **Tel** *0131 524 3200* **Fax** *0131 524 3210* **Rooms** *41*

Located just off the Royal Mile, these serviced apartments have been finished to the highest of standards, with sumptuous decor and every possible amenity. All have a fully fitted luxury kitchen. There is a 24-hour reception service, housekeeping service and secure parking. Continental breakfasts are also available. **www.holyroodaparthotel.com**

FURTHER AFIELD Airlie Guest House
29 Minto Street, Edinburgh, EH9 1SB **Tel** *0131 667 3562* **Fax** *0131 667 3562* **Rooms** *6*

Most rooms in this small three-star guesthouse with private parking are en suite; all are comfortably furnished and equipped. Located close to Holyrood Park and the Royal Commonwealth Pool, the Airlie is still only a short journey into the city centre. Full Scottish and continental breakfasts are served. **www.airlieguesthouse.co.uk**

FURTHER AFIELD Bield Guest House
3 Orchard Brae West, Edinburgh, EH4 2EW **Tel** *0131 332 5119* **Rooms** *3*

This small, family-run guesthouse offers comfortable accommodation in a location within easy reach of the West End, either by bus or on foot. All rooms are en suite or with private facilities, and they have been tastefully decorated and furnished to ensure a pleasant stay. Good breakfasts are also assured. **www.bieldbedandbreakfast.com**

FURTHER AFIELD Blinkbonny House
23 Blinkbonny Gardens, Edinburgh, EH4 3HG **Tel** *0131 467 1232* **Rooms** *3*

Located on the west side of the city, just a five-minute bus ride from the city centre, this charming 1930s bungalow has wooden flooring, cosy but stylish furnishings and spacious en-suite rooms. It is family-run, with a warm and relaxed attitude to guests. **www.blinkbonnyhouse.co.uk**

FURTHER AFIELD Granville Guest House

13 Granville Terrace, Edinburgh, EH10 4PQ **Tel** *0131 229 1676* **Fax** *0131 229 4633* **Rooms** *9*

This comfortable family-run guesthouse is set within an attractive Victorian house with many fine architectural features, such as a sweeping staircase. Both en-suite and standard rooms are available, all tastefully furnished and well equipped. Free parking on site. Full Scottish and continental breakfast served. **www.granvilleguesthouse.com**

FURTHER AFIELD Harvest Guest House

33 Straiton Place, Edinburgh, EH15 2BA **Tel** *0131 657 3160* **Fax** *0131 468 7028* **Rooms** *5*

Located right on the promenade in the Victorian seaside town of Portobello, this guesthouse is close to restaurants and pubs and a mere 15-minute drive from Edinburgh city centre. Parking is available, and there is a pretty garden area. Full Scottish and continental breakfasts are served. **www.edinburgh-guesthouse-accommodation.co.uk**

FURTHER AFIELD Ivy Guest House

7 Mayfield Gardens, Edinburgh, EH9 2AX **Tel** *0131 667 3411* **Fax** *0131 620 1422* **Rooms** *4*

Covered in lush ivy, as its name would suggest, this comfortable three-star guesthouse has its own private parking at the rear. It is also ideally located, on a regular bus route to the city centre and within easy reach of Arthur's Seat and Holyrood Park. All rooms have en-suite facilities. Try the delicious vegetarian breakfast. **www.ivyguesthouse.com**

FURTHER AFIELD Kaimes Guest House

12 Granville Terrace, Edinburgh, EH10 4PQ **Tel** *0131 229 3401* **Fax** *0131 228 1173* **Rooms** *12*

A ten-minute walk to the King's Theatre and 20-minute walk to Princes Street, this comfortable guesthouse is ideally located to offer a comfortable stay in Scotland's capital city. This is an old Victorian house that has been beautifully revamped. All rooms are freshly decorated; most are en suite. **www.kaimeshouse.co.uk**

FURTHER AFIELD Kariba Guest House

10 Granville Terrace, Edinburgh, EH10 4PQ **Tel** *0131 229 3773* **Fax** *0131 229 4968* **Rooms** *9*

This attractively refurbished Victorian townhouse with private parking is located only 15 minutes' walk from the city centre. All rooms are fully equipped with modern amenities, and most are en suite or have access to private showers. Full Scottish, continental or vegetarian options available for breakfast. **www.karibaguesthouse.co.uk**

FURTHER AFIELD Kelly's Guest House

3 Hillhouse Road, Edinburgh, EH4 3QP **Tel** *0131 332 3894* **Fax** *0131 538 0925* **Rooms** *4*

A welcoming guesthouse overlooking a secluded garden, Kelly's is within easy reach of the city centre by public transport. There is ample private parking on site. All rooms are en suite, with good amenities. Breakfast (Scottish or continental) is available. There is also a self-contained two-room family suite. **www.kellysguesthouse.co.uk**

FURTHER AFIELD Northumberland Hotel

31–33 Craigmillar Park, Edinburgh, EH16 5PE **Tel** *0131 668 3131* **Fax** *0131 667 5555* **Rooms** *16*

A comfortable hotel just 3 km (2 miles) from Edinburgh city centre, the Northumberland offers a high standard of accommodation. A full Scottish breakfast is included in the room rate, and the bar is a comfortable place to relax. Some rooms have access to a sunny rooftop terrace. Parking available. **www.thenorthumberlandhotel.co.uk**

FURTHER AFIELD Redcraig B&B

Redcraig, Mid Calder, EH53 0JT **Tel** *01506 884249* **Fax** *01506 884249* **Rooms** *3*

This friendly B&B is 20 minutes' drive to the west of Edinburgh. Tastefully decorated and furnished guest rooms are located in an extension, separate from the main house. There is ample private parking, and full Scottish and continental breakfasts are served; a vegetarian option is also available. **www.redcraigbedandbreakfast.co.uk**

FURTHER AFIELD Travelodge Edinburgh Learmonth

18–20 Learmonth Terrace, Edinburgh, EH4 1PW **Tel** *0871 984 6415* **Rooms** *79*

More characterful than many in the Travelodge chain, this hotel is housed in a sandstone Victorian terraced building, conveniently located near Haymarket railway station. Rooms are clean and have tea- and coffee-making facilities, and the staff are friendly. **www.travelodge.co.uk**

FURTHER AFIELD Allison House

17 Mayfield Gardens, Edinburgh, EH9 2AX **Tel** *0131 667 8049* **Fax** *0131 667 5001* **Rooms** *11*

Situated on the south side of Edinburgh, Allison House is a small but comfortable hotel suitable to both leisure and business guests. There is free parking on site, and all rooms are pleasant, with flat-screen TVs, a complimentary decanter of whisky and sherry, and a hospitality tray. **www.allisonhousehotel.com**

FURTHER AFIELD Crauchie Farmhouse

East Linton, East Lothian, EH40 3EB **Tel** *01620 860124* **Rooms** *3*

A delightful 200-year-old farmhouse hidden up a winding lane, the four-star Crauchie is within easy reach of the city yet a haven for those who value tranquillity. The house and the surrounding garden are lovely and peaceful. Excellent home cooking is available at breakfast, including a vegetarian option. **www.crauchiefarmhouse.co.uk**

FURTHER AFIELD Ellersly House

Ellersly Road, Edinburgh, EH12 6HZ **Tel** *0131 337 6888* **Rooms** *57*

Ellersly House is an attractive Edwardian property set in secluded gardens in the Murrayfield area. It is a popular place for conferences and weddings, but also suitable for individual travellers. Standard rooms are comfortable, and executive suites have extra luxuries. The restaurant offers a good variety of local fare. **www.ellerslyhousehotel.co.uk**

Key to Price Guide *see p168* **Key to Symbols** *see back cover flap*

FURTHER AFIELD Emerald Guest House

Gilmerton, Edinburgh, EH17 8QQ **Tel** *0131 664 5918* **Fax** *0131 664 1920* **Rooms** *3*

This family-run guesthouse in a Victorian villa on the outskirts of city is within easy reach of all the major attractions and the airport. Some rooms are en suite; others have access to pristine facilities. Full Scottish and continental breakfasts are served; early breakfast by prior arrangement. Ample parking. **www.emeraldguesthouse.co.uk**

FURTHER AFIELD Gerald's Place B&B

216 Abercromby Place, Edinburgh, EH3 6QE **Tel** *0131 558 7017* **Rooms** *2*

Walking into Gerald's Place is like walking into the house of a very good friend and knowing you are welcome. Gerald runs the place by himself; he provides generous extras and ensures your rooms are comfortable and clean. This B&B is within easy reach of all tourist attractions and the city centre. **www.geraldsplace.com**

FURTHER AFIELD Invertruin B&B

146 Ferry Road, Edinburgh, EH5 2AD **Tel** *0131 551 3580* **Fax** *0131 664 1920* **Rooms** *3*

This handsome, red-brick Victorian home offers a warm welcome and cosy rooms, including one for families. It's only a short stroll away from the Royal Botanical Garden and affords great views of the city. Breakfasts are substantial with plenty of choice. **www.invertruin.here2stay.org.uk**

FURTHER AFIELD Kew House

1 Kew Terrace, Murrayfield EH12 5JE **Tel** *0131 313 0700* **Rooms** *4*

An excellent B&B that's a good option for those visiting Murrayfield Stadium. The building is a fine 1860s villa, and rooms are soothingly decorated in pale colours. They also feature tea- and coffee-making facilities, fresh flowers and even a carafe of sherry. Locally sourced ingredients are used in the delicious breakfasts. **www.kewhouse.com**

FURTHER AFIELD Murrayfield Hotel

18 Corstorphine Road, Edinburgh, EH12 6HN **Tel** *0131 662 6800* **Fax** *0131 662 6822* **Rooms** *30*

This two-star hotel is within walking distance of Murrayfield Stadium, which makes it a popular choice with visiting rugby fans. It offers comfortable, if somewhat basic, accommodation, with a complimentary hospitality tray in each room. The popular bar serves traditional food until late. Close to Edinburgh Zoo. **www.festival-inns.co.uk**

FURTHER AFIELD Piries Hotel

4–8 Coates Gardens, Edinburgh, EH12 5LB **Tel** *0131 337 1108* **Fax** *0131 346 0279* **Rooms** *32*

Piries is a comfortable three-star hotel that offers good accommodation at reasonable prices. Situated in the West End of the city, it is ideally located for both business and leisure guests, with all types of transport, amenities and local attractions nearby. Close to the Edinburgh International Conference Centre. **www.thepiries.com**

FURTHER AFIELD Sandaig Guest House

5 East Hermitage Place, Leith Links, Edinburgh, EH6 8AA **Tel** *0131 554 7357* **Fax** *0131 554 7313* **Rooms** *6*

Within walking distance of the fashionable Edinburgh Waterfront, this guesthouse overlooking Leith Links Park offers a high standard of accommodation. All rooms are equipped and finished to a high standard, with attractive soft furnishings, hospitality trays and fluffy towels. Warm welcome and great value. **www.sandaigguesthouse.co.uk**

FURTHER AFIELD 20 Albany Street

20 Albany St, Edinburgh, EH1 3QB **Tel** *0131 478 5386* **Rooms** *3*

This exquisitely decorated B&B sits in a prime location on Albany Street, a wide New Town throughfare that's a short walk from the shops of Princes Street. The rooms have pretty colour schemes and amenities; one has a bathroom with a roll-top bath. The warm hospitality extends to the excellent breakfast on offer. **www.20albanystreet.co.uk**

FURTHER AFIELD 20 Elmview

15 Glengyle Terrace, Edinburgh, EH3 9LN **Tel** *0131 228 1973* **Rooms** *5*

Housed in a handsome Victorian terrace on the edge of Bruntsfield Links golf course – the owners can lend you golf clubs and balls so you can try it out yourself. Huge breakfasts are served by the lovely hosts, although note that they do not accommodate children. **www.elmview.co.uk**

FURTHER AFIELD Links Hotel

4 Alvanley Terrace, Edinburgh, EH9 1DU **Tel** *0131 229 3834* **Fax** *0131 622 6822* **Rooms** *26*

The Links comprises three townhouses and is located over three floors. It does not have a lift, so it is not suitable for the elderly or less able. The amenities are comfortable, however, and include a bar that is very popular with the locals. On occasion, noise from the bar can affect some of the bedrooms. **www.linkshoteledinburgh.co.uk**

FURTHER AFIELD Edinburgh Marriott Hotel

111 Glasgow Road, Edinburgh, EH12 8NF **Tel** *0131 334 9191* **Fax** *0131 316 4508* **Rooms** *245*

A modern four-star hotel with excellent leisure facilities and complimentary parking, the Edinburgh Marriott is only a 15-minute car/bus journey from the city centre. The hotel is also close to the airport and the city bypass, which grants easy access to the surrounding areas, such as the Borders and Fife. **www.marriott.co.uk**

FURTHER AFIELD Macdonald Marine Hotel

Cromwell Road, North Berwick, EH39 4LZ **Tel** *08704 008129* **Fax** *01620 894480* **Rooms** *83*

This refurbished hotel offers an extremely high standard of accommodation and amenities, in addition to its superb dining and leisure facilities. North Berwick has much to offer, sitting within close distance of both Edinburgh and beautiful surrounding countryside. **www.macdonaldhotels.co.uk**

FURTHER AFIELD Kilspindie House Hotel

Aberlady, East Lothian, EH32 0RE **Tel** *01875 870682* **Fax** *01875 870504* **Rooms** *20*

Located in the pretty East Lothian village of Aberlady, Kilspindie House boasts a particularly fine restaurant in the form of Ducks at Kilspindie, sister to Ducks in Edinburgh. The hotel offers very comfortable accommodation and is the perfect place to stay after enjoying the many pursuits that East Lothian has to offer. **www.kilspindie.co.uk**

SOUTHERN SCOTLAND

AYR 26 The Crescent

26 Bellevue Crescent, Ayr, KA7 2DR **Tel** *01292 287329* **Rooms** *4*

This elegant and pretty B&B offers luxury accommodation in a good location on a quiet terrace near the sea. Built in 1898, the house has been decorated with an eye for style and comfort; one room has a four-poster bed. The breakfast will set you up for the day. **www.26crescent.co.uk**

CLINTMAINS Clint Lodge

Clinthill, St Boswells, Melrose, Roxburghshire, TD6 0DZ **Tel** *01835 822027* **Fax** *01835 822656* **Rooms** *5*

This traditional country guesthouse and B&B has great views of the River Tweed. Its location close to Melrose Abbey makes it ideal as a base for exploring the surrounding areas. The rooms are tastefully decorated, with en-suite facilities and modern amenities. Clint Lodge serves excellent breakfasts. **www.clintlodge.co.uk**

EDNAM Edenwater House

Ednam, Kelso, Roxburghshire, TD5 7QL **Tel** *01573 224070* **Fax** *01573 226615* **Rooms** *4*

Quiet and family-run, this traditional guesthouse located on the edge of the village is comfortably furnished, offering lovely views of the surrounding Cheviot Hills. The delicious home-cooked meals are accompanied by a particularly interesting wine list. **www.edenwaterhouse.co.uk**

GRETNA Gretna Chase Hotel

Sark Bridge, Gretna, Dumfries and Galloway, DG16 5JB **Tel** *01461 337517* **Rooms** *20*

This hotel, which was built in 1856, is located on the English/Scottish border. Rooms are lovely, clean and spacious and traditional in style. There are large, private gardens, ideal for children to play in. The food is tasty and well-presented. Facilities include wheelchair access, parking and Wi-Fi. **www.gretnachase.co.uk**

GULLANE Mallard Hotel

East Links Road, Gullane, East Lothian, EH31 2AF **Tel** *01620 843288* **Fax** *01620 843288* **Rooms** *18*

The Mallard has a great location overlooking Gullane's famous golf courses. It is a family hotel which has built up an excellent reputation over the years. It is close to a sandy beach and nature reserve. A baby-sitting service is available, as well as room service and facilities for disabled guests. **www.mallard-gullane.co.uk**

GULLANE Golf Inn

Main Street, Gullane, East Lothian, EH31 2AB **Tel** *01620 843259* **Fax** *01620 842066* **Rooms** *14*

The Golf Inn is an intimate guesthouse decorated with pine furnishings and crisp colour schemes. It is set in a lovely village in East Lothian, a short drive from Edinburgh, which makes it popular for day trips to the city. Accommodation is comfortable and not too expensive. Meals are appetizing and excellent value. **www.golfinn.co.uk**

HEITON Roxburghe

Heiton, Kelso, Roxburghshire, TD5 8JZ **Tel** *01573 450331* **Fax** *01573 450611* **Rooms** *22*

Roxburghe is a grand Jacobean-style house set in acres of beautiful estate grounds. Luxuriously appointed, with comfortable rooms, the hotel is a perfect base from which to explore the scenic Borders area. It offers a range of outdoor activities such as golf, fishing, mountain-biking, walks and more. **www.roxburghe.net**

INNERLEITHEN Cardrona Hotel

Cardrona, Peebles, EH45 6LZ **Tel** *0870 1942114* **Fax** *01896 831166* **Rooms** *99*

On the banks of the River Tweed, just 5 km (3 miles) east of Peebles, this modern and luxuriously appointed hotel is a great place to stay and enjoy the Scottish Borders. The hotel has its own 18-hole golf course and comprehensive dining options, all set in luxurious surroundings and in a stunning riverside location. **www.macdonaldhotels.co.uk**

JEDBURGH Hundalee House

Hundalee, Jedburgh, Roxburghshire, TD8 6PA **Tel** *01835 863011* **Fax** *01835 863011* **Rooms** *5*

Set in 15 acres of woodland, this tastefully decorated Victorian manor house features all the modern conveniences. It has a classic interior and a welcoming ambience, it offers good home cooking and represents excellent value. Perfect for experiencing the scenic surroundings. Breakfast included. **www.accommodation-scotland.org**

LINLITHGOW Champany Inn

Champany, Linlithgow, West Lothian, EH49 7LU **Tel** *01506 834532* **Fax** *01506 834302* **Rooms** *16*

A stylish restaurant with rooms. The spacious sleeping quarters are tasteful and elegant, with en-suite bathrooms, and they all feature modern amenities. The Champany Inn serves an excellent Scottish breakfast. It is located close to several sightseeing attractions and golf courses. **www.champany.com**

Key to Price Guide *see p168* **Key to Symbols** *see back cover flap*

MELROSE Burts Hotel

Market Square, Melrose, Roxburghshire, TD6 9PL **Tel** *01896 822285* **Fax** *01896 822870* **Rooms** *20*

Situated close to several golf courses, this family-run traditional pub has developed a well-earned reputation, both locally and abroad. As well as serving superb local produce in both the restaurant and the bar, the Burts offers a warm welcome and good service. **www.burtshotel.co.uk**

MELROSE The Townhouse Hotel

3 Market Square, Melrose, Roxburghshire, TD6 9PQ **Tel** *01896 822645* **Fax** *01896 823474* **Rooms** *11*

This smart hotel is decorated in a classy, yet modern, style. The chic brasserie serves tasty contemporary cooking. The rooms are luxuriously appointed – some with Jacuzzi baths, others with views over the gardens. This is a good location from which to explore the Borders. **www.thetownhousemelrose.co.uk**

MOFFAT Seamore Guest House

Academy Road, Moffat, DG10 9HW **Tel** *01683 220404* **Rooms** *5*

Guests are assured a warm welcome at this family-run guesthouse located on the edge of Moffat town centre, in a listed Victorian house built around 1850. The en-suite rooms have been tastefully furnished in keeping with the style of the house, and a particularly good Scottish breakfast is available. **www.seamorehouse.co.uk**

ST BOSWELLS Buccleuch Arms

The Green, St Boswells, Dumfriesshire, TD6 0EW **Tel** *01835 822243* **Fax** *01835 823965* **Rooms** *19*

A popular meeting place for visitors, this 16th-century coaching inn is a great spot from which to explore the countryside. The accommodation is comfortable and unpretentious; the service is friendly and relaxed. The restaurant serves good bar food. **www.buccleucharmshotel.co.uk**

ST BOSWELLS Dryburgh Abbey Hotel

St Boswells, Melrose, Dumfriesshire, TD6 0RQ **Tel** *01835 822261* **Fax** *01835 823945* **Rooms** *38*

An imposing mansion in a picturesque setting on the edge of the River Tweed, this delightfully comfortable hotel offers high standards of hospitality, accommodation and dining. All rooms are en suite, and some have river views. Explore the surrounding area, fish in the river or simply relax and enjoy all the facilities on site. **www.dryburgh.co.uk**

STRANRAER Balyett B&B

Cairnryan Road, Stranraer, DG9 8QL **Tel** *01776 703395* **Fax** *01776 703395* **Rooms** *4*

This impressive Victorian house is close to the ferry ports and surrounded by a delightful garden. Bedrooms are spacious, tastefully decorated and comfortably fitted out. Guests enjoy a traditional Scottish breakfast in the luxurious dining room before setting off on their day. **www.balyettbb.co.uk**

TROON Lochgreen House

Monktonhill Road, Troon, Ayrshire, KA10 7EN **Tel** *01292 313343* **Fax** *01292 318661* **Rooms** *44*

A spacious, well-appointed Edwardian hotel with large, luxurious bedrooms and antique-filled public rooms. The innovative, award-winning restaurant is modern but baronial in style, and the cooking is superb. The hotel also has well-maintained grounds. **www.costleyhotels.co.uk**

TURNBERRY The Westin Turnberry Resort

Turnberry, Ayrshire, KA23 9LT **Tel** *01655 331000* **Fax** *01655 331706* **Rooms** *219*

One of the trendiest places to stay in Scotland, The Westin Turnberry boasts championship golf courses, a spa and superb conference facilities for business travellers. The en-suite rooms are elegantly furnished, and many have facilities for disabled guests. The restaurant serves excellent food. Pets allowed. **www.turnberryresort.co.uk**

WEST LINTON The Meadows

4 Robinsland Drive, West Linton, EH46 7JD **Tel** *01968 661798* **Fax** *01968 661798* **Rooms** *4*

A modern B&B located only a few minutes' walk from West Linton. Its location makes The Meadows ideal for those who want to explore the area, offering easy access to both Edinburgh and the Borders. Warm hospitality, comfortable accommodation and a hearty Scottish breakfast are on offer. **www.themeadowsbandb.co.uk**

GLASGOW

CITY CENTRE Alison Guest House

26 Circus Drive, Glasgow, G31 2JH **Tel** *0141 556 1431* **Rooms** *6*

This large Victorian house retains many of its original features. The accommodation is comfortable, and the location is ideal for visiting Glasgow Cathedral, St Mungo Museum and Glasgow's oldest house, Provand's Lordship. A full Scottish breakfast is available, and it can be served early if pre-arranged. **www.alisonguesthouse.co.uk**

CITY CENTRE Argyll Guest House

970 Sauchiehall Street, Glasgow, G3 7TH **Tel** *0141 357 5155* **Fax** *0141 337 3283* **Rooms** *20*

Centrally located, the Argyll is an ideal base for sightseeing. All rooms are en suite, and amenities include free Wi-Fi. A full Scottish breakfast is available in the adjacent Argyll Hotel. The latter hotel's restaurant, Sutherlands, is highly recommended. Free street parking at weekends. **www.argyllguesthouseglasgow.co.uk**

CITY CENTRE Claremont B&B

2 Broompark Circus, Glasgow, G31 2JF **Tel** 0141 554 7312 **Fax** 0141 554 7312 **Rooms** 2

Privately owned and run, this comfortable B&B is located in a large detached Victorian building in an established conservation area. Hosts are friendly and offer their guests a full Scottish breakfast. Continental and vegetarian options are also available. The Claremont has its own private parking. **www.claremont-guesthouse.co.uk**

CITY CENTRE Kelvingrove Hotel

944 Sauchiehall Street, Glasgow, G3 7TH **Tel** 0141 339 5011 **Fax** 0141 339 6566 **Rooms** 23

This hotel is adjacent to Kelvingrove Park, renowned for the Kelvingrove Art Gallery, and within easy reach of the West End and city centre. All the rooms are well appointed, and pets are welcome by prior arrangement. A self-contained apartment-style room is available for weekly lets. **www.glasgowhotelsandapartments.co.uk**

CITY CENTRE The Brunswick

106–108 Brunswick Street, Glasgow, G1 1TF **Tel** 0141 552 0001 **Fax** 0141 552 1551 **Rooms** 18

Situated in the restored Merchant City area, this hotel features an appealingly individual, contemporary style, with simple, clean lines and unfussy furnishings in the en-suite rooms. It is compact but comfortable, and very affordable. Those who feel like a special treat could check out the three-bedroom penthouse. **www.brunswickhotel.co.uk**

CITY CENTRE Kirklee Hotel

11 Kensington Gate, Glasgow, G12 9LG **Tel** 0141 334 5555 **Fax** 0141 339 3828 **Rooms** 9

The Kirklee is situated in Glasgow's leafy West End, amid award-winning gardens. The standard of accommodation is particularly high, and guests can be assured of a memorable stay here. All rooms are en suite, individually furnished and uniquely finished. Breakfast is served in the privacy of the guests' bedrooms. **www.kirkleehotel.co.uk**

CITY CENTRE Park Inn Hotel

2 Port Dundas Place, Glasgow, G2 3LD **Tel** 0141 333 1500 **Fax** 0141 333 5700 **Rooms** 100

This is a glamorous boutique hotel with two trendy restaurants, a beauty salon, and spa and leisure amenities. Bedrooms are comfortably minimalist. Excellently located for those who enjoy shopping, the hotel also offers meeting and conference facilities, thereby attracting both leisure and business travellers. **www.parkinn.co.uk**

CITY CENTRE The Premier Inn

80 Ballater Street, Glasgow, G5 0TW **Tel** 08702 383320 **Fax** 0141 5532719 **Rooms** 114

This city-centre budget hotel offers modern, spacious and well-equipped rooms with satellite TV and walk-in shower rooms. Families are well catered for, with children under 16 years of age staying for free. A delicious full Scottish breakfast is served in the trendy hotel bistro. **www.premierinn.com**

CITY CENTRE Radisson SAS

301 Argyle Street, Glasgow, G2 8DP **Tel** 0141 204 3333 **Fax** 0141 204 3344 **Rooms** 250

Recognized for its innovative design, this award-winning hotel has lavishly furnished rooms, suites and an apartment. There is also a popular bar and a good restaurant, making it the definitive choice for those who enjoy modern surroundings. A gym nearby offers massage treatments and a pool. **www.radissonblu.co.uk**

WEST END The Botanic Hotel

1 Alfred Terrace, Glasgow, G12 8RF **Tel** 0141 337 7007 **Fax** 0141 339 0477 **Rooms** 18

A stylish, small hotel offering a high standard of accommodation within easy reach of the city centre. All rooms are well equipped and en suite. There is a wide range of eating options available nearby, and the hotel serves a comprehensive Scottish breakfast menu with continental and vegetarian options. **www.botanichotel.co.uk**

WEST END The Wickets Hotel

52 Fortrose Street, Glasgow, G11 5LP **Tel** 0141 334 9334 **Fax** 0141 334 9334 **Rooms** 11

This family-run hotel occupies a country-house-style building in the West End, close to the Scottish Exhibition Centre and Glasgow University, but also in a convenient location for the motorway and for bus and train links, making it a suitable choice for those who wish to explore the area around Glasgow. **www.wicketshotel.co.uk**

WEST END Hotel Du Vin

1 Devonshire Gardens, Glasgow, G12 0UX **Tel** 0141 339 2001 **Fax** 0131 337 1663 **Rooms** 35

A beautiful townhouse located in the city's trendy and leafy West End. The rooms are glamorously furnished and opulently decorated, and the food in the restaurant is extremely refined. Well equipped, with a high standard of service to match, this is the place to treat yourself. **www.hotelduvin.com**

FURTHER AFIELD Abingdon Hotel

78 Carlisle Road, Abingdon, Lanarkshire, ML12 6DD **Tel** 01864 502467 **Fax** 01864 5022223 **Rooms** 29

Amid beautiful countryside in the heart of Abingdon is this former coaching inn, which numbers many famous historical figures among its former guests. The accommodation is comfortable, and the welcome genuine. A range of menus and eating options are available – food is well cooked, simply presented and tasty. **www.ab-hotel.com**

FURTHER AFIELD Ashtree House

9 Orr Square, Paisley, PA1 2DL **Tel** 0141 848 6411 **Fax** 0141 848 6411 **Rooms** 4

This 200-year-old listed Georgian townhouse is a luxuriously appointed family-run inn; great attention has been paid to quality and finish. Ashtree House is close to the airport and only 10 minutes to the city centre by train. There is a garden for residents' use, and evening meals are available by prior arrangement. **www.ashtreehousehotel.com**

Key to Price Guide see p168 **Key to Symbols** see back cover flap

FURTHER AFIELD Macdonald Crutherland Hotel €€€

*Strathaven Road, East Kilbride, G75 0QZ **Tel** 01355 577000 **Fax** 01355 577047 **Rooms** 75*

Luxurious accommodation and excellent dining facilities can be found at this hotel set in beautifully landscaped gardens, just 15 minutes from the heart of Glasgow. The leisure facilities are state of the art, as is the standard of the bedrooms. Dining options range from the formal restaurant to the cocktail bar and lounge. **www.macdonaldhotels.co.uk**

FURTHER AFIELD Bowfield Hotel €€€€

*Howwood, Renfrewshire, PA9 1DB **Tel** 01505 705225 **Fax** 01505 705230 **Rooms** 23*

The Bowfield is a country retreat popular with international and local visitors. Accommodation is of a superior standard, with rooms individually decorated and beautifully finished. The in-house restaurant offers imaginative, good-quality food, and the service is friendly and informal. **www.bowfieldcountryclub.co.uk**

CENTRAL SCOTLAND

AUCHTERARDER The Gleneagles Hotel €€€€€

*A9, Auchterarder, Perthshire, PH3 1NF **Tel** 01764 662231 **Fax** 01764 662134 **Rooms** 232*

This world-renowned château-style resort hotel with high standards of service, cuisine and amenities boasts a championship golf course and state-of-the-art spa and leisure facilities. It is well equipped to cater even for the most demanding of guests. Popular with both business travellers and families. **www.gleneagles.com**

BALQUHIDDER Monachyle Mhor €€€€€

*Balquhidder, Lochearnhead, Perthshire, FK19 8PQ **Tel** 01877 384622 **Fax** 01877 384305 **Rooms** 11*

A beautiful family-run hotel situated in the heart of Highland Perthshire, near the picturesque shores of Loch Voil, Monachyle Mhor offers luxury rooms and suites, some with log fires, as well as self-catering cottages. Service is outstanding. The hotel also features an award-winning restaurant. **www.mhor.net**

BIRNAM Waterbury House €€

*Murthly Terrace, Dunkeld, PH8 0BG **Tel** 01350 727324 **Fax** 01350 727023 **Rooms** 3*

This friendly, family-run guesthouse is on the main street of Birnam village. Not all rooms are en suite, but all are furnished and decorated to a high standard. The lounge has its own well-stocked bar and is where good home-cooked meals are served. Full Scottish and continental breakfasts are available. **www.waterbury.guesthouse.co.uk**

BLAIRGOWRIE Kinloch House €€€€€

*Nr Blairgowrie, Perthshire, PH10 6SG **Tel** 01250 884237 **Fax** 01250 884333 **Rooms** 18*

A family-run country-house hotel set in a scenic locale at the end of a remote lochside road, Kinloch House offers a warm and welcoming atmosphere. Rooms and suites are comfortable and well equipped with modern facilities. Amenities include a sauna and spa, as well as a restaurant serving good food. **www.kinlochhouse.com**

CALLANDER Leny House €€€

*Leny Estate, Callander, Perthshire, FK17 8HA **Tel** 01877 331078 **Rooms** 3*

This delightful B&B is a great base for exploring the Trossachs. Originally from the 16th century, the building retains both original features and Victorian finishes. Luxurious inside, it offers rooms and self-catering lodges and cottages. Ideally located for outdoor activities such as golf, cycling, fishing and watersports. **www.lenyestate.com**

CARNOUSTIE Duntrune House €€

*Carnoustie, nr Dundee, DD4 0PJ **Tel** 01382 350239 **Fax** 01382 350239 **Rooms** 4*

This lovely house set in a quiet wooded area close to Dundee has been decorated, furnished and finished to a very high standard. An excellent full Scottish breakfast is served, and dinner is also available if pre-arranged. An ideal base from which to explore this beautiful area. Free parking on the road. **www.duntrunehouse.co.uk**

CRIEFF Crieff Hydro   €€€€€

*Crieff, Perthshire, PH7 3LQ **Tel** 01764 651602 **Fax** 01764 653087 **Rooms** 254*

The Crieff Hydro is a vast family-run hotel with many amenities. You may choose to stay in the main building or in one of many self-catering lodges in the grounds. Either way, there is something for everyone here, which is why it is such a popular choice for families. There are also various options for dining. **www.crieffhydro.com**

CUPAR Peat Inn €€€€

*Peat Inn, nr Cupar, Fife, KY15 5H **Tel** 01334 840206 **Fax** 01334 840530 **Rooms** 8*

Located a short distance from St Andrews and several sightseeing attractions, the relaxed and informal Peat Inn is less a hotel and more a restaurant with rooms. It boasts elegantly decorated luxury suites. The renowned restaurant serves mouth-watering dishes accompanied by an extensive selection of wines. **www.thepeatinn.co.uk**

DOLLAR Castle Campbell  €€

*11 Bridge Street, Dollar, Clackmannanshire, FK14 7DE **Tel** 01259 742519 **Fax** 01259 743742 **Rooms** 9*

This simple but dignified Georgian building set in the town centre has spacious rooms, all with en-suite bathrooms. Modern amenities include colour TVs, tea and coffee makers and telephones. Castle Campbell is a good base from which to enjoy walks in the surrounding countryside. **www.castle-campbell.co.uk**

FAIRMONT ST ANDREWS St Andrews Bay Hotel   ©©©©©
St Andrews Bay, St Andrews, Fife, KY16 8PN **Tel** *01334 837000* **Fax** *01334 471115* **Rooms** *209*

A short distance from St Andrews, this resort hotel has everything one could look for: wonderful views, excellent facilities and an impressive standard of accommodation and service. It also boasts a conference centre for business travellers, as well as two world-class golf courses and a relaxing spa. **www.fairmont.com/standrews**

FALKLAND Edenshead Stables   ©©
Gateside, nr Cupar, KY14 7ST **Tel** *01337 868500* **Fax** *01337 868500* **Rooms** *3*

This is a stunning and charming five-star guesthouse set in three acres of woodland and mature gardens. All the rooms are en suite and have been beautifully furnished and decorated. Guests can relax in a separate lounge with patio doors leading out to the garden. Superb Scottish breakfasts are served. **www.edensheadstables.com**

GLENROTHES Balbirnie   ©©©©
Balbirnie Park, Markinch, Glenrothes, Fife, KY7 6NE **Tel** *01592 610066* **Fax** *01592 610529* **Rooms** *30*

Family-run and frequently acknowledged for its quality of service and dining, this elegant Georgian mansion evokes an air of hedonism. The ambience is luxurious and proves popular with both corporate and leisure travellers. The rooms are opulent and comfortable. **www.balbirnie.co.uk**

INVERSNAID Inversnaid Lodge   ©
Inversnaid, Aberfoyle, Stirlingshire, FK8 3TU **Tel** *01877 386254* **Fax** *01877 386254* **Rooms** *9*

Located on the eastern shores of Loch Lomond, this was once a hunting lodge for the Dukes of Montrose. These days Inversnaid Lodge offers photographic workshops and accommodation in simple, cottage-style bedrooms. The surrounding countryside includes a nature reserve. Good value for money. **www.inversnaidphoto.com**

KIRKCUDBRIGHT Gladstone House   ©©
48 High Street, Kirkcudbright, Kirkcudbrightshire, DG6 4JX **Tel** *01577 331734* **Fax** *01577 331734* **Rooms** *3*

This stylish B&B is located within an attractive Georgian townhouse. The interior is light and airy, and the hosts are friendly and welcoming. Gladstone House offers a good standard of accommodation and serves delicious Scottish breakfasts. **www.kirkcudbrightgladstone.com**

KIRRIEMUIR Falls of Holm   ©
Lower Welton Farm, nr Kirriemuir, Angus, DD8 5HY **Tel** *01575 575867* **Fax** *01575 575867* **Rooms** *3*

A lovely house built from local stone and set in a delightful rural location, the Falls of Holm has been finished to a very high standard, and the accommodation is comfortable and welcoming; all three rooms are en suite. There is much to do in this area for those who like exploring the outdoors. **www.fallsofholm.com**

LUNDIN LINKS Sandilands   ©©©
20 Leven Road, Lundin Links, KY8 6AH **Tel** *01333 329881* **Fax** *01333 329881* **Rooms** *3*

Located in the picturesque village of Lundin Links, the Sandilands is a convenient base for exploring the East Neuk of Fife. The tastefully decorated rooms are comfortable and en suite. The hosts are accomplished and friendly. Scottish and continental breakfasts are served, with a vegetarian option also available.

PITLOCHRY East Haugh Country House   ©©©
Pitlochry, Perthshire, PH16 5TE **Tel** *01796 473121* **Fax** *01796 472473* **Rooms** *13*

The East Haugh is a lovely family-owned and run hotel. The beautifully appointed rooms are very comfortable and tastefully furnished. Guests can choose to dine in the conservatory bar or at the restaurant, both of which serve the best local produce in menus that have been skilfully composed. **www.easthaugh.co.uk**

SALINE, DUNFERMLINE Kirklands House   ©©
Bridge Street, Dunfermline, KY12 9TS **Tel** *01383 852737* **Rooms** *2*

This beautiful 1832 home is surrounded by stunning gardens. Every amenity is provided to make your stay a pleasure. The standard of hospitality is high: the owners are proud of their home and enjoy sharing it with their guests. Full Scottish breakfast served, and there are also many good eateries nearby. **www.kirklandshouseandgarden.co.uk**

ST ANDREWS Old Course   ©©©©©
Old Station Road, St Andrews, Fife, KT16 9SP **Tel** *01334 474371* **Fax** *01334 477668* **Rooms** *134*

Situated on the edge of town, this hotel boasts splendid views over the Old Course, the legendary sea links. As well as glamorous and stylish public areas, the hotel has luxurious rooms and suites, decorated in a contemporary style. Specially designed rooms for disabled guests are also available. **www.oldcoursehotel.co.uk**

ST FILLANS Four Seasons   ©©
St Fillans, Perthshire, PH6 2NF **Tel** *01764 685333* **Fax** *01764 685444* **Rooms** *12*

Set in stunning countryside, with striking views of Loch Earn, this small hotel has comfortable rooms with en-suite facilities. Those who want a more intimate feel might prefer to stay in one of the six self-catering log cabins in the grounds. A cosy retreat for a romantic getaway. **www.thefourseasonshotel.co.uk**

STANLEY Ballathie House Hotel   ©©©
Kinclaven, nr Stanley, PH1 4QN **Tel** *01250 883268* **Fax** *01250 883396* **Rooms** *42*

The Ballathie is a relaxing and comfortable country hotel on the River Tay. The rooms are decorated and furnished to a high standard, as are the public areas and lounges. There is a cosy bar where excellent light meals are served, or you can eat in the more formal dining room. A great base to explore the countryside. **www.ballathiehousehotel.com**

Key to Price Guide *see p168* **Key to Symbols** *see back cover flap*

STRATHKINNES Mansedale House £

35 Main Street, Strathkinnes, St Andrews, Fife, KY16 9RY **Tel** *01334 850850* **Rooms** *5*

At this small B&B, tucked away in a small village 5 km (3 miles) from St Andrews, you are promised a warm welcome from owners Douglas and Elaine. The house itself is a former manse built in 1830, with a picturesque courtyard and tranquil garden. Rooms have exposed beams and stone walls, but also all mod-cons. **www.mansedalehouse.co.uk**

TIGHNABRUAICH An Lochan ⬛ £££

Shore Road, Tighnabruaich, Argyll, PA21 2BE **Tel** *01700 811239* **Fax** *01700 811300* **Rooms** *11*

The Royal is a family-run hotel offering comfortable and spacious accommodation. The welcome is warm, and the service friendly and efficient. At the on-site restaurant, residents can choose between formal and informal dining, safe in the knowledge that the quality of the food and ingredients is equally high. **www.anlochan.co.uk**

YARROW Tibbie Shiels Inn ⬛⬛⬛ £

St Mary's Loch, Selkirk, Selkirkshire, TD7 5LH **Tel** *01750 422231* **Fax** *01750 42302* **Rooms** *5*

Once a hostelry favoured by Sir Walter Scott, this 18th-century inn on the shores of St Mary's Loch remains a popular place to eat and stay while in the area. The hotel has several original features and is simply furnished, with clean rooms as well as camping facilities. Good food, warm service and a genuine welcome. **www.tibbieshiels.com**

THE HIGHLANDS AND ISLANDS

ABERDEEN Udny Arms ⬛⬛⬛ ££

Main Street, Newburgh, Ellen, Aberdeenshire, AB41 6BL **Tel** *01358 789444* **Fax** *01358 789012* **Rooms** *26*

Comfortable and traditional, the Udny Arms has bright and cheerful en-suite bedrooms. Although these are decorated with antique furnishings, they offer many modern conveniences. Located close to three championship golf courses, the hotel also offers facilities for biking and archery. **www.udnyarmshotel.com**

ABERDEEN Mercure Ardoe House Hotel £££

South Deeside Road, Aberdeen, Aberdeenshire, AB12 5YP **Tel** *01224 860600* **Fax** *01224 861283* **Rooms** *109*

Located 5 km (3 miles) from the city centre, this is one of Aberdeen's best hotels. Rooms are luxurious and lavish, but tastefully decorated. The suites have four-poster beds, and all rooms offer spectacular views of the countryside. Amenities include Jacuzzi baths, tennis courts and beauty salons. **www.mercure.com**

ABERDEEN Marcliffe at Pitfodels £££££

N Deeside Road, Pitfodels, Aberdeenshire, AB15 9YA **Tel** *01224 861000* **Fax** *01224 868860* **Rooms** *42*

Situated on the outskirts of the city, this upmarket hotel has beautiful interiors and a warm and welcoming ambience. The stylish bedrooms offer en-suite facilities and many other amenities. The conservatory is bright and airy, and the restaurant menus feature typically Aberdonian quality produce. **www.marcliffe.com**

ABERDEENSHIRE Craigellachie Hotel £££

Craigellachie, Speyside, Banfshire, AB38 9SR **Tel** *01340 881204* **Fax** *01340 881253* **Rooms** *26*

Located in the beautiful Craigellachie village next to the Fiddich and Spey rivers, this hotel has an old country-house feel, as well as all the modern comforts. The Spey Walk in front of the hotel provides impressive views over forest, river and mountains. **www.oxfordhotelsandinns.com**

ABERFELDY Farleyer Restaurant and Rooms ⬛⬛ £££

Aberfeldy, Perthshire, PH15 2JE **Tel** *01887 820332* **Fax** *01887 829879* **Rooms** *6*

This restaurant with rooms is situated in an attractive house in a beautiful countryside setting on the outskirts of Aberfeldy. Rooms are well appointed, with thoughtful extras that add to the pleasant experience. Appetizing food is served in relaxed and modern surroundings. **www.farleyerlodge.co.uk**

ACHILTIBUIE Summer Isles ⬛ £££

Achiltibuie, Ross-shire, IV26 2YG **Tel** *01854 622282* **Fax** *01854 622251* **Rooms** *13*

A remote and picturesque setting overlooking the Summer Isles makes this charming, low-key place an idyllic retreat. The hotel interior is sophisticated; the rooms are pleasant and well appointed. The restaurant serves food made with locally grown ingredients. **www.summerisleshotel.co.uk**

ARISAIG Old Library Lodge ⬛ ££

Road to the Isles, Arisaig, Perthshire, PH39 4NH **Tel** *01687 450651* **Fax** *01687 450219* **Rooms** *6*

This modest and well-run restaurant with rooms is set on the Road to the Isles. Housed in a 200-year-old former stable, the Old Library Lodge offers great views and comfortably furnished rooms. Dining here is a rich culinary experience, with five choices for each course. **www.oldlibrary.co.uk**

AULDEARN Boath House ⬛ ££££

Auldearn, nr Nairn, Inverness-shire, IV12 5TW **Tel** *01667 454896* **Fax** *01667 455469* **Rooms** *6*

Known as the "jewel in the Highland crown", this mansion is a must-see attraction. Rooms are elegantly furnished with antiques, works of art and modern amenities, and they all offer excellent views of the estate and gardens. Boath House also hosts a beauty salon and spa and serves award-winning cuisine. **www.boath-house.com**

AVIEMORE Ardlogie Guest House

Dalfaber Road, Aviemore, PH22 1PU **Tel** *01479 810747* **Rooms** *3*

A friendly family-run guesthouse on a quiet residential street with stunning views of the nearby Cairngorms. The Ardlogie is particularly suited to walkers, since there is much to explore in the area. Rooms are well equipped and comfortable. The hosts are friendly and welcoming and serve a superb Scottish breakfast. **www.ardlogie.co.uk**

BALLATER Morvada House

28 Braemar Road, Ballater, Royal Deeside, Aberdeenshire, AB35 5RL **Tel** *01339 756334* **Rooms** *6*

This is a traditional Victorian villa set in the beautiful village of Ballater. The rooms are decorated to a very high standard. All are en suite and have modern amenities. There is an excellent full Scottish and continental breakfast, available with early serving if pre-arranged. The hosts are most welcoming. A great place to explore the area. **www.morvada.com**

BALLATER Balgonie Country House

Braemar Place, Ballater, Royal Deeside, Aberdeenshire, AB35 5NQ **Tel** *01339 755482* **Fax** *01339 755482* **Rooms** *9*

The friendly, welcoming hosts play an important role in the success of this secluded hotel, which is a great place for a relaxing break. The interior is chic, and the rooms are decorated in a blend of traditional and contemporary styles; most overlook the golf course. Activities such as walks, biking and fishing are available. **www.balgonie-hotel.co.uk**

BALLATER Darroch Learg

Braemar Road, Ballater, Royal Deeside, Aberdeenshire, AB35 5UX **Tel** *01339 755443* **Fax** *01339 755252* **Rooms** *17*

Set on a hill in Ballater, amid attractive gardens, this charming Victorian hotel offers splendid views of Lochnagar. The accommodation is supremely cosy and comfortable: some rooms have canopied or four-poster beds. The cooking in the in-house restaurant is highly skilled, using the best local produce. **www.darrochlearg.co.uk**

BEAULY Lovat Arms Hotel

Beauly, Inverness-shire, IV4 7BS **Tel** *01463 782313* **Fax** *01463 782862* **Rooms** *22*

This family-run traditional hotel is more than 200 years old. Rooms are all en suite and equipped with modern facilities such as TV, coffee makers and more. It has a bar and two popular restaurants where good Scottish fare is served by friendly staff. Plenty of golfing and fishing opportunities are available nearby. **www.lovatarms.com**

BLACK ISLE Kincraig House

Invergordon, Ross-shire, IV18 0LF **Tel** *01349 852587* **Fax** *01349 852193* **Rooms** *15*

Many parts of this country house date back several centuries, giving it a great historic feel. All rooms are en suite, and many have views over the gardens and the Cromarty Firth. All the public areas are characterful and welcoming. Good food and fine Highland hospitality complete the pleasant experience. **www.kincraig-castle-hotel.co.uk**

BRAEMAR Schiehallion House

10 Glenshee Road, Braemar, AB35 5YQ **Tel** *01339 741679* **Rooms** *5*

The commitment to quality and to ensuring a high standard of experience for all guests is evident at this attractive B&B. Rooms are all well equipped and attractively furnished. Some are en suite. A full Scottish breakfast is served, with early serving available if pre-arranged. Packed lunches may be prepared by prior booking. **www.schiehallionhouse.com**

BUCKIE Rosemount B&B

Buckie, Banffshire, AB56 1ER **Tel** *01542 833434* **Rooms** *3*

This grand Victorian townhouse was built in 1890. It overlooks the Moray Firth and is at the beginning of the Speyside Way walking route. Sit with a dram whilst enjoying the sunset or watching for dolphins. Some rooms have sea views and fireplaces. **www.rosemountbb.co.uk**

CLACHAN SEIL Willowburn Hotel

Seil Island, nr Oban, Argyll, PA34 4TJ **Tel** *01852 300276* **Rooms** *7*

Located just over Clachan Bridge, this delightful family-run hotel is housed in a white-washed cottage. It offers magnificent views of the surrounding countryside. The decor is simple, and the rooms are well equipped. The on-site restaurant serves good food made with locally sourced produce. **www.willowburn.co.uk**

CRINAN Crinan Hotel

Crinan, Lochgilphead, Argyll, PA31 8SR **Tel** *01546 830261* **Fax** *01546 830292* **Rooms** *20*

A popular place from where to enjoy the panoramic views over Loch Fyne and the Jura Sound. The distinctive white-washed building accommodates a bar and restaurant where seafood is a renowned speciality. The bedrooms are simply but tastefully decorated. A friendly and bustling place. **www.crinanhotel.com**

DRUMNADROCHIT The Drumnadrochit Hotel

Loch Ness Exhibition Centre, Inverness, IV63 6TU **Tel** *01456 450218* **Rooms** *29*

The Drum, as it is affectionately known, is a family-run hotel on the northern shores of Loch Ness. It offers a comfortable lounge for relaxing in and a stylish bar. The hotel can arrange Loch Ness package trips and also has good facilities for disabled guests. **www.lochness.com**

DUNKELD The Pend

5 Brae Street, Dunkeld, Perthshire, PH8 0BA **Tel** *01350 727586* **Fax** *01350 727173* **Rooms** *3*

High-quality accommodation is on offer at this quiet Georgian townhouse, located just off Dunkeld's high street. The interiors are attractively furnished with many antiques and period pieces. The welcoming hosts offer the best in Scottish hospitality and serve imaginative and superbly prepared dishes. **www.thepend.com**

Key to Price Guide *see p168* **Key to Symbols** *see back cover flap*

DUNKELD Kinnaird

Kinnaird Estate, nr Dunkeld, Perthshire, PH8 0LB **Tel** *01796 482440* **Fax** *01796 482289* **Rooms** *9*

This charming country house is situated on an enormous Tayside sporting estate. The setting is tranquil, and the amenities are extensive. Kinnaird features elegantly furnished rooms with en-suite facilities, as well as self-catering cottages. Tennis courts and a croquet lawn are available for the more active guests. **www.kinnairdestate.com**

ERISKA Isle of Eriska Hotel

Ledaig, nr Oban, Argyll, PA37 1SD **Tel** *01631 720371* **Fax** *01631 720531* **Rooms** *17*

The Isle of Eriska Hotel is a luxurious, romantic hideaway located within tranquil and peaceful surroundings. Accommodation at this family-run country estate is offered within individually decorated rooms and in private cottages, all equipped with an extensive range of modern amenities. **www.eriska-hotel.co.uk**

FORRES Cluny Bank Hotel

69 St Leonard's Road, Forres, Inverness-shire, IV36 1DW **Tel** *01309 674304* **Fax** *01309 671400* **Rooms** *10*

Located in a quiet residential part of Forres, this historic, family-run hotel retains many of its original features. Bedrooms are comfortable and tastefully decorated, while public rooms are welcoming and airy. Staff can arrange outdoor pursuits such as golfing, fishing, cycling and more. **www.clunybankhotel.co.uk**

FORT WILLIAM The Grange

Grange Road, Fort William, Perthshire, PH33 6JF **Tel** *01397 705516* **Fax** *01397 701595* **Rooms** *4*

Guests at this historic B&B can enjoy lovely views across Loch Linnhe. Skilfully and lovingly restored, The Grange is run by welcoming hosts. The interior is beautifully decorated with attention to detail, and rooms are individually furnished, with antique beds and lavish en-suite bathrooms. Hearty breakfasts. **www.grangefortwilliam.com**

FORT WILLIAM The Inn at Ardgour

Nr Fort William, Inverness-shire, PH33 7AA **Tel** *01855 841225* **Fax** *01855 841214* **Rooms** *12*

All bedrooms, the restaurant and the bar in this beautiful family-run inn have stunning views across Loch Linnhe, towards the Great Glen. Rooms are well appointed, and the facilities are geared for those who pursue outdoor activities – drying facilities are available, for example. The friendly bar and restaurant serve good food. **www.ardgour.biz**

FORT WILLIAM Ashburn House

4 Archintore Road, Fort William, Perthshire, PH33 6RQ **Tel** *01397 706000* **Fax** *01397 702024* **Rooms** *7*

A traditional Highland B&B overlooking Loch Linnhe, Ashburn House is a short walk to the town centre. Its charming owners extend a typical Scottish welcome to their guests. The bedrooms of this Victorian house are attractively decorated and well equipped to ensure a comfortable stay. Hearty breakfasts. **www.ashburnhouse.co.uk**

FORT WILLIAM The Moorings

Banavie, Fort William, PH33 7LY **Tel** *01397 772797* **Fax** *01397 772441* **Rooms** *27*

The Moorings is situated on the banks of the Caledonian Canal. All rooms are individually designed and en suite, and many have panoramic views of Ben Nevis and Aonach Mor. The on-site Jacobean Restaurant serves good food that features locally sourced and skilfully prepared produce. **www.moorings-fortwilliam.co.uk**

INVERNESS Water's Edge

Canonbury Terrace, Fortrose, IV10 8TT **Tel** *01381 621202* **Fax** *08704 296806* **Rooms** *3*

Water's Edge has spectacular views over the sea and towards Culloden, and has access to a small private beach at the bottom of the garden. Each refurbished bedroom is individual in character and has antique furnishings and lovely views, sometimes of dolphins. **www.watersedge.uk.com**

INVERNESS Glenmoriston Town House

20 Ness Bank, Inverness, Inverness-shire, IV2 4SF **Tel** *01463 223777* **Fax** *01463 712378* **Rooms** *30*

This tastefully and luxuriously upgraded townhouse overlooks the River Ness and is located a few minutes' walk from the city centre. Rooms are furnished in a contemporary style and feature a wide range of modern amenities. The Glenmoriston boasts an award-winning French restaurant. **www.glenmoristontownhouse.com**

ISLE OF HARRIS Ceol Na Mara

7 Direcleit, Isle of Harris, HS3 3DP **Tel** *01859 502464* **Rooms** *4*

This cosy, modernized B&B offers great comfort to visitors. All of the rooms have views over Loch Kindeberg, and there is a pleasant wooden terrace for guests to enjoy on sunny days. All rooms are en suite and fitted with fridges and flat-screen TVs. Free Wi-Fi is also available. **www.ceolnamara.com**

ISLE OF IONA Argyll Hotel

Isle of Iona, Argyll and Bute, PA76 6SJ **Tel** *01681 700334* **Fax** *01681 700510* **Rooms** *16*

A relaxing retreat with views over the Sound of Iona, the traditional Argyll Hotel offers a comfortable, welcoming ambience, enhanced by cosy log fires. The bright and cheerful rooms are simply decorated and have a range of modern facilities. The hotel also features a sunny conservatory and serves good food. **www.argyllhoteliona.co.uk**

ISLE OF LEWIS Galson Farm

South Galson, Isle of Lewis, Outer Hebrides, HS2 0SH **Tel** *01851 850492* **Fax** *01851 850492* **Rooms** *4*

Set in a beautiful location on the west coast of Lewis, this charming 18th-century farmhouse is a working farm, with striking views of the surrounding area. The simple, homely accommodation includes a separate dormitory with eight bunks. Good home cooking with interesting vegetarian options is on offer. **www.galsonfarm.co.uk**

ISLE OF MULL Druimard Country House

Dervaig, Isle of Mull, Argyll, PA75 6QW **Tel** *01688 400345* **Fax** *01688 400345* **Rooms** *7*

Welcoming and cosy, this Victorian hotel is located in a quiet Glenside setting. Rooms are tastefully decorated and furnished with modern amenities. Britain's smallest professional theatre, the Mull Little Theatre, is situated within the hotel's grounds, with performances running from April to October. **www.druimardmull.co.uk**

ISLE OF MULL Glengorm Castle

Tobermory, Isle of Mull, Argyll, PA75 6QE **Tel** *01688 302321* **Fax** *01688 302738* **Rooms** *5*

Situated on the northern tip of Mull, this 1860 castle is occupied all year round by the owners and their family. Guests can opt for either B&B-style accommodation or a choice of self-catering cottages on the castle grounds. Evening meals are available by pre-arrangement. A superb place to enjoy the Hebrides. **www.glengormcastle.co.uk**

ISLE OF SKYE Duisdale

Sleat, Isle Ornsay, Isle of Skye, Inverness-shire, IV43 8QW **Tel** *01471 833202* **Fax** *01471 833404* **Rooms** *17*

Set on a hill, with magnificent views of the Sound of Sleat, Duisdale is a friendly establishment housed within a flamboyantly decorated Victorian building with lots of character. Rooms are spacious and comfortably furnished. The hotel also offers delicious food and lovely gardens. **www.duisdale.com**

ISLE OF SKYE Three Chimneys

Colbost, Dunvegan, Isle of Skye, Inverness-shire, IV55 8ZT **Tel** *01470 511258* **Fax** *01470 511358* **Rooms** *6*

Arguably the finest restaurant with rooms in Scotland, this intimate hotel is frequently recognized for the excellence of its cooking and the hospitality of its owners. The retreat's spectacular location makes for a truly memorable visit, and the rooms are modern and luxurious. **www.threechimneys.co.uk**

KILLIECRANKIE Killiecrankie Hotel

Killiecrankie, nr Pitlochry, Perthshire, PH16 5LE **Tel** *01796 473220* **Fax** *01796 472451* **Rooms** *10*

A relaxing and informal hotel located by the scenic wooded cliffs of the Killiecrankie Pass, a nature reserve run by the Royal Society for the Protection of Birds. The decor is stylish and bright, the accommodation comfortable and spacious. The Killicrankie also offers a series of two-day gourmet breaks. **www.killiecrankiehotel.co.uk**

KINGUSSIE The Hermitage

Spey Street, Kingussie, PH21 1HN **Tel** *01540 662137* **Fax** *01540 662177* **Rooms** *5*

This friendly guesthouse is comfortable, with plenty of character. All rooms are en suite, well furnished and attractively decorated. Evening meals are available, including a four-course menu that must be booked in advance. The chef uses fresh local produce, and the Scottish breakfast is excellent. **www.thehermitage-scotland.com**

KINGUSSIE The Cross

Tweed Mill Brae, Ardbroilach Rd, Kingussie, Perthshire, PH21 1TC **Tel** *01540 661166* **Fax** *01540 661080* **Rooms** *8*

The Cross is a highly acclaimed restaurant with rooms located in a converted tweed mill near the Cairngorms. The smartly refurbished and attractively decorated interior is light and bright. The hotel makes an ideal base for those who wish to explore this stunning area. Good food and an excellent wine list are available. **www.thecross.co.uk**

KIRRIEMUIR Thrums Hotel

Bank Street, Kirriemuir, Angus, DD8 4BE **Tel** *01575 572758* **Rooms** *9*

This small hotel, which sits in the heart of Kirriemuir, offers single, twin, double and family rooms. All are clean and comfortable, with TVs and tea- and coffee-making facilities. There's a lounge bar as well as a dining room, both of which serve meals made from local produce. **www.thrumshotel.co.uk**

LOCHINVER The Albannach

Lochinver, Sutherland, Inverness-shire, IV27 4LP **Tel** *01571 844407* **Fax** *01571 844285* **Rooms** *5*

Set on a hill on the outskirts of Lochinver, this hotel is ideal for those who enjoy the finer things in life, including superb views of the countryside. Cooking is also outstanding, innovative and fresh. Hosts Colin and Lesley are welcoming and hospitable. **www.thealbannach.co.uk**

LOCHRANZA Apple Lodge

Lochranza, Isle of Arran, Bute, KA27 8HJ **Tel** *01770 830229* **Fax** *01770 830229* **Rooms** *4*

Close to the Kintyre ferry, with beautiful views over the nearby castle, this charming guesthouse is an excellent base for exploring the sights of Arran. Bedrooms are prettily floral, and several are located in a self-contained cottage annexe. Good home-cooked food is served in the restaurant. **applelodge@easicom.com**

MUIR OF ORD The Dower House

Highfield, Muir of Ord, Inverness-shire, IV6 7XN **Tel** *01463 870090* **Fax** *01463 870090* **Rooms** *5*

This attractive 18th-century hotel is one of the best-kept secrets in the Highlands. It offers tastefully decorated, pleasant rooms equipped with modern amenities. The restaurant is renowned for its appetizing home-cooked meals, which emphasize the versatility of good local produce. **www.thedowerhouse.co.uk**

NORTH CONNEL Blarcreen House

Oban, Argyll, PA37 1RG **Tel** *01631 750272* **Fax** *01631 750132* **Rooms** *3*

Rooms at this lovely house on the shore of Loch Etive are tastefully and elegantly furnished. The Blarcreen is only 16 km (10 miles) from Oban, which makes it a comfortable base from which to explore the wonderful local area. Superb Scottish breakfasts are served. Dinner must be pre-arranged. No children under 16. **www.blarcreenhouse.com**

Key to Price Guide *see p168* **Key to Symbols** *see back cover flap*

OBAN Lerags House

Lerags, nr Oban, Argyll, PA34 4SE **Tel** *01631 563381* **Rooms** *6*

Located on the outskirts of Oban, this lovely country house is run by caring and welcoming hosts. As well as clean, simply furnished bedrooms with modern facilities, it provides a self-catering cottage. The restaurant serves tasty food, made from local produce. Scenic surroundings complete the experience. **www.leragshouse.com**

ORKNEY Castle Hill

Evie, Orkney, KW17 2PJ **Tel** *01856 751228* **Rooms** *4*

This modern home has a welcoming lounge, spacious rooms with sweeping views and immaculate bathrooms. The owners have an eco-friendly policy and use only locally sourced food, including plenty of fresh fish. They have their own smokery, and dinner is available on request. **www.castlehillorkney.co.uk**

ORKNEY Foveran

St Ola, Kirkwall, Orkney, KW15 1SF **Tel** *01856 872389* **Fax** *01856 876430* **Rooms** *8*

A fine, family-run hotel with splendid views over the Scapa Flow, the Foveran has been tastefully refurbished to a high standard. Offering superb cooking and pleasant accommodation, it is a wonderful base from which to explore these magical islands. **www.foveranhotel.co.uk**

PITLOCHRY Atholl Palace

Pitlochry, Perthshire, PH16 5LY **Tel** *01796 472400* **Fax** *01796 473036* **Rooms** *108*

This grandiose hotel is an excellent example of Scottish baronial architecture. The accommodation is on a large scale, with spacious bedrooms and vast public areas. The Atholl Palace features a wide range of leisure and spa facilities, as well as varying dining options to suit all tastes. **www.athollpalace.com**

PLOCKTON Plockton Hotel

Harbour Street, Plockton, Ross-shire, IV52 8TN **Tel** *01599 544274* **Fax** *01599 544475* **Rooms** *14*

Comfortable and tastefully furnished, the Plockton is set across the waterfront, with breathtaking views of the countryside. The bedrooms are stylishly simple, with immaculate en-suite facilities; many overlook the loch and the mountains. Good food made with local produce is served. **www.plocktonhotel.co.uk**

PORTREE Cuillin Hills

Portree, Isle of Skye, IV51 9QU **Tel** *01478 612003* **Fax** *01478 613092* **Rooms** *27*

Located on an elevated position that affords great views of the hills, this is a very comfortable and well-appointed hotel offering fine dining. The cooking is traditional and uses good local produce. All rooms are en suite and furnished and decorated to a superior standard. Welcoming staff. **www.cuillinhills-hotel-skye.co.uk**

SHETLAND Gord B&B

Fetlar, Shetland, ZE2 9DJ **Tel** *01957 733227* **Fax** *01957 733227* **Rooms** *2*

This family home set in a rural location 6.5 km (4 miles) from the ferries of Yell and Unst offers genuinely warm island hospitality. All rooms have superb views over the Wick of Tresta and en-suite facilities. Guests here can enjoy a particularly high standard of home cooking using locally sourced produce.

SHETLAND Westayre B&B

Muckle Roe, Brae, Shetland, ZE2 9QW **Tel** *01806 522368* **Rooms** *2*

This is a modern family home located on a working croft. It is close to the village of Brae, which has excellent amenities, including a swimming pool. Accommodation is of a very high standard, and both rooms are en suite. Guests can spend their time here relaxing, birdwatching, walking or painting. **www.westayre.shetland.co.uk**

STRATHPEFFER Ben Wyvis Hotel

Strathpeffer, Ross-shire, IV14 9DN **Tel** *08709 506264* **Fax** *01997 421228* **Rooms** *92*

The Ben Wyvis is located in tranquil Ross-shire, overlooking Strathpeffer. The architecture is particularly attractive, and the hotel is comfortable and welcoming. A range of rooms is available; all are well equipped and attractively decorated. There is a bar and lounge area, as well as a restaurant serving good food. **www.crerarhotels.com**

STRONTIAN Kilcamb Lodge

Strontian, Argyll, PH36 4HY **Tel** *01967 402257* **Fax** *01967 402041* **Rooms** *12*

This elegant country house located on the Ardnamurchan peninsula is a lovely place to relax and enjoy the remarkable views over the winding sea loch. The warm welcome from the charming hosts, the excellent food and the intimate ambience complete the pleasant experience. **www.kilcamblodge.co.uk**

TORLUNDY Inverlochy Castle

Torlundy, Fort William, Perthshire, PH33 6SN **Tel** *01397 702177* **Fax** *01397 702953* **Rooms** *17*

A grand, luxurious castle set amid beautiful grounds on the outskirts of Fort William, Inverlochy Castle offers high standards of food, accommodation and service. The interior is decorated in a traditional, classic style. Fishing, tennis and croquet facilities are available. Dining here is a truly memorable experience. **www.inverlochycastlehotel.com**

ULLAPOOL Tanglewood House

Ullapool, Ross-shire, IV26 2TB **Tel** *01854 612059* **Rooms** *3*

This modern, highly individual house commands panoramic views of Loch Broom from its large, picturesque windows. The hotel offers tastefully furnished and extremely comfortable rooms, and the restaurant serves imaginative and innovative cuisine. **www.tanglewoodhouse.co.uk**

WHERE TO EAT

Scotland's restaurant scene has moved far from its once-dismal reputation. This is partly due to an influx of foreign chefs and cooking styles. You can now sample a wide range of international cuisine throughout Scotland, with the greatest choice in Edinburgh and Glasgow. Home-grown restaurateurs have also risen to the challenge of re-deeming Scottish food, and the indigenous cooking has improved beyond all recognition in the last

Ryan's Bar in Edinburgh

decade. You can eat extremely well in Scotland regardless of your budget, and at most times of the day in the major towns and cities, although the more rural establishments are less flexible. Affordable, well-prepared but less elaborate food is making a mark in all types of brasseries, restaurants and cafés throughout the country. The restaurant listings on pages 185–97 feature some of the best places to eat. Be aware it is illegal to smoke in any Scottish restaurant, bar or café.

The vast selection of beer and whisky available in a typical Scottish pub

PRICES AND BOOKING

All restaurants are required by law to display their current prices outside the door. These amounts include VAT (value-added tax) at 20 per cent. Any service or cover charge should also be specified.

Wine can be pricey when dining out in Scotland, and extras like coffee and bottled water may be disproportion-ately expensive compared to the cost of the food. Service charges (usually between 10 and 15 per cent) are some-times added automatically to the bill. If service has not been included, you are expected to leave a tip – the amount will depend on the level of service that you have received. The majority of restaurants accept cheques with a cheque guarantee card, or credit cards. Pubs usually prefer cash to cards. It is advisable to book a table

before making a special jour-ney to a restaurant. City restau-rants are very busy, and some of the more renowned estab-lishments can be fully booked up to a month in advance. If you cannot keep a reserva-tion, cancel it by telephone.

BREAKFAST, LUNCH AND DINNER

Traditionally, breakfast in Scotland begins with cereal and milk, followed by bacon, eggs and tomato, and usually black pudding (blood sausage), haggis or white (oatmeal) pudding too. It finishes with toast and mar-malade, and a pot of tea. The alternative is a continental breakfast of black coffee, fruit juice and a croissant or two.

The most popular lunchtime foods are sandwiches, salads, baked potatoes and plough-man's lunches (a roll, hunk of cheese or ham and relishes),

found mainly in pubs. A trad-itional Sunday lunch of roast meat and vegetables is served in some pubs and restaurants.

Grand hotels can offer five or six courses for dinner, but usually there are only three. Dessert is often followed by a range of specialist cheeses and oatcakes. Outside the larger towns and cities, dinner is usually eaten between 6pm and 9pm, and no later. In Scotland lunch is sometimes called "dinner" and the even-ing meal may be called "tea".

AFTERNOON TEA

No visitor should miss the experience of a proper Scottish afternoon tea, which can rival breakfast as the most enjoyable meal of the day. There are hundreds of tearooms all over Scotland, offering a choice of delicious sandwiches and cakes. Dundee Cake, fruit scones and shortbread are particular favourites and are wonderful eaten with a cup of tea. Scotch pancakes swimming in butter are another appetizing speciality.

One of Glasgow's many fashionable Italian restaurants

Fast food in Edinburgh: a fish and chip shop on the Portobello promenade

CHILDREN

Many places now welcome junior diners *(see the listings for details)* and some actively encourage families, at least during the day or early evening. They may offer a separate children's menu, or simply adapt the portions to suit a child's appetite. Some will also provide highchairs. Italian, Spanish, Indian and fast-food restaurants nearly always welcome children, and even pubs, which are now non-smoking, are relaxing their rules and may provide special play areas.

VEGETARIAN FOOD

Britain is ahead of many of its European counterparts in providing vegetarian alternatives to meat dishes, and

The Mitre pub on Edinburgh's Royal Mile

Scotland is no exception. A few of the establishments listed in this guide serve only vegetarian meals, and most cater for non-meat-eaters *(see the listings for an indication of restaurants serving vegetarian dishes)*. Edinburgh and Glasgow have the widest choice, but smaller towns and villages are also beginning to experiment with meat-free dishes. Vegetarians wishing to find a wider choice than is offered by Scottish and English food should try South Indian, Chinese and other ethnic restaurants as they have a tradition of good vegetarian cuisine.

SEAFOOD

With more than 16,000 km (10,000 miles) of coastline, fish and shellfish play an important part in the Scottish diet and economy. North Sea cod, haddock (often smoked as kippers or Arbroath Smokies), herring and mackerel can all be found in shops and restaurants, while farms on the west coast rear much of Scotland's Atlantic salmon and rainbow trout. Lobsters, crabs and prawns are all common in Scottish waters, and more emphasis has also been placed on the cultivation and conservation of natural shellfish stocks including mussels, oysters and scallops.

FAST FOOD

Scotland is rightly famed for its "fish suppers" (fish and chips) and there are many seaside fish bars selling wonderfully fresh fish and chips (French fries). Most also offer chicken suppers. Away from the coast the fish may not be as amazingly fresh, but there are plenty of good places from which to choose.

Visitors will find the usual fast food chains, as well as sandwich bars and "greasy spoon" cafés that serve mainly fried food, particularly good for breakfast.

Taking afternoon tea in Scotland – an elegant and enjoyable pastime

PUBS AND STYLE BARS

Scottish licensing laws are different from the rest of Britain, most apparent in the closing times of pubs and bars. Whereas in England and Wales most places close at 11pm, many in Scotland, particularly in urban centres, stay open until midnight or even 1 or 2am. During the Festival in August *(see pp78–9)*, Edinburgh's bars often do not close until 3am, and some are open 24 hours a day.

While the old-fashioned, dark and occasionally shabby pubs still exist, a new breed of bar has now become popular in Scotland. In the towns and cities, "style" bars have become two-a-penny. They tend to be noisy, with a mostly young clientele. Unlike the traditional pubs, the choice of drink is not limited to a few beers. The emphasis is on variety, with lively happy hours and interesting cocktails.

The Flavours of Scotland

At its best, Scottish food is full of the natural flavour of the countryside. Served with few sauces or spices, its meat is lean and tasty. Beef doesn't get better than Aberdeen Angus, the lamb is full flavoured, and the venison superb. Scottish salmon and trout are renowned, but there are also excellent mussels, lobster and crabs. Wheat does not grow here, so oatcakes and bannocks (flat, round loaves) replace bread. The Scots have a sweet tooth, not just for cakes and shortbread but also for toffee and butterscotch.

Smoked salmon

Purebred Highland cattle grazing the Scottish moors

THE LOWLANDS

The pasturelands of southern Scotland nourish dairy cattle and sheep, producing cheeses such as Bonnet, Bonchester and Galloway Cheddar. To accompany them are summer fruits such as loganberries, tayberries and strawberries that ripen in the Carse of Gowrie beside the River Tay. Oats, the principal cereal, appears in much Scottish cookery, from porridge to oatcakes. Pearl barley is also a staple, used in Scotch broth (made with mutton and vegetables) or in a milk pudding. Oats are also used in the making of haggis, a round sausage of sheep or venison offal – the "chieftain o' the puddin' race", as the poet Robert Burns described it. It is often served with "neeps and tatties" (mashed swede (rutabaga) and potato).

THE HIGHLANDS

From the Highlands comes wonderful game, including grouse, partridge, caper-caillie (a large type of grouse) and deer. Fish are smoked around the coast, the west coast producing kippers, the east coast Finnan haddock, notably Arbroath Smokies. Smoked white fish is the main ingredient of Cullen Skink, a soup served on Burns' Night.

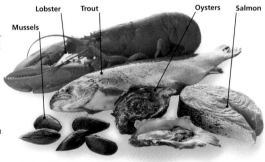

Lobster   Trout   Oysters   Salmon

Mussels

Selection of fresh Scottish fish and seafood

TRADITIONAL SCOTTISH FOOD

Kippers (oak-smoked herrings) are one way to start the day in Scotland, and porridge – traditionally served with salt rather than sugar – is another, although oatcakes or some other kind of griddled scone are usually present. A bowl of porridge would once last all week, just as one-pot Scotch broths bubbled in iron cauldrons over peat fires for days. Sometimes broths were made with kale or lentils, or they might contain an old boiling fowl and leeks, in which case they were known as cock-a-leekie. Any leftover meat went into making stovies, a potato and onion hash. The evening meal in Scotland is traditionally "high tea" taken in the early evening which might start with smoked fish, cold meats and pies, followed by shortbread, fruit cake or drop scones, all washed down with cups of tea.

Oats

Haggis with neeps and tatties
This is the definitive Scottish dish, traditionally served on Burns' Night (25 January).

Choosing a Restaurant

The restaurants in this guide have been selected across a wide price range for their good value, exceptional food and interesting location. Many are housed within recommended hotels. The chart lists the restaurants by region, starting with Edinburgh, and in ascending price order. For hotel listings, see pp168–81.

PRICE DETAILS
For a three-course meal for one, half a bottle of house wine and all unavoidable extra charges such as cover, service and VAT:
£ Under £20
££ £20–£35
£££ £35–£45
££££ £45–£55
£££££ Over £55

EDINBURGH

NEW TOWN The Cambridge Bar £

*20 Young Street, Edinburgh, EH2 4JB **Tel** 0131 226 2120*

The mismatched furniture, stone floors and subdued natural lighting give this bar a cellar-like feel. The clientele varies depending on the time of year and day, ranging from rugby fans to members of the local business community. The cuisine consists mainly of nicely cooked burgers, including the all-important and delicious vegetarian option.

NEW TOWN Karen's Unicorn £

*112 St Stephen Street, Edinburgh, EH3 5AD **Tel** 0131 220 6659*

Located in the elegant New Town, this cosy restaurant offers authentic Chinese cooking in a smart but informal setting. The extensive range of dishes includes chow mein and dim sum. Set menus offer excellent value, and there are also banquet menus for groups. Food can be ordered to take away, and a home delivery service is available.

NEW TOWN Queen Street Café £

*Scottish National Portrait Gallery, 1 Queen Street, Edinburgh, EH2 1JB **Tel** 0131 557 2844*

This delightful coffee shop is housed in the National Portrait Gallery, a magnificent Gothic redstone building dating from 1889. The café provides delicious and imaginative home-made lunches in interesting surroundings, as well as cakes, snacks and beverages. There are lots of vegetarian options. Closes at 5pm, later on Thursdays. Closed 25 & 26 Dec.

NEW TOWN Spice Pavillion £

*31A Dundas Street, Edinburgh, EH3 6QG **Tel** 0131 467 5506*

Occupying the basement of a New Town terrace, this restaurant specializes in the cuisine of northwest India. Dishes such as the popular *madras* (a spicy red curry) are full of flavour, while the atmosphere is both lively and welcoming. Set menus are available, and there is also a special children's menu.

NEW TOWN The Abbotsford ££

*3 Rose Street, Edinburgh, EH2 2PR **Tel** 0131 225 5276*

This is a good, fun place in central Edinburgh, where one can enjoy the lively atmosphere of Rose Street. An institution for several years, The Abbotsford is currently undergoing a range of worthwhile refurbishments. The place to come to for good bar food, a buzzing atmosphere and friendly staff.

NEW TOWN Centotre ££

*103 George Street, Edinburgh, EH2 3ES **Tel** 0131 225 1550*

Fast becoming an established icon in the city, Centotre is primarily an Italian bistro/restaurant where you can sit at the bar to enjoy a glass of good wine, or relax at a table with a light or a more substantial meal. The quality is superb, and the hosts are on hand to ensure you enjoy the experience. A deservedly popular dining destination.

NEW TOWN David Bann Vegetarian Restaurant & Bar ££

*56–58 St Mary's Street, Edinburgh, EH1 1SX **Tel** 0131 556 5888*

The food on chef David Bann's menu offers excellent value for money in a stylish setting just a short stroll from the Royal Mile. The food is eclectic and creative, ranging from curries to risottos and from crêpes to delicious desserts, including a decadent vegan chocolate ice cream. Brunch is served until 5pm on Saturdays and Sundays.

NEW TOWN Fishers in the City ££

*58 Thistle Street, Edinburgh, EH2 1EN **Tel** 0131 225 5109*

The sister restaurant to Fishers in Leith is a more contemporary version of the same. The split-level interior reveals a spacious dining area that still manages to remain cosy and intimate. This is an excellent choice for lovers of fresh, superbly cooked seafood. All dishes are prepared with care and innovative twists. Very popular; booking is essential.

NEW TOWN Henderson's Salad Table ££

*94 Hanover Street, Edinburgh, EH2 1DR **Tel** 0131 225 2131*

Established for 40 years, this vegetarian restaurant is a veritable Edinburgh institution. Open all day, the family-run eatery serves a wide range of snacks and complete meals. Favourites include chunky vegetable soup, baked lasagne, Moroccan stew and spring rolls. Henderson's also offers gluten- and dairy-free specialities.

NEW TOWN Petit Paris

17 Queensferry Street, Edinburgh, EH3 **Tel** *0131 226 1890*

Located on the first floor of the building and previously known as the French Corner Bistro, Petit Paris is now firmly established as one of the best French restaurants in the city. It also offers excellent value for money. The menus and food are firmly in the French tradition, and the staff are all French too, which adds to the authenticity of the place.

NEW TOWN Roti

73 Morrison Street, Edinburgh, EH3 8BU **Tel** *0131 221 9998*

The menus at Roti marry unusual, original Indian recipes with modern French cuisine, using only the best Scottish ingredients. It serves tiffin, for tapas-style sharing, and vegetarian and meat tasting menus are available. The range is complemented by top-class home-made desserts.

NEW TOWN Tigerlily

125 George Street, Edinburgh, EH2 4JN **Tel** *0131 225 5005*

A stylish establishment in Edinburgh's George Street, Tigerlily is a trendy bar, lounge and restaurant where you can enjoy superb cocktails, good food and an excellent atmosphere. The menus are contemporary, taking inspiration from both Europe and Asia and delivering quality fare. The staff are highly polished and friendly.

NEW TOWN Le Café St-Honoré

34 North West Thistle St Lane, Edinburgh, EH2 2ED **Tel** *0131 226 2211*

A traditional French restaurant with a Parisian-style interior, Le Café St-Honoré is located close to one of Edinburgh's main streets, but in a quiet lane where you can leave the traffic and the bustle of the city behind. The food is imaginatively and skilfully cooked, and the staff are friendly and helpful. All in all, a very satisfying experience.

NEW TOWN The Dome

14 George Street, Edinburgh, EH2 2PF **Tel** *0131 624 8624*

Housed in a magnificent building constructed for the Royal College of Physicians in 1775, The Dome incorporates the Grill Room & Bar, where you can have lunch or dinner; a cocktail bar that also serves morning coffee; and the Garden Café, where light lunches and afternoon tea are served alfresco in the courtyard. Closed 1 & 2 Jan; 25 & 26 Dec.

NEW TOWN VinCaffe

11 Multrees Walk, Edinburgh, EH1 3DQ **Tel** *0131 557 0088*

This Italian restaurant and wine bar is situated in the heart of the city. The pizzas, made on the premises from organic Canadian flour, are particularly recommended, and the bar stocks an award-winning wine range. The café downstairs serves panini and cakes, and there is even an on-site shop selling Italian food and wine. Closed 25 Dec–1 Jan.

NEW TOWN Hadrian's

The Balmoral Hotel, 1 Princes Street, Edinburgh, EH2 2EQ **Tel** *0131 557 5000*

This elegant restaurant is one of several housed within one of Edinburgh's finest hotels, and it enjoys a well-deserved reputation for excellence. The stylish Art Deco-influenced dining area is brightly coloured in a lime-and-violet palette. The kitchen produces superior brasserie fare as part of a cosmopolitan menu.

NEW TOWN Number One Princes Street

The Balmoral Hotel, 1 Princes Street, Edinburgh, EH2 2EQ **Tel** *0131 556 2414*

This classy and upmarket restaurant is located within the Balmoral Hotel but is also open to non-guests, with its own entrance on Princes Street. Acclaimed chef Jeff Bland is renowned for his skill, imagination and flair for fine Scottish cuisine. The service at this Michelin-starred and multiple award-winning dining venue is also exceptional.

OLD TOWN Always Sunday

170 High Street, Edinburgh, EH1 1QS **Tel** *0131 622 0667*

This welcoming café is a lively place from which to appreciate the atmosphere of the ancient part of Edinburgh. There are daily specials and a wide menu available from the counter – every dish is prepared with a nod to both health and taste. Try one of the many vegetarian options and wash it all down with a delicious smoothie. Closes at 6pm.

OLD TOWN Amber

The Scotch Whisky Experience, 354 Castlehill, The Royal Mile, Edinburgh, EH1 2NE **Tel** *0131 477 8477*

Hidden away in the bowels of the Scotch Whisky Experience, Amber is becoming more and more popular with visitors and local customers alike. The food is best described as innovative Scottish; dishes are executed well and presented attractively. The ambience is friendly and warm, and the amber nectar is never too far away.

OLD TOWN The Apartment

7–13 Barclay Place, Southside, Edinburgh, EH10 4HW **Tel** *0131 228 6456*

This is a popular restaurant that successfully blends a laid-back, relaxed ambience with efficient, unpretentious service. The menus are innovative, using great Scottish produce that is prepared and presented with flair and imagination. The flavours are superb. A place that deserves to stay put through all the trends and fads in eating.

OLD TOWN Barioja

19 Jeffrey Street, Edinburgh, EH1 1DR **Tel** *0131 557 3622*

Owner Iggy Campos first came to prominence for his restaurant next door, Iggs. Barioja has also proven a very popular dining destination. It is one of the most stylish tapas bars in town – its interior has even been featured in magazine articles. The food is superb, and the atmosphere and the service are authentically Spanish. A great place.

Key to Symbols *see back cover flap*

OLD TOWN Dubh Prais

123b High Street, Edinburgh, EH1 1SG **Tel** *0131 557 5734*

With a terrific Royal Mile location, this cellar restaurant provides an intimate atmosphere in which to enjoy refined and beautifully presented Scottish food with a modern twist. Venison, haggis, game and salmon feature regularly on the menu. Flavours are enhanced by herbs grown in the chef's own garden. A fine range of whiskies is also on offer.

OLD TOWN The Grain Store

30 Victoria Street, First Floor, Edinburgh, EH2 4DB **Tel** *0131 225 7635*

On the upper floor of an unusual building, this restaurant offers a modern menu that changes regularly and focuses on Scottish produce, such as locally produced beef and lamb, market-fresh fish and seafood, game, forest-picked mushrooms and seasonal fruit and vegetables. Informal atmosphere. Closed first week of Jan; 25 & 26 Dec.

OLD TOWN Atrium / Blue Bar Café

10 Cambridge Street, Edinburgh, EH1 2ED **Tel** *0131 228 8882*

Two restaurants run by consummate professionals. The formal Atrium is open for lunch and dinner and offers a fine, contemporary dining experience. The more relaxed Blue Bar Café is open all day for snacks, coffee, drinks, lunch and dinner. The cuisine is modern British, with a Mediterranean twist.

OLD TOWN The Witchery and The Secret Garden Restaurant

Castlehill, The Royal Mile, Edinburgh, EH1 2ED **Tel** *0131 225 5613*

Sample contemporary Scottish cuisine at this restaurant beside the entrance to Edinburgh Castle. Scottish lobster and rock oysters feature on the menu, alongside dishes such as smoked salmon with leeks and hollandaise sauce, and Angus beef fillet with smoked garlic broth. Theatre suppers and lunch menus are also available. Closed 25 & 26 Dec.

FURTHER AFIELD Avoca

4–6 Dean Street, Stockbridge, Edinburgh, EH4 1LW **Tel** *0131 315 3311*

The place to soak up authentic Stockbridge atmosphere, this pleasant bar is tastefully decorated in a brown-and-cream palette. It serves a good range of drinks, and the food is best described as good pub fare. Service is friendly and homely, which goes some way towards explaining Avoca's popularity. There are also good breakfast options.

FURTHER AFIELD Mimi's Bakehouse

63 Shore, Edinburgh, EH6 6RA **Tel** *0131 555 5908*

This irresistible family-run bakery in Leith has a loyal, local fanbase. Cakes, scones and tray bakes are available, as well as scrumptious chocolate beetroot cake. French toast and a full Scottish breakfast are among "Mimi's Belly Busting Breakfasts", while at lunchtime there are fishcakes, soups and savoury tarts.

FURTHER AFIELD A Room in Leith

1c Dock Place, Edinburgh, EH6 6LU **Tel** *0131 554 7427*

This restaurant, formerly called The Waterfront, has a nautical theme and overlooks the water of Leith. The menu is fun and imaginative and includes dishes such as a haggis starter with carrot and ginger marmalade. Local food is a priority. Expect to see rabbit, trout and Scottish beef on the menu. The banoffee pie and cheese board are both recommended.

FURTHER AFIELD Bells Diner

7 St Stephen Street, Stockbridge, Edinburgh, EH3 5AN **Tel** *0131 225 8116*

This tiny North American-style restaurant has been a local institution for more than 30 years. The menu is simple: burgers and steaks cooked to perfection. Since the restaurant is so small, booking is essential, and there is usually someone waiting to sit at your table after you. Desserts are excellent, if you have room for them. Well worth a visit.

FURTHER AFIELD The Boat House

22 High Street, South Queensferry, Edinburgh **Tel** *0131 331 5429*

A fish lover's paradise. The menu changes daily, depending on the best fish available at market on the day. Starters include a rich and creamy seafood bisque, Loch Fyne smoked salmon, mussels with a parsley cream sauce, and home-made smoked-haddock fishcakes. Quite simply a delightful little place that is worth seeking out.

FURTHER AFIELD Britannia Spice

150 Commercial Street, Leith, Edinburgh, EH6 6LB **Tel** *0131 555 2255*

Reputably one of the best Indian restaurants in Edinburgh, this vast, popular eatery is worth a visit if you enjoy the spicy flavours of the Orient. Friendly waiters, innovative menus and very convivial surroundings make Britannia Spice a truly memorable experience. The chef also prepares good Thai and Nepalese food.

FURTHER AFIELD Daniel's Bistro

88 Commercial Street, Leith, Edinburgh, EH3 6SF **Tel** *0131 553 5933*

Located in Leith's city centre, this restaurant can be relied upon to supply consistently good cooking, friendly, efficient service and a pleasant atmosphere. There is plenty of seating, too, so there is usually no need to make reservations in advance. The enormous, well-thought-out menu is served all day.

FURTHER AFIELD Indigo Yard

7 Charlotte Lane, Edinburgh, EH2 4QZ **Tel** *0131 220 5603*

Situated in the centre of the city's West End, this café-restaurant is a popular meeting place for the local community. Open all day for coffee, lunch, snacks and dinner, Indigo Yard offers a wide range of dishes designed to suit all tastes. The ambience is contemporary, the servings generous, and the service friendly and efficient.

FURTHER AFIELD Orocco Pier

17 High Street, S Queensferry, Edinburgh, EH30 9PP **Tel** *0870 118 1664*

Situated on the main street in South Queensferry, a short distance from Edinburgh city centre, Orocco Pier is open all day for light snacks, coffees and meals. Fish and seafood play a particularly prominent role on the menu. This elegant restaurant is a great place to enjoy the splendid views of the Forth estuary and its bridges.

FURTHER AFIELD Sangster's

51 High Street, Elie, Fife, KY9 1BZ **Tel** *01333 331001*

Located in a popular coastal village, this small, fine restaurant is run by one of Scotland's most recognized and skilled chefs, Bruce Sangster. Specialities include lightly spiced prawns, and pan-seared fillet of fresh halibut on a leek, potato and bacon chowder. Booking ahead is strongly advised. Closed Tue and Sat lunch, Sun eve, Mon.

FURTHER AFIELD Suruchi Too

121 Constitution Street, Leith, Edinburgh, EH6 7AE **Tel** *0131 554 3268*

Innovative Indian cuisine – often with a distinct Scottish flavour – is on offer at this spacious, airy restaurant. Among the highlights are the vegetable haggis fritters and a colourful menu written entirely in the Scots vernacular. A giant wooden camel from Rajasthan overlooks the dining room.

FURTHER AFIELD The Kitchin
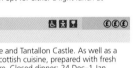

78 Commercial Quay, Leith, Edinburgh, EH3 6SF **Tel** *0131 555 1755*

The Kitchin quickly got the critics talking when it first opened. Tom Kitchin is a highly accomplished chef, having worked in some very well-known establishments and for renowned chefs such as Pierre Koffmann in London. While smart, the atmosphere in the restaurant is relaxed. Menus are well balanced, and the cooking is superb.

FURTHER AFIELD The Vintners Rooms Restaurant and Bar

The Vaults, 87 Giles Street, Leith, Edinburgh, EH6 6BZ **Tel** *0131 554 6767*

Housed in a wine warehouse, this charming candlelit restaurant is one of Leith's more established eateries. The Vintners Rooms offers a delicious contemporary Scottish menu, and guests can opt for either a light lunch at the bar or a complete meal in the more formal restaurant.

FURTHER AFIELD Whitekirk Golf Club and Restaurant

Whitekirk, near North Berwick, East Lothian, EH39 5PR **Tel** *01620 870300*

This restaurant has a pleasant rural setting, with lovely views over the coastline and Tantallon Castle. As well as a popular Sunday carvery, Whitekirk offers an elegant menu of contemporary Scottish cuisine, prepared with fresh seasonal and locally sourced ingredients. Good value and a friendly atmosphere. Closed dinner; 24 Dec–1 Jan.

FURTHER AFIELD Greywalls

Muirfield, Gullane, East Lothian, EH31 2EG **Tel** *01620 842144*

Located within a pretty walled garden, Greywalls is a famous historic hotel of Lutyens origins. The chef has an excellent pedigree, and his menus do not disappoint. The produce used is carefully selected for its quality, skilfully prepared and sensitively presented. A place for special occasions. Booking ahead is essential.

FURTHER AFIELD Restaurant Martin Wishart

54 The Shore, Edinburgh, EH6 6RA **Tel** *0131 533 3557*

Possibly the finest dining experience in all of Scotland. Chef Martin Wishart's creative and innovative cuisine is in great demand by lovers of fine food. On his restaurant's menu you will find modern French fare, created with the best available produce. The service is excellent, the ambience welcoming and the experience truly memorable.

SOUTHERN SCOTLAND

AYR Fouters Bistro

2a Academy Street, Ayr, KA7 1HS **Tel** *01292 261391*

Situated in a vaulted basement in Ayr town centre, Fouters is a popular, lively bistro where you can find a hearty meal at a decent price. It is set inside an old bank vault and still retains some of the original building's features. The menu offers classic French cuisine, making good use of fresh Scottish produce. Informal, warm and welcoming.

AYR Swallow Ivy House

2 Alloway, Ayr, KA7 4NL **Tel** *0845 351 9917*

Located in Burns Country, The Swallow Ivy House is set back from the road and overlooks the countryside and golf courses. Here you can enjoy a range of food, from simple lunchtime snacks to a superlative dinner overseen by a highly skilled chef. The setting is lovely, particularly on a sunny summer's day. Staff are well trained and hospitable.

DALRY Braidwoods

Drumastle Mill Cottage, nr Dalry, KA24 4LN **Tel** *01294 833544*

Keith and Nicola Braidwood have been recognized for the standards they have brought to the Scottish culinary scene. Located in a pleasant countryside setting, their restaurant is one of the best in Scotland. The two dining rooms are relaxed and intimate. Service is superb and, given the high quality of the food on offer, the prices are reasonable. Closed Monday.

Key to Price Guide *see p185* **Key to Symbols** *see back cover flap*

EAST LOTHIAN The Open Arms
Main Street, Dirleton, East Lothian, EH39 5EG Tel 01620 850241

Set on the edge of the village green, overlooking the 13th-century Dirleton Castle, this popular family-owned country hotel offers a welcome worthy of its moniker. Guests can choose between elegant dining or a more informal experience in the bright brasserie. Convivial surroundings add to the charm.

GATTONSIDE Chapters Bistro
Main Street, Gattonside, Melrose, TD6 9NB Tel 01896 823217

This spacious local restaurant is cosy and welcoming, and a popular destination for both locals and tourists. The service is always excellent and friendly, and the ambience warm. The menu reflects the high standard of local produce available, and the cooking is highly skilled, contemporary and delightfully unfussy.

GATTONSIDE Hoebridge Inn
Gattonside, Melrose, TD6 9LZ Tel 01896 823082

Bright and airy, this inn on the edge of the Borders village of Gattonside is particularly popular with the local community, since it offers a consistently high standard of welcome and service, ensuring repeat visits. Chef Maureen Rennie has been recognized for her commitment to local produce and imaginative use of said produce.

GULLANE La Potinière
Main Street, Gullane, East Lothian, EH31 2AA Tel 01620 843214

A superior restaurant situated in the pretty East Lothian village of Gullane, Le Potinière offers a seasonally changing menu. Rest assured that you will be able to sample well-prepared food using fresh local produce year-round. The caring and hospitable staff will see to your comfort. Private parking facilities. Closed Mon & Tue.

ISLE OF ARRAN Auchrannie Resort
Brodick, Isle of Arran, KA27 8BZ Tel 01770 302234

The restaurants at the delightful Auchrannie Resort offer both formal and informal dining options, with varied menus that will suit every taste. The surroundings are warm and welcoming, as are the well-trained, friendly staff. The chef makes good use of fresh, locally sourced fish, meat and produce.

KIPPFORD The Anchor Hotel
Main Street, Kippford, Dalbeattie, Kirkudbrightshire, DG5 4LN Tel 01556 620205

Offering great views of the maritime activity in the Solway Firth from its outside tables, this friendly hotel and pub on the waterfront serves superior pub food, made using seasonal, locally sourced produce. The Anchor is a popular spot to enjoy a pint of real ale and a filling, good-value seafood meal.

LAUDER Black Bull
Market Place, Lauder, TD2 6SR Tel 01578 722208

The Black Bull successfully combines a bar, a restaurant and a hotel. Its style is cosy and comfortable, and the atmosphere is welcoming and friendly. Good staple bar food options are available, along with many more interesting choices: you can eat anything from a sandwich to more sophisticated fare here, depending on the occasion.

MAIDENS The Wildings
Harbour Road, Maidens, Ayrshire, KA26 9NR Tel 01655 331401

Close to Turnberry golf course, this family-run operation is named after an aunt of chef and patriarch Brian Sage. It has a local following of regulars who come for the balance of seafood and meat dishes on the menu. Given the location, however, fish is the house speciality and well worth ordering. Good, unfussy food served in a relaxed ambience.

MAUCHLINE Sorn Inn
35 Main Street, Sorn, Mauchline, East Ayrshire, KA5 6HU Tel 01290 551305

This gastropub is set in native woodland in the tiny village of Sorn. Its reputation just keeps on growing – justifiably so. The food is indeed top class. Menus are varied and interesting, the dishes inspired by great flavours and made using only the best-quality ingredients. The restaurant is quite formal, but the atmosphere is still welcoming.

MELROSE The Station Hotel Restaurant
Market Square, Melrose, TD6 9PT Tel 01896 823147

At this little restaurant, the emphasis is very much on attention to detail. Scottish beef, chicken and seafood are always on the menu. There's a great choice of puddings including ice cream from the nearby Overlangshaw Farm. Combine all this with a warm welcome and attentive service, and you have a place well worth visiting.

MELROSE Burts Hotel
Market Square, Melrose, TD6 9PL Tel 01896 822285

There is something very welcoming about Burts, which is perhaps attributable to the real sense of it being a family-run business. The bar is cosy and comfortable, as is the more formal restaurant. The food is excellent, from hearty bar meals to more refined dishes in the dining area. Try the layered gâteau of smoked haddock and ratatouille.

MELROSE The Townhouse
Market Square, Melrose, TD6 9PQ Tel 01896 822645

This is a family-run business (managed by the same family as Burts Hotel) and a place where you can expect to enjoy the highest standards of hospitality, service and cooking. The stylish brasserie has been tastefully refurbished and draws both locals and visitors. The menus feature good local produce cooked in a modern fusion style.

MOFFAT Well View Hotel   ⓔⓔ
Ballplay Road, Moffat, Dumfriesshire, DG10 9JH **Tel** *01683 220184*

An intimate hotel situated in a residential area a few minutes' walk from Moffat's main street. On the menu you will find modern French cuisine with some Scottish elements, using best local produce. All meals are served in the dining room of this family establishment, which features a peaceful atmosphere and comfortable surroundings.

PORTPATRICK Knockinaam Lodge   ⓔⓔⓔⓔ
Off A77, nr Portpatrick, Dumfries and Galloway, DG9 9AD **Tel** *01776 81047*

Comfort and pampering are the top priorities at this stylish lodge in an idyllic location overlooking the sea. The dining room serves international cuisine with modern Scottish influences. Among the highlights: cauliflower and white garlic velouté, and grilled native salmon with a potato wafer. A welcoming ambience adds to the charm.

SELKIRK Philipburn House   ⓔⓔ
Linglie Road, Selkirk, TD7 5LS **Tel** *01750 20747*

This cosy, comfortable hotel offers a choice of dining options. The informal bistro serves traditional local fare, simply cooked and prepared. Named after the year of the Jacobite rising led by Bonnie Prince Charles, 1745 is a more formal dining room offering beautifully presented dishes such as roulade of sole and plaice.

SWINTON Wheatsheaf   ⓔⓔ
Main Street, Swinton, Berwickshire, TD11 3JJ **Tel** *01890 860257*

The Wheatsheaf is a restaurant with rooms that sits on Swinton's village green. Its specialities tend to be on the meat side. Cooking is superb, resulting in truly mouth-watering dishes such as pork fillet and chicken liver terrine on a red onion marmalade. The chef uses only tried and trusted local suppliers, thereby ensuring the quality of his ingredients.

TROON Highgrove House Hotel   ⓔⓔ
Old Loans Road, Troon Ayrshire, KA7 7HL **Tel** *01292 312511*

Perched high on Dundonald Hill, this hotel-restaurant is situated within a retired sea captain's house and enjoys magnificent views over the Firth of Clyde and the Mull of Kintyre. The atmosphere is comfortable and welcoming. Diners can enjoy a variety of informal dishes from an extensive menu.

TROON Macallums Oyster Bar   ⓔⓔ
Harbour Road, Troon, KA10 6DH **Tel** *01292 319339*

Located right down at the quayside, this is a good place to find and enjoy the freshest fish and seafood. The style of the restaurant is informal and unassuming, and the ingredients reign supreme: they are cooked with minimum fuss, but with great understanding and a light touch. A warm and welcoming atmosphere completes the picture.

TURNBERRY The Turnberry Restaurant   ⓔⓔⓔⓔⓔ
The Westin Turnberry Resort, Turnberry, Ayrshire, KA26 9LT **Tel** *01655 331000*

This place has charm and good taste in abundance. The award-winning chef is renowned for his superb skills, and his tutelage ensures that every dining experience here is a winning combination of French influence and excellent produce. Try the pan-roasted venison with artichoke gnocchi, or the grilled red mullet with crab cous cous, or the tasting menu.

GLASGOW

CITY CENTRE Café Hula   ⓔ
321 Hope Street, Glasgow, G2 3PT **Tel** *0141 353 1660*

Café Hula is designed to be an oasis in the heart of the city. Large sofas, dark wood, flickering candles and quirky decor make it an enticing place to show off. The food has a Mediterranean flavour, with pastas, risottos and a lovely chorizo stew on the menu. The service is relaxed, so be prepared to leave plenty of time for your meal.

CITY CENTRE The Doocot Café and Bar   ⓔ
The Lighthouse, 11 Mitchell Lane, Glasgow, G1 3NU **Tel** *0141 221 1821*

The Doocot sits five floors up in the design hub that is The Lighthouse, a Mackintosh-designed building. It is a bustling and popular place, with a charmingly bohemian clientele. It is open only during the day, when it is a good place to enjoy some good food, rest weary limbs and meet up with friends. All food is freshly prepared on site.

CITY CENTRE Baby Grand   ⓔⓔ
3–7 Elmbank Gardens, Glasgow, G2 4NQ **Tel** *0141 248 4942*

Named after the piano in the corner, this is a hard-working bar and supper club where you can enjoy good food from breakfast time until late at night. The menu successfully combines French brasserie-style food with New York deli-type dishes, and it also includes some continental classics. This place has buzz and real style.

CITY CENTRE Café Gandolfi   ⓔⓔ
64 Albion Street, Merchant City, Glasgow, G1 1NY **Tel** *0141 552 6813*

A local institution, Gandolfi has been in business for 25 years, operating from what was once the office of the Glasgow cheese market. The food ranges from light snacks to more substantial fare, with the emphasis on good local produce that is tastefully prepared and presented. Look out for great black pud. A bar occupies the loft space.

Key to Price Guide *see p185* **Key to Symbols** *see back cover flap*

CITY CENTRE City Café

City Inn, Finnieston Quay, Clydeside, Glasgow, G3 8HN **Tel** *0141 240 1002*

A hotel restaurant is not always the best choice for dining, but this café is the exception to the rule. The window seats look right on to the Clyde, and the hotel has its own parking, which is a considerable bonus. The contemporary menu is prepared and presented with great flair. Also look out for outdoor barbecues and Sunday buffets.

CITY CENTRE City Merchant

97 Candleriggs, Merchant City, Glasgow, G1 1NP **Tel** *0141 553 157*

Located in Glasgow's Merchant City, this friendly family-run restaurant is a bustling venue serving excellent maritime cuisine with a Scottish influence. Only the best local produce is used in the kitchen. The ambience is informal and rustic, and the restaurant, which can accommodate more than 120 guests, offers good value for money.

CITY CENTRE The Restaurant Bar and Grill

The Glass House, Springfield Court, Glasgow, G1 3DQ **Tel** *0141 225 5622*

The experience begins in a private glass lift (at the rear of Princes Square) and continues with a warm welcome. This restaurant is a stylish place to meet up and enjoy superb gastro-pub classics, such as pan-fried veal escalope with breaded mushrooms. Cosmopolitan and smart.

CITY CENTRE Brian Maule at Chardon d'Or

176 West Regent Street, Glasgow, G2 4RL **Tel** *0141 248 3801*

One of the finest restaurants in the city, the Chardon d'Or is the realm of highly acclaimed chef Brian Maule, who provides an innovative repertoire of French cuisine, using locally sourced ingredients. On his menu you will find fish, poultry and game. Stylish ambience and friendly, efficient staff. Closed Sundays.

CITY CENTRE Michael Caines at ABode

129 Bath Street, Glasgow, G2 2SZ **Tel** *0141 572 6011*

ABode is part of a chain of boutique hotels that has put Michelin-starred chef Michael Caines in charge of the food. The result is a super-stylish venue where diners can enjoy dishes such as raviolo of pheasant and foie gras with Stornoway black pudding and a red wine sauce. Menus use local produce that has been handled with panache.

CITY CENTRE Two Fat Ladies At The Buttery

652 Argyle Street, Glasgow, G12 2ND **Tel** *0141 221 8188*

Although it is located in a less-than-salubrious part of the city centre, this restaurant is well worth seeking out as it offers good value; there are fish specialities and a decadent dessert selection. It used to be called The Buttery but was taken over by Ryan James, who opened the original Two Fat Ladies in Glasgow.

CITY CENTRE Gamba

225a W George Street, Glasgow, G2 2ND **Tel** *0141 572 0899*

This popular seafood restaurant is widely acknowledged for its high-quality, varied cuisine. Food is meticulously prepared, using a wide variety of fresh seasonal ingredients, including fish, lobster and oysters. The interior of the restaurant is modern, stylish and comfortable.

WEST END Balbirs

7 Church Street, Glasgow, G11 5JP **Tel** *0141 339 7711*

Healthy is not often a word associated with Indian food, but Balbirs is the exception to that rule. Here the food is prepared without colourings and using only the best, freshest ingredients. The menus are varied and feature innovative takes on traditional dishes. The restaurant is spacious yet intimate, and the staff are informed and friendly.

WEST END Café Cherubini

360 Great Western Road, Kelvingrove, Glasgow **Tel** *0141 334 8894*

This traditional Italian café is located in Glasgow's West End. It prides itself on providing authentic Italian fare, including pasta, salads and a good tiramisu for dessert. The speciality of the house is the home-made salsiccia (Italian sausage). It has a licence, although you can still bring your own bottle. Service is friendly.

WEST END Mother India Café

1355 Argyle Street, Glasgow, G11 **Tel** *0141 339 9145*

Mother India looks out onto the Kelvingrove Gallery. Small tapas-sized portions allow you to enjoy a range of very good Indian food in a relaxed, Bohemian atmosphere. Their approach has garnered a loyal local following. They don't take bookings, so be sure to show up early – it is a popular place, and it does get busy.

WEST END The Ashoka

19 Ashton Lane, Glasgow, G12 **Tel** *0141 337 1115*

This established Ashton Lane restaurant continues to go from strength to strength. The superb-quality food is authentically Indian, and the atmosphere is warm and welcoming. One of the best places to enjoy a curry in Glasgow, The Ashoka is very popular, so it pays to book ahead.

WEST END La Parmigiana

447 Great Western Road, Glasgow, G12 8HH **Tel** *0141 334 0686*

This is a small but perfectly formed Italian restaurant that has been on this site for many years. It has a refreshingly welcoming ambience. The dining room is cosy and intimate, and there is a small bar for diners to use pre- or post-dinner. The food is simply superb and of the highest quality.

WEST END No. Sixteen
££

16 Byres Road, West End, Glasgow, G11 5JY **Tel** *0141 339 2544*

This restaurant is so popular that people travel from far and wide to enjoy a meal here. The simply decorated dining room is cosy and welcoming. The head chef has a light touch, and the portions are generous. The menu combines both modern and traditional approaches, with some innovative touches. However, the main emphasis is on flavour.

WEST END Ubiquitous Chip
 £££

12 Ashton Lane, Glasgow, G12 8SL **Tel** *0141 334 5007*

Celebrating its 40th birthday in 2011, the prestigious Ubiquitous Chip, is a Glasgow institution and remains as popular as ever. Serving traditional Scottish cuisine prepared with fresh local ingredients, its great atmosphere and friendly staff make this a justifiably notable place. It has a rooftop terrace and an extensive wine list.

WEST END Stravaigin
££££

28 Gibson Street, Hillhead, Glasgow, G12 8NX **Tel** *0141 334 2665*

Well located in the heart of Glasgow's university neighbourhood, this popular café-bar and restaurant serves award-winning pub fare. On the menu are such local favourites as whole mackerel with puy-lentil salad, Aberdeen Angus beef balls in peanut sauce, and appetizing haggis.

FURTHER AFIELD Art Lover's Café
 £

House for an Art Lover, Bellahouston Park, 10 Dumbreck Road, Glasgow, G41 5BW **Tel** *0141 353 4770*

The building housing this eaterie was originally sketched by CR Mackintosh in 1901 but only opened in the 1990s. The Art Lover's Café echoes the artful theme in the menu, with such dishes as pan-fried sea bass with sautéed juniper and kumquat potatoes, or warm minted cous cous with red pesto dressing.

FURTHER AFIELD The Kitchen Restaurant at Pollok House
£

Pollok House, Pollok Estate, 2060 Pollokshaws Road, Glasgow, G41 **Tel** *0141 616 6410*

This café-style restaurant is housed in the beautifully preserved kitchen of Pollok House. The food offered ranges from a selection of superb home bakes to good wholesome fare served simply and without fuss. There are also good choices for vegetarians. A great place to refuel after exploring the lovely gardens of the house and the lush Pollok Estate.

FURTHER AFIELD Barbarossa
££

3–5 Clarkston Road, Clarkston, Glasgow, G44 4EF **Tel** *0141 560 3898*

Head to Barbarossa for a truly authentic, good-quality Italian experience. The three-floor restaurant is owned and run by an Italian family and is popular with both the local community and visitors, thanks to its relaxed, friendly and lively ambience. The menu also includes some Scottish favourites cooked with Italian flair.

FURTHER AFIELD Dine
££

205 Fenwick Road, Giffnock, Glasgow, G46 6JD **Tel** *0141 621 1903*

Dine's small premises are situated on Giffnock's main strip of shops, and it is a genuine neighbourhood restaurant with a modern twist. Menus change monthly and use mostly seasonal ingredients, which are handled with care and without fuss. Booking is essential, since this is a very popular place with locals.

CENTRAL SCOTLAND

BALQUHIDDER Monachyle Mhor
 ££££

Balquhidder, Lochearnhead, Perthshire, FK19 8PQ **Tel** *01877 384622*

The Lewis family have a well-deserved reputation for offering a superb level of hospitality and a warm welcome to their guests. Set in the heart of Rob Roy country, Monachyle Mhor is a great place to unwind and enjoy Scottish fare. The beef is sourced locally, the vegetables come from the garden, and the seafood is from the West Coast.

BANKNOCK Glenskirlie House
 ££

Kilsyth Road, Banknock, Stirlingshire, FK4 1UF **Tel** *01324 840201*

A superb example of a well-run family business. The enthusiasm and commitment to customer satisfaction make this a place well worth seeking out. Food is served in the bar or in the more formal dining room – whatever your choice, you are assured of a memorable meal where local produce has been expertly cooked and prepared. Closed on Mondays.

BRIDGE OF ALLAN Allan Water Café
 £

15 Henderson Street, Bridge of Allan, Stirling **Tel** *01786 833060*

In spite of being landlocked in Bridge of Allan, this spacious, family-run restaurant has the definite feel of a seaside café. It is open all day, starting with hearty Scottish breakfasts. Don't come here looking for healthy options. The windows upstairs give a good vantage point of the hustle and bustle of Henderson Street.

BRIDGE OF ALLAN Clive Ramsay Café and Restaurant
 £

28 Henderson Street, Bridge of Allan, Stirling, FK9 4HR **Tel** *01786 822903*

This is a welcome addition to the popular delicatessen next door. The restaurant serves café, pre-theatre and dinner menus and is a great place to enjoy superb food and watch the world go by. A popular favourite is haggis served with sweet potato. Good, honest food has made this place a deservedly popular destination.

Key to Price Guide *see p185* **Key to Symbols** *see back cover flap*

BRIDGE OF ALLAN Chambo
Mine Road, Bridge of Allan, Stirling, FK9 4DT **Tel** *01786 833617*

Chambo, located in a former Victorian house with a large garden, is a superb eatery, with none of the hushed stuffiness that you would expect from a top restaurant. There is a cosy bar where you can relax and peruse the menu prior to being shown to your table. The restaurant is spacious, the menu is tempting and the food delicious.

BUCHLYVIE The Village Tea Room
Main Street, Buchlyvie, Stirlingshire, FK8 3LX **Tel** *01360 850150*

This is a lovely village tea room with a gallery and a post office attached; it is also the best place to stop on the A811 if you are driving to the National Park from Stirling. Take a seat and enjoy a good home bake or a bowl of freshly made soup. A wee gem that will fuel you up for a day of walking, sightseeing or whatever your pleasure may be.

CALLANDER Callander Meadows
24 Main Street, Callander, Stirlingshire, FK17 8BB **Tel** *01877 330181*

This wildly popular restaurant is owned and run by Nick and Susannah Parkes, who honed their culinary skills at Gleneagles. This is a relaxed, cosy eatery where the contemporary, innovative flavours in the menu mix well with the Victorian rooms in which the restaurant is located. The menu focuses on local quality produce.

CUPAR Ostlers Close
25 Bonnygate, Cupar, Fife **Tel** *01334 655 574*

Jimmy and Amanda Graham, who have been running this restaurant since 1981, share a real passion for good food. Jimmy has a strong interest in mushrooms and is in charge of the superb food. Amanda takes care of the front-of-house section, offering a superior standard of service and hospitality. Closed lunch (except Sun), Mon and Sun eve.

DUNDEE Best Western Invercarse Hotel
371 Perth Road, Dundee, Angus, DD2 1PG **Tel** *01382 669231*

The Best Western Invercarse is located just on the outskirts of Dundee, amid private woodland overlooking the River Tay. You can eat either at the bar or in the more formal restaurant, where some of the most popular dishes include salmon fillets and sirloin steaks. Simple but good food, accompanied by friendly, attentive service.

FALKLAND Kynd Kyttock's Kitchen
Cross Wynd, Falkland, KY15 **Tel** *01337 857477*

This small café is tucked away on a side street near the magnificent Falkland Palace. They serve traditional Scottish fare, with soups and home-made cakes and preserves, as well as soda bread. A simple but characterful spot to enjoy a refreshing afternoon tea with scones and pancakes.

FIFE The Cellar
24e Green, Anstruther, Fife, KY10 3AA **Tel** *01333 310378*

Housed in one of Fife's oldest buildings, The Cellar offers a cosy ambience and reasonably priced good food with lots of character. The award-winning chef prepares excellent seafood cuisine using only fresh local produce. The ideal destination for an intimate, romantic meal.

KINROSS Grouse and Claret
Heatheryford, Kinross, KY13 8YY **Tel** *01577 864212*

Just seconds from Junction 6 of the M90 turnoff at Kinross is the turning for the Grouse and Claret. For more than 15 years, David and Vicky Futong have been building their reputation for great cooking, with an emphasis on fresh, organic, GM-free ingredients. The restaurant has superb country views from the dining rooms.

KIPPEN The Inn at Kippen
Fore Road, Kippen, FK8 3DT **Tel** *01786 871010*

There is a real commitment to fresh produce at this delightful inn: the owner leaves every morning to work and stock up at Glasgow's fruit market. Choose to eat at the bar or in the dining room. Either way, the atmosphere and service are relaxed, and there is great attention to detail. The menu is varied, with well-cooked, imaginative dishes.

LARGS Nardini's
The Esplanade, Largs, Ayshire, KA30 8NF **Tel** *01475 674 4555*

Extremely popular with both tourists and locals, and a well-known icon of Largs, where it has been doing business since 1935, Nardini's is a seafront lounge café boasting a delightful Art Deco interior. Breakfasts, cakes and Italian and British dishes are served all day. A perfect place to relax, sit back and read the paper.

LINLITHGOW Champany Inn
Champany, nr Linlithgow, West Lothian, EH49 7LU **Tel** *01506 834532*

Located not far from Edinburgh, on the outskirts of Linlithgow, this charming restaurant offers the best steaks in Scotland. Diners can choose from different cuts – strip loin, rib-eye, fillet and porterhouse – all cooked to perfection. Other must-try specialities include Loch Gruinart oysters and succulent, hot smoked salmon.

PERTH Deans @ Let's Eat
77–79 Kinnoull Street, Perth, PH1 5EZ **Tel** *01738 643377*

Since taking over Let's Eat in 2005, Willie Deans and his wife Margo have firmly established themselves on the Scottish culinary scene. Willie is an incredibly skilled chef renowned for his attention to detail; Margo is a charming, welcoming host. The hardest part of dining here is deciding what you are going to have from the extensive menu.

PERTH The Roost

Forgandenny Road, Kintillo, Bridge of Earn, Perth, PH2 9A3 **Tel** *01738 812111*

This is a relaxed place with a warm welcome and an emphasis on exceptional Scottish produce prepared with a Mediterranean twist. The chef creates everything on the menu from scratch, including bread and ice cream – he sometimes even catches the fish that is served! There is a short but well thought-out wine list.

PERTH 63 Tay Street

63 Tay Street, Perth, Perthshire, PH2 8NN **Tel** *01738 643377*

The interior of this Perth restaurant run by a husband-and-wife team is minimalist and modern. Chef Jeremy Wares creates imaginative, high-quality, modern Scottish cuisine, while Shona skilfully manages the front-of-house section. Menus feature the best regional produce available, which is used as the basis for thoroughly enjoyable dishes.

PERTH Dunalastair Hotel

Dunalastair Hotel, The Square, Kinloch Rennoch, Perthshire, PH16 5PW **Tel** *01822 632218*

You will find classic Scottish cooking here; there are no novelties on the menu, but rather high-quality, simple, traditional dishes with ingredients taken from the Scottish Highlands. The emphasis is on local game. The atmosphere is relaxed and service is attentive.

ST ANDREWS The Tailend

130 Market Street, St Andrews, Fife, KY16 9PD **Tel** *01334 474070*

This popular local place comprises a packed takeaway counter and a seafood restaurant serving fresh and locally caught fish. Whitebait, cod, langoustine tails and arbroath smokies are all on the menu. Enjoy a relaxing meal with a glass of wine or get a takeaway and head to the beach on a sunny day.

ST ANDREWS The Peat Inn

On B940, Cupar, nr St Andrews, Fife, KY15 5LH **Tel** *01334 840206*

Highly accomplished modern cooking using seasonal produce has helped establish this small hotel-restaurant as one of the best in the whole of Britain. Renowned chef David Wilson is passionate about good Scottish fare, which is evident in the care and attention to detail he devotes to his dishes. The lunch menu offers particularly good value.

ST ANDREWS The Seafood Restaurant

Bruce Embankment, St Andrews, Fife, KY16 9AS **Tel** *01334 479475*

Located right on the seafront, this superb restaurant offers a memorable dining experience, along with striking views of the coastline. The menu features a wide variety of fish and seafood, all of which is carefully prepared and beautifully presented. The ambience of this stylish eatery is warm and cosy.

ST MONANS The Seafood Restaurant

16 W End, St Monans, Fife, KY10 2BX **Tel** *01333 730327*

Boasting a stunning water's edge location, this is an excellent place to enjoy the very best local seafood. This fine modern restaurant is attractive and elegant and serves fresh seasonal fish and seafood, including prawns, crabs, scallops and more. The food is meticulously prepared, and the staff are friendly and attentive.

STIRLING Scholars

Stirling Highland Hotel, Spittal Street, Stirling, FK8 1DU **Tel** *01786 272727*

Set in the old town of Stirling, at the foot of the entrance to the castle, this award-winning restaurant serves Scottish fare with an innovative twist. On the menu you will find creations such as terrine of black pudding, bacon and mushrooms with a fruit chutney, or seared salmon on lemon risotto with a balsamic reduction.

THE HIGHLANDS AND ISLANDS

ABERDEEN The Silver Darling

Porca Quay, Footdee, N Pier, Aberdeen, Aberdeenshire, AB11 5DQ **Tel** *01224 576229*

A well-established venue, The Silver Darling is a superb bistro/restaurant located on the north side of Aberdeen harbour. It is a superb place for a leisurely meal, on account of both the unforgettable views of the coastline and the excellent menu, which revolves around the daily catch.

ACHILTIBUIE Summer Isles Hotel

Achiltibuie, near Ullapool, Ross and Cromarty, IV26 2YG **Tel** *01854 622282*

Located in an idyllic setting overlooking the Summer Isles, this Michelin-starred restaurant is led by chef Chris Firth-Bernard, whose menu tantalizes with exceptionally fine fish and seafood fare. More informal – but still superb – seafood lunches and suppers are also available in the adjacent bar. Closed mid-Oct–Easter.

ALEXANDRIA Smolletts at Cameron House Hotel

off A82, Loch Lomond, Alexandria, West Dunbartonshire, G83 8QZ **Tel** *01389 755565*

Formal dining can be enjoyed at this luxurious country house, situated on the tranquil shores of Loch Lomond, surrounded by beautiful wooded parkland. This stylish yet informal restaurant offers exquisitely prepared meals. Choose from the à la carte menu or the three-course Market Menu. The experience of a lifetime.

Key to Price Guide *see p185* **Key to Symbols** *see back cover flap*

AUCHMITHIE But 'n' Ben

Off A92, 1 Auchmithie, nr Arbroath, Angus, DD11 5SQ **Tel** *01241 877223*

An unusual restaurant housed in twin cottages in a working fishing village, But 'n' Ben is open for lunch, dinner and high tea. It prides itself on the organic local produce used in the kitchen and is well renowned for its smokie pancakes. The great-value menus feature the fresh catch of the day. A small eatery with a welcoming ambience.

AUCHTERARDER InDulge

22 High Street, Auchterarder, Perthshire, PH3 1DF **Tel** *01764 660033*

The owners of this tiny café and deli are clearly passionate about what they do. They have a strong local following, but InDulge is popular with visitors too. The place is open during the day, as well as two evenings a week. All food is locally sourced, chosen for quality and flavour first and foremost.

AUCHTERARDER Andrew Fairlie @ Gleneagles

Gleneagles Hotel, Auchterarder, Perthshire, PH3 1NF **Tel** *01764 694267*

Set within the luxurious Gleneagles Hotel, this restaurant will provide one of the finest dining experiences in Scotland. Highly acclaimed chef Andrew Fairlie presents imaginative French cuisine with a Scottish twist. Must-try specialities include smoked lobster, roast Anjou squab with black-truffle gnocchi and delicious hot-chocolate biscuit dessert.

BALLATER Darroch Learg

Braemar Road, Ballater, Royal Deeside, AB35 AUX **Tel** *013397 55443*

Set within a Victorian shooting lodge, Darroch Learg offers a calm, relaxed setting. The chef creates imaginative and flavoursome modern British cuisine with the best local ingredients. One of the highlights is tortellini of Arbroath smokie, with roasted sea scallops, Sauterne sauce and curry oil. An adjacent conservatory adds to the charm.

BLACKFORD Café 1488

Tullibardine 1488 Visitor Centre, Stirling Street, Blackford, Perthshire, PH4 1QG **Tel** *01764 682252*

Located within a development next to the Tullibardine Distillery, this café is named in honour of the year James IV of Scotland stopped here to buy some supplies before his coronation. There is a good selection of food, ranging from simple home bakes to a roast of the day, light lunches and much more.

BLAIRGOWRIE Cargill's

Lower Mill Street, Blairgowrie, Perthshire, PH10 6AQ **Tel** *01250 876735*

Excellent Scottish fare is served here – try the steak, venison, scallops or Stornoway black pudding. There's a dedicated vegetarian menu, plus one for kids, and most of the food served is local and seasonal. Round things off with a tart, crème caramel or a selection of Scottish cheese.

CAIRNDOW Loch Fyne Oyster Bar

Clachan, Cairndow, Argyll, PA26 8BL **Tel** *01499 600236*

Highly renowned and a great draw with the locals, Loch Fyne serves an impressive array of fish and seafood. On the menu is an excellent selection of hot and cold meals, including oysters, mussels and seared tuna. The restaurant also caters for those who are not keen on fish, with chicken, lamb and vegetarian options.

CARNOUSTIE Titanic Pizza Company

104 High Street, Carnoustie, DD7 7EB **Tel** *01241 411912*

There's an impressive 53 pizzas on the menu here, but if you can't see the perfect combination, they'll tailor-make a pizza with your choice of ingredients. There's a smaller size available for kids, as well as a whopping 16-inch variety. There are a few tables and chairs, but takeaway is popular.

COLBOST The Three Chimneys

Colbost, Dunvegan, Isle of Skye, Inverness-shire, IV55 8ZT **Tel** *01470 511258*

Situated a short distance from Dunvegan, on the western shores of the loch, this award-winning restaurant offers excellent seafood and game dishes, all prepared with fresh, locally sourced produce. The ambience is peaceful and relaxed. One of the "not to miss" places in Scotland. Reservations are essential.

COLLISTON Colliston Inn

Forfar Road, Colliston, DD11 3RP **Tel** *01241 890232*

This family-run restaurant, located in a former manse, offers snacks, lunch and dinner. The focus is on Scottish cuisine, with local game and fish and a range of malt whiskies to round things off. The decor is a little dated, but the welcome is warm and the food delicious.

DRYMEN The Pottery

The Square, Drymen, Argyll, G63 OBJ **Tel** *01360 660458*

This bright and lively restaurant-cum-coffee shop is located in the village square and serves good home-cooked food all day long, as well as afternoon teas. It has a charming terrace for alfresco dining in clement weather and an open fire for the winter months. A popular stop-off point for tourists and locals.

DUFFTOWN A Taste of Speyside

10 Balvenie Street, Dufftown, Moray, AB55 4AB **Tel** *01340 820860*

Set amid the mountains and glens of the Spey Valley, this restaurant has been offering an enjoyable culinary experience to its customers for many years. The food is wholesome and simply prepared. There is a strong commitment to quality local produce, such as fish, poultry and game. Closed Mondays.

DUNKELD Kinnaird Estate
Kinnaird Estate, off B898, nr Dunkeld, Perthshire, PH8 0LB **Tel** *01796 482 2440*

Located in a beautifully maintained hotel, this stylish restaurant produces food of great taste and originality, which is accompanied by a superlative wine selection overseen by award-winning sommelier James Payne. The dining room is elegant and welcoming, and the staff are professional and friendly. Children aged ten and over only.

FORT WILLIAM Lime Tree
The Old Manse, Achintore Road, Fort William, Perthshire, PH33 6RQ **Tel** *01397 701806*

This highly praised hotel restaurant offers a warm welcome and well-presented, delicious dishes. Everything is cooked in the open kitchen, from the wood-pigeon starter to the slow-cooked Ayrshire pork belly with pear and star anise purée as well as the exquisite passion fruit soufflé.

INVERNESS La Tortilla Asesina
99 Castle Street, Inverness, IV2 3EA **Tel** *01463 709809*

Renowned for being one of the best tapas bars outside Spain, which is high praise indeed. The proprietor came up with the idea after touring Spain on his motorbike, and the result is a superb place to enjoy a wide selection of excellent tapas. As well as the usual staples, there are many interesting additions made using fresh Scottish produce.

INVERNESS River Café Restaurant
10 Bank Street, Inverness, IV1 1QY **Tel** *01463 714884*

This is a tranquil little riverside café that serves cooked breakfasts, lunch, coffee and cakes all day, as well as high teas. At lunch there is a vast menu, from filled croissants, baked potatoes and quiche to smoked-cod fishcakes; the daily specials are also good. The emphasis is on authentic Scottish cooking, and everything is home-made.

INVERNESS Rocpool
1 Ness Walk, Inverness, IV3 5NE **Tel** *01463 717274*

This is a vibrant eatery serving fresh, tasty food in a relaxed and stylish environment. The menus are contemporary and feature good, locally sourced produce that is then cooked and presented with flair. Service is friendly and efficient. This is popular with locals and visitors alike and well worth making the effort to visit when in the area.

INVERNESS Culloden House
Culloden, Inverness, IV2 7BZ **Tel** *01463 790461*

Culloden House is a Scottish country house situated within a historic building full of character and set in lovely grounds close to the visitors' centre. The chef prepares a hearty, appetizing menu featuring extraordinary dishes accompanied by sauces, jellies, sorbets and mousses. Accommodation is also available.

ISLE OF BUTE Chandlers Hotel
Ascog Bay, Isle of Bute, PA20 9ET **Tel** *01700 505577*

Chandlers is a substantial detached property in a superb location, with unsurpassed views over the Clyde to the Ayrshire coast and beyond. In the restaurant there is a selection of dishes lovingly prepared by chefs who have a real passion for food and use only the best local and seasonally available produce.

ISLE OF MULL The Highland Cottage Hotel
Tobermory, Isle of Mull, Argyll, PA75 6NT **Tel** *01688 302030*

This hotel is located in what was once a row of fishermen's cottages on the waterfront. A family-run concern, it is a great place to eat. The menu features the best of local produce, including salmon, seafood, venison, beef and lamb, not to mention a range of seasonal vegetables. There is also a good selection of vegetarian dishes.

KILBERRY Kilberry Inn
Kilberry, nr Tarbet, Loch Fyne, Argyll, PA29 6YD **Tel** *01880 770223*

Set within a traditional, red-tin-roofed "but and ben", the Kilberry Inn serves Scottish pub food at its best, with a constantly changing menu featuring locally sourced fish, seafood and game. There's a good selection of old favourites in a warm and cosy atmosphere, enlivened by a log fire and rustic stone walls. Closed Jan & Feb.

KILLIECRANKIE Killiecrankie Hotel
Off A9, nr Pitlochry, Perthshire, PH16 5LG **Tel** *01796 473220*

This attractive hotel has the cosy feel of a village inn. The food on offer is hearty and wholesome, yet somewhat unusual, with a few innovative twists. Excellent bar meals supplement the fine dinnertime fare, and both are served in warm and inviting surroundings. The staff are friendly and hospitable.

KINCRAIG The Boathouse Restaurant
Loch Insh, Kincraig, Inverness-shire, PH21 1NU **Tel** *01540 651 272*

Housed in a charming log cabin, this restaurant overlooking Loch Insh features a traditional Scottish menu with local fish, haggis and steak. The Boathouse also serves tea, coffee, snacks and home-baked dishes throughout the day. There is a special menu for children and an outdoor balcony for summer dining, as well as a gift shop and bar.

KYLESKU The Kylesku Hotel
On A894 nr lairg, Sutherland, IV27 4HW **Tel** *01971 502231*

Located on the quayside, against the backdrop of lochs and mountains, The Kylesku Hotel is Fairtrade- and RSPCA Freedom Food-accredited. Menus are extensive and feature an array of local dishes, the speciality being freshly caught fish. The tranquil surroundings create an excellent setting in which to unwind and relax. Closed Nov–Feb.

Key to Price Guide *see p185* **Key to Symbols** *see back cover flap*

OBAN Wide Mouthed Frog £
*Dunstaffnage Bay, nr Oban, Argyll, PA37 1PX **Tel** 01631 567005*

Situated between Coban and Oban, this restaurant is a popular meeting place, particularly with the sailing community. The courtyard and decking areas offer stunning views of Dunstaffnage Bay and Dunstaffnage Castle. This bustling venue's menu features a range of locally caught fish and seafood. Accommodation available.

OBAN The Gathering Restaurant ££
*Breadalbane Street, Oban, Argyll, PA34 5NZ **Tel** 07770 931967*

Centrally located, The Gathering Restaurant is popular with both locals and visitors. This is an informal place where you can enjoy simple, well-cooked local produce in convivial and lively surroundings. Everything is freshly prepared, and the menu offers enough choice to appeal to all tastes. The staff are friendly and welcoming.

OBAN Ee'usk – The Fish Café £££
*N Pier, Oban, Argyll, PA34 5QD **Tel** 01631 565666*

Ee'usk, or the Fish Café, is located within an impressive waterside setting. On the menu you will find mouth-watering seafood dishes, created using the fresh catch of the day. A must-visit for those who enjoy fish, this eatery also offers impressive views of the coastline.

OBAN The Knipoch Hotel £££
*On A816, nr Oban, Argyll, PA34 4QT **Tel** 01852 316251*

Situated on the outskirts of Oban, this traditional country hotel serves excellent bar food, as well as informal three- to five-course dinners, featuring a huge array of vegetables and puddings. There is also a remarkable selection of whiskies on offer, dating as far back as 1936.

ORKNEY Julia's Café and Bistro £
*Ferry Road, Stromness, Orkney, KW16 3AE **Tel** 01856 850904*

Whether you are looking simply for somewhere to refuel and refresh or for a more substantial meal, Julia's Café and Bistro is highly recommended. It is a superb place to enjoy great Orcadian produce, freshly prepared and presented. The place has been locally recognized for its excellent and consistent quality. A warm, friendly and welcoming place.

PITLOCHRY Fern Cottage ££
*Ferry Road, Pitlochry, PH16 5DD **Tel** 01796 473849*

This charming little place is located in a stone-built cottage in the heart of Pitlochry. They serve breakfast, lunch, tea and cakes, pre-theatre meals and dinner. The menu is simple, focusing on good Scottish ingredients and Mediterranean cooking, with dishes such as smoked salmon with balsamic vinegar.

PLOCKTON Plockton Shores £££
*30 Harbour Street, Plockton, Ross-shire, IV52 8NN **Tel** 01599 544263*

Nestling on the shores of Loch Carron, you can take in the spectacular views from across the bay here and enjoy fresh fish, shellfish and game as well as modern Scottish and vegetarian dishes. This restaurant serves local produce whenever possible. It is well known for its cullen skink (a Scottish soup).

PORT APPIN The Airds Hotel £££££
*Port Appin, Argyll, PA38 4DF **Tel** 01631 730236*

This hotel-restaurant is situated on the coast of Argyll and offers a well-balanced, daily changing menu based on a variety of fresh local seafood, poultry and game. Mealtimes are leisurely and peaceful. The excellent service, warm ambience and impressive wine list complete the experience. A vegetarian menu can be requested when booking.

ST MARGARET'S HOPE The Creel £££
*Front Road, St Margaret's Hope, Orkney, KW17 2SL **Tel** 01856 831311*

A front-runner for one of the best places to eat in Orkney. The food served at The Creel is emphatically Orcadian in style, with a commitment to the wonderful locally sourced seafood, which features frequently on the menu – as do beef and seaweed-fed lamb. The service is friendly and helpful. Accommodation is also available.

STONEHAVEN Lairhillock Inn ££
*Netherley, nr Stonehaven, Aberdeenshire, AB39 3QS **Tel** 01569 730001*

Tucked away just off the Aberdeen to Banchory road, this is a 200-year-old coaching inn with a log fire and a candlelit conservatory. The location is pretty, but the real draw here is the food: locally sourced beef, scallops, wild boar and venison are prime ingredients in the award-winning dishes. The bar stocks a great selection of real ales and whiskies.

TONGUE Borgie Lodge ££
*Skerray, Tongue, KW14 7TH **Tel** 01641 5 21332*

This lovely house on the banks of the River Borgie in North Sutherland is a great place to stay and explore or simply visit to enjoy the great food on offer. Whether you opt for a casual bar meal or a formal dinner in the restaurant, you will be assured of the best locally sourced produce – prepared, cooked and presented with great care and skill.

ULLAPOOL The Ceilidh Place £££
*14 W Argyle Street, Ullapool, Sutherland, IV26 2TY **Tel** 01854 612103*

This award-winning hotel, with its own bookshop, restaurant and bar, is located within an interesting building with a great atmosphere. The restaurant serves imaginative dishes made with locally sourced ingredients of the highest quality. Meals incorporate fish, meat, poultry, vegetables and fruits.

SPECIAL INTERESTS AND OUTDOOR ACTIVITIES

Scotland may not be able to guarantee sunshine or offer beach culture, but its popularity as a holiday destination is due in no small part to its opportunities for outdoor activities, as well as cultural pursuits. Over the years, the tourist industry has matured to occupy an important role in the Scottish economy, and local businesses have become adept at providing visitors with

A lone piper of the Highlands

what they are looking for. That could be playing golf by the sea, fishing on the Tweed, cruising to see whales off the west coast during the summer, skiing in the Cairngorms in winter, eating fresh oysters at a lochside restaurant or searching for information on ancestors who left the country 200 years ago. Facilities for all kinds of activities have never been better, and this section outlines some of the best.

Searching for records of ancestors, Edinburgh

TRACING GENEALOGY

From the time of the infamous Clearances of the 18th century onwards *(see p150)*, Scots have emigrated to Australia, Canada, New Zealand, South Africa, the US and elsewhere in search of an easier life. There are now millions of foreign nationals who can trace their heritage back to Scotland, and uncovering family history is a popular reason for visiting the country.

Professional genealogists can be commissioned, but those interested in conducting investigations themselves should try the **General Register Office for Scotland** (which has records of births, deaths and marriages dating from the 1500s), the **Scottish Genealogy Society** or the **National Archives of Scotland**, all in Edinburgh.

GAELIC STUDIES

The northwest of Scotland is the heartland for the Gaelic language. Historically, this was a Celtic language that spread

from mainland Europe to Ireland in the 4th century BC, and later into Scotland where it became the national language. By the 18th century, however, under English rule, Gaelic had become identified with a rebellious clan system that was persecuted after the Jacobite rising of 1745 *(see p45)*. It was marginalized and suffered a decline.

A renaissance aims to revive this once-dominant culture with Gaelic broadcasts and by teaching it to children. **An Comunn Gaidhealach**, Scotland's official Gaelic society, organizes the annual Royal National Mod *(see p38)*, a performing arts competition. Other Gaelic societies are **Comunn An Luchd Ionnsachaidh**

and **Comunn na Gàidhlig**. **Sabhal Mor Ostaig**, a college on the Isle of Skye, runs short Gaelic courses for visitors.

FOOD AND DRINK TOURS

Scotland has a justified reputation for fine produce, and there has been an upsurge in the number of noteworthy restaurants in Edinburgh and Glasgow. Indeed, Edinburgh has established itself as the number two city for eating out in the British Isles, after London.

One way of sampling Scottish cuisine is to book a holiday through **Connoisseurs Scotland**, which arranges stays at country house hotels with a reputation for top-class cooking, such as the Crinan Hotel in Argyll, or Gleneagles. The **Scotch Malt Whisky Society** has information for lovers of this spirit. Distilleries are a popular attraction *(see pp32–3 and p144)*, with

Learning about whisky, the "water of life", at a Speyside distillery

names such as **Glenfiddich Distillery** operating tours.

The production of cask-conditioned beers is explained at Edinburgh's **Caledonian Brewery**. An exhibition at **Inverawe Smokehouses**, near Taynuilt in the Highlands, shows the techniques used in smoking fish such as salmon.

VIEWING WILDLIFE

In comparison with much of the rest of the British Isles, Scotland still has large areas of moor and mountain wilderness and a long, relatively undeveloped coastline that supports a range of animals

Sighting a porpoise as it breaks the calm surface of a sea loch

Walkers on the lookout for red deer and birds of prey at Glen Coe

(see pp18–19). In the mountains near Aviemore, rangers from the **Cairngorm Reindeer Centre** take parties of people on to the mountain to also walk among a herd of reindeer.

A convenient way to see the abundant sealife is on a boat trip run by **Maid of the Forth Cruises**, which operates from South Queensferry on the Forth near Edinburgh – dolphins and common seals are resident in these waters. More adventurous are the trips in search of whales offered by **Sea Life Surveys** from the Isle of Mull, but even a casual tourist in the Highlands can spot birds of

prey, otters in the lochs and herds of red deer on the mountainsides. With a large share of Britain's resident and visiting birds, Scotland is also home to a number of important bird sanctuaries, the most celebrated being Handa Island off Scourie on the far northwest coast *(see p157)*. St Abb's Head *(see p84)* east of Edinburgh and Baron's Haugh near Motherwell (on the outskirts of Glasgow) are nearer the cities.

Many wildlife tours are small-scale private businesses that operate according to seasonal and daily demand, so always check the details with the local tourist information offices.

DIRECTORY

TRACING GENEALOGY

General Register Office for Scotland
New Register House, 3 West Register St, Edinburgh, EH1 3YT.
Tel (0131) 334 0380.
www.gro-scotland.gov.uk

Scottish Genealogy Society
15 Victoria Terrace, Edinburgh, EH1 2JL.
Tel (0131) 220 3677.
www.scotsgenealogy.com

The National Archives of Scotland
General Register House, 2 Princes St, Edinburgh, EH1 3YY.
Tel (0131) 535 1314.
www.nas.gov.uk

GAELIC STUDIES

An Comunn Gaidhealach
109 Church St, Inverness, IV1 1EY. *Tel (01463) 709 705.* www.acgmod.org

Comunn An Luchd Ionnsachaidh
1–4 Highland Rail House, Academy Street, Inverness, IV1 1LE. *Tel (01463) 226 710.* www.cli.org.uk

Comunn na Gàidhlig
5 Mitchell's Lane, Inverness, IV3 2AQ.
Tel (01463) 234138.
www.cnag.org.uk

Sabhal Mor Ostaig
Teangue, Sleat, Isle of Skye, IV44 8RQ.
Tel (01471) 888000.
www.smo.uhi.ac.uk

FOOD AND DRINK TOURS

Caledonian Brewery
42 Slateford Rd, Edinburgh, EH11 1PH.
Tel (0131) 337 1286.
www.caledonian-brewery.co.uk

Connoisseurs Scotland
PO Box 26164, Dunfermline, KY11 9WQ.
Tel (01383) 825800.

Glenfiddich Distillery
Dufftown, Keith, Banffshire, AB55 4DH.
Tel (01340) 820373.
www.glenfiddich.com

Inverawe Smokehouses
Taynuilt, Argyll, PA35 1HU.
Tel (0844) 847 5490.

Scotch Malt Whisky Society
The Vaults, 87 Giles St, Edinburgh, EH6 6BZ.
Tel (0131) 554 3451.
www.smws.com

VIEWING WILDLIFE

Cairngorm Reindeer Centre
Glenmore, Aviemore, PH22 1QU. *Tel (01479) 861228.*

Maid of the Forth Cruises
Hawes Pier, South Queensferry, EH30.
Tel (0131) 331 5000.
www.maidofthe forth.co.uk

Sea Life Surveys
Ledaig, Tobermory, Isle of Mull, PA75 6NU.
Tel (01688) 302916.
www.sealifesurveys.com

Outdoor Activities at a Glance

Only a handful of inland lochs and coastal waters
have been exploited by commercial boating and
watersports companies, though it is possible to use
private vessels on many minor lochs in wilderness
areas. Likewise, organized skiing is confined to just
five centres. Of the country's several hundred golf
courses, most are concentrated in central and
southern Scotland. This map plots the main centres
for various popular activities. For further information
about particular
sports across
Scotland, see
pages 202–11.

Handa Island, off the
far northwest coast, is
one of a number of
seabird reserves.

**Rock climbers and
mountaineers** (see
p208) *usually head
for Glencoe, the
Cairngorms and the
Cuillin Hills on Skye.
The Torridon range
and other formations
further north are also
popular choices.*

The five skiing centres (see p209)
*are White Corries (Glencoe), the
Nevis Range, Cairngorm, Glenshee
and the Lecht. The skiing season
usually gets under way in
December and lasts until April.*

**The West Highland
Way** is the most
famous long-distance
walk in Scotland,
encompassing a
wonderful variety
of terrain.

Culzean Castle

KEY

Watersports	
Sailing	
Major golf course	
Birdwatching	
Mountaineering	
Skiing	
Fishing	
Pony trekking	
Major walking area	
Long-distance walk route	

Sailing (see p211) *is
popular off the west coast
and the islands. The
calm waters of sheltered
bays are suitable for be-
ginners, while the open
sea can be both exhila-
rating and treacherous.
Inland, Loch Ness offers
sailing opportunities.*

SHETLAND

ORKNEY

• John o'Groats

Bird-watching (see p199) *is in itself a reason to visit Scotland. The best sanctuaries are in remote coastal areas where such delightful species as puffins make their home on the sheer, wave-lashed cliffs.*

SPEYSIDE

• Cairngorms

GRAMPIAN MOUNTAINS

Watersports (see p211) *include canoeing, surfing, windsurfing and diving. Visitors can book equipment and courses through activities centres scattered around the country.*

GLASGOW EDINBURGH

Golf *(see pp202–5)* attracts thousands of visitors every year, especially to the most famous courses in Central Scotland, such as St Andrews and Carnoustie.

PENTLAND HILLS

CHEVIOT HILLS

Walking (see pp206–7) *is tremendously popular in Scotland, and vast swathes of the countryside are open to the public.*

Fishing *(see p210)* is well catered for on the River Tweed in southern Scotland, and on Loch Ness in the Highlands.

Pony trekking *opportunities (see p210) are within easy reach of the cities, in the gentle countryside of southern and central Scotland, and in the great moor and mountain wilderness of the Highlands.*

0 kilometres   50

0 miles   50

Golf in Scotland

The ancient game of golf is synonymous with Scotland and has been played here for hundreds of years. Wherever you choose to stay, there will be a golf course not far away. Few countries can rival Scotland for the number, quality and variety of courses – over 550 at the last count, with new ones opening every year. Similarly, few golfing destinations can lay claim to such magnificent, unspoilt scenery. Golf is played by people of all ages and capabilities in Scotland – it's a game for everyone to enjoy. Whether your game is suited to one of the legendary championship courses or to a less daunting challenge, you will find a hearty welcome here.

British-made golf tees

EARLY HISTORY

Variations on the game of golf as we know it today were being played across Europe as long ago as the 14th century, and possibly even in Roman times. However, it is the Scottish who must be credited with establishing the official game and encouraging its development across the world. It was in Scotland that the passion for golf was born. By the middle of the 16th century, the game had become a popular pastime at the highest levels of society – James VI himself was a keen player, as was his mother, Mary, Queen of Scots.

In the late 1800s, wealthy middle-class Englishmen began to follow the example of the Royal Family by taking their holidays in Scotland. The expansion of the railway system at this time allowed people to get to the seaside courses, and the English became so infatuated with the game of golf that they took it home with them. In 1744 the Gentlemen Golfers of Leith, led by Duncan Forbes, drew up the first *Articles & Laws in Playing at Golf.* Although later revised and updated, these original rules, set down by the Scottish professionals of the time, formed the framework for the modern game of golf.

TOOLS OF THE TRADE

The Scottish influence on golf was not to end there. Many of the professionals playing at the time were also skilled carpenters, instrumental in developing the clubs and balls used in the game. Willie Park Senior was a master clubmaker, and winner of the first Scottish Open in 1860, while Old Tom Morris became a legend in the game for both his playing and craftsmanship. In the days before machinery, the wooden clubs were made entirely by hand. The earliest irons were also fashioned by hand, followed by aluminium-headed clubs that differ very little from clubs today. The "guttie" ball was invented in 1848, replacing the expensive and easily damaged "feathery", thus making the game more affordable. The modern, rubber-core ball in use today appeared at the beginning of the 20th century.

A scenic view of Gleneagles, one of Scotland's championship courses

ARRANGING A GAME

Nearly all Scottish golf clubs welcome visitors, although there may be restrictions on non-members at popular times. Check booking arrangements carefully. Most clubs have websites, many with online booking facilities; others require a formal written application. To be certain of a round on the more famous courses, book well in advance, or take a golfing package that includes guaranteed tee times at your chosen venues.

For a comprehensive list of all Scotland's golf courses, including prices and amenities and other useful golfing information, order a free copy of the annual *Official Golf Guide to Scotland* brochure, produced by VisitScotland (Tel: 0845 22 55 121).

ETIQUETTE

Scotland isn't a snobbish place to play golf, but some clubs are more conservative than others. Some frown on jeans or trainers, and a few insist on jackets and ties in the clubhouse lounge. Remember to bring your handicap certificate along each time you visit.

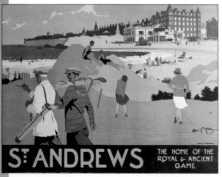

St ANDREWS THE HOME OF THE ROYAL & ANCIENT GAME

An old railway poster illustrating the lure of St Andrews as a paradise for golfing enthusiasts

WHEN TO PLAY

It's easier (and cheaper) to get a game during the week rather than at a weekend, and outside busy holiday periods. The main golfing season runs from about April to mid-October, but most clubs stay open all year round, especially the links (coastal) courses, where the climate is milder. May and September are ideal times to play: temperatures are moderate and the scenery is at its most beautiful. The further north you go, the more variable the hours of daylight are. At midsummer, you can tee off at midnight on Orkney and Shetland.

GOLFING EVENTS

Many keen golfers combine a visit to Scotland with a well-known golfing event. Besides the famous Open Championship, held at least every other year, professional fixtures attracting visitors to Scotland are the Barclays Scottish Open, staged at Loch Lomond in late summer; the Dunhill Links Championship (Oct); and two women's championships: the Women's British Open and the Ladies' Scottish Open. Popular amateur events include the St Andrews Links Trophy (Jun) and the Scottish Amateur Championship (Jul–Aug). "Golf Weeks" are held at St Andrews (Apr), Royal Deeside and Machrihanish (both in May), and Pitlochry (Jun). The Fife, Ayrshire and Highland Classics are held at multiple venues.

Sunset at Royal Troon, Ayrshire

FACILITIES

A scheme called "Visiting Golfers Welcome", operated by VisitScotland, indicates which clubs provide facilities for non-members. Smarter clubs offer on-site accommodation; this can be extremely luxurious, with many leisure amenities, as at **Gleneagles** or the **Carnegie Club**'s Skibo Castle. Others can suggest hotels or bed and breakfasts nearby, many of which offer special rates or discounted green fees for golfers, along with storage facilities, drying rooms and early or late mealtimes. Look out for the "Golfers Welcome" logo, which indicates accommodation specially geared to golf lovers.

Clubs and hand trollies can be hired at most courses, but book ahead if you need a caddy. Buggies (ride-on golf carts) may be available if pre-booked at the larger courses, but the norm in Scotland is to walk the course unless you have a medical condition or physical disability.

LONG TRADITIONS

Many of Scotland's courses are steeped in history and tradition. Without a doubt, **St Andrews** in Fife is the true home of golf, where the game originated in the 15th century (records date back to 1457). The St Andrews Links Trust now operates seven superb courses on this hallowed stretch of seaside, the most venerable of which is the Old Course. Every golfer dreams of playing here. If you are lucky, your dream may come true – this legendary course is accessible to visitors at short notice via a democratic ballot system. Simply contact the Trust the day before you want to play, and your name will be included in the daily draw (successful applicants are posted on the club's website).

St Andrews's resident Royal and Ancient Golf Club (R&A), founded in 1754, is the official ruling body of world golf.

The R&A organizes the famous British Open Championship, traditionally hosted by St Andrews every five years. The winner of this prestigious contest is awarded the coveted Claret Jug trophy, crafted and hallmarked in 1873. The British Golf Museum, opposite the R&A clubhouse, is a must-visit attraction for any keen player.

Not far from St Andrews is the **Crail Golfing Society**, which began life in 1786. Its Balcomie links course is a tough seaside test. The **Royal Burgess**, instituted in 1735, is the oldest golfing society in the world. Upholding time-honoured golfing rules, it features a picturesque tree-lined course on the north side of Edinburgh. Visitor tee times are available.

The Claret Jug trophy

The Barclays Scottish Open at Loch Lomond Golf Club

CHAMPIONSHIP COURSES

Other famous courses on the Open circuit include **Carnoustie** in Angus (which hosted the championship in 2007), **Turnberry** and **Royal Troon**. **Prestwick** and **Royal Musselburgh** are splendid but no longer used because of the difficulty of accommodating large crowds. Other stunning courses used as Open qualifying venues are **Gullane** (No. 1), **North Berwick** and **Glasgow Gailes**. **Downfield** in Dundee hosts the Scottish Open from time to time, while up in the Highlands, **Royal Dornoch** is an all-time great links course designed by Tom Morris. Another famous name is **Gleneagles**, a luxurious resort home to four courses. The Johnnie Walker Championship is held here annually in late summer.

DESIGNER GOLF

Carnoustie, Royal Musselburgh and the King's and Queen's courses at Gleneagles were designed by the great 1920s player James Braid, five-time winner of the Open. VisitScotland's James Braid Trail explores some of the 250 or so courses he created or modified throughout the country, introducing features such as dog-legs and pot bunkers. Famous Braid courses include **Nairn**, **Boat of Garten**, **Crieff**, **Haggs Castle**, **Brora** and **Dalmahoy**. Braid cut his golfing teeth on the links at **Elie**, where he was born, though he had little influence on the present course.

The tranquil landscape at Cruden Bay golf course, near Aberdeen

Aerial view of Machrihanish, a golf course overlooking the Atlantic Ocean

More recently, Dave Thomas has achieved great success as a course designer. Among his creations are **Deer Park** in Livingston, **Roxburghe** in the Borders and the **Spey Valley** championship course near Aviemore, dramatically set against the backdrop of the Cairngorm mountains.

ARRESTING SCENERY

It's a rare Scottish golf course that doesn't boast a glorious setting. **Elgin** is one of the finest inland courses, in lush parkland surroundings, while **Kingussie** takes advantage of an amazing Cairngorm backdrop. **Pitlochry** is an ideal holiday course, and nine-hole **Traigh**, on the Road to the Isles, features a magnificent panorama towards the Inner Hebrides. **Shiskine** on the Isle of Arran is an unusual and little-known gem with 12 holes in a wonderful setting. The **Isle of Skye** is another small but beautiful course with sea and island views, while Orkney's **Stromness** is a demanding holiday course with superb vistas of Scapa Flow.

However, it is perhaps the classic links, or coastal courses, that are most typical of the Scottish game. Links courses present infinitely varied challenges: a dramatic opening drive across the Atlantic at **Machrihanish** in Argyll, or the lunar landscape at **Cruden Bay**, near Aberdeen. One of the newest top-flight courses is **Kingsbarns**, near St Andrews, which opened in 2000 with stunning sea views.

CUTTING COSTS

Golf can be an expensive hobby, but it is possible to enjoy a round for under £20 – for example, at **Braid Hills** in Edinburgh, a superb public course with amazing views of the castle and city, or at **Merchants of Edinburgh**. If you don't want to spend too

Golfing at the Isle of Skye course

much at Fife's **Leven Links**, try the adjoining James Braid-designed nine-hole **Lundin Ladies** course, which costs a third of the price and welcomes visitors of either gender, or **Colvend**, overlooking the Solway Firth.

Another way to keep costs down is to take up one of the many deals and passes available through specialist operators, or listed in the Official Guide to Golf. These include the Freedom of the Fairways, which allows discounted play at 21 courses in the Borders, and the Aviemore & Cairngorms Golf Pass, which offers seven days' golf at eight different courses in the central Highlands.

DIRECTORY

USEFUL WEBSITES

www.scotlands-golf-courses.com
www.scottishgolf.com
www.golf.visitscotland.com

GOLFING ORGANIZATIONS

Scottish Golf Union
Tel (01382) 549500.

Scottish Ladies Golfing Association
Tel (01738) 442357.

SPECIALIST OPERATORS

Adventures in Golf
Tel 001 (877) 424 7320. www.adventures-in-golf.com

Golf International
Tel (800) 833 1389. www.golfinternational.com

Links Golf St Andrews
Tel (01334) 478639. www.linksgolfstandrews.com

Premier Golf
Tel 001 (866) 260 4409. www.premiergolf.com

Scottish Golf Tours
Tel (0131) 657 1984. www.scottish-golftours.com

EDINBURGH AND SOUTHERN SCOTLAND

Braid Hills
22 Braid Hills Approach, Edinburgh. **Tel** (0131) 447 6666. www.edinburghleisuregolf.co.uk

Colvend
Sandyhills, Colvend. **Tel** (01556) 630398. www.colvendgolfclub.co.uk

Dalmahoy
Marriott Hotel & CC, Kirknewton, Edinburgh. **Tel** (0131) 333 1845.

Deer Park
Golf Course Rd, Livingston, West Lothian. **Tel** (01506) 446699.

Gullane
West Links Road, Gullane, East Lothian. **Tel** (01620) 842255. www.gullanegolfclub.com

Merchants of Edinburgh
10 Craighill Gardens, Edinburgh. **Tel** (0131) 447 1219. www.merchantsgolf.com

North Berwick
New Clubhouse, Beach Rd, North Berwick. **Tel** (01620) 895040. www.northberwickgolfclub.com

Prestwick
2 Links Road, Prestwick, Ayrshire. **Tel** (01292) 671020. www.prestwickgc.co.uk

Roxburghe
Village of Heiton, Kelso, Borders. **Tel** (01573) 450 333. www.roxburghegolfclub.co.uk

Royal Burgess
181 Whitehouse Road, Barnton, Edinburgh. **Tel** (0131) 339 9440. www.royalburgess.co.uk

Royal Musselburgh
Prestongrange House, Prestonpans, East Lothian. **Tel** (01875) 810276. www.royalmusselburgh.co.uk

Royal Troon
Craigend Road, Troon, Ayrshire. **Tel** (01292) 311 555. www.royaltroon.com

Turnberry
The Westin Turnberry, Turnberry, Ayrshire. **Tel** (01655) 331000. www.turnberryresort.co.uk

GLASGOW AND CENTRAL SCOTLAND

Carnoustie
Links Parade, Carnoustie, Angus. **Tel** (01241) 802 270. www.carnoustiegolflinks.co.uk

Crail
Balcomie Clubhouse, Fifeness, Crail, Fife. **Tel** (01333) 450686. www.crailgolfingsociety.co.uk

Crieff
Perth Road, Crieff, Perthshire. **Tel** (01764) 652909. www.crieffgolf.co.uk

Downfield
Turnberry Avenue, Dundee. **Tel** (01382) 825595. www.downfieldgolf.co.uk

Elie
Golf Course Lane, Elie, Fife. **Tel** (01333) 333301. www.golfhouseclub.org

Glasgow Gailes
Gailes, Irvine. **Tel** (0141) 942 2011. www.glasgowgolfclub.com

Gleneagles
Gleneagles, Auchterarder, Perthshire. **Tel** (01764) 662 231. www.gleneagles.com

Haggs Castle
70 Dumbreck Road, Dumbreck, Glasgow. **Tel** (0141) 427 1157. www.haggscastlegolfclub.com

Kingsbarns
Kingsbarns, St Andrews, Fife. **Tel** (01334) 460860. www.kingsbarns.com

Leven Links
The Promenade, Leven, Fife. **Tel** (01333) 428859. www.leven-links.com

Lundin Ladies
Woodielea Road, Lundin Links, Fife. **Tel** (01333) 320832. www.lundinladiesgolfclub.co.uk

St Andrews Links
St Andrews Links Trust, Fife. **Tel** (01334) 466666. www.standrews.org.uk

Shiskine
Blackwaterfoot, Shiskine, Isle of Arran. **Tel** (01770) 860226. www.shiskinegolf.com

THE HIGHLANDS AND ISLANDS

Boat of Garten
Boat of Garten, Inverness-shire. **Tel** (01479) 831282. www.boatgolf.com

Brora
Golf Road, Brora, Sutherland. **Tel** (01408) 621417. www.broragolf.co.uk

Carnegie
Skibo Castle, Dornoch, Sutherland. **Tel** (01862) 894600. www.carnegieclub.co.uk

Cruden Bay
Aulton Road, Cruden Bay, Peterhead. **Tel** (01779) 812285. www.crudenbaygolfclub.co.uk

Elgin
Birnie Road, Elgin, Moray. **Tel** (01343) 542338. www.elgingolfclub.com

Isle of Skye
Sconser, Isle of Skye. **Tel** (01478) 650333. www.sconserlodge.co.uk

Kingussie
Gynack Road, Kingussie. **Tel** (01540) 661600. www.kingussie-golf.co.uk

Machrihanish
Campbeltown, Argyll. **Tel** (01586) 810277. www.machgolf.com

Nairn
Seabank Road, Nairn. **Tel** (01667) 453208. www.nairngolfclub.co.uk

Pitlochry
Golf Course Road, Pitlochry. **Tel** (01796) 472792. www.pitlochrygolf.co.uk

Royal Dornoch
Golf Road, Dornoch, Sutherland. **Tel** (01862) 810219. www.royaldornoch.com

Spey Valley
Dalfaber Golf & Country Club, Dalfaber Village, Aviemore. **Tel** (0845) 601 1734. www.macdonaldhotels.co.uk/resorts/dalfaber

Stromness
Ness, Stromness, Orkney. **Tel** (01856) 850772. www.stromnessgc.co.uk

Traigh
Traigh Golf Club, Arisaig. **Tel** (01687) 450337. www.traighgolf.co.uk

Walking in Scotland

Thermos flask

It can truly be said that Scotland is a paradise for walkers. The scenery is superb without being overwhelming, and the variety of terrain encompasses everything from craggy mountains to gentle river valleys, not to mention a magnificent coastline. In recent years there has been an increase in the number of walks available to the public. The local tourist information centre is always a good first port of call if you are looking for advice or suggested routes. Whether you wish to walk for an hour or spend a day on the trail, you will find that Scotland can satisfy all of your walking needs.

Long-distance trail signpost for walkers in the Spey river valley

RIGHT OF ACCESS

In Scotland there is a statutory right of access to most land for recreational purposes. Access laws implemented in 2005 are balanced by a Scottish Outdoor Access Code giving guidance on responsible conduct for users and managers of such land.

Scotland's long tradition of open access has resulted in few routes being shown on Ordnance Survey or other maps, although historic rights of way are usually marked. **Scotways** hold the definitive maps showing these routes.

Guidebooks available at large bookshops such as **WHSmith** or **Waterstone's** describe easily walkable routes, many of which are signposted. Outdoor chain **Tiso** also sells maps and hiking guides.

There may be access restrictions in mountain areas during the stag stalking season (August to October), but not on any areas owned by the **National Trust for Scotland** *(see p209)*.

CLOTHING AND EQUIPMENT

The weather in Scotland is fickle. It can snow in June or be balmy in February, and conditions are liable to change rapidly. This makes selecting the right clothing and equipment tricky. Even in summer, you should take a waterproof jacket if venturing far from shelter. When going on a day walk, take waterproof trousers and a fleece or warm sweater.

The art of being comfortable is to make your clothing adaptable; several thin layers are better than one thick one. Head covering is worth considering – a cap for sunny days or a warmer hat for cold days.

For any walk of more than a couple of hours' duration, take a drink and snack. If you are going to be out all day, take energy foods and liquids.

Good footwear is essential. Countryside walks generally demand strong shoes or boots. Sturdy trainers can be worn on roads or firm tracks, but not on rough ground where you may need ankle support. Lightweight walking boots are suitable for most seasons.

WALKING OPPORTUNITIES

This section deals with low-level walking; mountain activities are covered on pages 208–9, and you can also obtain information from the **Mountaineering Council of Scotland**.

In recent years, greatly improved path networks have been developed, some through the national **Paths for All Partnership**. The networks provide excellent, safe walking opportunities for visitors. Some of the best networks are in the Borders and around Galloway, in Perthshire (around Dunkeld and Pitlochry), in Aberdeenshire (around Huntly), at Braemar and on the island of Bute.

Local authorities and other agencies have created paths and published walking guides for remote areas, such as Wester Ross, the Western Isles, Orkney and Shetland. Some of these walks tie in with ferry services. Most have a cultural or natural history theme, or incorporate a castle, waterfall or other place of interest. The walks are generally from 6 to 12 km (4 to 7 miles) in length.

Walking boots

Summer walking in Glen Etive

Above the clouds in Knoydart, looking to the Cuillin Hills on Skye

Tourist information centres are good starting places for more details, or you can contact **VisitScotland** to obtain their *New Walking Scotland* brochure, which describes

Compass of the type commonly used by walkers

walks in all parts of Scotland. Their brochure also lists walking festivals. These events, that last up to a week, offer a wide range of guided walks along with a programme of evening entertainment. The first such festival, held in the Borders, started in 1995. Others are now held in the Highlands, Deeside and Perthshire, with more starting up each year.

For information on organized walks, contact the **Ramblers' Association Scotland**. There are also hundreds of miles of forest trails and walks across the country. The **Forestry Commission** can provide you with general information.

Longer low-level routes being developed include the Fife Coastal Path, the Clyde Walkway and the Speyside Way extension to Aviemore. All of these can easily be sampled as day walks.

Spring and autumn are especially lovely times of the year for walking in Scotland. The colouring is superb, and there is often a wider choice of accommodation available.

LONG-DISTANCE WALKS

Scotland has relatively few formal long-distance routes, though the potential for making up your own is limitless. The three "official" routes are the 152-km (95-mile) West Highland Way from Glasgow to Fort William, the 340-km (211-mile) Southern Upland Way from Portpatrick to Cockburnspath, and the 84-km (52-mile) Speyside Way from Spey Bay to Tomintoul.

Other routes developed by local authorities include the 100-km (62-mile) St Cuthbert's Way from Melrose to Lindisfarne, and the Fife Coastal Path from North Queensferry to Tayport near the bridge over the Tay to Dundee.

The three principal routes are shown on the activities map *(see pp200–1)*. For information about them, and others being developed, contact **Scottish Natural Heritage** and local tourist information centres.

Surveying the scenery on a wintry day in the Cairngorms

DIRECTORY

Forestry Commission
231 Corstorphine Rd,
Edinburgh EH12 7AT.
Tel (0845) 367 3787.
www.forestry.gov.uk

Mountaineering Council of Scotland
The Old Granary, West Mill St,
Perth PH1 5QP.
Tel (01738) 493942.
www.mcofs.org.uk

National Trust for Scotland
28 Charlotte Square,
Edinburgh EH2 4ET.
Tel (0844) 493 2100.
www.nts.org.uk

The Paths for All Partnership
Inglewood House,
Tullibody Rd, Alloa FK10 2HU.
Tel (01259) 218888.
www.pathsforall.org.uk

Ramblers' Association Scotland
Kingfisher House,
Auld Mart Business Park,
Milnathort KY13 9DA.
Tel (01577) 861222.
www.ramblers.org.uk

Scottish Natural Heritage
Great Glen House, 1 Leachkin
Rd, Inverness IV3 8NW.
Tel (01463) 725067.
www.snh.org.uk

Scotways
24 Annandale St,
Edinburgh EH7 4AN.
Tel (0131) 558 1222.
www.scotways.com

Tiso
123–125 Rose Street
Precinct EH2 3DT.
Tel (0131) 225 9486.

VisitScotland
23 Ravelston Terrace,
Edinburgh EH4 3TP.
Tel (0845) 225 5121.
www.visitscotland.com

Waterstone's
83 George Street, Edinburgh
EH2 3ES. *Tel (0131) 225 3436.*
153–157 Sauchiehall Street,
Glasgow G2 3EW.
Tel (0141) 332 9501.

WHSmith
10B Queensferry St,
Edinburgh EH2 4PG.
Tel (0131) 225 9672.

Activities in the Mountains

Although Scotland's highest mountains rise to little over 1,200 m (4,000 ft), they offer a true challenge to the hill walker and rock climber alike. Noted worldwide for their beauty of form and variety of character, the mountains of Scotland command respect among all mountaineers, not least because the climate is so variable. During the winter, conditions can be arctic. Long days in the hills offer a sense of satisfaction and refreshment that is highly valued as a contrast to the hectic pace of modern life.

west, many of which command superb sea views. Narrow ridges such as the Aonach Eagach above Glencoe, and the peerless Cuillins of Skye, offer exhilarating sport and a special challenge. Given the right conditions, most hills can be climbed in a day, but more remote peaks may demand an overnight camp, or a stay in one of the simple huts known as a "bothy". Winter mountaineering needs extra skills but it also reaps the fantastic reward of the most breathtaking scenery.

Rock and ice climbing in Scotland has a long and distinguished history stretching back over a century. The main climbing areas, including Glencoe, the Cairngorms and Skye, have provided tough training grounds for many climbers who later gained world renown. All year the huge northern faces of Ben Nevis (*see p135*) offer a multitude of climbs at all levels. New areas, including the far northwest and the islands, have been developed more recently, as have particular disciplines such as sea-stack climbing. Techniques are being continually extended and skills refined, so that ever tougher routes can be completed. The mountains of

A rucksack for carrying provisions

Scotland may be small, but the maritime climate and frequently wild winter weather produce ice climbs that are among the most serious and demanding in the world. The only "closed season" on Scotland's mountains is the short period between mid-August and late October, when restrictions apply in certain areas during the stag shooting season. *Heading for the Scottish Hills*, published jointly by the **Mountaineering Council of Scotland** and the Scottish Landowners' Federation gives estate maps and telephone numbers to call for local advice. See the Directory opposite for details of the **Hillphones** message system.

MUNROS AND CORBETTS

Scottish mountains rising just above 914 m (3,000 ft) are often called "Munros" after Sir Hugh Munro, first president of the Scottish Mountaineering Club (SMC). In 1891 Munro published the first comprehensive list of mountains fulfilling

Hard hats and safety ropes – vital equipment for rock climbing

SAFETY IN THE MOUNTAINS

The mountains of Scotland demand respect at any time of the year, and this means being properly prepared. You should always take with you full waterproofs, warm clothes (including hat and gloves), and food and drink. Take a map and compass and know how to use them. Good boots are essential. Winter mountaineering demands knowledge of ice-axe and crampon techniques. **Glenmore Lodge** in Aviemore is a good centre offering courses in skiing, hill craft and mountaineering.

MOUNTAINEERING IN SCOTLAND

Recreation in the mountains takes several forms. Many people aim for the higher hills, known as "Munros" and "Corbetts". These vary in character from the rounded heathery domes of the Monadhliath or the Southern Uplands to the steep, craggy eminences of the

Rock climbers ascending Polldubh, Glen Nevis

Enjoying a superb mountain panorama in the northern Highlands

this criterion. The list has been maintained by the SMC ever since, and the hills are now officially classed as Munros. Normally, the principal summits on a hill are Munros; the lesser summits are called "Tops". Revised several times, the list now totals 284 Munros.

The first known Munroist was the Rev AE Robertson in 1901. He finished his tour of the Munros on Meall Dearg, above Glencoe, and it is recorded that he kissed the cairn before kissing his wife, such was his enthusiasm as the first of many dedicated Munroists.

In the 1920s, J Rooke Corbett published a list of the summits that measured 760–915 m (2,500–3,000 ft). These 221 "Corbetts", as they became known, have a clearer definition than the Munros – they must be single summits.

A third list is available, of summits of 610–760 m (2,000–2,500 ft) called "Grahams". All summits in Scotland over 610 m have now been categorized and published. The hills are described, with ascent routes, in the SMC guides *The Munros* and *The Corbetts, and other Scottish Hills*, and in *The Munros Almanac* and *The Corbetts Almanac*. The third set is listed in a publication called *The Grahams*.

SKIING IN SCOTLAND

There are five ski centres in Scotland: **White Corries** at Glencoe, **Nevis Range** *(see pp135)*, **The Lecht, Cairngorm** *(see pp140–41)* and **Glenshee**. The Lecht tends to have the gentlest runs, while White Corries has the steepest.

These two centres are more informal than the others. Nevis Range, Glenshee and Cairngorm offer good facilities and runs for skiers of all abilities, including nursery slopes.

Ski centres are usually open from December to April, depending on the amount of snow cover. Unfortunately, snow is not wholly reliable in Scotland but when it does snow, the skiing is exhilarating. Hotels and guesthouses in the ski areas offer weekend and midweek packages, and there are ski schools in all the areas. The best advice is to keep an eye on the weather and take your chance as it arises.

Cross-country or Nordic skiing is a popular, informal sport in Scotland. Given good snow cover, there are many suitable areas, ranging from the Southern Uplands to the hills of the north and west, as well as hundreds of miles of forest trails all over Scotland.

Downhill skiing on the Scottish slopes

DIRECTORY

SAFETY IN THE MOUNTAINS

Scotland has a well organized network of voluntary mountain rescue teams. Calls for rescue should be made to the police on **999**.

Weather Forecasts
(the Highlands)
Tel 0870 900 0100.

Mountaineering Council of Scotland
The Old Granary, West Mill St, Perth PH1 5QP.
Tel (01738) 493942.
Fax (01738) 442095.
www.mcofs.org.uk

Hillphones
www.snh.org.uk/
hillphones
This service offers hill-walkers a recorded telephone message detailing daily stag stalking in various parts of the Highlands from 1st Jul until 20th Oct. It is organized by the Mountaineering Council of Scotland, Scottish Natural Heritage and participating estates.
Athol and Lude
Tel (01796) 481740.
Balmoral–Lochnagar
Tel (01339) 755532.
Callater and Clunie
Tel (01339) 741997.
Drumochter
Tel (01528) 522300.

Glen Clova
Tel (01339) 755532.
Glen Dochart/Glen Lochay
Tel (01567) 820886.
Glen Shee
Tel (01339) 741911.
Grey Corries/Mamores
Tel (01397) 732362.
Invercauld
Tel (01339) 741911.
North Arran
Tel (01770) 302363.
Paps of Jura
Tel (01496) 820323.
South Glen Shiel
Tel (01599) 511425.

Glenmore Lodge
Aviemore,
Inverness-shire PH22 1QU.
Tel (01479) 861256.

SKI CENTRES

www.visitscotland.com

Cairngorm
Aviemore, Inverness-shire.
Tel (01479) 861261.

Glenshee
Cairnwell, Aberdeenshire.
Tel (01339) 741320.

The Lecht
Strathden, Aberdeenshire.
Tel (01975) 651440.

Nevis Range
Torlundy, Inverness-shire.
Tel (01397) 705825.

White Corries
King's House,
Glencoe, Argyll.
Tel (01855) 851226.

Other Outdoor Activities

Scotland has a few surprises up its sleeve for people who still associate the country with old-fashioned tourist images. While traditional pursuits such as deerstalking or salmon fishing still thrive, they are now complemented by a wide range of more contemporary sports including mountain biking and even surfing. Flanked by the North Sea and the Atlantic, Scotland has ample water for sailing, windsurfing and fishing, while horse riding and cycling present excellent ways to explore the country's varied and dramatic landscapes.

Dunkeld fishing fly

Splendid catch of the day from the River Tweed, southern Scotland

Mountain biking on low-level tracks

CYCLING AND MOUNTAIN BIKING

Cycling around Scotland is one of the best ways to view the country. The trails of the Highlands are near perfect mountain bike territory and **Forest Enterprise** has opened a lot of the forest road network to mountain bikers. There is also an expanding national cycle path network to explore. Edinburgh has a system of cycle paths on old train tracks. **Edinburgh Central Cycle Hire** is just one of many hire shops in the city. The **Scottish Cyclists Union** has information on cycling events and races in and around the capital.

A *Cycling in Scotland* booklet is available from tourist offices. For details of cycling trips in Scotland, contact the **C.T.C. National Cyclists Organisation** and **Scottish Cycling Holidays**.

FISHING

Although Scotland is most associated with salmon fishing, there are opportunities for sea angling, coarse fishing, and game fishing for trout too.

The **Salmon and Trout Association** has information on game fishing – the season runs from mid-February to the end of October. For coarse fishing and sea angling a landowner's permission is required before casting off. The **Scottish Federation for Coarse Angling** and **Scottish Federation of Sea Anglers** provide all the necessary information. Contact the **Scottish Anglers National Association** for general advice.

HUNTING

The tradition of recreational hunting can be traced back to the mid-1800s, when Queen Victoria and Prince Albert set up residence in Balmoral on Deeside. It became fashionable for British aristocrats to spend the autumn shooting in Scotland. Large parts of the Highlands became sporting estates.

Scotland is recognized as providing Europe's best game-shooting and deerstalking. Red deer and grouse are plentiful, while many estuaries and firths are wintering grounds for birds.

Over the last 30 years or so, hunting in Scotland has also attracted overseas visitors. For information on gun licensing and where to shoot, contact the **British Association for Shooting and Conservation**.

PONY TREKKING AND HORSE RIDING

There are more than 60 trekking and riding centres across Scotland, catering to a wide range of abilities, including trips deep into the Highlands for experienced riders. Some offer accommodation, tuition and trail riding, others provide trekking by the hour. The **Trekking and Riding Society of Scotland** has a complete list of all the centres. **Pentland Hills Icelandics**, south of Edinburgh, offers rides on rare Icelandic ponies. On Deeside is the **Glen Tanar Equestrian Centre**, and visitors to Skye should try **Skye Riding Centre**.

Visitors taking in the Scottish scenery on horseback

SAILING

Scotland is a country of firths, islands and sea lochs, and the best way to explore them is by boat. You do not necessarily have to be a skilled sailor to do this, as some companies now offer supervised yachting holidays for novices. Visitors also have the option of chartering a yacht. Centres such as **Port Edgar Marina** near Edinburgh or the **Scottish National Watersports Centre** on Cumbrae in the Firth of Clyde offer tuition for beginners, while experienced sailors will find serviced moorings for their own craft in beauty spots up and down the west coast and among the islands.

Wooden sailboat in the Sound of Sleat, just off the Isle of Skye

Kayaking on Loch Eil in the shadow of magnificent Ben Nevis

WATERSPORTS

Surfing is not an activity normally associated with Scotland, but a good wetsuit and a sense of determination are all that is needed. Pease Bay in East Lothian is a popular spot, as are some north coast locations such as Dunnet Bay by Thurso and the northwest tip of Lewis. September to October is the best time for the waves. Windsurfing is also a favourite activity. The **Royal Yacht Association** has information on sites across the country. The top venue is the remote island of Tiree, which hosts a major windsurfing event in October every year.

Canoes and kayaks can be rented on lochs and in sheltered bays. The **Scottish Water Ski Centre** has details on the best places to water ski.

DIRECTORY

CYCLING AND MOUNTAIN BIKING

C.T.C. National Cyclists Organisation
Parklands, Railton Rd,
Guildford, Surrey GU2
9JX. *Tel (0844) 736 8450.*
www.ctc.org.uk

Edinburgh Central Cycle Hire
13 Lochrin Place,
Edinburgh EH3 9QX.
Tel (0131) 228 6633.

Forest Enterprise
1 Highlander Way,
Inverness IV2 7GB.
Tel (01463) 232811.
www.forestry.gov.uk

Scottish Cycling
Caledonia House, South
Gyle, Edinburgh EH12
9DQ *Tel (0131) 317 9404*
www.britishcycling.org.
uk/scotland

Scottish Cycling Holidays
87 Perth St, Blairgowrie,
Perthshire PH10 6DT.
Tel (01250) 876100.
www.scotcycle.co.uk

FISHING

Salmon & Trout Association
National Game Angling
Centre, The Pier, Loch
Leven, Kinross KY13 8UF.
Tel (01577) 861116.
www.salmon-trout.org

Scottish Anglers National Association
National Game Angling
Centre, The Pier, Loch
Leven, Kinross KY13 8UF.
Tel (01577) 861116.
www.sana.org.uk

Scottish Federation for Coarse Angling
8 Longbraes Gardens,
Kirkcaldy,
Fife KY2 5YJ.
Tel (01592) 642242.
www.sfca.co.uk

Scottish Federation of Sea Anglers
Stitchill House, Kelso,
TD5 7TB.
Tel (01573) 470612.
www.fishpal.com

HUNTING

British Association for Shooting and Conservation (Scotland)
Trochry, Dunkeld,
Perthshire PH8 0DY.
Tel (01350) 723226.
www.basc.org.uk

PONY TREKKING AND HORSE RIDING

Glen Tanar Equestrian Centre
Glen Tanar, Aboyne,
Royal Deeside AB36 8XJ.
Tel (01339) 886448.
www.glentanar.co.uk

Pentland Hills Icelandics
Windy Gow Farm,
Carlops,
Midlothian EH26 9NL.
Tel (01968) 661095.
www.phicelandics.co.uk

Skye Riding Centre
Suladale, Portree,
Isle of Skye, IV51 9PA.
Tel (01470) 582419.
www.skye-riding-
centre.co.uk

Trekking and Riding Society of Scotland (TRSS)
Druaich Na-H Abhainne,
Killin, Perthshire
SK21 8TN. *Tel (01567)
820909.* www.
ridinginscotland.com

SAILING

Port Edgar Marina
South Queensferry,
Edinburgh EH30 9SQ.
Tel (0131) 331 3330.
www.portedgar.co.uk

Scottish National Watersports Centre
Cumbrae KA28 0HQ.
Tel (01475) 530757.

WATERSPORTS

Royal Yacht Association
Caledonia House,
South Gyle,
Edinburgh EH12 9DQ.
Tel (0131) 317 7388.
www.ryascotland.org.uk

Scottish Water Ski Centre
Town Hill Loch, Townhill,
Dunfermline KY12 0HT.
Tel (01383) 620123
www.waterskiscotland.
co.uk

SURVIVAL
GUIDE

PRACTICAL INFORMATION

To enjoy Scotland fully, it is best to know something about the workings of everyday life. The range of facilities for tourists in Scotland has never been better – indeed tourism has become a major part of the country's economy – and VisitScotland is continually promoting better services around the country. This chapter gives advice about when best to visit Scotland; customs and immigration requirements; where to find tourist information; what

Logo of VisitScotland

to do or whom to turn to if things go wrong; banking and communications; and how to get around the country by public and private transport, including ferries to the islands.

Whether or not you find Scotland an expensive country will depend on the exchange rate between the pound and your own currency. Visitors travelling from London will find that costs are generally lower in Scotland's capital. Glasgow offers even better value for money.

Visitors' Centre in Callander, at the heart of the Trossachs

WHEN TO VISIT

Scotland's climate is very changeable *(see pp36–9)*. May and June are usually drier than July and August, although the latter are usually the warmest months. The west coast tends to be mild and wet, while the east coast is cool and drier.

Scotland's towns and cities are all-year destinations, but many attractions open only between Easter and October. The main family holiday months, July and August, and public holidays *(see p38)* are always busy. Hotels are crammed at Christmas and New Year, particularly in Edinburgh for the Hogmanay street party *(see p39)*. Spring and autumn offer a moderate climate and a lack of crowds. Whatever

Sign for the Mountain Rescue

the time of year, it is wise to get an up-to-date weather forecast before you set off on foot to remote hills or mountainous locations. Walkers and climbers can be surprised by the weather, and the Mountain Rescue services are frequently called out due to unexpectedly severe conditions. Weather reports are given on television and radio, in newspapers and by a weather phone service *(see p209)*.

INSURANCE

It is sensible to take out travel insurance before travelling, to cover cancellation or curtailment of your holiday, theft or loss of money and possessions, and the cost of any medical treatment *(see p218)*. If your country has a reciprocal medical arrangement with the UK you can obtain free treatment under the National Health Service. Australia, New Zealand and everywhere in the European Union (EU) has this arrangement. North American health plans, and student identity cards may give some protection against incurred costs, but always check the small print.

If you want to drive a car in Scotland, it is advisable to take out fully comprehensive insurance. You must carry a valid driver's licence. If you are not an EU citizen, you must have an international driver's licence, available through the AAA for those in the US.

ADVANCE BOOKING

Out of season, you should have few problems booking accommodation or transport at short notice, but in high season always try to book ahead if possible. Before you travel, contact **VisitScotland**, www.visitscotland.com, or a travel agent, for advice and information.

CUSTOMS AND IMMIGRATION

A valid passport is needed to enter the United Kingdom. Visitors from the European Union (EU), the United States, Canada, Australia and New Zealand do not require visas to enter the UK, nor any inoculations or vaccinations. Once within the UK, visitors are free to travel to and from Scotland, England, Wales and Northern Ireland without passing any other frontier formalities.

When you arrive at any international air or sea port in the UK, you will find separate queues at immigration control: one for EU nationals and several others for everyone else. Scotland is a member of the EU, which means that anyone arriving from an EU member country can pass through a blue channel. Random checks are still made, however, for illegal goods, especially drugs.

Standard tourist information sign

◁ **The busy Royal Mile in Edinburgh, with the Firth of Forth in the distance**

Travellers entering from outside the EU have to pass through the usual customs channels. Go through the green channel if you have nothing to declare over the customs allowances for overseas visitors, and the red channel if you have goods to declare. If you are unsure of importation restrictions, go through the red channel. Full details of these restrictions are available from HM Customs and Excise in London. Beware – never carry luggage or parcels through customs for someone else.

TOURIST INFORMATION

Tourist bookings in Scotland are handled by **VisitScotland** via its call centre and website. The organization also has a base in central London. In addition to these, every region of Scotland has its own tourist board, providing information about local accommodation, entertainment and places of interest. Smaller, subsidiary tourist information offices can be found in many towns and public places, and at some of the principal locations of historical interest. Look out for the tourist information symbol, indicating an office. Often the best source of information for events in the area, these offices will also book accommodation for visitors. Pick up one of their brochures that give comprehensive

listings of Tourist Board-accredited places to stay. The British Tourist Authority operates offices overseas.

DISABLED TRAVELLERS

The facilities on offer in Scotland for disabled visitors are steadily improving. An increasing number of hotels and guesthouses now offer wheelchair access. This information is given in the headings for each entry throughout the guide. Given advance notice, FirstScotRail *(see p227)*, ferry or coach (long-distance bus) staff will help any disabled passengers. Ask a travel agent about the Disabled Persons Railcard, which entitles the holder to discounted rail fares on services across the country.

Specialist tour operators, such as **Holiday Care**, cater for the physically handicapped visitor. You can contact them on (0845) 1249971, www.holidaycare.org.uk. **Hertz Rent A Car** offers hand-controlled vehicles without any extra cost *(see p231)*. For permission to use any disabled parking space, you need to display a special sign in your car.

Visitors from the US can telephone the **Society for the Advancement of Travel for the Handicapped (SATH)** on (212) 447 7284 or visit www.sath.org before leaving. SATH publishes *ACCESS to Travel*, a magazine full of information.

DIRECTORY

VISITSCOTLAND

For brochures to any area in Scotland, or to book accommodation contact:
Tel (0845) 225 5121.
www.visitscotland.com

VisitScotland Centre
19 Cockspur St, London SW1Y 5BL

REGIONAL TOURIST BOARDS

Aberdeen & Grampian
Tel (01224) 288828.
www.aberdeen-grampian.com

Angus & Dundee
Tel (01382) 527527.
www.angusanddundee.co.uk

Argyll, The Isles, Loch Lomond, Stirling & The Trossachs
Tel (0845) 225 5121.
www.visitscotland.com

Ayrshire & Arran
Tel (08452) 255121.
www.ayrshire-arran.com

Dumfries & Galloway
Tel (01387) 253862.
www.visitdumfriesand galloway.co.uk

Edinburgh & Lothians
Tel (0845) 225 5121.
www.edinburgh.org

Greater Glasgow & Clyde Valley
Tel (0141) 556 0800.
www.seeglasgow.com

Highlands of Scotland
Tel (0845) 225 5121.
www.visithighlands.com

Kingdom of Fife
Tel (0845) 225 5121.
www.standrews.co.uk

Orkney Islands
Tel (01856) 872856.
www.visitorkney.com

Perthshire
Tel (0845) 225 5121.
www.perthshire.co.uk

Scottish Borders
Tel (01835) 863170.
www.scot-borders.co.uk

Shetland Islands
Tel (01595) 693434.
www.visitshetland.com

Western Isles
Tel (0845) 225 5121.
www.visithebrides.com

Tobermory harbour on the Isle of Mull, popular with tourists

Glamis Castle, one of the sights that charge admission to visitors

TRAVELLING WITH CHILDREN

Public holidays and school holidays (July–mid-August) have most to offer in the way of children's entertainment. Many places have activities suitable for children over the Christmas period, particularly pantomimes. Discounts for children and family tickets are available for travel, theatre and other entertainments. ScotRail allows two children aged between 5 and 15 to travel for free with an adult.

Choose accommodation that welcomes children (see pp166–81), or opt for self-catering (efficiency apartments). Many hotels provide baby-sitting or baby-listening services, and offer reductions or free accommodation for the very young.

Nowadays restaurants are better equipped for children; many provide highchairs and special menus (see pp182–97).

Playing with interactive exhibits at Edinburgh's Museum of Childhood

Pubs often admit children, if accompanied by an adult. The legal drinking age is 18.

ADMISSION CHARGES

These vary widely, from a nominal fee to a more substantial charge for popular attractions. Reductions are often available for groups, senior citizens, children or students. The majority of local churches, museums and art galleries are free, unless a special exhibition is showing, but donations are frequently expected. Some attractions in Scotland are run privately, either as commercial ventures or on a charitable basis.

OPENING HOURS

Many shops in Scotland open on Sundays, particularly in the city centres. In the Western Isles, however, Sunday is still very much regarded as a day of rest, and shops, cafés and restaurants are likely to be closed. Monday to Friday hours are around 9am to 6pm, but shop hours do vary, opening late one evening a week – usually Thursday. Museums and art galleries generally open for fewer hours on Sundays, and many attractions open on public and bank holidays, especially on Christmas Day and New Year's Day.

VAT AND REFUNDS

Value added tax (VAT) is charged at 20 per cent on most goods and services. When leaving the UK, non-residents can redeem VAT on goods purchased from shops in the Retail Export Scheme. Refunds will be given if goods are faulty and are returned with the receipt as proof of purchase.

STUDENT TRAVELLERS

Full-time students who have an International Student Identity Card (ISIC) are often entitled to discounts on travel, sports facilities and entrance fees.

Student ISIC card

North American students can also get medical cover but it may be very basic (see p218). ISIC cards are available from **STA Travel**, or the **National Union of Students**. Inexpensive accommodation is also available (out of term time) at the university halls of residence in the main cities. This is a good way of staying in central locations when on a tight budget.

An **International Youth Hostel Federation** card enables you to stay in one of Scotland's many youth hostels. Contact the **Scottish Youth Hostels Association** directly (see Directory) for more detailed information.

NATIONAL TRUST FOR SCOTLAND

Many of Scotland's historic buildings, parks, gardens, and vast tracts of countryside and coastline are cared for by the **National Trust for Scotland** (NTS). Entrance fees can often be relatively high compared to fees at other sights, so if you plan on visiting several NTS properties, it may be worth taking out annual membership, which allows free access thereafter to all NTS properties, as well as free admission to National Trust properties in England, Wales and Northern Ireland. Membership also includes a sticker for free parking at all NTS sites, along with a Trust magazine three times a year.

Charlotte Square, Edinburgh, home of the National Trust for Scotland

Be aware, however, that many NTS properties close during the winter months, so check ahead before visiting.

MEDIA

National newspapers in Scotland fall into two categories: serious publications, such as Edinburgh's *The Scotsman* or Glasgow's *The Herald*; and those that are heavy on gossip, such as *The Sun* or *The Daily Record*. Weekend newspapers, such as *Scotland on Sunday* and the *Sunday Herald*, are more expensive than dailies, with many supplements including sections on arts, restaurants, entertainment, travel and reviews.

Newsagents sell a huge range of specialist periodicals. In major towns, main train stations and some larger book stores stock foreign magazines and newspapers.

The BBC (British Broadcasting Corporation) operates nine TV channels and produces

Buying newspapers at a stand in Glasgow

programmes without commercial breaks. The BBC's main rivals are ITV, Channel 4 and Channel 5. The BBC operates a number of radio stations including the national station, BBC Radio Scotland. There are many local radio stations.

ELECTRICITY

The voltage in Scotland is 220/240 AC, 50 Hz. The electrical plugs have three square pins and take fuses of 3, 5 and 13 amps. In order to use your foreign appliances, such as hair dryers, you will need an adaptor. Most hotel bathrooms have two-pronged sockets for electric shavers.

SMOKING AND ALCOHOL

It is illegal to smoke in all public places in Scotland, including public transport systems, taxis, train stations, theatres and cinemas, bars, restaurants and shops.

There is a general ban on drinking in public in Greater Glasgow and the Clyde Valley area, although public drinking is discouraged throughout Scotland. This ban is usually lifted for the New Year street party at Hogmanay (31 December).

CONVERSION CHART

Britain is officially metricated in line with the rest of Europe, but imperial measures are still in common usage, including road distances (measured in miles). Imperial pints and gallons are 20 per cent larger than US measures.

Imperial to metric
1 inch = 2.5 centimetres
1 foot = 30 centimetres
1 mile = 1.6 kilometres
1 ounce = 28 grams
1 pint = 0.6 litres
1 gallon = 4.5 litres

Metric to imperial
1 millimetre = 0.04 inch
1 centimetre = 0.4 inch
1 metre = 3 feet 3 inches
1 kilometre = 0.6 mile
1 gram = 0.04 ounce
1 kilogram = 2.2 pounds

TIME

Scotland is on Greenwich Mean Time (GMT) during the winter months – that is, five hours ahead of Eastern Standard Time and ten hours behind Sydney. From the middle of March to the end of October, the clocks go forward one hour to British Summer Time (which is one hour ahead of GMT). To check the correct time, you can dial 123 to contact the Speaking Clock service.

DIRECTORY

National Trust for Scotland (NTS)
Tel (0844) 493 2100.
www.nts.org.uk

STUDENT TRAVELLERS

International Youth Hostel Federation
Tel (01707) 324170.
www.hihostels.com

National Union of Students
Tel (0131) 556 6598.
www.nus.org.uk/scotland

Scottish Youth Hostels Association
Tel (0871) 230 0040.
www.syha.org.uk

STA Travel
Tel (08701) 600599.
www.statravel.co.uk

EMBASSIES AND CONSULATES

Australian High Commission
Australia House, Strand, London WC2B 4LA.
Tel (0207) 379 4334.
www.uk.embassy.gov.au

Canadian Consulate
30 Lothian Rd, Edinburgh EH1 2DH.
Tel (0131) 220 4333.

New Zealand High Commission
New Zealand House, 80 Haymarket, London SW1Y 4TQ.
Tel (0207) 930 8422.

United States Consulate
3 Regent Terrace, Edinburgh EH7 5BW.
Tel (0131) 556 8315.
www.edinburgh.usconsulate.gov

Personal Security and Health

Pharmacy Sign

Like any other country, Scotland has its share of social problems, but it is very unlikely that you will come across any violence. If you do encounter difficulties, do not hesitate to contact the police for help. The UK's National Health Service (NHS) can be relied upon for an emergency or routine treatment. However, you may have to pay for treatment if your country has no reciprocal arrangement with the UK. Below is some guidance for enjoying a trouble-free visit.

HOSPITALS AND MEDICAL TREATMENT

All visitors to Scotland, especially those from outside the European Union (EU), are strongly advised to take out medical insurance against the cost of emergency hospital care, repatriation and specialists' fees. Emergency medical treatment in an NHS Accident and Emergency department is free, but additional medical care could prove expensive. US visitors should check with their insurance companies to be sure they are covered.

EU residents and nationals of some other Commonwealth and European countries are entitled to free medical treatment under the NHS, though the process is bureaucratic. Before travelling, obtain a European Health Insurance Card (EHIC) from a post office; show this to anyone treating you. Be aware, however, that some treatments are not covered, and repatriation is not included, so medical insurance is preferable. For advice, or if you're unsure whether to call an ambulance, call the NHS Direct helpline *(see Directory).*

If you need to see a dentist, you will have to pay. The cost will vary depending on your entitlement to NHS treatment. Emergency dental treatment is available in some hospitals.

PHARMACISTS

You can buy a wide range of medicines without prescription from pharmacies in Scotland. Boots is the best-known and largest supplier, with branches in most towns.

A traditional, privately owned pharmacy in Leith, Edinburgh

Many medicines are available only with a doctor's prescription, which you must take to a dispensing chemist (pharmacist). Either bring your own supply or ask your doctor to write out the generic name of the drug (as opposed to the brand name). If you are entitled to an NHS prescription, you will be charged a standard rate; without this, you will be charged the full cost. Ask for a receipt for any insurance claim. Some pharmacies stay open until midnight. Doctors' surgeries (offices) are usually open mornings and early evenings. Hospital Accident and Emergency departments are always open.

THE MIDGE

Being bitten by midges is one of the most common hazards for visitors to Scotland. The chance of encountering these tiny biting flies is particularly heightened around lochs and on the coast, as they love damp conditions. They breed between April and October, and are at their worst at the start and end of the day. There is no way of escaping them altogether, but to ensure that you suffer only the minimum of bites, apply insect repellent (such as Autan) and avoid sitting near bright lights after dark. If they really are a nuisance you may want to invest in a midge net.

CRIME AND SUITABLE PRECAUTIONS

Scotland is not a dangerous place for visitors, and it is most unlikely that your stay will be blighted by crime. There are, however, practical steps that can be taken to help you avoid loss of property or personal injury. Take good care of your belongings at all times. Make sure your possessions are adequately insured before you arrive. Never leave them unattended in public places. Keep your valuables well concealed, especially in crowds. In cinemas or theatres, keep handbags on your lap, not on the floor. It is advisable not to

Woman police constable

Police constable

Traffic police officer

carry too much cash or jewellery with you; leave it in the safe in the hotel instead. Pickpockets tend to frequent crowded places like bustling markets, busy shops and rush-hour public transport.

By far the safest way of carrying large amounts of cash around is in traveller's cheques (see p221). Alternatively, you can withdraw small amounts of cash from cashpoints (ATMs). If you are travelling alone at night try to avoid deserted and poorly lit buildings and places such as back streets and car parks. When driving, try to park in well-lit areas where it will be difficult for someone to tamper with your car without being noticed. A steering wheel lock is also a good visual deterrent to thieves. If you are the victim of crime, contact your local police station. It is often necessary to report a crime in order to claim on insurance.

WOMEN TRAVELLING ALONE

It is not unusual in Scotland for women to travel unaccompanied, or to visit a bar or restaurant with a group of female friends. Nor is it especially dangerous. But caution is advisable in deserted places, especially after dark. Try to avoid using public transport when there is just one other passenger or a group of young men. It is best to summon a licensed taxi (see p231) rather than walk through a lonely area of a city at night, especially if you do not know the area well. It is illegal to carry any offensive weapons, including knives, guns, mace or tear-gas, even for self-defence. Personal alarms are permitted, however.

Police car

Ambulance

Fire engine

POLICE

The sight of a traditional British bobby patrolling the streets in a tall hat is now less common than the police patrol car, usually with wailing sirens and flashing lights. But the old-fashioned police constable does still exist in Scotland, particularly in rural areas and crowded city centres, and continues to be courteous, approachable and helpful. Unlike in many other countries, the police in Scotland do not carry guns. If you are lost, the traditional advice to ask a policeman or woman still applies. Traffic wardens may also be able to help with directions. If you have lost property it is worth contacting the local police station as someone may have handed it in.

In a crisis, dial 999 to reach police, fire and ambulance services who are on call 24 hours a day. Calls are free from any public or private phone, but they should only be made in real emergencies. In Scotland's coastal areas this number will also put you in touch with Britain's voluntary coastguard rescue service, the RNLI (Royal National Lifeboat Institution).

Logo of the Royal National Lifeboat Institution

LOST PROPERTY

If you are unlucky enough to lose anything or have anything stolen, go straight to the nearest police station to report your loss. If you want to claim on insurance for any theft, you will need a written report from the local police. All of the main bus and train stations have lost property centres. Most hotels disclaim all responsibility for valuables not kept in their safe.

It is advisable to make photocopies of your vital documents such as passports and travel papers. If you lose your passport, contact your embassy or consulate in either Edinburgh or London (see p217).

DIRECTORY

POLICE, FIRE AND AMBULANCE SERVICES

Tel 999. Calls are free (24-hour phoneline).

HOSPITAL ACCIDENT AND EMERGENCY DEPARTMENTS

Aberdeen Royal Infirmary
Tel (0845) 456 6000.

Edinburgh Royal Infirmary
Tel (0131) 536 1000.

Glasgow Royal Infirmary
Tel (0141) 211 4484.

Inverness Raigmore
Tel (01463) 704000.

NHS Direct Helpline
Tel (0845) 4647.

Perth Royal Infirmary
Tel (01738) 473838.

EMERGENCY DENTAL CARE

Edinburgh Dental Hospital
Tel (0131) 536 4900.

DISABLED HELPLINE

The Disability Helpline
Tel (01302) 310123.
www.dialuk.info.

Banking and Local Currency

Visitors to most Scottish cities and large towns will find a number of options for exchanging currency and cashing travellers' cheques. High-street banks, travel agencies and bureaux de change all offer this service at different exchange and commission rates. Cashpoints (ATMs) can be found at many locations and can be used to dispense cash via your debit card. Credit cards and traveller's cheques are the safest methods of bringing currency with you to Scotland.

One of many banks to offer bureau de change facilities

BUREAUX DE CHANGE

Although bureaux de change are often more convenient-ly located than banks and have longer opening hours, the exchange rates can vary considerably and commission charges can be high.

The reputable firms such as **International Currency Exchange**, **Thomas Cook** and **American Express** offer good exchange facilities. International Currency Exchange has just one branch at Edinburgh Airport; both Thomas Cook and American Express have branches throughout Scotland.

Scottish Banks
Branches of the three main Scottish banks (Royal Bank of Scotland, Bank of Scotland and Clydesdale), will be found in all cities and many towns. English banks such as NatWest and Barclays are rare outside the main cities. Most banks offer exchange facilities, but proof of identity may be required and the commission charges will vary.

BANKS

Every large town and city in Scotland should have a branch of at least one of the following banks – Bank of Scotland, Royal Bank of Scotland, Lloyds TSB Scotland, Girobank and Clydesdale.

Most banks have a cash-point (ATM), as do many building societies, shops and garages, from which you can obtain money with a bank or credit card and your personal identification number (PIN). Some of the most modern machines have easy-to-read computerized instructions in

several languages. Card-holders from principal English banks, such as NatWest, HSBC, Lloyds TSB and Barclays, can withdraw money from most banks in Scotland. Check that your bank card is compatible with the cashpoint you are us-ing or you may be charged a fee or have your card rejected.

You can also obtain money by contacting your own bank and asking them to wire cash to the nearest Scottish bank. Branches of Thomas Cook or American Express will do this for you. Visitors from the US can have cash dispatched through **Western Union** to a bank or post office. Take your passport as proof of identity. Banking hours vary from bank to bank, but the mini-mum opening times are 9:30am to 3:30pm Monday to Friday.

CREDIT CARDS

Credit and store cards are widely accepted through-out Scotland, but some smaller shops, guesthouses and cafés may not take them. VISA is the most widely used card, but MasterCard, Access, Diners Club and American Express are also accepted. For a small fee you can get cash advan-ces with a credit card at any bank displaying the card sign.

TRAVELLER'S CHEQUES

Traveller's cheques can be purchased at American Express, Travelex or your bank. All are accepted in Scotland. If you exchange American Express cheques at an American Express office, commission is not charged.

DIRECTORY

EXCHANGE FACILITIES

International Currency Exchange
Tel (0844) 800 3974.

Thomas Cook
Tel (0845) 308 9309.

American Express
Tel (0131) 718 2505.

Western Union
Tel (0800) 833833.

Clydesdale Bank logo

Bank of Scotland logo

Royal Bank of Scotland logo

NatWest logo

CURRENCY AND TRAVELLER'S CHEQUES

Britain's currency is the pound sterling (£), which is divided into 100 pence (p). There are no exchange controls in Britain, so you may bring in and take out as much cash as you like. Scotland has its own notes. Although they are legal tender throughout Britain (with the exception of the £1 note), you are likely to encounter difficulties when using Scottish notes in England. Bank of England and Northern Ireland notes can be used throughout Scotland. Traveller's cheques are a safer alternative to carrying large amounts of cash. Be sure to keep the receipts separate from the cheques so you can easily obtain a refund if your cheques are lost or stolen. Some high-street banks issue traveller's cheques free of commission to their account holders, but the normal charge is around 1 per cent.

Bank Notes
Scottish notes are produced in denominations of £1, £5, £10, £20, £50 and £100. Always get small denominations, as some shops may refuse the larger notes. Although Scotland has a £1 note, the English £1 coin, and all Bank of England currency, is legal tender.

£100 note

£20 note

£10 note

£5 note

£1 note

Coinage
Coins currently in use are £2, £1, 50p, 20p, 10p, 5p, 2p and 1p. The same coins are produced and accepted throughout the UK.

2 pounds (£2)

1 pound (£1)

50 pence (50p)

20 pence (20p)

10 pence (10p)

5 pence (5p)

2 pence (2p)

1 penny (1p)

Communications

Modern BT phone box

With continuously improving telecommunication systems and the spread of email, staying in contact and making plans while travelling has never been easier. The telephone system in Scotland is efficient and inexpensive. Charges depend on when, where and for how long you talk. The cheapest time to call is between 6pm and 8am Monday to Friday, and throughout the weekend. Local calls made on public payphones, however, are charged at a fixed rate per minute.

PAYPHONES

You can pay for a payphone using coins or a card. Payphones accept 10p, 20p, 50p and £1 pieces, while newer phones also accept £2 coins. The minimum cost of a call is 60p. If you expect a call to be short, use 10p or 20p pieces, as payphones only return unused coins. Some payphones accept credit and debit cards. The minimum fee for local and national calls is £1.20 and £1.50 for international calls, calls to premium rate numbers, mobile phones and calls made through the operator.

TELEPHONE DIRECTORIES

Directories, such as *Yellow Pages* and *Thomson Local*, list local businesses and services. They can be found at local Post Offices, libraries and often at your hotel. A number of operators now offer telephone directory enquiry services at different levels of cost to the caller.

USING A CARD AND COIN PHONE

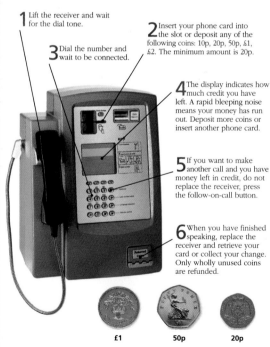

1 Lift the receiver and wait for the dial tone.

2 Insert your phone card into the slot or deposit any of the following coins: 10p, 20p, 50p, £1, £2. The minimum amount is 20p.

3 Dial the number and wait to be connected.

4 The display indicates how much credit you have left. A rapid bleeping noise means your money has run out. Deposit more coins or insert another phone card.

5 If you want to make another call and you have money left in credit, do not replace the receiver, press the follow-on-call button.

6 When you have finished speaking, replace the receiver and retrieve your card or collect your change. Only wholly unused coins are refunded.

£1   **50p**   **20p**

USEFUL NUMBERS

A number of telephone services exist to help you find or reach a specific phone number.

Emergency Calls
Tel 999. Police, Fire, Ambulance, Coastguard, Mountain and Cave Rescue.

Directory Enquiries
Tel 118500 (BT).

International Directory Enquiries
Tel 118505 (BT).

International Operator
Tel 155.

Operator Assistance
Tel 100.

Overseas Calls
Tel 00 followed by country code: Australia (61), Canada (1), Ireland (353), New Zealand (64), South Africa (27), United States (1).

Talking Pages
Tel 118247. Provides numbers for specific kinds of shops or services in any area.

ACCESSING THE INTERNET

Most cities and towns now have some form of public access to computers and the Internet. Free Internet access is often available at main library branches, although you may have to book a time slot. Internet cafés usually charge by the minute for computer use.

Access is very cheap and is most reasonable during off-peak times. Most hotels and many B&Bs and hostels provide Wi-Fi, sometimes free, as do several cafés and restaurants. There are Wi-Fi hotspots throughout the main cities – look out for the black-and-white symbol.

24-hour Internet access at the easyInternetcafé

Sending a Letter

The distinctive Post Office logo

Besides main Post Offices that offer all the mail services available, there are many sub-Post Offices in newsagents, grocery stores and general information centres, particularly in more isolated areas and smaller towns. In many villages the Post Office is also the only shop. Post Offices are usually open from 9am to 5:30pm Monday to Friday, and until 12:30pm on Saturday. Mailboxes – in all shapes and sizes but always red – are found throughout cities, towns and villages.

Postbus collection in rural Scotland

MAIL SERVICES

Stamps can be bought at many outlets, including supermarkets and petrol stations. Hotels often have mailboxes at their reception. When writing to an address anywhere in the UK always include the postcode. Letters and postcards can be sent either first or second class within the UK. First-class

1st-class aerogramme

1st-class stamp   2nd-class stamp

Greetings stamps featuring characters from children's fiction

service is more expensive but quicker, with most letters reaching their destination the following day (except Sunday); second-class mail takes a day or two longer.

POSTE RESTANTE

Large urban Post Offices have a *poste restante* service where letters can be sent for collection. To use the service be sure to print the surname (last name) clearly so it will be filed correctly. Send it to Poste Restante followed by the address of the Post Office. To collect your mail you will have to show your passport or other form of identification. Mail will be kept for one month. One of the most central Post Offices in Edinburgh is the one situated in the St James Centre, EH1, close to the main bus station. This Post Office also offers the *poste restante* service.

MAILBOXES

These may be either freestanding "pillar boxes" or wall safes, both painted bright red. Some pillar boxes have separate slots, one for overseas and first-class mail, another for second-class mail. Initials on older mail boxes indicate who was monarch at that time.

Mailboxes are often embedded in Post Office walls. Collections are usually made several times a day during weekdays (less often on Saturdays and rarely on Sundays and public holidays); times are marked on the box.

A rural mailbox, embedded in a stone wall

MAILING ABROAD

Airmail provides a speedy and cost-effective method of communication. Aerogrammes go first class anywhere in the world and cost the same regardless of destination. They take about three to four days to reach European cities, and between four and seven days for destinations elsewhere. All mail sent within Europe goes via airmail, while overseas mail rates are classed by weight. Sending post overseas by surface mail may be more economical, but it can take anywhere up to 12 weeks for it to reach its final destination. The Post Office offers an express delivery service called **Parcelforce International**. Available from most main Post Offices, Parcelforce is comparable in price to many private companies such as **DHL**, **UPS**, **Crossflight**, or **Expressair**.

Pillar box

Crossflight
Tel (01753) 776000.

DHL
www.dhl.co.uk

Expressair
Tel (0207) 781 0036.

Parcelforce International
www.parcelforce.com

UPS
Tel (08457) 877877.

TRAVEL INFORMATION

As the UK is an international gateway for air and sea traffic, travelling to Scotland poses few problems. There are direct flights from North America and continental Europe. Coach travel from Europe via the ferries is a cheap, albeit slow, form of transport. Travelling by train using the Channel Tunnel is an efficient way of crossing to the UK. Travelling within Scotland itself is fairly easy. Internal

A British Airways plane in mid-flight

flights are available between cities on the mainland, and also to the island groups. Another way to island-hop is to take the ferries. There is an extensive network of roads in urban areas and renting a car can be the best way of travelling. The inter-city rail network is limited in Scotland, but a small network of trains serves the country, some with scenic routes. Coach travel is the cheapest option; services run between most cities.

Check-in desks at Glasgow International Airport

INTERNATIONAL FLIGHTS TO AND FROM SCOTLAND

Edinburgh and Glasgow are the principal airports in Scotland. The four other international airports are Prestwick, Aberdeen, Inverness and Sumburgh on Shetland.

Air France, **bmi** and **KLM UK** (formerly AirUK) offer direct flights from continental Europe. Glasgow and Edinburgh have the most frequent services, with direct and indirect flights to many major

European destinations including Paris, Dublin and Brussels.

A number of transatlantic airlines offer direct services to Glasgow airport, including **British Airways**, **American Airlines**, **Continental Airlines** and **Air Canada**. Flights to Edinburgh and Glasgow are available from long-haul destinations such as North Africa, South Africa, Australia and the Far East. These are routed via a European capital, often Brussels or Amsterdam.

A more economical option can be to fly to London and then take a domestic flight north. These flights can cost as little as £29 one way. If you plan to take the scenic train journey, it is advisable to book in advance for the best deals *(see p227)*.

The airports at Glasgow, Edinburgh and Aberdeen offer good facilities, including banking, shops, cafés, hotels and restaurants, as well as parking. Each of these airports is connected to the nearest city centres by regular and reliable shuttle bus services.

TRAVELLING WITHIN THE UK FROM SCOTLAND

Flights from Scotland to other British destinations operate from all the mainland international airports. British Airways offers express services to London's Heathrow and Gatwick airports. bmi also flies direct to Heathrow. **easyJet**, **Ryanair** and KLM UK operate between Scotland and the English airports of Luton, Stansted and London City.

There are also direct flights to other major cities in the UK, including Manchester, Newcastle upon Tyne, Leeds, Birmingham, Belfast and Cardiff, and to some of the

Passengers from abroad passing through International Arrivals

AIRPORT	ℂ INFORMATION	DISTANCE TO CITY CENTRE	TAXI FARE TO CITY CENTRE	PUBLIC TRANSPORT TO CITY CENTRE
Aberdeen	(0870) 040 0006	7 miles (11 km)	£12	Bus: 30 min / Taxi: 20 min
Edinburgh	(0870) 040 0007	8 miles (13 km)	£16	Bus: 25 min / Taxi: 20 min
Glasgow	(0844) 481 5555	8 miles (13 km)	£16.50	Bus: 25 min / Taxi: 20 min
Prestwick	(0871) 223 0700	29 miles (47 km)	£40	Train: 45 min / Taxi: 40 min

The terminal at Glasgow International Airport

smaller ones such as Bristol and Southampton, but the relatively high cost of these flights can sometimes outweigh the time saved.

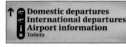

Sign directing passengers to locations within an airport

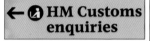

Directions to the department for information on customs

TRAVELLING WITHIN SCOTLAND BY AIR

Scotland's size means that internal air travel is quick, but it can prove an expensive mode of travel compared to rail, coach or car. There are good air connections between the Highlands and central Scotland. When travelling to the islands off the coast of Scotland, flying becomes a particularly viable option. **Flybe** and **Loganair**, both subsidiaries of British Airways, provide regular flights from all the major cities on the mainland to the Western Isles, Orkney Islands and Shetland Islands.

TRANSPORT FROM THE AIRPORTS

Scotland's main international airports lie on the outskirts of Glasgow, Edinburgh and Aberdeen, where there are efficient transportation links. Taxis are the most convenient form of door-to-door travel,

but they are also fairly expensive. Coaches or buses provide cheaper transport to the town centres, though during rush hour or heavy traffic, coaches, buses and taxis may be slow. **National Express** as well as **Scottish Citylink** *(see p227)* provide direct coach services from the major airports to various destinations.

Prestwick International is served by its own train station; a service runs to Glasgow city centre every half an hour.

AIR FARES

Air fares to Scotland are usually at their highest from June to September. The best deals are available from November to April, excluding the Christmas period – if you want to travel then, you should book well in advance.

Apex (Advance Purchase Excursion) fares are often the best value, though they must be booked a month ahead and are subject to restrictions, such as minimum and maximum stays and no refunds. Charter flights offer even cheaper seats, but with less flexibility.

Promotional fares are often available, and it is worth checking direct with the airlines for special offers. Cheap deals are sometimes offered by package operators and are

advertised in newspapers and travel magazines. Students, those under 26 years old and senior citizens may be eligible for a discount. Children and babies travel for less.

If you choose a discount fare, always buy from a reputable operator, and check with the airline to ensure your seat has been confirmed. Packages may also be worth considering for cost-savings, even if you enjoy independent travel. Airlines and tour operators can put together a great range of flexible deals to suit your needs, sometimes with car rental or rail travel included. This can often be cheaper than arranging transport once you have arrived. A small airport tax is imposed on all those departing from British airports.

DIRECTORY

AIRLINE INFORMATION

Air Canada
Tel (0871) 220 1111.
www.aircanada.ca

Air France
Tel (0871) 663 3777.
www.airfrance.co.uk

American Airlines
Tel (0844) 499 7300.
www.aa.com

British Airways
Tel (0844) 493 0787.
www.british-airways.com

bmi
Tel (0844) 848 4888.
www.flybmi.com

Continental Airlines
Tel (0845) 607 6760.
www.continental.com

easyJet
Tel (0871) 989 1366.
www.easyjet.com

Flybe
Tel (0871) 700 2000.
www.flybe.com

KLM UK
Tel (0871) 222 7474.
www.klmuk.com

Loganair
Tel (0141) 848 7594.
www.loganair.co.uk

Ryanair
Tel (0871) 246 0000.
www.ryanair.ie

Rental car collection point at Glasgow International Airport

Travelling by Rail and Coach

Scotland has a privatized rail network, FirstScotRail, that covers most of the country and is generally efficient and reliable. A quarter-hourly service operates between Edinburgh and Glasgow, and lines radiate from both cities, with frequent services to many Scottish destinations and to most parts of England. Journey times to London are just over four hours from Edinburgh and just over five from Glasgow. Scotland also has a good coach (long-distance bus) service that is generally cheaper than the trains, although journeys can be slow. Weekend rail and coach services are popular, so book ahead.

The Flying Scotsman, one of the many swift inter-city train services

The Virgin Superfast train at Edinburgh's Waverley station

TRAIN TICKETS

Allow plenty of time to buy your ticket, and always ask about any special offers or reduced fares. Try to buy your tickets for intercity routes at least 14 days in advance. The best offers are online. For shorter trips, reasonable fares are available from station ticket booths and machines on the day of travel. First-class tickets cost about one-third more than standard fares, and it's usually cheaper to buy two singles on long-distance routes. ScotRail has some discounted fares; up to two children aged between 5 and 15 can travel free with each adult who purchases a "kids go free" ticket. Groups of more than three should enquire about discount fares.

RAIL PASSES

If you plan to travel a lot by train, it is a good idea to buy a rail pass. These can be purchased from agents such as **Rail Europe**, which operates in Europe, the US and Canada.

There are different passes available to suit every need. The Freedom of Scotland pass allows unlimited rail travel around the country for a set period. The Highland Rover permits travel on the West Highland lines and the Inverness-to-Kyle line. The Festival Cities Rover, available during the Edinburgh International Festival in August, is for use between Glasgow's Queen Street and Edinburgh's Waverley station on any three out of seven consecutive days. The passes are also valid on some coach and ferry services and on the Glasgow Underground (see p96).

One-third price discounts are available for 16- to 25-year-olds using a Young Person's Rail Card. The Senior Railcard and Disabled Railcard entitle the holder to a one-third discount on most fares. There are also railcards for 16- to 18-year-olds and families.

A leaflet about the steam train

GENERAL TIPS

Britain's fastest and most comfortable trains are those on the inter-city routes. These popular services book up quickly. It is always advisable to reserve your seat in advance, especially if you want to travel at peak times such as Friday evenings and Sunday afternoons. Inter-city trains are fast, with a limited number of stops. The trip from Edinburgh to Glasgow, for example, takes around 50 minutes. A reduced service is usually in operation on Sundays and public holidays. Porters are often scarce at British stations, although trolleys are usually available for passengers to help themselves. If you are disabled and need assistance, contact the relevant train company before the day you travel.

RAIL MAP OF SCOTLAND

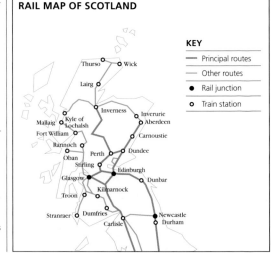

KEY

— Principal routes

— Other routes

● Rail junction

○ Train station

Thurso · Wick
Lairg
Inverness · Inverurie
Mallaig · Kyle of Lochalsh · Aberdeen
Fort William · Carnoustie
Rannoch · Dundee
Oban · Perth
Stirling · Edinburgh
Glasgow · Dunbar
Kilmarnock
Troon · Newcastle
Stranraer · Dumfries · Durham
Carlisle

SCENIC TRAIN RIDES

When motor transportation made many rural railways redundant in the mid-20th century, picturesque sections of track, and many of the old steam engines, were rescued and restored to working order. Tourist offices or train ticket offices can provide you with information on where the lines are, and how much it will cost to take a ride on the trains.

Ride the Jacobite steam train from Fort William to Mallaig, passing over a spectacular viaduct at Glenfinnan; or take the Strathspey Steam Railway from Aviemore to Boat of Garten.

The Jacobite steam train on its picturesque journey to Mallaig

INTERNATIONAL COACH TRAVEL

Although travelling by coach (long-distance bus) is cheap compared with other methods of transport, it is not the most comfortable way of crossing Europe. If you have a lot of spare time, however, and want to stop off en route at other destinations, it can be a convenient mode of transport. The ticket usually covers all parts of the journey, including the ferry or Channel Tunnel.

NATIONAL COACH NETWORK

The largest coach operators in Scotland are **Scottish Citylink**, **Stagecoach** and **National Express**, which runs services only between the main cities and to destinations in the rest of Great Britain. Buy a reserved ticket to guarantee a seat.

Discounts are available for full-time students or anyone under 25 with a coach pass. Over-50s and children aged between 5 and 15 years also qualify for reductions. Under-5s travel free on Scotland's national coaches. The Tourist Trail Pass is ideal for those planning to cover many destinations over a limited period. It allows unlimited travel on all National Express services in Scotland and the rest of Britain. You can buy the pass in the UK at major international airports, at Glasgow's Buchanan Bus Station and at Edinburgh's Tourist Information Centre. The Scottish Explorer Pass, available from Scottish Citylink agents and from Glasgow Airport, allows travel only within Scotland and only on Scottish Citylink services.

COACH AND BUS TOURS

Dozens of coach tours are available in Scotland, catering for all interests, age groups and a host of different destinations. They may last anything from a couple of hours for a city tour to several days for a national tour.

OctopusTravel.com offers scheduled sightseeing tours of Edinburgh, Glasgow and Inverness, or can arrange a tour to your own itinerary for Edinburgh and Glasgow. The Edinburgh-based **Scotline Tours** offers half- and full-day tours, while **Rabbie's Trail Burners** offers tours of three days or more.

Ask at your hotel or tourist office for details of local bus and coach tours. Most major towns and cities offer open-top bus tours.

Local buses are generally a cheap way to get about. In the more remote rural areas not served by public transport, **Royal Mail** operates the Postbus. Fare-paying passengers travel in the postal delivery van – an interesting if rather slow way to travel around. Details of routes are available from the Royal Mail and via its website.

The Postbus provides transport in remote parts of the Highlands

Open-top bus tour on the Royal Mile in Edinburgh

DIRECTORY

UK AND OVERSEAS RAIL NUMBERS AND WEBSITES

Train Information
www.thetrainline.com

Disabled Information
Tel (08457) 443366.

Lost Property
Tel (0141) 335 3276 (Glasgow).

National Rail Enquiries
Tel (08457) 484950.
www.nationalrail.com

Rail Europe
Tel (08448) 484 064 (UK).
Tel (1800) 622 8600 (US).
Tel (1800) 361 7245 (Canada).
www.raileurope.co.uk

First ScotRail Telesales
Tel (0845) 601 5929 (bookings).
www.scotrail.co.uk

COACH AND BUS INFORMATION

British Travel Associates
Tel (800) 327 6097 (US only).

National Express
Tel (08717) 818178.
www.nationalexpress.com

OctopusTravel.com
Tel (0207) 136 2856.
www.octopustravel.com

Rabbie's Trail Burners
Tel (0131) 226 3133.
www.rabbies.com

Royal Mail
Tel (0845) 601 5726.
www.royalmail.com

Scotline Tours
Tel (0131) 557 0162.
www.scotlinetours.co.uk

Scottish Citylink
Tel (0871) 266 3333.
www.citylink.co.uk

Travelling by Ferry

If you are travelling to Scotland from continental Europe by foot, car, coach or train, you will need to cross the English Channel or North Sea by ferry or Channel Tunnel. Ferry services operate between several ports on the Continent and Scotland and England, while the Channel Tunnel provides a nonstop rail link from France and Belgium. Fares between ferries and the Channel Tunnel are fiercely competitive. Island-hopping by ferry is an enjoyable and economical way to visit the beautiful islands situated off the coast of Scotland.

Caledonian MacBrayne
Hebridean and Clyde Ferries

Logo of a Scottish ferry company

A car ferry travelling from Oban to Lochboisdale on South Uist

TRAVELLING DIRECT TO SCOTLAND BY FERRY

Scotland's only ferry link to Europe is provided by **Superfast Ferries**. This service links Rosyth on the opposite side of the Firth of Forth to Edinburgh, with Zeebrugge in Belgium. The overnight sailing takes about 17 hours 30 minutes. From Northern Ireland, there is a frequent service operated by **Stena Line**, which runs between Belfast and Stranraer. **P&O Ferries** also offers daily crossings between Larne and Cairnryan, just north of Stranraer. Check the company's website for details.

SERVICES TO ENGLAND FROM THE CONTINENT

A network of ferry services regularly crosses the North Sea and the English Channel from northern Europe to ports in the UK. Of those travelling to the north of England, **P&O Ferries** runs a daily crossing from Rotterdam or Zeebrugge to Hull, and **DFDS Seaways** runs from Kristiansand, Gothenburg and Amsterdam to Newcastle.

An alternative way to travel to Scotland from the Continent via England is the Channel Tunnel, which links the UK with France.

Passengers travelling by coach or car board the **Eurotunnel** train, and remain in their vehicle throughout the 35-minute journey from Calais to Folkstone. For those travelling on foot, the **Eurostar** train runs frequent services between Paris, Brussels and London.

Any visitors from outside the European Union should allow plenty of time for immigration control and customs clearance at British ports (*see pp214–15*).

ISLAND-HOPPING IN SCOTLAND

Scotland has just under 800 islands scattered off its coastline, and travelling by ferry is a wonderful way to experience their rugged beauty. The islands can be roughly divided into two main groups: the Hebrides, situated off the west coast, and Orkney and Shetland, lying to the northeast of the mainland.

Caledonian MacBrayne has 30 ships, linking 23 of the westerly isles to the mainland and to each other. Destinations include Arran, Islay, Mull, Barra, Lewis, Harris, Skye, Raasay, Coll, Tiree and Eigg. The summer timetable runs from Easter to mid-October with a reduced service for the rest of the year. Most of the routes have two or three trips a day, but some have only one, so be sure to call ahead and check. Single, return and five-day tickets are available.

In addition, there are two special travel tickets. Island Hopscotch tickets are valid on a choice of fifteen routes for one month from the date of the first journey. The Island Rover gives you the freedom to choose your own route between the islands for 8 or 15 consecutive days from the date of the first journey. Although the Island Rover ticket is valid on all of Caledonian's services, it does not ensure a place on any particular sailing, and it is advisable to make vehicle reservations.

Northlink Ferries, a venture between Caledonian MacBrayne and The Royal Bank of Scotland has ferry routes from the Scottish mainland to Orkney and Shetland. All routes have large capacity purpose-built roll-on roll-off ferries with modern facilities including restaurants, cabins, shop and children's play area.

Passengers on the deck of a ferry leaving Tobermory on the Isle of Mull

A Caledonian MacBrayne ferry
leaving the port of Mallaig

NorthLink sails from Scrabster, north of Thurso, to Stromness on Orkney Mainland and direct from Aberdeen to Orkney or to Shetland. Another service links Orkney and Shetland.

Pentland Ferries also offers a car service to Orkney. This runs between Gill's Bay west of John o' Groats and St Margaret's Hope on South Ronaldsay. This island is linked to Orkney Mainland via the Churchill Barrier causeways. The vehicle capacity of this older ferry is limited to 46 and booking in advance is recommended.

During the summer, **John o' Groats Ferries** runs a 40-minute passenger-only crossing to Burwick on South Ronaldsay with a coach link to Kirkwall on Orkney Mainland. Small passenger and car ferries link Orkney's nine large outer islands with Orkney Mainland.

CRUISES

A cruise is a leisurely way to see the many different Scottish islands. Caledonian MacBrayne offers various non-landing, evening cruises departing from a number of locations on the west coast.

John o' Groats Ferries offers day cruises to Orkney Mainland from John o' Groats and Inverness. These can be extended to include accommodation in Kirkwall and a tour of the island's historic sites by bus.

It is also possible to take a cruise on some of Scotland's lochs and rivers. **Caledonian Discovery** offers six-day cruises along the Caledonian Canal from Fort William to Inverness.

DIRECTORY

Caledonian Discovery
Tel (01397) 772167.
www.fingal-cruising.co.uk

Caledonian MacBrayne
Tel (0800) 066 5000.
www.calmac.co.uk

DFDS Seaways
Tel (0871) 522 9955.
www.dfdsseaways.co.uk

Eurostar
Tel (08432) 186 186.
www.eurostar.com

Eurotunnel
Tel (08443) 353535.
www.eurotunnel.com

John o' Groats Ferries
Tel (01955) 611353.
www.jogferry.co.uk

NorthLink Ferries
Tel (0845) 600 0449.
www.northlinkferries.co.uk

P&O Ferries
Tel (08716) 642121.
www.poferries.com

Pentland Ferries
Tel (01856) 831226.
www.pentlandferries.co.uk

Stena Line
Tel (08447) 707070.
www.stenaline.co.uk

Cruising on Loch Ness with Caledonian Discovery's *Fingal of Caledonia*

CAR FERRY ROUTE	INFORMATION	DAYS	LAST CHECK-IN	JOURNEY TIME
Aberdeen–Kirkwall (Orkney)	(0845) 600 0449	alternate days	30 mins	6 hrs, 30 mins
Aberdeen–Lerwick (Shetland)	(0845) 600 0449	daily	30 mins	13 hrs
Ardrossan–Brodick (Arran)	(01294) 463470	daily	30 mins	55 mins
Gill's Bay–St Marg's Hope (Ork.)	(01856) 831226	daily	30 mins	1 hr
Kennacraig–Port Ellen (Islay)	(01880) 730253	daily	45 mins	2 hrs, 10 mins
Kilchoan–Tobermory (Mull)	(01688) 302017	Mon–Sun	30 mins	35 mins
Lerwick (Shet.)–Kirkwall (Ork.)	(0845) 600 0449	alternate days	30 mins	5 hrs 30 mins
Mallaig–Armadale (Skye)	(01687) 462403	daily	30 mins	30 mins
Oban–Castlebay (Barra)	(01631) 566688	daily ex. Wed	45 mins	5 hrs, 15 mins
Oban–Craignure (Mull)	(01631) 566688	daily	30 mins	45 mins
Scrabster–Stromness (Orkney)	(0845) 600 0449	daily	30 mins	1 hr, 30 mins
Uig (Skye)–Tarbert (Harris)	(01470) 542219	Mon–Sat	30 mins	1 hr, 35 mins
Ullapool–Stornoway (Lewis)	(01854) 612358	Mon–Sat	45 mins	2 hrs, 40 mins

Travelling by Car

In Scotland, and the rest of the UK, driving is on the left-hand side of the road, and distances are measured and signposted in miles. A network of toll-free motorways exists in the south and between Edinburgh and Glasgow; using these can reduce travelling time. In the larger towns traffic density can cause delays, and during public holiday weekends heading north to the Highlands is often slow work. Rural Scotland, with its striking scenery, is an enjoyable place to drive, and the roads to even the remote parts are generally good.

The A68 from Northern England to Scotland

WHAT YOU NEED

To drive in Scotland you need a current driving licence, with an international driving permit if required. In any vehicle you drive, you must carry proof of ownership or a rental agreement, plus insurance documents.

A motorway sign

ROADS IN SCOTLAND

Peak rush-hour traffic can last from 8–9:30am and 5–6:30pm on weekdays in the cities. Radio Scotland and local radio stations broadcast regular reports of road conditions throughout the day. You can also contact **Keep Moving** for information on road conditions. You can save vital travel time by knowing which routes should be avoided.

Outside the cities, a good touring map is essential; the AA or RAC motoring atlases are straightforward to use. For exploration of more remote areas, the Ordnance Survey series is the best. Such areas often have only single-track roads with passing places and blind bends, that demand cautious driving.

On all road maps, motorways are indicated by an M followed by a number, such as the M8. Major roads, which are often dual (2-lane) carriageways, are labelled A roads. Secondary roads, often less congested than A roads, are called B roads. There are fewer roads in the Highlands.

Disabled drivers can contact the **AA Disability Helpline** for general motoring information.

ROAD SIGNS

Signs are now generally standardized in line with the rest of Europe. Directional signs are colour-coded: blue for motorways, green for major (A) roads and white for minor (B) roads. In the Highlands and islands, road signs display both English and Gaelic names. Brown signs with a blue thistle give visitor information on attractions and tourist centres. Warning signs are usually triangles in red and white, with easy to understand pictograms. Watch for electronic notices on motorways that warn of road works, accidents or dangerous driving conditions. Level crossings at train tracks often have automatic barriers. If the lights are flashing red, it means a train is approaching; you are required to stop.

No stopping Speed limit (mph)

No entry No right-turn allowed

Railway level crossing Yield to all vehicles

One-way traffic Gradient of a road

RULES OF THE ROAD

Speed limits are 50–65 km/h (30–40 mph) in built-up areas and 110 km/h (70 mph) on motorways or dual carriageways – look out for speed signs on other roads. Wearing seatbelts is compulsory in Scotland and it is illegal to drive and use a hand-held mobile phone. Severe penalties are imposed for drinking and driving.

PARKING

In Scotland's towns and cities, on-street parking is often paid for by purchasing a ticket from a roadside machine. The ticket is then left on display inside the car. Some cities have "park and ride" schemes, where you take a bus from an out-of-city car park into the centre. Other towns have a "disc" parking scheme; ask the tourist office or a local newsagent for a disc to mark your arrival time. Many car parks operate on a pay-and-display system. Avoid double yellow lines at all times; you can park on single lines at evenings and weekends, but check roadside signs for variations to the rule. Traffic wardens will not hesitate to ticket, clamp or tow away your car if in breach of the rules. If in doubt, find a car park. Outside urban and popular visitor areas, parking is not such a problem. Look out for the letter P, which indicates legal parking spaces.

It is best to avoid driving in Edinburgh, as cars have limited access to the centre and the vast majority of sights can be reached on foot. Taxis, which you can hail on the street or find waiting at a taxi rank, are another option. Licensed cabs must display a "For Hire" sign. Mini-cabs must display a card proving the identity of the licensed driver. If there is no meter, ask the fare in advance.

One of Glasgow's black cabs

FUEL

North American visitors to Scotland may find petrol (gasoline) very expensive, particularly at motorway service stations. It is the large supermarkets that often have the lowest prices. Petrol is sold in four grades: diesel, 4-star (regular) super unleaded and premium unleaded. Most modern cars use unleaded petrol. Diesel and unleaded fuel are cheaper than 4-star. Most petrol stations are self-service but instructions at the pumps are easy to follow. Green hoses denote unleaded fuel pumps and deliveries are in litres.

BREAKDOWN SERVICES

Britain's major motoring organizations, the **AA** (Automobile Association) and the **RAC** (Royal Automobile Club), provide a comprehensive 24-hour breakdown and recovery service. Both motoring organizations

RAC logo

The busy M8 motorway on the outskirts of Glasgow

offer reciprocal assistance for members of overseas motoring organizations – before arrival check with your own group to see if you are covered. You can contact the AA or RAC from roadside SOS phones on all motorways. Most car rental agencies have their own cover, which includes membership of either the AA or the RAC while you are driving. Even if you are not a member of an organization, you can still call out a rescue service, although it will be expensive.

Always take the advice given on the insurance policy or rental agreement. If you have an accident that injures you or damages a vehicle, contact the police straight away.

CAR RENTAL

Renting a car can be costly, but one of the more competitive companies is **Autosabroad**. Others include **Arnold Clark**, **Budget**, **Hertz Rent A Car**, **Europcar** and **National Car Rental**.

Many companies require a credit card number or a substantial cash deposit as well as your driving licence and passport. The normal age requirements are over 21 and under 70. Major airports, train stations and city centres have car rental outlets. Value for money car hire can also be found in some smaller towns.

DIRECTORY

BREAKDOWN SERVICES

AA
Tel (0800) 887766.
www.theaa.com

RAC
Tel (0844) 891 3111.
www.rac.co.uk

CAR RENTAL

Arnold Clark
Tel (0844) 815 2129.
www.arnoldclark.com

Autosabroad
Tel (0844) 826 6536.
www.autosabroad.com

Avis
Tel (08445) 445566.
www.avis.co.uk

Budget
Tel (0844) 544 3470.
www.budget.co.uk

**Europcar/
British Car Rental**
Tel (08457) 222525.
www.europcar.co.uk

Hertz Rent A Car
Tel (0843) 309 3032.
www.hertz.com

National Car Rental
Tel (0871) 384 1140.
www.nationalcar.co.uk
www.nationalcar.com *(in US)*.

GENERAL
INFORMATION

AA Disability Helpline
Tel (0800) 262050.

Keep Moving
Tel 401100.

General Index

Acknowledgments

Dorling Kindersley would like to thank the following people whose contributions and assistance have made the preparation of this book possible.

Design and Editorial Assistance
Claire Baranowski, Hilary Bird, Emer FitzGerald, Claire Folkard, Camilla Gersh, Alrica Green, Kathleen Greig, Lydia Halliday, Carolyn Hewitson, Jessica Hughes, Donnie Hutton, Marie Ingledew, Laura Jones, Elly King, Kathryn Lane, Nicola Malone, Sue Megginson, Sonal Modha, Catherine Palmi, Clare Pierotti, Tom Prentice, Rada Radojicic, Alice Reese, the Scottish Tourist Board (especially Vineet Lal), Pamela Shiels, Helena Smith, Susana Smith, Stewart Wild, Alice Wright.

Cartography
Uma Bhattacharya, Mohammad Hassan, Jasneet Kaur

DTP
Vinod Harish, Azeem Siddiqui, Vincent Kurien

Additional Photography
Sarah Ashun, Joe Cornish, Andy Crawford, Philip Dowell, Chris Dyer, Andreas Einsiedel, Peter Gathercole, Steve Gorton, Paul Harris, Dave King, Cyril Laubscher, Brian D. Morgan, Ian O'Leary, Stephen Oliver, Tim Ridley, Kim Sayer, Karl Shore, Clive Streeter, Kim Taylor, Mathew Ward, Stephen Whitehorne.

Additional Picture Research
Rachel Barber

Photographic and Artwork Reference
Aerographica: Patricia & Angus Macdonald; London Aerial Photo Library.

Photography Permissions
City of Edinburgh Council Heritage and Arts Marketing/ People's Story Museum; Royal Botanic Garden, Edinburgh; House for an Art Lover, Glasgow; Glasgow School of Art; Glasgow Botanic Gardens.

Picture Credits
a = above; b = below/bottom; c = centre; f = far; l = left; r = right; t = top.

The publisher would like to thank the following individuals, companies and picture libraries for their kind permission to reproduce their photographs:

3x1 PUBLIC RELATIONS/HIGHLAND SPRING: 75clb. ABERDEEN TOURIST BOARD: 51cra; ABERDEEN UNIVERSITY LIBRARY: George Washington Wilson Collection 163t; Action Plus: 14t; AEROGRAPHICA: Patricia & Angus Macdonald 16t/b, 17tl, 18cra; ALAMY IMAGES: archphotography 219ca; Serda_ikrumoki 219tc; Bertrand Collet 184cl; Bill Coster 161br; Tim Gainey 158tr; Doug Houghton 160tr; Nick Kirk 8tc; Iain Masterton 99bl; David Robertson 8br; Skyscan Photolibrary 204tr; David Tipling 161cr; Worldwide Picture Library/ Iain Sarjent 161bl; ALLSPORT: Craig Prentis 36b; T & R ANNAN & SON (D): 101br. BANK OF SCOTLAND: 220cb; BRIDGEMAN ART LIBRARY, London/New York: 27t, 146b, 147b (d); City of Edinburgh Museums & Galleries 28bl; Fine Art Society, London 101 clb; Robert Fleming Holdings Limited, London 43c; National Gallery of Scotland, Edinburgh 40; National Museet Copenhagen 42c; Collection of Andrew McIntosh Patrick, UK 101cla; Smith Art Gallery and Museum, Stirling 120b; South African National Gallery, Cape Town 101cra; Trinity College Library, Dublin 42t; BRITAINONVIEW.COM: 203tc; Duncan Shaw 9br; BRITISH AIRWAYS: 224t; BT PAYPHONES: 222bl, 222tl; BURT GREENER COMMUNICATIONS: 76crb. LAURIE CAMPBELL: 18clb/bl, 127b, 157t/c; Peter Evans 140tl; Gordon Langsbury

141t; Hans Reinhard 116tl; Dr. Frieder Sauer 152t; DOUG CORRANCE: 12, 23br, 29b, 30c, 30bc, 31br, 38t, 52, 90t, 108l/r, 110, 133b, 139t, 144b, 146t, 147t, 200c, 201ca/cb/b, 206br, 208cl, 210tr/b, 214c, 228b; ERIC CRICHTON PHOTOS: 23cl/cr; CROWN COPYRIGHT: Historic Scotland 60tr/c, 61bl, 121c; Ordnance Survey/Photo, Scotland in Focus 208tl; EDINBURGH FESTIVAL FRINGE SOCIETY: 36t; Empics: 109r; ET ARCHIVE: Bibliothèque Nationale, Paris 6–7; MARY EVANS PICTURE LIBRARY: 7 (inset), 26t/c/b, 44c, 45cr, 86bl, 88c, 123b, 153br, 165 (inset), 213 (inset). FALKIRK WHEEL: 125b; LOUIS FLOOD: 28br. GARDEN PICTURE LIBRARY: John Glover 22tr; GETTY IMAGES: Stanley Chou 203c; Richard Heathcote 203bl; GLASGOW MUSEUMS: Art Gallery & Museum, Kelvingrove 102t, 134b, 150b; Burrell Collection 104–105 except 104tl; Museum of Transport 24br, 25bl; RONALD GRANT ARCHIVE: 27c; V. K. GUY LTD: Mike Guy 18cla, 34cl, 133t, 3 (Inset); Paul Guy 2–3; Vic Guy 118–119. ROBERT HARDING PICTURE LIBRARY: 130t, 209b; Van der Hars 142t; Michael Jenner 162c; Julia K. Thorne 20bl; Adina Tovy 20br; Andy Williams 126; Adam Woolfitt 140tr; DENNIS HARDLEY: 34cr, 35t/cb, 80, 82, 84c/b, 90b, 91t, 113, 114t/b, 115b, 136b, 137b, 156b, 163b, 215b; GORDON HENDERSON: 19cra, 34t, 35ca/b, 148c, 157b, 162b, 229t; HOUSE OF LORDS RECORD OFFICE: Reproduced by permission of the Clerk of the Records 45t; HULTON GETTY COLLECTION: 25cra, 46t, 92tl, 117br, 149c; (c) HUNTERIAN ART GALLERY, UNIVERSITY OF GLASGOW: 103tl; Mackintosh Collection 94, 101crb; HUTCHISON LIBRARY: Bernard Gerard 15t. ANDREW LAWSON: 22bl, 23tl/tr, 156t. MUSEUM OF CHILDHOOD, EDINBURGH: 58b. NATIONAL GALLERIES OF SCOTLAND: Scottish National Gallery of Modern Art Study For Les Constructeurs: The Team At Rest by Fernand Leger 1950 (c) ADAGP, Paris And DACS, London, 2011 69t; NATURAL HISTORY PHOTOGRAPHIC AGENCY: Bryan & Cherry Alexander 37tr; Laurie Campbell 13t, 19bla, 36c; Manfred Danegger 19br/ bra; Scottish National Portrait Gallery 63t; NATIONAL MUSEUMS OF SCOTLAND: 62b; NATIONAL PORTRAIT GALLERY, LONDON: 64b; NATIONAL TRUST FOR SCOTLAND: 50b, 56b, 92tr, 93tl/tr/br, 124b, 125c, 216cr; Lindsey Robertson 93bl; Glyn Satterley 100br; NETWORK PHOTOGRAPHERS: Laurie Sparham 14b. ORTAK JEWELLERY, EDINBURGH: 74ca, 106t. PA NEWS: 31t/bl; Chris Bacon 39c; Roslin Institute 25br; (c) 1996 POLYGRAM FILMED ENTERTAINMENT: 27b; THE POST OFFICE: 223tl, 223cla, 223clb; Glyn Satterley 227b; POWERSTOCK/ZEFA: 20c; RBS GROUP: 220br, 220crb; REX FEATURES: J. Sutton Hibbert 47c; ROYAL AUTOMOBILE CLUB (RAC): 231b; ROYAL BOTANIC GARDEN, EDINBURGH: 23bl; ROYAL COLLECTION (c) 1999, HER MAJESTY QUEEN ELIZABETH II: 29tc; ROYAL PHOTOGRAPHIC SOCIETY: 25tl. SCIENCE PHOTO LIBRARY: M-SAT Ltd 10; SCIENCE & SOCIETY PICTURE LIBRARY: Science Museum 25crb; ALASTAIR SCOTT: 17b, 19cla, 31cb, 207b, 211l; SCOTTISH HIGHLAND PHOTO LIBRARY: 19tc, 135t; SCOTTISH VIEWPOINT: 158c; Iain McLean 9tl; Ken Paterson 8cla; Paul Tomkins 158c; VisitScotland 158bl; 204bl; VisitScotland/ P Tomkins 204cr; VisitScotland/ Paul Tomkins 9c, 204cr; PHIL SHELDON GOLF PICTURE LIBRARY: 202tr; James Shuttleworth: 227c; STILL MOVING PICTURE COMPANY: Gordon Allison 30br; Marcus Brooke 17tr; Wade Cooper 47t; Doug Corrance 30t, 81b, 130b, 199cl, 206cl, 210c; Peter Davenport 18br; Distant Images 89t; Derek Lairs 41c; Robert Lees 39b, 200t, 207t; Paisley Museum 89b; Ken Paterson 65t; David Robertson 22cl, 149b; Glyn Satterley 201t; Colin Scott 31cl; Scottish Tourist Board 30bl, 140br, 141c, 198c, 199t; Paul Tomkins/STB 162t, 198b, 200b; Stephen J. Whitehorne 117t; Harvey Wood 139b. STRATHCLYDE PASSENGER TRANSPORT (SPT): Richard McPherson 96bl. TRON THEATRE: Keith Hunter 108cr. CHARLIE WAITE: 131t; DAVID WARD: 134t; STEPHEN J. WHITEHORNE: 1, 19tl, 31cra, 34b, 37c, 62tl, 63c, 66b, 83, 111b, 115t, 132t, 148b, 163c, 183c, 198t, 208b, 209t, 211r, 221t, 223cl, 229c. Front Endpaper: DOUG CORRANCE: cl, br; ROBERT HARDING PICTURE LIBRARY: Andy Williams tl; DENNIS HARDLEY: bl; HUNTERIAN ART GALLERY, UNIVERSITY OF GLASGOW: Mackintosh Collection tr.

JACKET FRONT - PHOTOLIBRARY: Andy Williams. Back - ALAMY IMAGES: Jon Arnold tl; AWL IMAGES: Paul Harris ca, Travel Pix Collection bl; DORLING KINDERSLEY: Linda Whitwam. Spine - PHOTOLIBRARY: Andy Williams t.
All other images © Dorling Kindersley.
For further information see www.dk.com

Scottish Vocabulary

Gaelic is a Celtic language that is still spoken as a second language in the Highlands and Western Isles of Scotland. Estimates put the figure of Gaelic speakers throughout the country at around 80,000. The last decade has seen something of a revival of the language, due to the encouragement of both education and broadcasting authorities. However the majority of people are most likely to come across Gaelic today in the form of place names. Words such as glen, loch, eilean and kyle are all still very much in use. English remains the principal language of Scotland. However the country's very distinct education, religious, political and judicial systems have given rise to a rich vocabulary that reflects Scottish culture. Many additional terms in current usage are colloquial. English as spoken by the Scots is commonly divided into four dialects. Central Scots can be heard across the Central Belt and the southwest of the country. As around a quarter of the population lives within 32 km (20 miles) of Glasgow, West Central Scots is one of the most frequently heard subdivisions of this dialect. Southern Scots is spoken in the east of Dumfries and Galloway and the Borders; Northern Scots in the northeast; and Island Scots in the Orkney and Shetland Islands.

Pronunciation of Gaelic Words

Letters	Example	Pronunciation
ao	craobh	this is pronounced similar to **oo**, as in cool
bh	dubh	"h" is silent unless at the beginning of a word in which case it is pronounced **v**, as in vet
ch	deich	this is pronounced as in the German composer Bach
cn	cnoc	this is pronounced **cr**, as in creek
ea	leabhar	this is pronounced **e**, as in get or **a**, as in cat
eu	sgeul	this is pronounced **ay**, as in say or **ea**, as in ear
gh	taigh-òsda	this is silent unless at the beginning of a word, in which case it is pronounced as in get
ia	fiadh	this is pronounced **ea**, as in ear
io	tiocaid	this is pronounced **ee**, as in deep or **oo**, as in took
rt	ceart	this is pronounced **sht**
th	theab	this is silent unless at the beginning of a word in which case it is pronounced **h**, as in house
ua	uaine	this is pronounced **oo**, as in poor

Words in Place Names

ben	mountain
bothy	farm cottage
brae	hill
brig	bridge
burn	brook
cairn	mound of stones marking a place
close	block of flats (apartments) sharing a common entry and stairway
craig	steep peak
croft	small plot of farmland with dwellings in the Highlands
dubh	black
eilean	island
firth	estuary
gate/gait	street (in proper names)
glen	valley
howff	a regular meeting place, usually a pub
kirk	a Presbyterian church
kyle	a narrow strait of river
links	golf course by the sea
loaning	field
loch	lake
moss	moor
Munro	mountain over 914 m (3,000 ft) high
strath	valley/plain beside river
wynd	lane
yett	gate

Food and Drink

Arbroath smokie	small haddock that has been salted and then smoked
breid	bread
clapshot	mashed turnips and potatoes
clootie dumpling	rich fruit pudding
Cullen skink	fish soup made from smoked haddock
dram	a drink of whisky
haggis	sheep's offal, suet, oatmeal and seasonings, usually boiled in the animal's intestine
Irn-Bru	popular soft drink
neeps	turnips
oatcake	a savoury oatmeal biscuit
porridge	a hot breakfast dish made with oats, milk and water
shortie	shortbread
tattie	potato
tattie scone	type of savoury pancake made with potato

Cultural Terms

Burns Night	25 January is the anniversary of the birth of the poet Robert Burns, celebrated with a meal of haggis
Caledonia	Scotland
ceilidh	an informal evening of traditional Scottish song and dance
clan	an extended family bearing the same surname (last name)
first foot	the first person to enter a house after midnight on New Year's Eve
Highland dress	Highland men's formal wear including the kilt
Hogmanay	New Year's Eve
kilt	knee-length pleated tartan skirt worn as traditional Highland dress
Ne'erday	New Year's Day
pibroch	type of bagpipe music
sgian-dubh	a small blade tucked into the outside of the sock on the right foot worn as part of the traditional Highland dress
sporran	pouch made of fur worn to the front of the kilt
tartan	chequered wool cloth, different colours being worn by each clan

Colloquial Expressions

auld	old
auld lang syne	days of long ago
Auld Reekie	Edinburgh
aye	yes
bairn	child
barrie	excellent
blether	chat
bonnie	pretty
braw	excellent
dreich	wet (weather)
fae	from
fitba	football
hen	informal name used to address a woman or girl
ken	to know; to have knowledge
lassie	a young woman/girl
lumber	boyfriend/girlfriend
Nessie	legendary monster of Loch Ness
Old Firm	Celtic and Glasgow Rangers, Glasgow's main football teams
wean	child
wee	small